THE GREAT WAR AND WOMEN'S CONSCIOUSNESS

The Great War and Women's Consciousness

Images of Militarism and Womanhood
in Women's Writings, 1914–64

By Claire M. Tylee

University of Iowa Press Ψ Iowa City

Dedicated to my Heroines of the Past

Edith Cavell
Sylvia Pankhurst
Virginia Woolf

and to my heroines of the future

Jessica and Hannah Matthew

The purblind policy of shielding women against their will from a knowledge of truths, however unpleasant they may be, is disastrous not only for women, but for the community at large.

Mrs St Clair Stobart, War and Women, 1913

Contents

Preface

One August, when I was a little girl of about six, my parents, my elder brother and I spent a day in Brighton with my grandparents. After lunch we went for a stroll along the Front. Out of the cloud of rules that floated above my head two were selected for attention: 'Walk *properly*, and don't keep asking "why?" all the time!' Then my mother and granny took my brother, who could be 'a bit of a handful', off in one direction, and I was left, most unusually, alone with my father and grandfather. Grandad, who was my mother's father, was strict and rather fierce. With a hand firmly grasped on either side, I concentrated on getting my small feet in their white socks and sandals to keep up with the large, polished shoes on both sides of me. All six feet strode down a flight of steps. Mine watchfully did not jump the last couple.

At the bottom Grandad let go of my hand to go over to a rather shabby man selling matches from a tray around his neck. He was a long time. My father gazed out to sea, his hands carefully not in his pockets, 'a bad habit' my brother had been copying. My grandmother not being there to notice ('it's rude to stare at people'), I kept my eyes fixed on my grandfather. Like all his generation his back was extremely straight. He held himself upright and rather rigid. Now, from behind, he seemed animated, laughing and gesticulating in a way I had never seen.

'Daddy, is that man a friend of Grandad's?' It seemed unlikely, Grandad was clean and always very correctly dressed.

'I shouldn't think so.'

'Then why are they talking for so long?'

'I expect they were in the War together.'

'Oh.' I already knew what that meant: not the Second-rate war Daddy had been in, but the earlier one, the *real* one, the 'Great' War; the one where Grandad had got his medals and his arthritis, and since which he had 'never been the same again'.

Then I saw Grandad take out of an inside pocket and unfold one of those large white pieces of paper that he and Daddy always carried 'for emergencies' (like Granny carried an extra hankie), but which were rarely seen: one of the old five pound notes. As he walked back towards us, he turned and held up his hand to shake a box of matches at the man, who waved his one arm in reply.

When he rejoined us, Grandad still had a smile on his face.

'Grandad, you didn't get any change.' I had watched scrupulously. Sometimes my brother and I got a silver threepenny bit out of the spare change in Grandad's pocket.

'No.'

'That was a very expensive box of matches.'

'Not to me.'

I pondered this sublime piece of adult logic. Whatever would Granny have said? Then, with undreamt of temerity, I chanced my arm:

'Grandad?'

'Yes?'

'*Why* did you buy the matches? – You've got a lighter.'

'One day, when you're grown-up, you'll understand.'

But I think I had already realised, incoherently, that on the contrary it was not until I did understand that I ever should be grown-up. So I continued to step out of line and to ask awkward questions.

Developing that strategic refusal to be ladylike, this book marks one more impatient skip along my progress to adulthood.

Claire M. Tylee
University of Málaga

Acknowledgements

This book had two midwives to coax it into the open: Angela Ingram and Joe Marsh. I relied on their emotional support which never failed me.

For the intellectual push and pull that kept me under way, I am indebted to Pilar Hidalgo and Esteban Pujals. Other people sparked off ideas and encouraged me theoretically: Catalina Montes gave me insights into Virginia Woolf's aesthetics, Roger Poole stimulated my biographical approach, Bill Schwarz provided the political bedrock; John Hazlett argued with me about generational autobiography and sent me references, and Pete Messent discussed the idea of cultural zones. Beth L'Oiseaux gave me the lead to banned books, Esther Newton and Helen McNeil answered queries, and Alan Bishop commented constructively on my views about Vera Brittain. Just as importantly, George, Anne and Ken at the second-hand bookshop offered enthusiasm and practical advice, and Carlos Alba and Marcos Espinosa waved adamantly and provocatively from the other side of the gender barrier.

I am grateful to Kenneth Graham for enabling me to carry out research at Sheffield University Library and to Bryan Burns for helping me with it, and I want to express my gratitude to the librarians there, and at Birmingham Public Reference Library, Friends House Library and Leicester University Library for their energetic help and interest. Without the resources of the Imperial War Museum and the care of its staff, particularly Dr Bayliss, I could not have written this book at all, and I want to thank them especially for their time and patience.

Indirectly I am indebted to the Centre for Cultural Studies at the University of Birmingham, the root of many of my ideas about the relation between literature, ideology and cultural hegemony. More directly, I am indebted to feminist literary historians such as Jane Marcus and Elaine Showalter for blazing the trail.

For permission to reproduce the illustrations in the plates section I am indebted to the following: The Imperial War Museum (1), (2), (3), (6), (7), (9) and (17); Mary Evans/Fawcett Library (8), (10) and (12); McMaster University Library (13); Tate Gallery (5); Walker Art Gallery (4). [The publishers have tried to contact all copyright holders but in cases where they may have failed will be pleased to make the necessary arrangements at the first opportunity.

Finally I want to thank the person whose unflagging conversation and hospitality have enabled me to explore my ideas: Una Flett; and the person whose moral courage gave me strength when I most needed it: Dr Lorenzo Valderrama.

I hope they all find this book an adequate outcome for so much generosity.

List of Plates

Terminology and Abbreviations

The British term 'The Great War' refers to what Americans call 'The European War, 1914–18', or World War I. I have used the phrase 'The Great War' where I wanted to stress the emotional reverberations which that war has in British consciousness, or, for brevity, I have written 'the War' as people of the time did. Where I wanted to be dispassionate I have used the terms 'the 1914–18 War' or 'World War I'. Otherwise I have spoken less neutrally of 'The First World War', an idea charged with apprehension of the Second.

DORA = The Defence of the Realm Act, 1914. (See Appendix 2.)

ELFS* = East London Federation of Suffragettes. Founded by Sylvia Pankhurst in 1913, this split from the WSPU (see below) in 1914, became the Workers' Suffrage Federation in 1916, and then Workers' Socialist Federation in 1918. It had provincial branches and was uniquely democratic in organisation and proletarian in membership.

ILP = Independent Labour Party.

NCF** = No Conscription Fellowship (later the National Council for Civil Liberties). Founded in 1915 on the principle of conscientious objection to killing for the state. Reached a membership of 12 000, mainly male, of conscription age, religious-pacifist and belonging to ILP.

NUWSS* = National Union of Women's Suffrage Societies. Founded in 1897, with roots back to 1866. By 1914 it had 480 affiliated societies and 53 000 members. It had a democratically-elected president, Mrs Fawcett, and a national executive committee, several of whom resigned in 1915 to work instead for WIL (see below).

UDC** = Union of Democratic Control (of Foreign Policy). Founded in August 1914 to work for a non-vindictive peace treaty and post-war disarmament, it grew from an individual membership of 5000, through an affiliated membership of 300 000 in 1915, to an affiliated membership of 650 000 by 1918.

VAD = Voluntary Aid Detachment. Detachments, consisting of 23 people, were established from 1910, under the British Red Cross or St John Ambulance Brigade, to assist the professional military nursing services in case of war. A 'VAD' came to mean an individual female nurse who was a war-time volunteer.

WFL* = Women's Freedom League. Under the leadership of Charlotte Despard, broke away from the increasingly autocratic and conservative WSPU in 1907. With strong links to ILP, it had 53 branches in 1908, but only 4000 members by 1914.

WIL** = British Section of the Women's International League for Peace and Freedom (founded as a result of the 1915 International Women's Congress at The Hague). Affiliated to UDC, WIL had an official membership of 3687 in 1918.

WSPU* = Women's Social and Political Union, the 'Suffragettes'. Founded in Manchester in 1903, specifically to adopt militant tactics; under the increasingly autocratic leadership of Mrs. Emmeline Pankhurst and her daughter Christabel it broke away from ILP and moved its headquarters to London in 1906. By 1907 it had over 70 branches (but no membership figures). From 1914 it was nationalistic, xenophobic and war-mongering.

WWSL = Women Writers' Suffrage League. Founded in 1908 with Elizabeth Robins, the actress/writer, as president, with the aim of using the pen to further feminist aims non-violently.

* = discussed in Garner, Les (1984), *Stepping Stones to Women's Liberty*.
** = discussed in Wiltshire, Anne (1985), *Most Dangerous Women*.

Introduction
'We Will Remember'

The year 1964 was both the 50th anniversary of the declaration of World War I and the 25th anniversary of the declaration of World War II. Arriving during the Viet-Nam War at a time of increasing hostility between the world powers, the two anniversaries had a signal effect on British cultural awareness. The First World War, emotively remembered as 'The Great War', was the more prominent focus of public attention. Not that it had ever been forgotten. The annual celebration of Armistice-day, 11 November 1918, by two minutes' silence followed by the sounding of the last post at the 11th hour, of the 11th day, of the 11th month (now 'Remembrance Sunday'), in front of the war-memorials 'To Our Glorious Dead' with their lists of name upon name, in every city, town and village throughout Britain, ensured that the Great War was a permanent monument within British culture. But the question was: exactly what did that monument perpetuate?

The years 1964–68 became the central years of a period of cultural re-assessment. The post-war generation (of which I was one) saw the personal memories of their parents and grandparents as no longer publicly petrified into part of an annual ceremony commemorating the war-dead. They listened as those memories contributed to a public debate about the national culture. What were we responding to when we committed ourselves to be ever mindful of the dead? Whose values were we corroborating?

The polarity of the cultural response to the First World War was already in evidence in the years leading up to 1964. It can be gauged by comparing two examples of the performing arts: on the one hand, the political satire, *Oh, What a Lovely War*, first performed by the Theatre Workshop in London's East End in 1963, and on the other hand, Benjamin Britten's elegiac *War Requiem*, which was given its first performances in 1962 and issued on records in 1963. Recollection typically veered between the pole of grief and pity, and the pole of withdrawal and protest.

The Theatre Workshop group suited their art to the music-hall in which they performed, to recapture the popular response of the common people. This had been immortalised in British culture by

1

the soldiers' songs of the First World War, parodies (often obscene) of traditional hymns and of famous music-hall hits of the day. Britten's *Requiem*, based on the war-poetry of Wilfred Owen, was first performed in Westminster Abbey and in the new anglican cathedral in Coventry. (This cathedral was itself designed as a symbol of Christian reconciliation; the raising of it alongside the ruins of the medieval cathedral bombed in the Second World War, embodied the hope of a decision not to forget the destructive power of war.) Both musical works were political. They both maintained a strongly anti-war stance. But whereas Britten's work was a spiritual affirmation of pacifism, which emphasised the pathos of war in the traditional form of the mass for the dead, and was performed within the establishment setting of the Church of England by a choir and orchestra in evening-dress, Joan Littlewood's troupe of circus pierrots utilised the street-theatre techniques of the workers' theatre of the 1930s, to parody the religious and political establishment of the First World War era and to forestall any indulgence in nostalgia. Britten's art was solemn and elevating; the Theatre Workshop event was deliberately comic and irreverent.

The two works not only addressed the War differently; they addressed themselves differently to different audiences. Calling for three major soloists, two choirs, an organ, a chamber music group and a full symphony orchestra, Britten's *War Requiem* requires large resources to be repeated in public. It is available on a set of two records, at a price that probably restricts it to enthusiasts of classical music. However, its stress on the pity of war, with the central theme of war as the sacrifice of the innocent, was shared by a play which was to reach a less exclusive public: John Wilson's *Hamp*. (This was based on a First World War novel, *Return to the Wood*, by J. Lansdale Hodson, 1930.) First performed in Newcastle in 1964, *Hamp* was a success at the Edinburgh Festival of the same year, being described by one critic as: 'A strong bid for sentiment and even tear-jerking ... which had its audience very clearly moved'. The play reached a far wider audience as an equally successful film under the title, *For King and Country* (1965).

Oh, What a Lovely War also reached a mass audience. The play having won wide critical acclaim, culminating in the *Grand Prix* of the *Théâtre des Nations* festival in Paris in 1963, the script was published in 1965, and a cheap, illustrated, paperback edition brought out in 1967 was reprinted repeatedly thereafter. The play was adapted for the cinema in 1969. Richard Attenborough's film adaptation used famous stars of theatre, television and cinema, and parodied the techniques of the Hollywood musical. This simultaneously forestalled superficial emotional responses and satirised the glamorising portrayal of war by the mass media, which had followed the Second World War. It was a more sophisticated exposé of propaganda than was possible in the original music-hall setting, and it had a more up-to-date concern. The play had encouraged the audience to see the songs they knew as the soldiers' rejection of the official picture of the War. Jostling its audience out of inert grief, the film tried to alert them to the fact that political motives still lay behind the lies that lead people into war.

Controversy about the First World War was not only stimulated by the performing arts. A number of new historical studies were published during the same period. *The Guns of August – August 1914* by the popular American historian Barbara W. Tuchman appeared first in hardback in 1962, and then in paperback in 1964. Supported at every point by quotation from contemporary documents, Tuchman's account is strongly influenced by the propaganda and fulsome rhetoric of the period. Her story began in 1910, with the funeral of Edward VII: 'On history's clock it was sunset, and the sun of the old world was setting in a dying blaze of splendor never to be seen again' (Tuchman 1964: 15). The social misery and political tensions beneath this surface of lavish pageantry were outlined by Arthur Marwick in *The Explosion of British Society 1914–62* (1963). His thesis was that the impact of the First World War in transforming the social and economic structure of Britain could be described as explosive. Two forces in that explosion were the rise of the working class and the rise of the female sex.

A. J. P. Taylor's *The First World War: an Illustrated History* (dedicated to Joan Littlewood) was also published in 1963, and then brought out by Penguin. The text runs side by side with photos because the photos show anonymous Everyman: 'The unknown soldier was the hero of the First World War. He vanished, except as a cipher, from the written records. He lives again in photos' (Taylor 1963: 9). Claiming that 'This war was our war too', Taylor hoped that, by understanding it better, 'we can come nearer to being, what the men of that time were not, masters of our own destiny' (9). He followed this in 1965 by his *English History 1914–1945* which was also published in paperback by Penguin, in 1970. In 1967

Arthur Marwick published *The Deluge: British Society and the First World War*. Taylor's emphasis was on political decisions and their effects on the army of working-class 'Tommies'. Marwick was more interested in the War's effects on the home front, and he devoted one chapter to 'New Women: 1915–1916'. Drier in tone than Tuchman's, the British works have become set texts at the level of higher education. Through the Penguin imprint they reached a wide readership beyond educational institutions.

Naturally publishers noticed the potential market. Famous war-memoirs from the 1930s were reissued. Robert Graves's facetious *Goodbye to All That* (1929) was already still in print, and so was Edmund Blunden's *Undertones of War* (1928); but new paperback editions were issued of such works as Richard Aldington's *Death of a Hero* (1929, republished 1965), Frederick Manning's *Her Privates We* (1930, republished 1967), Guy Chapman's *A Passionate Prodigality* (1933, republished 1965), V. M. Yeates's *Winged Victory* (1934, republished 1961) and Cecil Lewis's *Sagittarius Rising* (1936, republished 1965). *Vain Glory*, Guy Chapman's anthology of extracts from writings about the First World War, which first appeared in 1937, was reissued in 1968.

New anthologies of poetry from the First World War were brought out. In 1963 there appeared a new edition of Wilfred Owen's poetry, edited by C. Day Lewis: *The Collected Poems of Wilfred Owen*. *Up the Line to Death: The War Poets 1914–1918* edited by Brian Gardner, with a foreword by Edmund Blunden, was published in 1964. *Men Who March Away: Poems of the First World War*, edited by I. M. Parsons, appeared in 1965. These were followed by two collections specifically intended for use in schools: M. Hussey's *Poetry of the First World War* (1967) and E. L. Black's *1914–18 in Poetry* (1970).

Alongside this retrieval of First World War literature came academic studies of it. In America in 1964, J. H. Johnston published *English Poetry of the First World War*, and Stanley Cooperman published *World War I and the American Novel* in 1967. (This included an important chapter on the war-propaganda written by British men of letters specifically to be directed at America.) In England, Bernard Bergonzi published *Heroes' Twilight: A Study of the Literature of the Great War* in 1965; and *Promise of Greatness: The War of 1914–1918*, a collection of critical essays edited by George A. Panichas, appeared in 1968.

As Donald Davie perceptively pointed out in 1964, Johnston's efforts to judge the literary merits of works about the War, to adjudicate between, say, Blunden and Aldington, or Sassoon and Owen, rather missed the point. The disagreement that emerged over the value of the war-poets in particular, was essentially a disagreement between an 'inside' (British) view, and an 'outside' (American) view which had little to do with the skill or artistry of the writing at issue. Pieces by Rosenberg, Owen or Sassoon, were 'not poems at all, but something less than that and more; they are first-hand and faithful witnesses to a moment in the national destiny . . . high-water marks in the national psychology' (Davie, 1964: 282). In Davie's opinion, poems written out of the experience of the Flanders trenches and the 'battles' on the Western Front, documented a crisis in the life of the British nation, a shock from which the British imagination has never recovered. This opinion pin-pointed one aspect of the general idea which Cooperman was to explore with regard to American culture: 'we are all creatures of World War I, both in aesthetic and political terms' (Cooperman, 1967: viii).

Yet the imaginative memory of that national crisis was not conveyed in unison. As A. J. P. Taylor emphasised, the poets only spoke for a minority; they were mainly officers, even Wilfred Owen, who saw their 'men' from the outside. 'Literary' compositions presented the Tommy with affectionate contempt. To adopt Davie's rhetoric, the Somme and Passchendaele are scars on the national memory. That traumatic memory comes down to us from a divided society. The children born with no personal memory of the First World War had to find some way to circumvent the underlying pain, and the social resentment, if they were to make their own sense of the national past and of their own present. This they began to do.

In the 1970s a new crop of studies appeared. Every year of the decade brought at least one significant new book, from Martin Middlebrook's *The First Day on the Somme: 1st July, 1916* in 1971, to Robert Wohl's *The Generation of 1914* in 1980. Although the traditional historian, G. M. Trevelyan had barely mentioned the battle of the Somme in passing (Trevelyan, 1942: 547), A. J. P. Taylor pointed out that 'the Somme had set the picture by which future generations saw the First World War' (Taylor, 1963: 105), as a senseless, callous massacre due to the way in which blundering, obstinate, old generals misused the patriotic enthusiasm of brave, helpless, young men. Middlebrook, a Lincolnshire farmer, interviewed as many survivors of the battle of the Somme as he could still locate, 546 of them. He used their testimony to supplement the official records in his reconstruction of this, the biggest battle Britain had ever fought, and the most disastrous in terms of dead and wounded. Wohl, an American, examined in depth one of the main cultural myths to be found in all the countries that took part in the First World War. This myth as it existed in Britain had been detailed by Reginald Pound in *The Lost Generation* (1964): that those who died were 'the best, in body and spirit, of their generation' (Cole and Postgate, 1949: 535).

These two books represent one of the dimensions of the revision being attempted in the history of the First World War: in one direction to adjust the official, written history by appeal to personal memory; in the other to subject the popular myths about the War to an 'objective' analysis. An interest in myth became the dominant feature of books focussing on the First World War. The most influential work to appear at this time, and the one with the most powerful thesis, was Paul Fussell's *The Great War and Modern Memory* (1975). As he explained in his Preface, it was a book about the reciprocal relationship between literature and life. In particular it was about the Great War as a determinant of subsequent life: 'At the same time that the war was relying on inherited myth, it was generating new myth, and that myth is part of the fiber of our own lives' (Fussell, 1975: ix). His specific argument was: 'that there seems to be one dominating form of modern understanding; that it is essentially ironic; and that it originates in the application of mind and memory to the events of the Great War' (35). Fussell would not be at all surprised to discover that his book has itself become a major stimulus to literary imagination.

It was mythopoeic in other ways, too. Not merely did Fussell treat time, memory and the past as if entirely separate from the political and economic developments of any concrete society. He treated memory and culture as if they belonged to a sphere beyond the existence of individuals or the control of institutions. This enabled him to move indiscriminately between the British experience on the Western Front, and contemporary American novels, with no explanation at all of why or how the myths of modern Europe should be inherited by the New World. Above all it divorced war literature from the bed of propaganda within which, as Cooperman had shown, it gained its sense. Fussell ignored the fact that certain British writers (such as Richard Aldington and

C. E. Montague) had made it quite clear that their ironic detachment was a result of political disenchantment. Graves had waved his 'Goodbye' to a whole ideological world – although, as he later found, 'a conditioning in the Protestant morality of the English governing classes . . . is not easily outgrown' (Graves, 1957: 282). The relation between that conditioning and the 'medieval' values which Fussell explored and Cooperman had found to dominate British propaganda, Mark Girouard was to display as intimately connected with the ideology of British imperialism, in Chapter XVIII of *The Return to Camelot: Chivalry and the English Gentleman* (1981).

There is one myth Fussell does not consider, although it is one which he shares. Concentrating in general on the British experience on the Western Front from 1914 to 1918, and taking the first day on the Somme in particular as an 'archetypal original', Fussell quite unselfconsciously perpetuated the myth promoted by Homer in the story of Andromache and Hector in *The Illiad*: that during war women's best place is at home, for 'War is men's business'. A story recounted by Ray Strachey and often repeated concerns Dr Elsie Inglis's offer to the War Office of fully staffed medical units in 1914. Inglis and the other women doctors were told 'To go home and keep quiet' for the commanding officers 'did not want to be troubled with hysterical women' (Strachey, 1928: 338). (Inglis formed the NUWSS Scottish Women's Hospitals, which raised £500 000 and sent 14 hospital units abroad to help Britain's allies instead.)

Whereas Bergonzi's book managed without any reference to a woman writer whatsoever, even in the chapter entitled 'Civilian Responses', Fussell did mention the names of some dozen women within lists, or as the recipients of letters, or where they corroborated points made by one of his *500* literary sources. Those few exceptions prove the rule. Only two of the four new anthologies of poetry about the period 1914–18 contained any poetry by women, despite including sections of contributions from the Home Front and comments from remoter points in place and time. Hussey and Parsons included respectively one and two poems written by women. Like M. Greicus' *Prose Writers of World War One* (1973), Holger Klein's critical anthology, *The First World War in Fiction* (1976), only studied male authors. War is still generally conceived of by men as belonging to that zone of cultural experience which is exclusively male. Fussell was not alone in that view, but because of his choice of 'archetypal original', his thesis had the most extreme implications for women's share in the formation of modern culture.

Of course women lived through the First World War, and suffered; and many served on the Western Front. Yet although the First World War is seen and presented as the main determinant of modern British culture, the crucial area of that War, the experience of trench warfare and of one battle in particular, was a zone forbidden to women. Women were only attached to the Army as auxiliaries. They were not permitted within the firing-lines, and did not bear arms. That means, if Fussell can substantiate his thesis, that women were prohibited from direct participation in their national culture. In other words, although in Western culture the First World War is imaginatively seen to mark a shift as decisive as the loss of Eden, the flood, or the birth of Christ, one matter has remained unchanged since the time of the Ancient Greeks: the access of women to the crucial sphere of culturally significant experience. For an understanding of 'modern understanding' we remain dependent on men.

This 'men-only' construction of the Great War also came under challenge. If class was one dimension of the rewriting of national history, the other main dimension was gender. In 1977 the Imperial War Museum mounted an exhibition on the role of women in the First World War. To coincide with the exhibition (which went on tour, and resulted in one permanent showcase in the Museum), Arthur Marwick was commissioned to produce a book, which, with some excusable embarrassment at being 'a mere male', he did. The book, *Women At War 1914–1918*, drew on the notable archives amassed by the Women's War Work Sub-Committee of the Museum, established in 1917, and the records of women's suffrage organisations at the Fawcett Library. Marwick claimed to fill a lacuna in modern histories, by relating women's activities during the First World War to the women's movement for female suffrage, which had crescendoed before the War and partially achieved its goal in 1918.

This was somewhat disingenuous of him. Between 1957 and 1975 there had been a number of books on the women's suffrage movement, mostly concentrating on the spectacular suffragettes led by Mrs Pankhurst, whose movement ceased its guerrilla warfare in 1914. It is true that the books themselves also rather lamely halted with 1914, allocating only a few pages to the events between 1914 and 1918. They had therefore failed to make any reasoned connection between the War and the attainment of the vote for women. This is mainly because they seem to have been in ignorance of the original history of the Women's Movement, Ray Strachey's *The Cause*. This was first published in 1928. While referring to Mrs Pankhurst and the WSPU, it relied upon the personal memories of Mrs Fawcett, the president of the far larger and older organisation, the NUWSS. Ray Strachey made Mrs Fawcett's view of the link between women's war-work and the 1918 Act quite explicit. This view was specifically contested by Sylvia Pankhurst in 'Votes for Women', Chapter LI of *The Home Front* (1932). Although Marwick makes use of her examples, he does not mention his indebtedness to either Pankhurst or Strachey.

The nature of the link between women's war-work and female suffrage is far more complicated than either Strachey or Marwick makes out. One reasoned discussion, by Martin Pugh in the journal *History* in 1974, argued that the War actually hindered the progress of the women's franchise. Marwick simply dismisses this as 'an absurd contention'. Marwick then, like a previous popular historian, David Mitchell, in *Women on the Warpath: the Story of the Women of the First World War* (1966), traces the history of women's work during the First World War by means of the mountains of propaganda put out by women of the period to advertise how necessary they were to the successful prosecution of the War. It seems they believed their own propaganda. 'Inflated by the wind of patriotic romanticism purveyed by the press, the women of Britain became a gigantic mutual admiration society; now that they knew their worth, they knew they were worthy of the vote . . . By 1916 the anti-suffragist was a negligible figure' (Marwick 1965: 96). But so was the suffragist. What most women had wanted was public equality with their brothers. During the War they apparently gained as much as they desired. Then, according to women's autobiographies, in the stress of the War the vote seemed to have become an irrelevant issue.

Television also contributed to the women's memory of the First World War. In 1974 the award-winning London Weekend Television series, *Upstairs, Downstairs*, featured women's work during the Great War. Upstairs the ladies exchanged their society life for voluntary nursing, and the problems of refugees and relief committees. Downstairs, the female domestic servants faced the choice

of working for higher wages in munitions factories. A book based
on this part of the series, *'The War to End Wars'* by Mollie Hardwick,
was published in paperback in 1975. In 1978, a television adaptation of the most famous woman's autobiography of the First World
War was broadcast as a serial. This was so popular that it was
repeated, and sold abroad. Vera Brittain's *Testament of Youth* had
been a best-seller on publication in 1933, and remained a great
favourite, although, unlike the autobiographies of Graves, Blunden
and Sassoon, it did not qualify for a place in A. G. S. Enser's
comprehensive *A Subject Bibliography of First World War Books in
English, 1914–78* (1979). *Testament of Youth* was republished in
paperback in 1978, and reissued annually again thereafter. Of all
the women who wrote about their experiences during the Great
War, Vera Brittain was the only one who had remained well
enough known to be asked to contribute to the memorial volume
edited by George A. Panichas in 1968: *Promise of Greatness*. Either
Bergonzi had never heard of her, or he did not regard her work as
'literature'.

From the late 1970s there began to appear a number of books by
women which studied the female dimension of the memory of the
Great War. In 1978 Mary Cadogan and Patricia Craig published
Women and Children First: The Fiction of Two World Wars, which
included a consideration of the way in which women were portrayed in the fiction of the First World War, especially in writing by
women. *Roses of No Man's Land*, Lynn Macdonald's history of the
First World War Red Cross nurse, appeared in 1980. The title of
this account of a generation of nursing volunteers, 'gently nurtured
girls who walked straight out of Edwardian drawing-rooms into
the manifold horrors of the First World War', was taken from a
music-hall hit of the time. Avoiding earlier written reports, Macdonald based her account directly on women's recollections in
interview with her. These books were followed in 1981 by two
scholarly studies by women, based on work for professional
qualifications. *Scars Upon My Heart: Women's Poetry and Verse of the
First World War* was selected by Catherine Reilly, using bibliographical research she had carried out for a fellowship of the
Library Association. Having identified over 2000 individuals who
had published verse on the theme of the First World War, she had
found that at least five hundred of them (about 25 per cent) were
women, including such famous poets as Dame Edith Sitwell. *Scars
Upon My Heart* republished works by 79 of these women. *Women*

Workers in the First World War: The British Experience was an analysis by Gail Braybon of the statistical evidence concerning the effect that the War had on women's employment. She was awarded a doctorate for this research. She followed it in 1987 with a more popular book of social history, which relied largely on what women themselves had written and remembered about their experience of war work. A whole issue of the journal *Oral History* had been devoted to this topic in 1977, and Braybon frequently cited a work first published in 1978: Peggy Hamilton's *Three Years or the Duration: Memoirs of a Munitions Worker 1914–1918*. Braybon's book, jointly authored with Penny Summerfield, was called *Out of the Cage*. Dealing with both World Wars, it extended the ongoing argument about just how liberating war-work had been and felt for women.

In the first months of the War unemployment amongst working-class women had risen rapidly as the wealthy upper classes economised. But once conscription became law in 1916 women were called upon to take men's places. Braybon's analysis shows that by the end of the War there had been a increase of about 1.5 million women in the industrial labour force, from 3 276 000 to 4 808 000. Of these perhaps half a million had changed from domestic service. The figures include one million working in munitions factories (in jobs which virtually disappeared after the War). Numbers in other areas of employment are less spectacular, but they include a rise of 300 000 in commerce, 54 000 in banking, and nearly 100 000 in the civil service. Transport also saw a rise of nearly 100 000, from 18 000 to 117 000. Many middle-class women found public work for the first time. There was a women's Land Army of 23 000 helping in agriculture. By 1917 there were 100 000 extra voluntary nurses, 45 000 in military hospitals. They encountered antagonism from established nurses similar to the prejudice shown to women in factories by male industrial workers. The armed forces were supported by a body of uniformed auxiliaries, of about 40 000 women, some 8500 of whom served abroad in addition to 5000 nurses and VAD's. Women lost the comparatively well-paid employment to men when the War ended, many being forced reluctantly back into domestic service. Of course, all voluntary and military jobs disappeared altogether.

The philosopher Genevieve Lloyd has demonstrated that Western political thought has specifically associated women with the sphere of domestic, private values, requiring men alone to act in the public sphere and to sacrifice their lives for the State (Lloyd, 1986). Women nurtured individuals and were expected to be the guardians of certain personal needs and obligations, which were safeguarded in the home. Only men could become citizens, playing their role in situations which rejected personal, private considerations. Containing women was a way of containing what they were held to stand for – the importance of personal life. The State required this to be of secondary importance to the needs of the nation as a whole. As the public world became ever more inhuman, so the pressure was stronger for women to represent the excluded human values in the private sanctuary of the home. Women themselves came to symbolise those values, and had to be protected and fought for on their behalf. A threat to the special position of women was a threat to the values they stood for. The masculine and feminine worlds became ever more demarcated and exclusive.

Women spoke out against this situation, both on their own behalf as individuals, and on behalf of the 'feminine sphere of influence' which they believed should be extended into the public, masculine arena. Or rather, as Susan Kingsley Kent expresses it: 'Nineteenth-century feminists argued that the public and the private were not distinct spheres, but were inseparable from one another; the public was the private, the personal was the political' (Kent, 1987: 5). Whilst acting individually on various fronts from the 1850s onwards, to show that women's abilities were not exhausted by motherhood, and that even mothers might benefit from the opportunity of university education, women also campaigned collectively for the right to vote and stand in Parliamentary elections. They wished to be able to control their legal protection against their so-called protectors. Women were divided as to how far they identified with the cultural definitions of femininity and their expected role as wives and mothers. Nor were they in agreement as to how to achieve changes in the *status quo*, or who were their best allies. But what was inescapable was that women wanted their voice to be heard. And one of the matters they wanted their voice to be heard about was war.

During the same year as Marwick's book about women's contribution to the government's war aims in 1914–18, an article appeared in the journal *History*, by the Cambridge historian Jo Vellacott Newberry: 'Anti-war Suffragists' (Newberry, 1977). This was a seminal paper which drew on a book published in 1965, *The Women's International League for Peace and Freedom*, by Gertrude

Bussey and Margaret Tims. Vellacott countered the emphasis placed on the suffragettes in the recent history of how women got the vote, by concentrating on the activities of constitutional, non-militant suffragists during the First World War. Believing in non-violence, several important members of the NUWSS worked during the War for the Union of Democratic Control (of Foreign Policy), for the Non-Conscription Fellowship, and for the WILPF. These were the main organisations working for a negotiated peace settlement in place of armed conflict and 'a fight to the finish'. Vellacott's paper stimulated a number of other works on women's involvement with pacifism, and the retrieval of women's anti-war writings. In America a collection of papers edited by Judith Stiehm, *Women and Men's Wars* (1982) included several on the topic of the First World War. The activities by women at Greenham Common led to an increased interest in this aspect of women's history, and sparked off Anne Wiltsher's comprehensive account: *Most Dangerous Women: Feminist Peace Campaigners of the Great War* (1986).

This is the conceptual framework within which I propose that 'war literature' must be defined and understood. While war was taken to mean 'armed conflict', with the assumption that physical combat is natural (and even desirable) between males, since to be truly masculine is to be prepared to kill other men, women would hardly be able to write about war. They would be specifically excluded from direct acquaintance with it, by the very way their feminine nature was conceived. If, on the other hand, war is taken to be a state of hostility between human beings, and the whole way of life where such a state of hostility exists and is taken for granted, even actively promoted, then women certainly know about it and can write about it and its consequences.

Most studies of so-called 'war-literature', in poetry or prose, have been primarily concerned with descriptions of the battlefront. They seem to be covertly devoted to the vicarious thrills of danger and the erotic myth of the fellowship of warriors. Women's literary responses to war, however, tend to be much wider and more subtle in scope than battle-tales, since they are interested in the social context of belligerence and its connection with personal relations and the quality of ordinary life. Women have always been the sufferers in wartime, their peacetime way of life inevitably disrupted as they become nurses, widows, refugees, slaves. As a result they are less intrigued with the excitements of battle. Women's writing about war before the Great War concentrated on

the effects of militarism, nationalism and patriotism, and on the
definition of masculinity and femininity. Women were concerned
with what men and women were expected or allowed to do or to
become.

Although it is not clear quite what effect the First World War had
on British women's consciousness and the movement for women's
rights in Britain, it is clear that this is a matter of supreme
importance to the history of women, and thus to the proper
understanding of British society. It would not be absurd to argue
that the creation of women's citizenship in 1918 (and its extension
in 1928) was at least as important a determinant of modern
consciousness as the Battle of the Somme. What is curious is that
many women who lived through that period saw the War itself as
overriding their interest in women's suffrage. With the War came
the opportunity for them to achieve what they had struggled for:
entry to what had been seen before as male centres of power. The
female dimension of the history of the First World War concerns
politics, employment, national service. Women's war-literature
reflects these concerns.

If we adapt the model used by Elaine Showalter in 'Feminist
Criticism in the Wilderness' (1981), we could say that women's
writing of that period was not concerned with the 'wild zone' of
women's culture. Women were not then so concerned to express that
imaginary area of their experience which was literally 'no-man's-
land', off-limits to men and so outside the dominant culture.
Rather, their literature is concerned with women's entry into that
exclusive part of the national culture which had previously been
forbidden to women, all that area of public privilege and power to
which men had access, and women did not, such as politics, the
professions, skilled industrial work, sexual adventure. Above all, it
concerns their access to military institutions and the martial zone.
Which is why it is all the more important for an understanding of
our cultural past that women's writings of the Great War should
not be excluded from the cultural debate as to what we remember.

What I proposed to do when I first embarked on this study was
to modify and extend Paul Fussell's thesis, in order to include
women among the possessors of 'modern memory'. There were
two highly acclaimed novels by women from the 1970s which
would make good test cases: Susan Hill's *Strange Meeting* (1971)
and Jennifer Johnston's *How Many Miles to Babylon?* (1974). The
feature which the books shared was that they were both written as

men's war biographies. These women had used the common cultural memory of the trench experience as a way of representing a fundamental emotional truth about British social relations. The field of Great War imagery became a way for them to understand male homoeroticism as a response to the hostility and alienation endemic to British imperial society. However, what came to perplex me was why women's imagination should rely on cultural myths based on men's experience. Were there no memoirs by women to fire people's imagination; were women not the source of cultural myths too?

My study required a much wider empirical groundwork. Catherine Reilly's bibliographical work, and the study by Cadogan and Craig, as well as a later book by Nicola Beauman, *A Very Great Profession: The Women's Novel 1914–39* (1983), all indicated that there was a great deal of writing by women which was failing to be considered by male critics such as Fussell, Bergonzi, Klein. What I decided to do was to go back to base and try to see what was characteristic of women's writing, of all types, in response to the First World War. Had it been, like the men's, idealistic to begin with and had it only become ironic as a result of the reports of men's experience in the war zone forbidden to women? Was the Battle of the Somme the determining factor for women too? Did they share the cultural myths based on men's tales, or did they have tales of their own?

Taking the notion of 'myth' to indicate a story or motif which is felt to be significant in a particular culture, this work addresses the following question: is women's writing about the Great War mythopoeic? In other words, does there exist an imaginative memory of the First World War which is distinctively women's? If so, has it influenced the form of modern (British) understanding? My answers are an effort to see what part women's writing plays in the construction of a national culture.

Women's written memory was not homogeneous. Nor was the men's. The first great flood of famous 'war-books' came ten years after the propaganda and poetry of the War-period. They were memoirs written by young men with experience of the front-line, to correct the official military histories written by the old men, either generals well behind the lines, or elderly civilians at home such as Masefield and Kipling. With few exceptions (such as Ivor Gurney, Isaac Rosenberg and David Jones), the famous young poets and memoirists of the War were mainly middle-class and officers. The second aspect of the revision was the emphasis on the oral and written literature of the ordinary soldier, in such works as *The Long Trail: Songs and Slang of the British Soldier, 1914–1918* (1931; reprinted 1965), edited by J. Brophy and E. Partridge. Auto-biographies by common soldiers such as Frank Richards were scanter, but several were eventually written 50 years after the War. Their diaries and letters were also retrieved in the 1970s, resulting in several volumes edited by Michael Moynihan. Together with this interest in working-class memory came a revival of the story of pacifists and conscientious objectors, and of the trade union activity that matched the mutinies and anti-conscription movements. The fourth dimension of the reaction to the dominant 'official histories' was internationalist. Anthologists made a deliberate effort to cross national boundaries in such collections as *The Soldier's War* (1929), an anthology of prose extracts edited by J. Brophy, and Eugene Löhrke's *Armageddon: The World War in Literature* (1930).

The parameters of androcentric history were age, class and political or religious commitment. The over-riding factor was nationality, obfuscated by ideas of race, and ambiguities between 'English' and 'British'. These are also the parameters of gynocentric history. However, although historians are now investigating the oral history of working women, most of the first-hand accounts and imaginative responses to the First World War were written by middle-class women. The main 'class' difference and conflict which writing women were aware of was not between middle-class and working-class females; it was between the 'Lady' of the upper- and middle-class, and the educated 'New Woman'. ('Class' is a notoriously elusive category. At the time Margaret Bondfield determined women's class position by education: women who had only been to elementary school were working-class, the rest were middle-class. I should add that women who had only had governesses and possibly never been to school at all were 'Ladies'.) The generational conflict between fathers and sons was paralleled by the envious expectations and demands made on young women by older women. This was associated with a distinct women's history. Women's literature about the First World War was deeply affected by the pre-War women's movement, especially the struggle for female suffrage, but that is a huge and controversial topic which could well swamp this study. I adopt a procedure of Virginia Woolf's, of tunnelling back into that ground where it seems enlightening.

For my factual knowledge of the general pre-War culture of Britain, I have relied on research by Samuel Hynes, John MacKenzie and Mark Girouard; for my theoretical understanding of women's politics I have followed Jo Vellacott and Les Garner; and for my ideas about the nature of women's literary history I am indebted to Jane Marcus and Elaine Showalter. For the empirical data of published texts, I drew on bibliographies by Cyril Falls, A. G. S. Enser, and Philip E. Hager and Desmond Taylor, and on the critical studies by Catherine Reilly, Nichola Beauman, and Mary Cadogan and Patricia Craig; I studied the *Times Literary Supplement* for the years 1915–35, when it published lists of new fiction; and I scoured second-hand bookshops for the modern paperbacks that do not reach library catalogues or critical bibliographies. About the whole question of Great War myth and modern consciusness I was stimulated by the books by Stanley Cooperman, Eric J. Leed, and, above all, Paul Fussell.

It is beyond my scope to deal with American imagination, or to discuss the relative contribution to 'modern' understanding of British or American experience. I have limited myself to works that were written by women with experience of Europe during the First World War, published in English, and available in England. Since all written material can generate and transmit myths, I have not bogged myself down in trying to distinguish fiction from non-fiction. What is important to this study is not so much whether tales were true or false, but what ideas and incidents have been seen as 'significant'. To try to gauge cultural significance precisely would be like grabbing at a rainbow. I have relied on general indicators such as wide sales and reprinting; notices in literary reviews; prizes and censorship. Paul Fussell's aim was to guess at the imaginative impact of myths; my study turned out to have a less nebulous goal. It became more concerned with what cushioned the imaginative drive of women's writing so that their myths were stifled.

1

The Heroic Pageantry
of War

JOURNALISM, WOMEN WAR-CORRESPONDENTS 1914–16,
AND THE IDEOLOGY OF WAR

In his book *Realities of War*, not published until 1920, Philip Gibbs
referred to the spirit of adventure in which young writing men set
out to the Continent in 1914. They went to see 'what war meant in
civilised countries', and made 'wild, desperate efforts to break
through the barrier that had been put up against them by French
and British staffs in the zone of war' (Gibbs, 1920: 3). That was not
the only barrier they had to overcome. When these young men
returned to Fleet Street, they were still unable to write the things
they had seen. They were unable to tell them to people who had
not seen and could not understand.

> Because there was no code of words which would convey the
> picture of that wild agony of peoples, that smashing of all
> civilised lands, to men and women who still thought of war in
> terms of heroic pageantry. (4)

It was not until June 1915 that Gibbs received full credentials as a
war correspondent with the British armies on the Western Front. It
took a further six months for the Commander-in-Chief, recognising that civilian support was necessary 'to hearten the troops',
to agree to relax the censorship a little. Thereafter, Gibbs 'wrote all
that was good to write of the actions day by day' although he 'had
to leave out something of the underlying horror of them all' (24). In
1920 he was still having difficulty with more than an appropriate
'code of words'; continuing to write about 'German hordes',
'punctilious chivalry', and 'the beau ideal of knighthood', he was
revealing his retention of a whole cast of thought which the War
had revealed as archaic. In 1920 he himself was *knighted* for his war
work.

Many women also reacted to the declaration of war in a spirit of adventure. They too found the same problems as Gibbs was still manifesting in 1920, not only in creating a language adequate to what they actually encountered, but in reconciling what they saw of the War with their preconceptions about the 'heroic pageantry' of war. This was more than a matter of the nice choice of vocabulary by which to convey the smashing of civilisation while omitting the underlying horror. The idea of war was intimately connected with many other values of Western culture. To challenge its heroic image was to undermine ideas fundamental to their world and to their conception of history.

One of the first books to be published about the War was by an elderly American woman, Mildred Aldrich. In June 1914 she had given up working as a newspaper critic in Paris to retire peacefully to a house on a hill in the countryside 20 miles outside Paris. She called her war-book *A Hilltop on the Marne* (1915). Typically of much women's writing of the period, this is not a novel. It is in that early form of 'journalism' which gained popularity at the turn of the century with *Elizabeth and her German Garden* (1898), a book in the form of a journal of events and impressions. Indeed, Aldrich's book gains from the ironic field of force thrown out by Elizabeth von Arnim's well-known work, in which a woman finds peace and happiness by escaping from the artificiality of town-life to the solitary creation of a beautiful garden in the German countryside. Elizabeth's tranquillity was only disturbed by visits from her bullying German husband. Aldrich's peaceful solitude was immediately threatened by the German invasion, and she found her hilltop garden involved in the Battle of the Marne. This was the decisive encounter that saved Paris in the first days of the War and led to the four-year entrenchment of the opposing armies.

Like Elizabeth's, Aldrich's tone is familiar, and the book becomes a self-portrait as much as a narrative. Like the best journalism it demonstrates how difficult it is to discover facts or reach an objective view, to write 'history' while it is taking place. The stress on the writer's personality, wrily conscious of the advantages of her age but the vulnerability of her sex, marks the awareness that is absent from, say, Barbara Tuchman's *The Guns of August – August 1914*, for all the historian's use of documentation. Aldrich's hilltop home not only gives her a spatial panorama of the battlefield of the Marne; it is also a metaphor for the perspective on life that she has attained with age. It comes to symbolise her outlook on war, which is essentially that of a spectator – but not one who is impartial.

The journal runs from 3 June 1914 to 8 September 1914. Although probably based on letters written by Aldrich to her friend Gertrude Stein, who had got caught in England at this time, the fictional work is addressed to a young, unnamed American who has returned to 'The Land of the Free and the Home of the Brave', by a woman of over 60, for whom 'the end is the most interesting event ahead'. On 2 August the *garde champêtre* drums out the mobilisation order: 'War again!' Not war as her friend will read about it in the newspapers in the States, but 'war right here' (44). She is not entirely innocent: 'It will be the bloodiest affair the world has ever seen' – a war in the air, under the sea as well as on it, and carried out with 'the most effective man-slaughtering machines ever used in battle' (41). She becomes not only 'reconciled to living a long time now' in order to see what happens; she is actually 'excited over this ugly business' (47).

By 10 August, with the planes still flying overhead, and with stern, silent groups of men walking past her hedge, accompanied by their women and leading children by the hand, she writes revealingly: 'It has all been so thrilling that I find myself forgetting that it is tragic'. What she finds thrilling is not the blatant intoxication of war-fever but the idea of a people silently united.

> I am old enough to remember well the days of our Civil War, when regiments of volunteers, with flying flags and bands of music, marched through our streets in Boston, on the way to the front. Crowds of stay-at-homes, throngs of women and children lined the sidewalks, shouting deliriously, and waving handkerchiefs, inspired by the marching soldiers, with guns on their shoulders, and the strains of martial music, varied with the then popular 'The girl I left behind me,' or, 'When this cruel war is over.' But this is different. (51)

If she is thrilled it is rather because of than despite her sense of the seriousness of war. 'Since the day when war was declared ... I have seen sights that have moved me as nothing I have ever met in life before has done. Day after day I have watched the men and their family pass silently, and an hour later have seen the women come back leading the children' (52).

The apparent denial of sensationalism is what makes her account so compelling. It is, nevertheless, emotionally highly charged. She remarks on one musician who, like his father, is very timid, 'But he accepted the war without a word, though nothing is more foreign to his nature'. What she calls 'this rising up of a Nation in self-defence' she finds is 'not the marching into battle of an army that has chosen soldiering. It is the marching out of all the people – all classes shoulder to shoulder – all men, because they happen to be males, called on' (57). But she finds the women remarkable, too, together with the old men and the children going to the fields to get the crops in. The get-up of the unprepared soldiers amused her 'almost to tears': 'in their patched trousers and blouses and *sabots*, with a band round the left arm, a broken soldier cap, and a gun on the shoulder' (64). Her mundane descriptions are also amusing, despite her sense of the seriousness of it all. She catches a train into Paris, that is crowded with evacuees and wounded soldiers: 'It was packed as the Brookline street cars used to be on the days of the baseball game. Men were absolutely hanging on the roof; women were packed on the steps that led up to the imperials to the third-class coaches. It was a perilous-looking sight' (78).

When the first tired remnants of the British Expeditionary Forces arrive at her doorstep, she begins to understand the danger she is in, on her prominent hilltop above the main route towards Paris. She learns from their officer that these exhausted men had been in four actions in the retreat: 'Saint-Quentin was pretty rough luck. We went into the trenches a full regiment. We came out to retreat again with four hundred men' (95). There are Germans in the vicinity, but she manages to ask him what she should expect, just as if it were 'the sort of tea-table conversation' to which she was accustomed. Shortly afterwards she is visited by a stray group of perfectly civil German Uhlans, and then by a randy Irish scout on a bicycle who gives her more trouble than the Germans. She had recounted the scorn and bitter feeling in the locality against Germans, but for herself, she merely finds it hard to be polite to them. Further on she is to repeat a common-sense blow to propaganda atrocity-tales of the Germans deliberately firing on the Red Cross: 'If we screen our hospital behind a building and a shell comes over and blows us up, how can we swear that the shell was aimed at us?' Her method for getting rid of the Irishman diverts her from the booming of the cannon.

In the afternoon of Saturday, 5 September, the cannonading gets heavier and the battle advances to where she could watch it on the plain. She had imagined long lines of marching soldiers, detachments of flying cavalry, 'like the war-pictures at Versailles and Fontainebleau' but an actual battle was nothing like that. 'There was only noise, belching smoke, and long drifts of white clouds concealing the hill' (126). Her expectations were conditioned by the type of war-painting popular with the Victorians, which depicted war as a heroic spectacle. One of the most successful painters of military themes at the end of the 19th century was Lady Elizabeth Butler, a soldier's wife, who described her views about war and war-art in her autobiography: 'War . . . calls forth the noblest and basest impulses of human nature. The painter should be careful to keep himself at a distance, lest the ignoble and vile details under his eyes should blind him irretrievably to the noble things that rise beyond' (Butler, 1922: 46).

Mildred Aldrich also keeps herself at a distance. 'To my imagination every shot meant awful slaughter, and between me and the terrible thing stretched a beautiful country, as calm in the sunshine as if horrors were not' (127). She could see in the field below the wheat being cut, and women and children stacking and gleaning. The 'awful slaughter' of her imagination remains out of sight. It was not until sunset, at about six o'clock, that the first bomb that she could really see came over the hill.

> For two hours we saw them rise, descend, explode. Then a little smoke would rise from one hamlet, then from another; then a tiny flame – hardly more than a spark – would be visible; and by dark the whole plain was on fire, lighting up Mareuil in the foreground, silent and untouched. There were long lines of grain-stacks and mills stretching along the plain. One by one they took fire, until, by ten o'clock, they stood like a procession of huge torches across my beloved panorama. (128)

That calm simple prose grants full force to the destructive power of war, by contrast with the vulnerable, productive scene that precedes it. But it concentrates on the visually dramatic destruction of objects rather than on the slaughter of people. Despite pretty references to 'the poor fellows lying dead out there in the starlight', the 'horrors' for the wounded and their families cannot be seen from her hillside.

What we do not know is whether she herself did not know, or decided to omit, what Gibbs later revealed about those fields:

> The German dead had been gathered into heaps like autumn leaves. They were soaked in petrol, and oily smoke was rising from them. (Gibbs, 1920: 6)

Of the fighting itself she sees nothing, but she responds ironically to what she hears. The English Tommies did not speak of the War at all, so the first real battle tales she is treated to are from a French lad of the ambulance corps. Laughingly, 'with his Latin eloquence' he told her graphic stories that 'made me see how war affects men, and how often the horrible passes across the line into the grotesque'. At one point he claims, 'It was so awful that it became comic': in the battle for Charleroi, the French *mitrailleuses* made such havoc in the German ranks that

> the air was so full of flying heads and arms and legs, of boots, and helmets, swords, and guns that it did not seem as if it could be real – 'it looked like some burlesque'; and that even one of the gunners turned ill and said to his commander, who stood beside him: 'For the love of God, colonel, shall I go on?' and the colonel, with folded arms, replied: 'Fire away.' (145–6)

She comments, 'Perhaps it is lucky, since war is, that men can be like that. When they cannot, what then? But it was too terrible for me' (146).

She finds the domineeringly courteous French billeted on her less sensitive to her feelings than the British, but her irony is finely placed. She is reluctant to look again at the battlefield but good manners require her to point out the towns to the French officers, and answer their questions. Disregarding the cannon booming in the northeast, they confront the view as smilingly as one would go into a ballroom. Observing her emotion one responds: 'The day will come . . . when you will look with pride, not pain, and be glad that you saw what may prove the turning of the tide in the noblest war ever fought for civilization' (152). She was not convinced by this grandiloquence, and later marks with inverted commas their judgement of the duel of heavy artillery which the battle had become: 'magnificent' (153). She does not share their excitement over attempts to shoot down a Taube, 'treating it as if it were a Fourteenth of July show'. One was sorry she missed seeing it come down: 'It is a beautiful sight' (154). Not commenting directly she records her silent preference for the plane not to come down in her garden, and only later caustically picks up the idea of the beautiful sight. Picturing the men sleeping on the hillside in the moonlight, she comments: 'It was really very beautiful if one could have forgotten that tomorrow many of these men would be sleeping for good'. She had already, in reference to the boys of the neighbourhood swimming the Marne to see the previous Saturday's battlefield, remarked on 'the hilarious, *macabre* spirit of the French untried lads crossing the river to look on horrors as if it were a lark' (141). Later, recording her 'strange sensation' about the men who passed so rapidly in and out of her life, she wrote: 'I did wish I could see only the picturesque side of it' (159).

When the French soldiers leave, again 'no bands played. No drum beat'. As she says, she tried in her book to make as clear a statement of facts as she could. What comes over is her own practical courage, shared by her near neighbours, and, despite her emotional responsiveness, her determination not to find war glamorous. She remains equally unimpressed by ghoulishness or heroics. Her own courage she describes simply as not having 'been sufficiently afraid to run away and leave my house to be looted unless I had to'. She pays tribute to the determination of ordinary men and women, is stirred by the horror, but reports as faithfully as she can the sheer banality and disorder of war. Her pointed reminders that this is not a tea-party, ballroom, or fireworks display, a baseball game or cricket match, ironically leave us to remember that these 'old friends' she makes under the stress of war are engaged in a deadly activity, and their passing is likely to be final. She does not encourage the reader to indulge in any vicarious emotion for them, but on the other hand neither does she bring herself to examine the nature of what she refers to as 'the horrors' of war. She relies on euphemisms such as 'sleeping' to avoid peering too closely.

As the War progressed she was encouraged to bring out further books. Although she continually claimed 'I can only speak of what I see and hear' she became increasingly affected by Allied propaganda, until when the Lusitania was sunk in May 1915 she wrote: 'Germany is the most absolute synonym of evil that history has ever seen' (Aldrich, 1917: 90). She might have said with Gibbs:

My duty was that of a chronicler, not arguing why things should have happened so, nor giving reasons why they should **not** happen so, but describing faithfully many of the things I saw, and narrating the facts as I found them, as far as the Censorship would allow. (Gibbs, 1920: v)

She would have been equally deceived. Attempting to chronicle only what she witnessed, without overt argument or explanation, she treats the War like a thrilling spectacular, with the nationalism inherent to the genre.

For over a century variety theatres had presented war spectaculars. For instance, in 1804 *The Siege of Gibraltar* was represented at Sadler's Wells on an artificial lake 40 feet deep and nearly 100 feet in length. Real ships of 100 guns were built. They were fully rigged and manoeuvred correctly. Floating batteries took fire, some blowing up with a dreadful explosion, while British tars plunged into the water to save drowning Spaniards (Willson Disher, 1942: 38). In 1825 Astley's Royal Amphitheatre performed both *The Burmese War*, 'a grand naval and military melo-drama' and *The Burning of Moscow*, 'a grand military and equestrian spectacle' (28–9, 17). Throughout the 19th century equestrian dramas formed the climax to circus programmes, and from the 1880s these became re-enactments of British military triumphs, such as Waterloo, the Afghan war, the relief of Ladysmith, and the Sudanese campaign. The greatest spectacle of Sanger's circus in the 1890s was the Relief of Khartoum, which employed '700 men, 100 camels, 200 real tribesmen, the fifes and drums of the Grenadier Guards and the pipes of the Scots Guards'. Real rifles and field guns were used, and the 'wounded' were carried off in real, horse-drawn ambulances (Beaver, 1979: 44–5, 54–5). So commonplace were these theatrical events that the novelist Sarah Macnaughton had difficulty in shaking off the idea that what she saw at a railway station in Flanders had been staged by a demented impresario:

> At Drury Lane one would have said that the staging had been overdone, that the clothes were *too* ragged, the men *too* gaunt and obviously wounded, and that by no stretch of the imagination could a band be playing God Save the King while a painted train called Lou-Lou steamed in, looking like a child's giant gaudy toy, and an aeroplane fussed overhead. (Macnaughtan, 1915: 125).

Circus promotional cavalcades of the period featured dazzlingly splendid tableaux of mythical figures such as St George and the dragon, or Britannia (with a live lion). Amateur productions re-enacting the glories of the past were also popular, both in villages and cities, and the suffragettes used massive street parades of famous women to publicise their campaign for the vote. Pageantry with its medieval associations suggests that the past is colourful and attractive and linked in a gradual progress to the present. It ignores what is not picturesque; by reflecting only surface appearances it evades the controversial nature of historical change and actually obscures any explanation of the underlying political issues.

Aldrich's writing amply demonstrates the impossibility of being an independent observer, and the contradictions inherent in the idea of the 'innocent eye'. Having experienced war before, but a civil war, she was thrilled by the idea of an international war which would unite a nation against a common enemy, rather than accentuate internal divisions. While she did not glorify the destruction entailed, she tended to idealise the social effects of the War: 'I know that a long peace makes for weakness in a race' (69). In all this she was voicing the ideas of the period in which she grew up, the Victorian belief in the ennobling, unifying, evolutionary aspects of war. The War did break down social barriers, and she found herself able to meet and speak on an equal footing with a range of people which pre-war conventions would have forbidden. That was exciting, as the danger was thrilling. But it did not signify any fundamental change in the system of privilege on which European society was based. With no strong grasp of the political background to the War, no understanding of how imperialist rivalry and treaty-making induced a sense of threat that led to nationalism and aggression, she simply accepted war as a natural phenomenon. This made her an easy target for the British propaganda specifically aimed at Americans.

Aldrich's is one of the earliest of a rash of 'eye-witness' war-reports by women, ostensibly published to raise money for various war-efforts. It is of interest to compare it with another journal kept in September 1914 by another middle-aged woman, which was also published in 1915. The well-known English novelist May Sinclair (who was probably 50, she kept her age secret) was one of the first English women to arrive on the Continent after war was declared. She went as secretary and publicist to a Motor Ambulance Unit, and based her *Journal of Impressions in Belgium* on the Day Book she kept to record its activities. Parts of the journal were first published in *The English Review* in May, June and July 1915 under the general heading 'The War of Liberation – From a Journal', and a fuller version appeared as a book at the end of that year.

She gained a good deal of amusement from the early appearance and exploits of the 13 members of the corps, two of whom went on to become 'the Heroines of Pervyse', but this levity is sobred by her first encounter with thousands of the destitute refugees that the War had already produced, whose misery evades her descriptive powers:

> [The Palais] is an immense building, rather like Olympia. It stands away from the town in open grounds like the Botanical Gardens, Regent's Park. It is where the great annual shows were held and vast civic entertainments given. Metres of country round Ghent are given up to market-gardening. There are whole fields of begonias out here, brilliant and vivid in the sun. They will never be sold, never gathered, never shown at the Palais des Fêtes. It is the peasants, the men and women who tilled these fields, and their children that are being shown here, in the splendid and wonderful place where they never set foot before. (Sinclair, 1915: 176)

Sinclair attempts to make the reader a voyeur at this exhibition of picturesque 'final and supreme' desolation, with hyperbole that overleaps itself: 'there are no words for it, because there are no ideas for it ... you are stunned, stupefied'. She then stoops to sentimentalise her account by dwelling on one of the 'little things [that] strike you': an absurd little mongrel terrier that a family has brought with it.

Journal of Impressions is an apt title, for Sinclair makes little effort at any kind of factual accuracy; her concern becomes increasingly the emotional effect that her experiences have on her, and these are almost gloated over. Already on the first day after her arrival in Ostend, whilst driving to Ghent, she sees 'the first visible intimation that the enemy may be anywhere':

> A curious excitement comes to you. I suppose it is excitement, though it doesn't feel like it. You have been drunk, very slightly drunk, with the speed of the car. But now you are sober. Your heart beats quietly, steadily, but with a little creeping, mounting

thrill in the beat. The sensation is distinctly pleasurable. You say to yourself, 'It is coming. Now – or the next minute – perhaps at the end of the road.' You have one moment of regret. 'After all, it would be a pity if it came too soon, before we'd even even begun our job.' But the thrill, mounting steadily, overtakes the regret. It is only a little thrill, so far (for you don't really believe that there is any danger), but you can imagine the thing growing, growing steadily, till it becomes ecstasy. Not that you imagine anything at the moment. At the moment you are no longer an observing, reflecting being; you have ceased to be aware of yourself; you exist only in that quiet, steady thrill that is so unlike any excitement that you have ever known. Presently you get used to it. 'What a fool I should have been if I hadn't come. I wouldn't have missed this run for the world.' (170–1)

This description parallels her first encounter with a 'hero', a 'magnificent' figure, 'tall and handsome', who is said to 'have accounted for nine Germans with his own rifle in one morning': 'Drenched in the glamour of the greatest possible danger, he gives it off like a subtle essence' (93). Intoxicated by the scent of danger, Sinclair's journal, constantly impressed, strikes off at a tangent from that war at which Aldrich gazed so fixedly, resistant to its charms.

This is presumably what early critics were hinting at when they felt Sinclair wrote as a poet and artist. Kinder critics claimed her book was 'somewhat hampered by delicacy and sensitiveness', or that she was 'supersensitive'; less kind ones found the book 'too personal' and 'meagre in historical fact', finally judging that 'the front was no place for a person of highly artistic temperament'. This judgement had evidently already been reached by Dr Munro, the leader of the group, who, after a clash of opinions, found a pretext for returning her permanently to England after only 17 days. Mrs Knocker, who went on to become one of the Heroines of Pervyse and Baroness de T'Serclaes, and whose high spirits are responsible for the humorous note of the early part of the journal, later wrote about that early expedition:

May Sinclair, an older woman, was well-known as a novelist; she was a very intellectual, highly strung woman who managed to survive only for a few weeks before the horrors of war overcame her and she was sent home. Her functions were not entirely clear: I think she was to act as a secretary to Dr Munro though she could only have had the effect of making his own confusion slightly worse. (T'Serclaes, 1964: 37)

Trained and hardy nurses such as Mrs Knocker, and G. A. McDougall whom May Sinclair encountered in Belgium, were somewhat contemptuous of the eccentric Scottish psychologist who led the expedition, of the amateur nature of the corps, and of the timid sallies that it ventured. However, the modest, retiring May Sinclair was profoundly inspired by her 17 days in Belgium, and the experience was worked and reworked in her imagination, giving rise to three separate novels which tried to analyse and evaluate the nature of courage in the face of danger.

Although it is now conventional to disparage Victorian rhetoric about the glory of war, there is no doubt that shared physical danger exerts a powerful allure. It was not merely that 'an idealized notion of war offered romantic and vicarious excitement as a complete contrast to their humdrum working lives' (Bond, 1964: 72). In fact war was one of the opportunities for ecstasy actually encouraged by the Victorian culture in which Sinclair was raised. To lives of strict emotional repression the war was a time of heightened experience, of exaltation. Julian Grenfell bears witness to this in his poem 'Into Battle', where he exults in the 'frenzy' and 'joy' of battle; Duff Cooper, in his letters to Diana Manners following his first engagement at the Front in 1918, claims that war *is* what the old poets said it was, that there is romance in it. He experienced 'a feeling of wild and savage joy', the 'most glorious moment' of his life (Cooper, 1958: 197). Even, surprisingly, Wilfred Owen, in 'Apologia pro Poemate Meo', challenges the reader to know such merriment and 'exultation' as he shared in battle, as he 'dropped off Fear'.

For the modern reader who is so burdened with the later lists of those who 'fell in the Great War', Sinclair's absorption in her own emotional reactions to the wounded, the self-indulgence of the detailing of her own doings, appear narcissistic and myopic. But the near mystical nature of her inner experiences so overwhelmed her that we cannot doubt it was genuine. In 1916, when she read Hugh Walpole's novel, *The Dark Forest*, based on his experiences with a medical group on the Russian Front, May Sinclair wrote to him, calling it 'the best war-novel, in its own way, that has been written yet':

You alone of all the writers who've touched on the War, have seen and felt it as it is . . . I don't know anybody but you who has realised the ecstasy and joy that came whenever you got into what they call 'the danger zone' – that's the nearest to perfect happiness we're likely to reach in this world. It *is* perfect happiness, and it has nothing to do with 'doing your duty,' (I'm not at all sure that my duty wasn't to stop at home lest I should get ill and become a nuisance) it's deeper than all that. (Boll, 1973: 112)

H. D. Zegger, finding Sinclair 'disarmingly frank' about her impressions and reactions during her time in Belgium, says of the experience of 'a sense of intense happiness' which she had described in the full Journal as 'touching Reality at its highest point in a secure and effortless communication' (168), that she had 'what can perhaps be described as a religious experience' (Zegger, 1976: 83). Sinclair was, philosophically, an idealist. She tells in the Journal of practising the same kind of faith-healing on a wounded man as she had attributed to female characters in some of her novels. However, I would not call the state of stimulation induced by danger 'religious', and Sinclair herself had come to very different conclusions about it by the time she published *The Romantic* in 1920.

Whether enthralled by the War or trying to be ironically detached from it, Aldrich and Sinclair remained essentially spectators. Other women demanded and took a far more active role. When women's volunteer hospital-units were turned away by the British authorities, many had their services warmly accepted on the Russian or Serbian Fronts, or by the Belgians. Florence Farmborough's autobiography, *Nurse at the Russian Front* (unpublished until 1974), tells how, as a volunteer nurse on the Eastern Front, she was caught up in the Russian Revolution. Mairi Chisholm and Mrs Knocker left Dr Munroe's ambulance unit, to set up an advanced dressing-post immediately behind the Belgian front-line. 'When in March 1915 a decree was passed by the commanders of the Allied armies in Paris forbidding the presence of any women in the firing-line, at the request of the Belgian authorities an exception was made for these two, mentioned by name, who were then officially attached to the Third Division of the Belgian army in the field' (McLaren, 1917: 49). King Albert decorated them for their courage. The only British women living within the 'forbidden zone' of masculine experience on the Western Front, not at the base camps to the rear but right up by the trenches, these two 'Chevaliers of the Order of Leopold' became mythical heroines in the imagination of other British women.

Unfortunately, unlike Florence Farmborough, most of the more adventurous women had scant imagination themselves and a poor gift for words. G. E. Mitton made what 'splendour and romance' she could out of the brief diaries kept by the two 'Heroines of Pervyse', but they provided meagre material. She records without qualification the 20-year-old Mairi Chisholm's characterisation as 'a very curious incident', of the finding of the brains of one man in the pockets of the overcoat of another, a boy of 19, where they had been blown by the force of an explosion. Her quotation from 'Gypsy' (Mrs Knocker) is equally dispassionate: 'It requires nerve to drive an ambulance steadily under fire, but to sit still doing nothing with the shells bursting around takes it out of you worst of all'. To heighten such matter-of-factness, Mitton claims that: 'visions of the grey-clad Germans, lust-mad, bestial, pouring in like a herd of wild beasts, haunted the women' (Mitton, 1916: 202). This reads strangely when placed alongside the report of the American writer Mary Rinehart, who visited their first-aid post in a cellar-room early in 1915, as part of a fact-finding tour to raise money for the American Red Cross. According to her they were more inclined to treat the Germans as 'a bit of a joke' (Rinehart, 1915: 113).

The War enabled another young Englishwoman, Flora Sandes, to escape the life of a provincial vicar's daughter. She actually ended up (by way of nursing) as an armed and uniformed soldier in the Serbian army, and received a decoration for her part in a skirmish in which she was wounded. She left an account of her exploits, based on her letters and diaries, in a short autobiography published in 1916 to raise funds for the Serbians: *A Woman Sergeant in the Serbian Army*. A not untypical extract gives some idea of its imagination and style: 'Under some circumstances you feel you would most willingly barter the most gorgeous panorama of scenery for a cup of hot tea' (Sandes, 1916: 204–5). The book ends by looking forward to the time 'when we could get another whack at the enemy' (242). Appropriately, Alan Burgess recently constructed a romance worthy of G. A. Henty out of her literary scraps.

While society and social values only permitted a life of initiative and enterprise to men, it was inevitable that many women who wanted an active share of life would imagine themselves vicariously as men. Children's books in which girls were equal protagonists with boys, as in those written by Edith Nesbit, were exceptional, and the adventures of her heroines, like the adventures of Alice, were never dangerous. Adventure proper was defined by boys' books, particularly those by G. A. Henty, where a life of risk was normal, even desirable, and undertaken in the company of real national heroes at epic moments of Britain's history, such as *With Clive in India*. In such tales boys did heroic deeds on girls' behalf. A girl who even considers asserting herself, such as Elise in 'In the Hands of the Malays', who thanks her hero from rescuing her from a fate worse than death at the hands (sic) of pirates, by murmuring: 'but it would not have been so, for I would have killed myself', is firmly reminded that: 'I do not think that he would have given you much opportunity for doing that' (Henty, 1905: 47). It is little wonder that women of courage should think of fulfilment as coming from doing whatever men did, from sharing the historical limelight by taking part in the men's game of militarism as Flora Sandes had. The 'New Woman' would simply be another one of the chums.

Flora Sandes had no doubt that Serbia had more need of her with a gun in her hands than a surgeon's scalpel. Other women would energetically have disagreed.

Another early book of the war, *The Flaming Sword [in Serbia and Elsewhere]* by Mrs St Clair Stobart, takes its arresting title (a reference to *Genesis* iii 24) from the impassioned plea for peace with which the book concludes. The frontispiece shows Mrs Stobart at the age of 53 heroically on horseback during the great Serbian retreat of the winter of 1915–16, when her ambulance unit acted as a field hospital and crossed the mountains with the desperate Serbians. Mrs Stobart already knew war at first hand, for in 1907 she had founded a Women's Convoy Corps which helped in the Balkan War in 1912–13, and she had gone straight to the Continent in August 1914 to set up medical help in Belgium and France. There she had suffered bombing, and imprisonment by the Germans, before answering a call to help in Serbia in April 1915.

She believed that formerly women could only 'express sentiments concerning war', but that having obtained some experience of war gave her the right to give opinions as to the meaning of war; and for Mrs Stobart, 'war means the failure of society'. Aldrich accepted (without enthusiasm) that 'War is'. Sinclair, in an article on 'Women's Sacrifices for the War' (1914), claimed that women wanted the war to be fought to a victorious finish. But unlike Mildred Aldrich, Mrs Stobart did not believe war to be natural. In Stobart's opinion war is fought for 'paltry purposes' and ought to be suppressed. It is a cosmic blunder, but 'wars will never be supressed by men alone':

> The more 'natural' it seems for man to fight his fellow-man, in order to acquire supremacy, the more urgent it is for society to intervene . . . Society has failed in its primary function of preserving life. But society has hitherto been controlled by men only . . . Nature, in her benificence, generally arranges that side by side with the poisonous plant, the antidote shall grow, and thus, side by side with the growth of militarism, has also grown the woman's movement. (Stobart, 1916: 315–16)

In 1910, well before the War, Norman Angell had commented that: 'a sedentary, urbanized people find the spectacle of war even more attractive than the spectacle of football. Indeed, our Press treats it as a sort of glorified football match'. Mrs Stobart quotes from recent newspapers 'The spirit of our boys was splendid. They simply loved the fun' – to justify her claim that, despite the fact that experience of the present War validates the truism that 'war means blood, slaughter, brutality, deformities, and always death, death, death', yet 'Men still regard battles as magnified football scrums; war is still for many men a glorified sport' (315). According to I. F. Clarke this was more than a superficial attitude: 'the language of sport was often the language of war', and he instances Captain Guggisberg's *Modern Warfare, or How our Soldiers Fight,* where the analogy between war and football is spelt out:

> The army *fights* for the good of its country as a team *plays* for the honour of its school. Regiments *assist* each other as players do when they *shove together* or *pass the ball* from one to another; exceptionally gallant *charges* and heroic *defences* correspond to brilliant *runs* and *fine* tackling. All work with one common impulse, given to the army by its general, to the team by its captain. (Clarke, 1966: 132)

The Georgian view of the logic of the connection was made clear by E. B. Osborn: 'sportsmanship is our new homely name . . . for the *chevaleries* of the Middle Ages' (Osborn, 1917: ix). Clarke's point is further substantiated by Paul Fussell, as an example of what he calls 'the prevailing innocence of mind' of the period. He traces it back to the ethics of the Victorians: 'The classic equation between war and sport – cricket, in this case – had been established by Sir Henry Newbolt in his poem "Vitaï Lampada", a public-school favourite since 1898' (Fussell, 1975: 25). Newbolt had raised into verse the guiding ideas of Thomas Hughes's book for boys, *Tom Brown's Schooldays*, the classic apologia for public school education. At the heart of the book is the belligerent injunction to boys to learn to box, as they learn to play cricket and football: 'Fighting with fists is the natural and English way for English boys to settle their quarrels... After all, what would life be without fighting, I should like to know? I am dead against peace when there is no peace and isn't meant to be'.

It was that idea that war was natural, together with the 'sporting' sense of national pride, which disguised imperial rivalry to carry Britain into the War by 'common impulse', and maintained the War in being despite all calls for peace. Apparently the ethos of the public-school, particularly enthusiasm for 'playing the game', persuaded young officers to lead their men into certain death in futile assaults against gun-batteries, as if dying were simply a matter of losing an innings. This is the ethos of 'The Charge of the Light Brigade', and it seems to me less 'innocence' than delusion. It was a deluded belief in unquestioned authority, which those in power were determined to maintain: 'Theirs not to question why / Theirs but to do and die'. Modern warfare encouraged methods which were not 'cricket' – and neither were they football. As Peter Parker observed, the fact that war was not a game may be judged from the fact that rain did not stop play (Parker, 1987: 84).

The delusions as to the fair-play of war, the sporting opportunities it offered, and the significance of personal character in deciding the outcome of this muddy, bloody-kneed spectacle, were shared by many women. May Sinclair refers ironically to the 'game of war', but only to show that she intends to participate in it, a desire held by many women:

It is with the game of war as it was with the game of football I used to play with my big brothers in the garden. The women may play it if they're fit enough, up to a certain point, very much as I played football in the garden. The big brothers let their little sister kick off; they let her run away with the ball; they stood back and let her make goal after goal; but when it came to the scrimmage they took hold of her and gently but firmly moved her to one side. (Sinclair, 1915: 122)

Rose Macaulay was probably voicing quite accurately the views of many girls of her generation in her ironic little poem, 'Many Sisters to Many Brothers': 'Oh, it's you that have the luck, out there in blood and muck: / / But for me . . . a war is poor fun' (Trotter, 1920).

But war meant something more than fun, even poor fun. The spiritual value of war had been elucidated by Wordsworth in his *Character of the Happy Warrior*, a poem which formed part of the education of public schoolboys. For Wordsworth, the happy warrior 'that every Man in arms should wish to be', was able to transmute the bad influence of Pain, Fear, and Bloodshed, into glorious gain; the more he was exposed to suffering and distress, the more he would be able to endure, and the more compassionate he would become. Such a man is as 'happy as a Lover' in the heat of conflict, and 'equal to the need'. He is the man who 'Plays, in the many games of life, that one / Where what he most doth value must be won'. One man who chose to play the military game of life was Oscar Wilde's elder son. His guiding purpose in life was 'to retrieve a name no longer honoured in the land', to wipe away the stain of his father's name. To do this, 'first and foremost, I must be a *man*. There was to be no cry of decadent artist, of effeminate aesthete, of weak-kneed degenerate'. Having been an outstanding athlete at school, winning the *victor ludorum*, he joined the army, arduously grinding himself forward to achieve what he most did value: the honour of masculinity. Part of his military duties involved spying in Germany. In June 1914, foreseeing the War, he wrote to his brother about his 'Purpose': 'I ask nothing better than to end in honourable battle for my King and Country'. He was killed on the Western Front in May 1915 (Holland, 1954: 122–7).

Not all women were convinced that war was 'fun' either. But neither would they necessarily have agreed with Wordsworth or Thomas Hughes that it was the most honourable method of achieving manhood:

From the cradle to the grave, fighting, rightly understood, is the business, the real highest, honestest business of every son of man. Every one who is worth his salt has his enemies, who must be beaten . . . who will not let him live his life in quiet till he has thrashed them.

Mrs Stobart believed that such militarism had reached a climax in modern warfare, which was a 'bloody business; a business for butchers, not for high-souled gentlemen . . . Militarism is maleness run riot' (Stobart, 1916: vii). What society needed was the more forceful promotion of 'womanly' values, of what 'women feel in our souls', in order to channel the courage required by militarism away from the battlefield and into moral, social, spiritual purposes that 'might create a new heaven and earth'.

Whilst many young men saw the war as an opportunity to prove their manhood, women argued over it as the opportunity to demonstrate what womanhood was. This argument, the continuation of years of debate as to the nature of women, was at the beginning of the 20th century inextricable from the issue of women's suitability to exercise political power. That issue was not only a matter of domestic legal reforms with regard to women's rights to divorce, professional opportunities, or contraception. It concerned the management of the Empire and the power to redefine the nature of international relations.

Britain's declaration of war in August 1914 had immediately revealed the underlying rifts in the movement to gain women's suffrage. Certain women, such as Mrs Pankhurst and Mrs Fawcett, put their nationalism first: they were British first, women second. For them, the most important matter was to win the war. Whether or not women's wartime help would aid them to get the vote, hindering the war effort would certainly not. Other feminists saw a fundamental contradiction between any sort of aggression and womanly values. For them, the most important matter was to stop the war, and they tried to show solidarity with all women, regardless of their nationality, in order to bring about a negotiated peace. Some of these women were (international) socialists and also worked with men, many of whom were 'male feminists', to prevent conscription. For them what was at stake were human values which were neither specifically feminine nor masculine, but were crucial for both men and women. For many other women, the issues were never consciously argued out, and no connection was made between the subordination of women by force and the use of force to subordinate one nation or one class to another.

The war-writings of women display the polarities in feminist thought, especially with regard to the prestige attached to masculinity and the 'manly' virtues of war. Mildred Aldrich, trying to remain a neutral bystander, succumbed to the dominant propaganda. May Sinclair, a pre-War campaigner for women's suffrage, wrote that the war demonstrated that a great many jobs held by men could be filled in an emergency by women, and this showed that women 'would not collapse into preferring peace at any price, but wanted the war to be fought to a victorious finish' and should therefore be awarded the right to vote (Sinclair, 1914). Like other writers such as Cicely Hamilton, May Sinclair had turned her back on the traditional role of wife and mother. She had remained single and earned her own living by writing. For her the war was a chance to show that women could be as good as men. In this she followed the lead of Mrs Pankhurst, the founder of the Women's Social and Political Union, which had campaigned militantly for the suffrage since 1903.

On the declaration of war the government announced a national truce, and released Emmeline Pankhurst from prison. She ceased hostilities, and her daughter, Christabel, returned from exile in Paris. In 1915, they allied themselves with Asquith to organise a march demanding women's right to work for the war. With many other political feminists they believed that the War was the opportunity to demonstrate that women were not essentially different from men. The leadership of the older organisation, the non-militant National Union of Women's Suffrage Societies, was split over what policy to follow. Half of the committee resigned over the decision taken by the president, Mrs Fawcett, which was to support the government in the belief that 'the British Empire is fighting the battle of representative government and progressive democracy'. They left to found the Women's International League which worked with other pacifist groups throughout the world to achieve a permanent peace (Wiltsher, 1985).

Mrs Stobart, who like other women had demonstrated her heroism, claimed that democracy had failed, but democracy was not yet democracy, for it consisted of men only. Men were not superior to women. Like the members of the Co-operative Women's Guild, she was a social feminist, believing that women were essentially different from men and that society needed to allow full recognition to women's nurturing instincts. She had heard that recently 'from one trench, 800 men were killed within three minutes' and responds sardonically: 'To this end has the wisdom of Man brought Man. Could the wisdom of Woman bring us to a worse abyss than this?' In her view women must share in the control of society in order to preserve life. War must be suppressed. She did not conceive of that as a 'collapse' but as an *advance*.

In order to substantiate her view that 'The glamour, the adventure, the chivalry, which of old gilded the horrors of war, have vanished', she drew on her own experience, on a summer's night in Serbia, of the kind of horrors war means:

> I stumbled unawares upon an open grave. It was three-quarters full of naked corpses. They were typhus victims. They had been prisoners of war, and the grave would not be closed until there were enough dead to fill it. Heavy rain had fallen, and the bodies were half-submerged in water; but I saw one man above all the others. His body, long and strong-limbed, was all uncovered, but his face, fine featured, proudly ignorant of the ignominy, his face was covered with – flies; filthy, bloodsucking flies. Round his finely-cut nostrils, his mouth, his half-opened eyes, squatting, buzzing, sucking, shunting one another for best place – flies, flies, flies, and no one to beat them off. Flies in thousands, squabbling for his blood, and no one to beat them off. Only flies knew where he was. His mother was, perhaps, at this moment, picturing him as a hero, and he was – food for flies. / The night, in old parlance, would have been called glorious. But is there glory on this blood-stained earth? (Stobart, 1916: 313)

This is *The Red Badge of Courage* rewritten from the point of view of Henry's mother. It amply illustrates Stobart's claim that the results of war are not glorious but bestial and humiliating.

This vigorous pacifist voice was not new. Mrs Stobart's writing and arguments form part of a tradition of women's peace-propaganda that stretched at least as far back as Bertha Von Suttner and her best-selling novel *Die Waffen nieder! Eine Lebensgeschichte* (*Lay Down Your Arms!*), which was first published in German in 1889. This book appeared in English in an authorised translation in 1894, and by 1905, when Suttner was awarded the Nobel Peace Prize, the work had run to 37 editions and was available in every European language (Kempf, 1972: 24–5). It was, as she describes in her memoirs, specifically written to promote the ideals of the

International Arbitration and Peace Association, which had been founded in London in 1880 and which she joined in Paris at the end of the 1880s (21ff). This association was distinguished from other peace organisations by being specifically political in character. It aimed to promote a new norm for international relations with an idea of peace as the accepted state of harmonious co-existence between nations, in place of the existing idea of peace as a precarious armistice during intermissions in the normal state of war. This new state of international relations was to be achieved by treaties and an international tribunal to arbitrate disputes, much like the present United Nations Organisation. Suttner offered her talents as a radical, campaigning novelist in the 'service' of the IAPA. If *Uncle Tom's Cabin*, a novel written by a woman, could influence the public conception of slavery, then another novel might help to reconstruct the traditional conception of war.

Suttner's very long, deliberately emotional, work was based on careful research of the four European wars of 1859, 1864, 1866 and 1870–71. It is told from the point of view of a woman, Martha von Tilling, who lives through the wars and suffers the loss of close relatives in consequence. In place of the accounts of exciting deeds of courage and heroism in the face of danger, which are the focus of the 'great' literary epics from Homer onwards, Suttner concentrates on descriptions of the agony of the wounded and the effect on the minds of soldiers of the horrific events of the battlefield, and stresses the contrast between the pre-war happiness of peacetime and post-war misery and sense of loss.

The narrator, Martha von Tilling, having lost her first husband in battle in the 1859 war, miscarries her first child at the news that her second husband has been called up to fight in the war of 1864. This is an extract from a letter she receives from him at the front:

Smoking ruins of villages, ravaged cornfields, weapons and knapsacks lying about, spots where the land was ploughed up by shells, blood stains, bodies of horses, trenches filled with the slain – such are the features of the scenes through which we have been moving in the rear of the victors, in order, if possible, to add more victories to the account – i.e., to burn more villages, and so forth . . . The butchery lasted more than two hours, and we remained in possession of the field. The routed enemy fled. We did not pursue. We had work enough to do on the field. A hundred paces distant from the village stood a large farm-house, with many empty dwelling-rooms and stables; here we were to rest for the night and hither we have brought our wounded. The burial of the dead is to be done to-morrow morning. Some of the living will, of course, be shovelled in with them, for the 'stiff cramp' after a severe wound is a common phenomenon. Many who have remained out, whether dead or wounded, or even unwounded, we are obliged to abandon entirely, especially those who are lying under the ruins of the fallen houses. There they may, if dead, moulder slowly where they are; if wounded, bleed slowly to death; if unwounded, die slowly of famine. And we, hurrah! may go on with our jolly, joyous war! (Suttner, 1894: 153–4)

This lacks the particularity of Stobart's description, but its sarcastic message is the same. Suttner's book is, like Stobart's, particularly addressed to mothers. Like other writers of the period they were conscious of the important role women had in educating children. Not believing that militarism is an innate characteristic of boys, or that girls are immune from the 'mystico-historico-political consecration' of war in the patriotic system of education in Western culture, Suttner is critical not only of the soldiers' games boys play, which instil the idea of 'enemy', but also of corporal punishment or any other form of cruelty (3–4). The book ends at the christening of Martha's grandson, with a toast to the future in which universal disarmament and an international 'League of Peace' may be established.

Like many other works which have turned out to be popular 'best-sellers', *Lay down Your Arms!* was only accepted for publication after overcoming initial reluctance on the part of the publishers. Despite its success it did not set a fashion for anti-war literature, although there were other examples of literature which opposed militarism, such as G. B. Shaw's play *Arms and the Man* (1894). There were also serious works of non-fiction by women, which analysed the connection between gender and war. In 1911 the American Charlotte Perkins Gilman published *The Man-Made World*, which included a chapter on 'War'. Propounding a thesis about the congenital inferiority of men to women, she found in warfare 'maleness in its absurdest extremes'. In war could be studied the whole gamut of masculinity, 'from the initial instinct of combat, through every form of glorious ostentation, with the loudest possible accompaniment of noise'. Her views were somewhat different from those of Olive Schreiner in *Women and Labour*, published in the same year. This book was a plea for equal partnership between men and women. Women were no less courageous than men, nor morally superior to them, in Schreiner's opinion, and with the developments in armaments women were just as capable of fighting in battle as men. Women might even have the gift to be supreme general. However, in her chapter on 'Women and War', Schreiner argued that the day that women shared in government with men would be the day that heralded the death of war. This was because women, the bearers of men's bodies, know the cost of human flesh. Yet although writing against war continued right up to the last minute, with Douglas Newton's novel *War* (1914), it was relatively powerless against the flood of pro-war literature. This confirmed the prevailing ideology of war as not only normal, natural and inevitable, but as romantic and even glorious.

I. F. Clarke's research shows that, with the publication of fiction such as George Chesney's pamphlet *The Battle of Dorking* (1871), the serial 'The Great War of 1892' in the weekly *Black and White* (1892), and the novel by Erskine Childers, *The Riddle of the Sands* (1903) (amongst much else), the period from the 1880s up until the outbreak of the Great War of 1914–18 itself, 'saw the emergence of the greatest number of tales of coming conflicts ever to appear in European fiction'. These predictions of an imaginary war were marked by a desire for adventure and an aggressive spirit of nationalism. 'Save for rare exceptions, they are distinguished by a complete failure to foresee the form a modern war would take' (Clarke, 1966: 68). Such works had helped to create the jingoistic mentality of the older generation of decision-makers. For instance, Newbolt wrote that he had for many years the conviction that 'our Country must pass through the trial of a great European war: much of our effort we spent in preparing for it, some in military training, some of us in preparation of the heart' (Newbolt, 1942: 187).

The young men who provided the fodder of the Great War had been nourished on a diet of children's stories that were equally xenophobic. E. S. Turner has given an account of the 'remorseless spate of serials which described the descent of foreign hordes upon these shores and their subsquent bloody repulse', that appeared in boys' newspapers in increasing volume from 1897 to 1914 (Turner, 1975: 176). In Clarke's opinion the authors of such tales of future warfare helped to raise the temperature of international disputes and were partly responsible for the War that did take place, by sustaining and fomenting the 'self-deception, misunderstanding, and downright ill will that often infected relations between the peoples of Europe' (Clarke, 1966: 135). Turner is more inclined to lay the blame with the publisher, Lord Northcliffe, who owned such junior papers as *Boys' Friend*, *Boys' Herald* and *Marvel*, as well as the *Daily Mail*. Turner quotes from an American newspaper of 1910:

> It will be a marvel if relations with Germany are not strained until war becomes inevitable as a direct result of the war-scare campaign inaugurated and carried on with the most reckless and maddening ingenuity by the Northcliffe syndicate of papers. (176)

Turner instances only a single war-story, published by Aldine, which ran counter to the vindictive campaign. It ended with a peace treaty that guaranteed international arbitration in place of future war.

It was not just light fiction that prepared people for war. Following Matthew Arnold's *Culture and Anarchy*, poetry had taken on the role of moral and spiritual guide formerly reserved to religion. After Wordsworth published his characterisation of the warrior that every Man would like to be, other poets, such as Scott, Tennyson and Newbolt, had promoted the idea that war would purify and enoble the nation too. The hero of *Maud*, wishing for a cause 'pure and true' is awaked by the battle-cry of the Crimean War 'to the higher aims / Of a land that has lost for a little her lust for gold'. In W. E. Henley's song, war is an agent of social evolution: the Sword sifts the nations, 'the slag from the metal, / The waste and the weak / From the fit and the strong'. War would purge society not only of materialism, but of its weaker human members. In fact the near fiasco of the Boer War had convinced many Edwardians of the degeneracy of the nation. In 1937 Elinor Glyn, looking back on the death of Queen Victoria, wrote that, influenced by Gibbon's *Decline and Fall of the Roman Empire*, she had felt she was witnessing 'the funeral procession of England's greatness and glory'. Samuel Hynes comments that, 'the idea of imperial decline and fall haunted imaginations of the time' (Hynes, 1968: 17). E. Glyn was not alone in finding signs of national decadence.

When articles in the *Contemporary Review* (1901–02) related Britain's military inadequacies to the physical fitness of the population, the government set up a Committee on Physical Deterioration. There was already ample evidence that the poor physical development of the lower classes was directly related to the deterioration in urban living conditions. Yet, despite the fact that the Committee investigated the worsening of city slum life, the report was referred to in Parliament as 'the recent report upon the degeneracy of our race'. In 1890 the social explorer William Booth had satirised the idea of imperial progress by applying the descriptions of Stanley's exploration of Darkest Africa to the city slums of 'Darkest England'. Claiming that civilisation could breed its own barbarians, he asked rhetorically, 'The ivory raiders who brutally traffic in the unfortunate denizens of the forest glades, what are they but the publicans who flourish on the weakness of our poor?' In 1899, in *Heart of Darkness*, Joseph Conrad portrayed the hollowness that lay at the heart of ivory-trading imperialism, revealing the savage exploitation idealised by the myth of the torch of progress. Setting his tale of the Dark Continent in a framework of a boat moored in the Thames estuary, and referring back to the Roman Empire, he clearly implied that the British Empire was not superior to any other. However, the Victorians had disguised the armed force upon which the Empire relied, by the Christian mythology of chivalry. The Edwardians continued to justify the British Empire by likening the peace and stability guaranteed by the British Army to the *Pax Romana*.

In 1905 an anonymous pamphlet once again satirised the British imperial dream with an account of *The Decline and Fall of the British Empire*. This 'fall' it largely attributed to the inability of the British to defend themselves and their Empire, due to the gradual decline of the physique and health of the English people (Hynes, 1968: 24–6). Baden-Powell took the pamphlet seriously, and it seems to have been a motivating force behind his setting up the Boy Scout Movement. In the first edition of *Scouting for Boys*, he claimed that 'The same causes which brought about the fall of the great Roman Empire are working to-day in Great Britain ... One cause which contributed to the downfall of the Roman Empire was the fact that the soldiers fell away from the standard of their forefathers in bodily strength'. He concluded that 'recent reports on the deterioration of our race ought to act as a warning to be taken in time before it goes too far' (Baden-Powell, 1908: 335, 208).

Samuel Hynes relates the literature of invasion to this anxiety about national strength and imperial defence. One of the most popular of such books, *The Invasion of 1910*, was published in 1905. Two pertinent facts Hynes reveals are that the author, William le Queux, was helped to write it by Lord Roberts, and that their background research for the book was financed by Lord Northcliffe, for its publication first as a serial in his paper the *Daily Mail*. The story promotes anti-socialist propaganda and paranoia about the German invaders, who inhumanly massacre children after forcing them to dig their own graves. It explicitly states that the government 'should have listened to Lord Roberts'. Lord Roberts had been Commander-in-Chief of the army between 1901 and 1904 but had resigned in order to criticise the Liberal government's military policies and to promote universal military training. Hynes concludes: 'certainly it is obvious that the militaristic group around Roberts and Northcliffe worked to induce anxiety in the English people for political reasons' (Hynes, 1968: 53).

The cultural emphasis on racial superiority, national identity, and heroic manliness, stimulated by anxiety about invasion, was politically motivated. The rationale was spelt out by Baden-Powell:

> The Damoclesian sword of war ever hanging over a country has its value in keeping up the manliness of a people, in developing self-sacrificing heroism in its soldiers, in uniting classes, creeds and parties, and in showing the pettiness of party politics in true proportion. (Reynolds, 1942: 180)

Militarist propaganda had clear aims, first, to disguise the exploitation and class inequality on which British imperialism was based, both abroad and 'at home'; second, to relegate to secondary importance any political belief that arose out of an awareness of that injustice; and third, to deflect onto an external enemy the resentful aggression of political movements, such as trade unionism and suffragism, which threatened to disrupt the *status quo* of British society. Literature was one area where the struggle for political hegemony was waged. The beliefs of the older generation were challenged or passed on to the younger generation in fiction and non-fiction, as part of an entire cultural system.

The mental preparedness for war of a whole population was directly related not only to the fiction of the period, and to the popular press, which 'fanned the flames of self-righteous jingoism' in older men and women. As historians like Ann Summers have demonstrated, it was also due to the zealous work of patriotic pressure groups. Such organisations as The National Service League, of which Lord Roberts became president in 1906, had been inculcating a militaristic spirit in boys and girls since 1901 (Summers, 1976). The literature of the Edwardian period formed part of a total cultural network of institutions, publications, artefacts, still promoting the values of Imperialism inherited from Victorian Britain (MacKenzie, 1986). The dominant ideology was a sense of national and racial superiority. It was bolstered by the aggressive self-righteousness of a religious belief in Britain as the greatest force for good in the world. Francis Younghusband was not alone in holding 'the greatest possible faith in our race and its high destiny'. The public-school ethic was but one aspect of a general system of norms and beliefs which ran right through English society, from the King as Head of the Armed Forces and the national Church of England, down to Empire Day, and the sale of memorial teacups and matchboxes sporting union jacks, to justify economic rivalry and the exploitation of 'lesser breeds' (MacKenzie, 1984).

It was such dominant cultural beliefs which formed the very fabric of social reality. Organisations for international co-operation would have to unpick that whole tapestry into which the heroic pageantry of war was woven. Unable to control the institutions which reinforced those beliefs – the press, the churches and the schools – pacifist and feminist organisations were working from a very weak position indeed.

Whether consciously or unconsciously, women's writing about the War was inextricably bound into these cultural conflicts.

2

Mental Flannel

The social conventions of the Edwardian era not only prevented a
woman from taking part in public affairs by denying her the legal
right. They also defined what was womanly in such a way that it
seemed actually unnatural for a woman to have any life beyond her
family. It was still more unnatural for her to question this. Later
writings, by speaking about what could not even be mentioned at
the time, make plain the ways in which the First World War
resulted in a breakdown of such social rules. Autobiographies, in
particular, elucidate the character of the mental restrictions set up
by the social taboos of the period. These taboos formed obstruc-
tions to women apprehending what it might be to become a full
individual and take a knowledgeable part in public activities. By
reading the diaries of the Great War period with this hindsight, an
immediate sense can be gained of the effects that social rules and
cultural definitions had on women's experience and self-knowl-
edge. Diaries and journals unwittingly exemplify the precise
nature of the mental barriers set up to women's independent
thought and awareness, and especially to their comprehension of
those very barriers. If the Great War resulted in the breakdown of
old social forms, it also resulted in the eventual gate-crashing of
forbidden zones, for women as well as for young men.

Vera Brittain wrote her autobiography, *Testament of Youth*, as a
memorial to 'those misguided dupes, the boys and girls of the War
generation' (Brittain, 1933: 37). Although it was not completed until
1933, it was based on diaries that she had kept since before the War.
In order to display 'how abysmally ignorant, how romantically
idealistic and how utterly unsophisticated' (43) she and her contemporaries had been at the time of the War, Vera Brittain tried to
make the experiences recorded in her diaries comprehensible
to a later generation by relating them to the culture in which she
had been raised. She ends Chapter 1 by hoping that she has

managed to make it clear that, having been reared in a country without conscription, boys and girls like herself with their naïve generosities and enthusiasm left uninformed fell easy victims to the war-propagandist. It was hardly possible for a young woman to have been less fore-armed against war than Vera Brittain.

In order to show how she was kept naïve, one of the matters she comments on is the effectiveness of the cultural idea of 'decency' in restricting her exposure to experience. She illustrates this by describing girl's clothing of the period, which seems to have been designed on the assumption that 'decency consisted in leaving exposed to the sun and air no part of the human body that could possibly be covered with flannel' (34). She still resents the conventions of 20 years before, which had wrapped up her comely body in woollen combinations, cashmere stockings, a 'liberty' bodice, stockinette knickers, a flannel petticoat, and a long-sleeved, high-necked, knitted woollen 'spencer', not to mention the various hampering garments that were expected to be worn over this 'conglomeration of drapery'.

As her diary demonstrates, the idea of 'decency' also wrapped up her mind. In an effort to induce a prudish suspicion of the opposite sex, she was subjected to vague rules about not going 'too far' with men, not travelling alone with men in railway carriages, or even 'publicly' conversing with her brother's friends – at about the age of 11. Her efforts to gain some sort of information about 'the facts of life' left her in a state of half-knowledge. The result was that her immediate reaction to the idea of physical relationship 'insofar as this happened to be separable from romance' was one of shame, humiliation and disgust. At the age of 20, when the Great War was declared, she did not clearly understand what was meant by homosexuality, incest or sodomy, and had only hazy ideas about the precise nature of the sexual act or what venereal disease was.

That this sort of ignorance was typical can be seen from other autobiographies of the period, such as Storm Jameson's, which relates the efforts she made in 1915 when pregnant to find out what might be involved in childbirth. Her own mother did not enlighten her, and her husband, a doctor's son, advised her to read *Anna Karenina*: 'These things were not talked of, no more than the sexual act, or abortion, or any of the body's daily habits' (Jameson, 1969: 90). Kathleen Dayus became pregnant in the street in the slums of wartime Birmingham without understanding how (Dayus,

1986); her sister and mother had left her in ignorance of even the meagre knowledge Vera Brittain had achieved through 'the decorous elucidations' of *Household Medicine*. It was not merely knowledge of facts that these young women lacked, but the knowledge that would have given them power over their own bodies and the capacity to understand their emotions and the emotions of the men they knew (Dyhouse, 1981: 11–12).

The distance between that generation and our own can be measured by the extent of Vera Brittain's physical inexperience, which reveals itself in the recounting of certain events in the Journal. Vera first met Roland Leighton, a public-school friend of her brother's, in June 1913. Her diary records: 'I like him immensely' (Brittain, 1981: 42), but she only began to know him well when he came to spend a few days with her family in April 1914, and they spent hours talking together. She was then 20, 15 months older than Roland or her brother, Edward. At that time, the few young men she knew she had met through the tennis club in provincial Buxton. Having had the benefit of a single-sex education at a girls' school with a feminist headmistress, she was anxious to be able to earn her own living and avoid the marital tyranny her mother was subjected to. Her diaries deal impatiently with the reactions of local people to her desire to go to Oxford. She records one particularly trying conversation in which a man who had proposed to her reproaches her for not learning to be a woman. He insisted that by wishing to go to Oxford she was not acting like one (90). She met Roland again in July when she and her mother spent a weekend in Uppingham for her brother's Speech Day. The young pair started to correspond. Influenced by his mother, a successful novelist, Roland declared himself to be a feminist who shared Vera's interest in Olive Schreiner. He gave her a copy of *The Story of an African Farm*, and they were both inspired by the likeness he found between Vera and Schreiner's idealistic heroine, Lyndall. Like Edward, Roland supported Vera's ambition to go to Oxford, and they all three hoped to be up at the same time.

However, on the outbreak of war Roland enlisted (with considerable difficulty owing to his poor eyesight); Vera had initially to be content with knitting, which she did badly, although she progressed to darning, which she did well (107, 215). At the end of December, well chaperoned by her Aunt Belle, she met Roland on leave for several days in London, where she was introduced to his mother. By this time Vera was 21. Having overcome her father's opposition and, against the odds, won a scholarship to Somerville, she was now an Oxford undergraduate. Already writing in her diary of her love for Roland, she said goodbye to him by shaking hands.

In January, by subterfuge they 'defied conventions' and managed to meet and have lunch alone together in Leicester, and to travel alone on the train together between Leicester and Oxford. Just as they were arriving in Oxford she put out her hand to say goodbye: 'He took it quite collectedly and then suddenly raised it to his lips and kissed it'. Taken by surprise she only 'resisted a little but quite unavailingly in his strong grip', and after all she 'did not really want to resist' (182). She turned her face from him and then hurried away when the train stopped. The exact nature of this physical encounter that she 'ought never to have allowed' (183) is only brought home to the modern reader by the entry for March 1915. By this time Vera and Roland had known each other closely for a year; they had met each other's mothers and been on familiar speaking and writing terms. When he heard he was due to go to the Front, Roland came up to Buxton to spend the night of 18 March at Vera's home again. Naturally they talked about the war and his possible death, and sitting up late after everyone else had gone to bed, they mentioned marriage. Finally: 'He took my hand and kissed it again as he did in the train once before – but this time there was no glove upon it' (197). Her gloves are the material manifestation of the conventions of decency: they were barriers placed in the way of her receptiveness to emotional experience, barriers to any direct awareness of other people, or knowledge of her own body.

These proprieties were also expressed as linguistic conventions about what could be said between men and women. In 1965 Charles Carrington published his memoirs *Soldier from the Wars Returning*. In 1930 he had been the pseudonymous author of a Great War autobiography: *A Subaltern's War*, and he commented on the difference as to what he could write about sexual conduct in the two works. In the 50-year period since the outbreak of the Great War there had been a relaxation in both the class-structure of English society and the structure of taboos which restrained the relation of the sexes. Fifty years before, there had been two distinct moral codes: men might lapse privately from the moral standards of public propriety and decency; for women this was unpardonable. In that world:

the female sex was permanently divided into two classes: those who 'did' and those who 'didn't'. It was assumed that the women one met in 'decent society' lived on a plane of such exalted virtue that the slightest allusion, however obscure or oblique, to the functions of the body was an insult; and it was equally assumed that elsewhere, on another plane, was a class of women who were not so ethereal and not so restricted in their conversation. (Carrington, 1965: 160)

A man might consort with women of either 'class', on distinct occasions, but no woman could move freely across the barrier; 'a single sexual lapse consigned her irrevocably to the class that "one could not possibly meet in decent society"' (160).

Half a century later it had become possible to discuss in print the fact that during that War Carrington experienced a marked change in what he called his 'own mental make-up' (168). Soldiers on active service were released from the taboos of civil life – neither property nor life were *sacred*, and nor were women. What soldiers fought for was 'glory' – which Carrington could now define to be the glorious prize of women's sexual favour. Once a man became a soldier, even for an inexperienced 18-year-old member of the professional middle class such as Carrington, 'nothing prevented an approach to the other world of women who "did", except a fastidious timidity' (163). During his upbringing, Carrington had received 'no instruction of any kind from parents or teachers upon what are called the facts of life, nothing but a clear conviction that they must never be mentioned in the company of respectable women' (162). In France brothels were well advertised, and 'Amiens and Boulogne swarmed with prostitutes and semi-prostitutes, some of them refugee girls . . . they did not lack custom from men who had not seen a woman's face for months' (164). When he returned from the Front to London in 1917, he found himself leading a double life. After his experiences in France, where death and bloodshed were accepted as commonplace events, and the approach to women was uninhibited, he felt estranged from his quietly respectable family, where the old taboos still prevailed, and 'women who did' were still sharply divided from 'women who didn't'.

The gulf that opened up between the men who fought at the Front and the people back home became proverbial; it has become a cliché in criticism of First World War literature. As early as 1916 an anonymous writer on leave from the Front (actually R. H. Tawney) spoke in *The Nation* (21 October 1916) of the 'dividing chasm' between the strangers at home, with their 'reticence as to the obvious physical facts of the war!' and 'the people with whom I really am at home, the England that's not an island or an empire, but a wet populous dyke stretching from Flanders to the Somme'. Women became only too aware of this gulf, and much of the writing about that War by women struggles to chart it. They were hampered by their own enforced ignorance of human emotions, and by the linguistic taboos that maintained that ignorance, and perverted it. Their culture retained women not so much in childish innocence, as in a world glamorised by veils of romantic fantasy.

Vera Brittain started to glimpse what lay behind those veils when Roland Leighton was home on leave after five months at the Front. They went shopping together, and he bought 'a vicious-looking short steel dagger' which she thought he took an almost morbid delight in playing with, despite claiming that he probably could not use it 'except under the fierce excitement and madness of hand-to-hand fighting'. Vera wrote afterwards that 'To see the thing in cold blood & think of its use made me shudder ... The sight of this dagger in the hand of one of the most civilized people of these ironically-named civilized times depressed me to morbid-ness also' (Brittain, 1981: 329). If the War itself brutally wrenched young men out of the construction of 'civilisation' that their education and childhood reading had created for them, for women it set up new conflicts with the petrified Victorian stereotypes that the New Woman and Modern Girl were still trying to escape.

Men themselves found it difficult to articulate the effect of the War on their lives. This was partly due to the social and linguistic conventions that governed expression, particularly literary ex-pression; but it was also because war-events had frequently been traumas so shocking that they were repressed, and resulted in neurotic reactions. Since these responses conflicted with the cultural stereotypes of manliness that soldiers were expected to live up to, and because the whole front-line experience was so remote from the standards of 'normal' civilised life, it was hard for either men or women to conceptualise them. Moreover, the effects of propaganda and censorship made it especially difficult for women to deal with such emotional responses to the war, by disguising what had given rise to them and might have made sense of them.

It seems that women's inability to understand actually contributed to the trauma for men, but the cultural determination of women's 'feminine frailty' (as well as loving concern not to increase their anxiety) imposed a further constraint on what men could try to reveal to them in order to explain their reactions. Roland Leighton's account of the first death of one of his men is typical of many letters home: 'It is cruel of me to tell you this. Why should you have the horrors of war brought any nearer to you? And you have more time to think of them than I. At least, try not to remember: as I do' (Brittain, 1981: 244). He must have noticed Vera's response when he was home on leave later and she encouraged him to tell about the trenches, '– but all the same it makes me feel sick to hear about it' (305). Their time in the trenches could only be contemplated by many of the survivors from the refuge of some years' distance, when the effort of writing about it helped to control and structure the experience; and when changes in conventions enabled them to give new literary significance to the War and to the culture that had produced it.

The ordinary social pressures to conform to the majority (militaristic) view are well demonstrated by the public vilification of even objectors of such standing as G. B. Shaw and Bertrand Russell (Vellacott, 1980). The threats of prison or firing squad were used to reinforce the pressure to conform, and even though it was legal it was never easy to be a conscientious objector or to help one. Nevertheless, there were men who resisted the pressure and women who supported them. They were correspondingly critical of their society and its values but it became increasingly difficult to get such views stated or published openly. They were impeded by the layers of social camouflage that were turned out by the patriotic press, abetted by the government's Bureau of 'Information' (Wright, 1978). The Defence of the Realm Act (DORA), introduced early in August 1914, prevented the camouflage from being detected, or identified in print (Pankhurst, 1932: Hopkin, 1970). Groups opposed to the war were harassed, books were suppressed, and printers intimidated by the police. News about the results of the fighting was delayed and falsified. Conditions in the trenches and hospitals were romanticised in photographs and films, which appeared to be documentaries and were validated by the King himself, but which were specially posed and staged (Reeves, 1986).

Edmund Blunden characterised the resultant alienation felt by those at the Front as an 'impassable gulf' which cut the combatants off from those behind and away from the trenches, 'who, not being there, kept up the war' (Brereton, 1930: 13–24). There was felt to be more sympathy between English and German soldiers than between Englishmen at the Front and all other English women and men. As John Bayley remarked later: 'This division, between Us who have had the experience and You who have not, was deeply and terribly apprehended ... overriding all national feelings'. It resulted in an unjust antagonism which tended to divide 'beyond the reach of sympathy or understanding' (Bayley, 1963: 419).

The new meaning thus given to the notion of England as Two Nations that were mutually incomprehensible has retained widespread currency. It seems to me an appropriate metaphor, not so much because of the emotional estrangement it is taken to signify, or the hostility felt by the combatants to all those behind the front-line, but because two languages were being used, which represented two competing constructions of reality. Two quite distinct ideologies, with two distinct vocabularies, bounded what Edgell Rickword called 'two incommunicable worlds' (Rickword, 1940: 29). In Pamela Hinkson's Great War novel, *The Ladies' Road* (1932), a silence grows up between Nancy Creagh and her son Guy, who has been invalided home after being gassed. One morning, wanting to comfort him, she stands at his bedroom door:

> Guy moved about and talked to himself unintelligibly. She listened, holding her breath for a word, a clue that must help her. But she was shut outside as though he was a stranger speaking a strange tongue. (Hinkson, 1932: 186).

Richard Aldington, in his novel *Death of a Hero* (1929), which was based on his own wartime experiences fictionalising his relationship with his wife, Hilda Doolittle, and his mistress, also spoke of 'the widening gulf which was separating the men of that generation from the women':

> He still clung desperately to Elizabeth and Fanny, of course. He wrote long letters to them trying to explain himself, and they replied sympathetically. They were the only persons he wanted to see when on leave, and they met him sympathetically. But it was useless. They were gesticulating across an abyss. The

women were still human beings; he was merely a unit, a murder robot, a wisp of cannon-fodder. (Aldington, 1965: 228).

If men on leave appeared strange and slightly insane to civilians, the emotional support that the men needed and found in each other came partly from their sense that it was England that was mad, suffering from a mass illusion and speaking strangely. Graves expresses this clearly in *Goodbye To All That* (1929):

England looked strange to us returned soldiers. We could not understand the war-madness that ran wild everywhere, looking for a pseudo-military outlet. The civilians talked a foreign language . . . Our best place would be back in France, away from the more shameless madness of home-service. (Graves, 1957: 190–2)

I took the line that everyone was mad except ourselves and one or two others, and that no good could come of offering common sense to the insane. (215)

This was to confirm the view of the anonymous writer in *The Nation*, 1916: 'Yet I don't think I'm mad, for I find that other soldiers have somewhat the same experience as myself' (Chapman, 1937: 380).

It does not seem to me to be accurate of Vera Brittain to say, 50 years later, that it was the War itself that came between men at the Front and the women who loved them, 'putting a barrier of indescribable experience between the two sexes, thrusting horror deeper and deeper inward' (Brittain, 1968: 374). Rather, it was the construction of the reality of the War that came between men and women. As her own diaries illustrate, many women were unable to grasp the descriptions offered them in place of the flannel blindfolds fabricated by the government's propaganda apparatus. Plain descriptions not only implied the futility of the men's deaths, but the utter degradation of the 'civilised' values which the men were supposedly dying to preserve. It was perhaps harder for women to recognise the shams of their society because they were more subject to cultural coercion. But everyone behind the front-lines (and women were soon forbidden in the combat-zone altogether) was subjected to linguistic constructions of the war which it was difficult to resist.

Early in the War, Edward Thomas, reviewing the volumes of war-poems already appearing, made a qualitative distinction between 'poetry' and mere 'verse', in order to distinguish propaganda from what was more likely to endure (Thomas, 1914). According to Thomas, verses, like hymns, are not 'great poetry'; they are the 'downright stanzas' in which popular ideas or phrases, common ideas which most people have in their heads at the time, are dished up to thrill by looking noble and lofty. They are the 'noisy stuff' which, like 'Tipperary', unites people by drowning their thoughts in popular sentiment. He qualifies them as 'bombastic, hypocritical, or senseless' because they have nothing to do with 'experience, reality, truth'. One rhetorical feature such verses share is their archaic style, and Thomas cites G. K. Chesterton's 'Hymn of War' which is reminiscent of Anglicised psalms. Another of Thomas's examples, written to express surprise at the Anglo-French alliance, briefly refers to 'Harry with his Crispins' and ends with the following lines:

> A sword to strike the Dragon of the slime,
> Bidding St Denis with St George stand fast
> Against the Worm. St Denis and St George!

The same medieval commonplaces are drawn upon by the popular versifier Jessie Pope in her poem 'St George and the Dragon' ('There's a dragon loose *now*, and all of us know it') written to encourage recruitment:

> Of gallant St Georges today we have legion,
> As sturdy and game as the knight of Romance.
>   (Pope, 1915: 40)

The strengthening of stock responses to familiar values by emphatic rhymes and hypnotic rhythm is particularly obvious in what Bergonzi calls 'the unspeakable verses' of William Watson (Bergonzi, 1980: 63). 'Sons of Britain', for instance, simply uses terms from a public-schoolboy's moral vocabulary, such as 'Bully', 'shame' and 'honour', in combination with a selection from the sub-religious 'poetic' repertoire reiterated by hymns: 'Rally', 'foe', 'warrior', 'crown', as triggers to an enthusiastic response. Here are two stanzas:

> Heed not overmuch when she is slandered;
> Yours to guard her from a Bully's blow:
> Yours to rise, and rally to her standard:
> Yours to arm, and face the brutal foe.

> Would you sit at home, and watch and ponder,
>> While the warriors agonise and dare?
> Here for you is shame, but glory yonder:
>> Choose the glory – yea, a hero's share.
>>> (Hussey, 1967: 142)

As Fussell argued, such clichés acted as euphemisms. They contributed to the general prophylaxis in thought by shielding users from the blunter language of 'dead' for 'fallen', 'run away' for 'swerve', 'cowardly' for 'base' and 'the blood of young men' for 'the red / Sweet wine of youth' (Fussell, 1975: 21–3).

What Fussell did not point out was that the archaic shields acted by virtue of their chivalrous connotations. They did not so much ward off brutal reality as magically transform imperialist rivalry into a crusade; so that German peasants became 'foes' like 'heathen dogs' or 'the Dragon', threatening the 'New Jerusalem' of England, or the purity of English maidens. As Douglas Goldring said, shortly after the War, the mental equipment which such conceptions provided to the young men just out of school 'for withstanding the shock of experience was as useless as the imitation suit of armour, the dummy lance and the shield of the actor in a pageant' (Goldring, 1920). These chivalrous conceptions, implicitly assigning to females the passive role of 'damsels in distress', were equally useless to young women. Conceiving of themselves as essentially in need of protection, without which they were nakedly helpless, women's mental submissiveness left them as vulnerable as the young men to the real obscenity of war.

The total construction of the War as a Christian crusade against the barbaric Hun was not accidental, but part of a careful propaganda campaign by the British government. The campaign was mainly directed towards America, and its effect on American literature has been analysed by Cooperman, (Cooperman, 1967: chapter 1). Some of the propaganda was crude lying, such as the Bryce Report; some German 'atrocities', such as the sinking of the *Lusitania*, were actually engineered (Simpson, 1972). The use of respected British Men of Letters to provide the rhetoric was partly responsible for its effectiveness, on the English public as much as on the American. Two examples will suffice.

G. K. Chesterton's *The Barbarism of Berlin* was published in 1914, and translated by the British government's secret Wellington House propaganda department for distribution in neutral counties.

It compared barbarous German war with ungentlemanly German eating habits, claiming that butchery and gobbling had 'ruined all the real romance of war'. As D. G. Wright remarked, translations of such gems of rhetoric as 'We fight for the trust and for the tryst' must not have been easy. In 1917 Chesterton supplied texts to accompany a collected edition of Raemaker's cartoons of German bestiality. So did Hilaire Belloc. Belloc's use of cultural semi-religious clichés such as 'chivalric', 'high', 'glorious', together with the snobbish connotations of 'noblest', 'inheritance' and 'business', to trigger a patriotic response was typical of orations from press and pulpit:

> The edges of the Germanies have, in the past, been touched by the chivalric tradition: Prussia never. That noblest inheritance of Christendom never reached so far out into the wilds. And to Germany . . . soldier is no high thing, nor is there any meaning attached to the word 'glorious'. War is for that nation a business . . . (Raemaker, 1917: 18)

One of the most popular of the professional war-poets was Robert Nichols, a poseur, who after a few weeks' brief service in France was employed by the Ministry of Information to lecture on British war-poetry. His first book of war poems is characterised by Bergonzi as consisting 'largely of the Brooke-pastiche so prevalent in the first year of the war' (Bergonzi, 1980: 63). This was more than the second-hand use of expression or style; it betrays the un-reflective adoption of a whole cast of thought. The phrase quoted above by Fussell from Brooke's 'The Dead': 'the red sweet wine of youth', equates the death of young men with the crucifixion of Christ, in a nearly subliminal metaphor which stemmed from a whole cultural conception of Christian heroism. This conception, actively promoted by the Church of England and the National Service League, is crystallised in a pamphlet first published by the League in 1903, and still being disseminated in 1911: 'Leaflet L', *Religious Thought and National Service*, written by Canon J. H. Skrine of Merton College, Oxford. It contains the following sentiments:

> Fighting and killing are not of the essence of [war], but are the accidents, though the inseparable accidents; and even these, in the wide modern fields where a soldier rarely in his own sight sheds any blood but his own, where he lies on the battle sward not to inflict death but to endure it – even these are mainly

purged of savagery and transfigured into devotion. War is not murder but sacrifice, which is the soul of Christianity. (Playne, 1928: 149)

The dominance of this set of values is amply illustrated in Vera Brittain's diaries, although she has tried to edit it out of the autobiography. It provided one construction of the reality of the war which Roland Leighton, like other young soldiers with experience of the Front, tried in vain to dismantle.

In August 1915 Vera recorded in her diary that while he was home on leave the 20-year-old Roland gave her and her brother a detailed account of 'the usually unmentioned and more unpleasant aspects of the war, such as the condition of the charnel-house trenches, or the shooting of sentries who go to sleep on duty' (Brittain, 1981: 305). If he was trying to impress them that ceased to be the case when he returned to the Front. In September, by which time she had left Oxford to serve as a VAD and had become engaged to Leighton, Vera reported in her diary the receipt of a letter from him which gave her 'a fine, if somewhat morbid description of the charnel-house condition of his present trenches – poor darling!' She quoted from the letter which told how:

among [this] chaos of twisted iron and splintered timber and shapeless earth are the fleshless, blackened bones of simple men who poured out their red, sweet wine of youth unknowing, for nothing more tangible than Honour or their Country's Glory or another's Lust of Power. Let him who thinks that war is a glorious golden thing, who loves to roll forth stirring words of exhortation, invoking Honour and Praise and Valour and Love of Country ... let him look at a little pile of sodden grey rags that cover half a skull and a shin bone and what might have been Its ribs, or at this skeleton lying on its side, resting half-crouching as it fell, supported on one arm, perfect but that it is headless, and with the tattered clothing still draped around it; and let him realise how grand & glorious a thing it is to have distilled all Youth and Joy and Life into a foetid heap of hideous putrescence. (Brittain, 1981: 344).

This deflation of Brooke-style bombast was copied out by Vera without further comment. Just three days later, contemplating her fiancé's possible death even as she writes, Vera exalts to

Brooke-sublimity the idea that Roland may already be 'just one lifeless thing among thousands of others, upon the battlefield, and all that is left to us who worship him is just

> . . . some corner of a foreign field
> That is forever England'. (345)

The rhetoric is more than a mere form of words. It is the spell that dazzles her imagination, blinding her to Leighton's likely reduction to the sort of smashed and rotting corpse he had recently pictured for her, or even to one of the suppurating amputees she was daily treating in her drudgery at the hospital. It is surprising that he had persevered in trying to convey to her what death at the Front was like, considering her response to an earlier reaction of futility on his part. Then she 'bade him' not to quote from Olive Schreiner in likening the death of a soldier friend to that of a beetle; she had recommended instead some lines of Francis Thompson's:

> They passed, they passed, but cannot pass away,
> For England feels them in her blood like wine. (267)

These heady words are less an embrocation for Leighton's sore mind than an intoxicating potion for Vera's. He gave up his correspondence altogether for over a month, shortly before he was killed. Twenty years later, in her autobiography, Vera still claimed dramatically that she would never know the explanation for this silence: 'was the explanation to be found in that terrible barrier of knowledge by which the War cut off the men who possessed it from the women who, in spite of the love that they gave and received, remained in ignorance?' (Brittain, 1933: 215). Leighton had tried to dispel that 'ignorance'. It is small wonder that, finding the disparity between her sanitised, gauzed world and his own barbaric existence too great, Leighton began like others to speak of the unreality of England.

The gulf between the two nations was born less of ignorance or innocence than of illusion, the transfiguring of the unceremonious death of young soldiers by means of hack poeticisms. Roland is far gentler with Vera than the writers of later autobiographies were to be with their readers. Suppressing the 'gruesome details' he realises have upset her, he writes of coming across unburied human remains in No Man's Land, ' "which, without going into

further details, is decidedly unpleasant"' (Brittain, 1981: 262).
Stuart Cloete was more explicit about the work of a burial party:

> As you lifted a body by its arms and legs, they detached
> themselves from the torso, and this was not the worst thing.
> Each body was covered inches deep with a black fur of flies,
> which flew up into your face, into your mouth, eyes and nostrils
> as you approached. The bodies crawled with maggots ... the
> bodies had the consistency of Camembert cheese. (Cloete, 1972)

General Crozier managed with grim humour to convey an alternate
horror:

> In the main communication trench we passed a man carrying a
> sandbag full of something. Thefts of rations and minor stores
> from the line are increasing. I therefore asked, 'What have you in
> that bag?' 'Rifle-man Grundy, sir,' came the unexpected reply.
> (Crozier, 1930)

Sometimes there wasn't even an identifiable bagful, as H. S.
Clapham remembered:

> We dug about, but did not seem to be able to find the body, and
> when I seized the sleeve and pulled, the arm came out of the
> ground by itself. We had to dig deeper for our own sake, but
> there was nothing else left, except messy earth, which seemed to
> have been driven into the side of the trench. (Clapham, 1930)

Such experiences gave an ironic meaning to the cliché of 'some
corner of a foreign field' which was unimaginable to those at
'home'.

The psychological effects on men of enduring such experiences
often resulted in extremely abnormal behaviour. 'Shellshock' was
the new euphemism designed to camouflage soldiers' madness.
Wilfred Owen first met Siegfried Sassoon when they were both
being treated at Craiglockhart Hospital for shellshock victims,
where the director, W. H. Rivers, was a psychologist who encouraged the writing of poetry as therapy. He diagnosed the cause
of much war-neurosis to be the repression of war-time memories.
As an example he cited a patient who had been flung by shell-blast
face down into the distended abdomen of a German several days

dead. The young officer realised before losing consciousness that 'the substance which filled his mouth and produced the most horrible sensations of taste and smell was derived from the decomposed entrails of an enemy' (Rivers, 1918: 176). Rivers considered that this polluting experience had left him almost incurable. It had polluted not only his body, but his mind. As Owen wrote in 'Mental Cases': '– These are men whose minds the Dead have ravished'. Even those who regained sufficient 'normality' to return to the trenches were not thoroughly cleansed, and continued to have what Sassoon called 'dreams from the pit':

The rank stench of those bodies haunts me still,
And I remember things I'd best forget.

It was not only poetry which sublimated the nauseating encounter with death in war. One of the best-selling tales of the War was an account of a fictitious Scottish battalion of Kitchener's volunteer army, *The First Hundred Thousand*. First serialised in *Blackwood's Magazine* in 1915, it was still in print as a paperback in 1985. Its author, 'John Hay' (Ian Hay Beith), was involved with recruiting and moved to the Ministry of Information in 1916. His arch style manages to convey the idea that death is slightly humorous. Narrated knowingly by an unidentified 'We', events are shown through the unquestioning perception of 19-year-old Bobby Little, whose first days as a newly-joined subaltern are 'very like one's first days at school'. The first death, of an underdeveloped, over-eager 16-year-old, is from pneumonia. The death of 'Wee Pe'er' is patronisingly described as the promotion of his 'simple soul' to another company: 'the great Company of Happy Warriors who walk the Elysian Fields'. Bobby Little's first encounter with a dead body in the trenches is decently camouflaged by mock-ceremony which the narrator does nothing to penetrate: Bobby meets

a slow-moving procession – a corporal, followed by two men carrying a stretcher. On the stretcher lay something covered with a ground-sheet. At one end projected a pair of regulation boots, very still and rigid.

The burlesque is emphasised by an account of the man's death in comic Scots: 'That last shot from the trench-mortar got him. It came in kin' o' sideways. He was sittin' at the end of his dug-oot, gettin' his tea'. Then the procession disappears 'round the curve of Shaftesbury Avenue'. The music-hall staginess of the event prevents us from considering what might lie under the ground-sheet.

The common soldier dies like a clown; the officer like a tragic hero. A subaltern, Lochgair, having 'climbed in leisurely fashion upon the parados' to encourage his men, is apparently shot down, in mid-speech:

> He stopped suddenly, swayed, and toppled back into the trench. Major Trench caught him in his arms, and laid him gently upon the chalky floor. There was nothing more to be done. Young Lochgair had given his platoon their target, and the platoon were now firing steadily upon the same. He closed his eyes and sighed, like a tired child.
> 'Carry on, Major!' he murmured faintly. 'I'm all right.'
> So died the simple-hearted, valiant enthusiast whom we had christened Othello. (220)

The theatrical presentation of these two deaths encourages the reader to regard them with the same lack of involvement as an evening's entertainment; clearly the men will return to take their bow when the performance is over. It was with shock that those who were left came to realise at the time of the Armistice that 'One will have to look at long vistas again, instead of short ones, and one will at last fully recognise that the dead are not only dead for the duration' (Asquith, 1968: 480).

That death in a muddy trench was a little less clean and orchestrated than Hay suggests can be seen from any first-hand account. Most memoirs refer to the author's first experience of death. George Coppard's *With a Machine-gun to Cambrai* (1969) makes a good comparison because of its artlessness. Having left school to work at the age of 13, Coppard enlisted as a common soldier in August 1914 when he was 16, and served for four and a half years on the Western Front. During that time he (illegally) kept a diary in notebooks, and after he retired in 1962 he used them as the basis of his narrative of those four years. He recalled in detail the sniping of a friend at breakfast-time in the trench; the fire was going nicely and the bacon was sizzling:

> Just as I was about to tuck in Bill crashed to the ground. I'll never forget the sound of that shot as it found its billet . . . A moment

before, Bill had been talking to us, and now, there he was, breathing slightly, but otherwise motionless. (Coppard, 1969: 25)

'The back of the cranium [was] gone, and the grey brain flecked with red [was] splashed out.' While they waited for stretcher-bearers, Coppard 'for decency's sake put some bandages round Bill's head to hide the mess' and then helped a friend in the arduous work of carrying Bill down the narrow twisting trench to the first-aid post. When Coppard got back he was ravenous.

My bacon and bread was on the fire-step, but covered with dirt and pieces of Bill's brain. I looked down the front of my tunic and trousers and there were more bits there; my boots were sticky with blood.
I felt the passing of Bill acutely. (26)

It was the gulf between this reality and the civilian idea of it, which drove Sassoon to counter-attack by publishing his soldier's declaration:

I believe that I may help to destroy the callous complacence with which the majority of those at home regard the continuance of agonies which they do not share, and which they have not sufficient imagination to realise. (*Bradford Pioneer*, 27 July 1917)

However, it was less indifference that those at home suffered from than propaganda, which constricted their knowledge, their comprehension and their imagination. The shift necessary in the whole cultural framework which supported the 'theatre of war' would require fundamental alterations in the apparatus of church, press and education which maintained it in being. Declarations alone would not effect a change.

If women could not understand what men were going through, neither could women understand themselves. Propaganda had constructed not only women's conception of the War, but women's conception of themselves in relation to it. Although Vera Brittain was 21 and exceptionally intelligent, she was naïve and subject to many influences. She well exemplifies Storm Jameson's later remarks:

Why do not women know that in any war, the enemy is not on the other side? their enemy is war itself – which robs them of their identity: and they cease to be clever, competent, intelligent, beautiful, in their own right, and become the nurses, the pretty joys, and at last the mourners of their men. (Jameson, 1933: 211)

Vera's histrionic reactions and her surrender of her personal ambitions were encouraged by her women tutors at Oxford, and by Leighton's mother, and sanctioned by the publications of the establishment. Official war-propaganda, heightened by the poetry of Rupert Brooke, replaced Olive Schreiner's writing as the dominant construction of her reality. Instead of continuing to see herself as a powerful rebel like Lyndall, or identifying with Schreiner's public support for conscientious objectors, Vera Brittain subordinated her own identity in hero-worship of Roland Leighton. This became a religion in which letter-writing and nursing the wounded formed the ritual, her nurse's uniform the vestments, and the propaganda of chivalry and Brooke's poetry the liturgy (Brittain, 1933: 248).

In September 1915, quoting in her diary from an anonymous article in *The Times*, 'Smiling through her tears', that described the courage of women waiting for news from the Front, she responds: 'Oh! if I can only get him back to hold and kiss and worship once more, how tenderly, how strongly, how reverently I shall love him!' This echoes Leighton's own language in an earlier letter to her, which speaks of the 'sweet sacrilege' of having kissed her photograph, and of the 'reverence' which governs his behaviour towards her. After his death Vera began to elevate him even further, capitalising the pronouns and adjectives when referring to him as is conventional for Jesus, and speaking of his mother and herself as the Virgin Mary: 'Blessed art thou among women' (Brittain, 1981: 391). This hystrionic tendency had been encouraged at school where, at the age of 16, she had played the part of the Madonna in a Christmas mystery play called *The Eager Heart*: 'Temperamentally at least, I was thoroughly suited to the rôle' (Brittain, 1933: 43). The tendency was strengthened by the melodramatic wartime propaganda, which inspired Vera's vision of Roland in death, 'lying amid a heap of fallen soldiers with his white face upturned to the glory of the Eastern sky, and the Archangel in the Heavens with his wings spread protectingly over them' (Brittain, 1981: 378).

Such use of religious language and the deifying of a **young** officer can be located within her culture's general admiration for the ideal of nobly heroic self-sacrifice: 'Greater love hath no man than this, that a man lay down his life for his friends'. Vera first quotes this biblical tag in February 1913, with reference to Captain Oates, but it became a commonplace of the War, and is inscribed on many war-memorials. The image of the soldier as a Christ-figure was expressed by poets as diverse as Sassoon (in 'the Redeemer') and Studdert-Kennedy (in 'Solomon in All his Glory'). One of the tritest forms is by a Corporal J. H. Jarvis ('At a Wayside Shrine'). Although there is no hint in the memoirs of common soldiers that the rank and file were taken in by his view, an essay written for the *Spectator* by a New Army officer encouraged middle-class readers to believe that the troops saw their 'Beloved Captain' as Christ Himself tending their feet (Hankey, 1916). In a letter to Osbert Sitwell in 1918, Wilfred Owen subverts this image by identifying his men with Christ and himself as their crucifier: 'I ... inspected his feet to see that they should be worthy of the nails'. Turning the (female) reader into Mary Magdalene – 'noli-me-tangere' – he produced a sardonic version of the whole idea in his poem 'Greater Love' (Hibberd, 1973: 37).

The idea that the suffering Christ was himself present on the Western Front was the subject of the most widely reprinted poem of the war, Lucy Whitmell's 'Christ in Flanders', which first appeared in the *Spectator*, 11 September 1915: 'You helped us pass the jest along trenches – / You touched its ribaldry and made it fine'. It was also a theme of the visual propaganda, such as the painting by James Clark, *The Great Sacrifice* (1914), copies of which were given away with the Christmas supplement of the *Graphic* in 1914. This dilution of the sacred into bromides is the imaginary aspect of that society's real trivialisation of human anguish. After the war, O'Casey based his play of outrage against war, *The Silver Tassie* (1928), on Owen's poem 'Disabled'. The play transformed the war-time commonplace into a condemnation of the profanity of the Great War: 'Christ, who bore the cross, still weary, now tracks a rope tied to a field gun' (Ayling, 1985: 214).

The image of Christ Crucified is linked with the image of the Mater Dolorosa. Mary Rinehart found in this tradition an emblem for the nature of war: 'War is an old woman burning a candle before the Mater Dolorosa for the son she has given. For King and country' (Rinehart, 1915: 7). In the popular mind the grieving mother/fiancée could idealise her dead or mutilated son/lover as the pierced sacred body, and identify herself with the ambiguous Virgin Mother. Perhaps the most moving expression of this is Mary J. Henderson's poem, 'An Incident':

And the boy turned when his wounds were dressed,
Held up his face like a child at the breast,
Turned and held his tired face up,
For he could not hold the spoon or cup;
And I fed him . . . Mary, Mother of God,
All women tread where thy feet have trod.

(Reilly, 1981: 52)

The European icon of the Pietá was reworked grotesquely in Alonzo Earl Foringer's war relief poster, published for the American Red Cross at Christmas 1918. It displays a gigantic, soulful nurse-Madonna cradling a child-sized bandaged soldier helpless on a stretcher that resembles a crucifix, in order to symbolise the Red Cross as 'The Greatest Mother in the World' (Darracott, 1972: 28).

In fact the social role of mother was one of the areas of greatest conflict for women once their sons began enlisting for the War. Spurred by growing unemployment and the need to breed an imperial race, a 'cult of motherhood' had been developed before the War, promoting a view of women as naturally maternal beings whose place was in the home. Voluntary organisations such as the Women's League of Service for Motherhood were encouraged in 1903 by Major General Sir Frederick Maurice's belief that 'for the raising of a virile race, either of soldiers or citizens, it is essential that the attention of the mothers of the land should be mainly devoted to the three K's – Kinder, Kuche, Kirche' (Davin, 1978: 16). And in 1910 Lord Cromer opposed women's suffrage by asking how Britain could hope to compete with a nation such as Germany, 'if we war against nature, and endeavour to invert the natural role of the sexes' (Garner, 1984: 9). Mrs Humphry Ward, the first president of the Anti-Suffrage League from 1908, suggested in her novels that self-realisation and rebellion against motherhood would 'un-sex' women. (She was the most famous woman writer engaged by the war-time Bureau of Propaganda.) Unsurprisingly then, when Vera Brittain recognised that she loved Roland

Leighton, she conceptualised the outcome of this love in the way which her society provided for her:

> I would give all I had lived or hoped for during the brief years of my existence, not to astonish the world by some brilliant and glittering achievement, but some day to be the mother of Roland Leighton's child. (Brittain, 1981: 175)

However, the ideal of patriotic duty placed demands on women which were in direct contradiction to the conception of a mother's duty, which was to nurture the life of her children and husband. This was to some extent officially 'reconciled' by playing on the duty of self-sacrifice which was expected of all citizens: since a mother's life was to be devoted to tending her family, with the concomitant sacrifice of her own life or desires if necessary, the death of her son was portrayed as the greatest sacrifice she could offer. In this respect the novel by the popular woman writer, E. M. Delafield, *The Pelicans*, which was published in September 1918 yet did not mention the war at all, can be seen as firmly of its time. It preached the spiritual virtue of the heroine's voluntarily relinquishing the happiness and life of the people that she held dearest. This 'self'-sacrifice was presented as 'the key' to finer happiness. Brittain reduced this to a catch-phrase when she recorded that 'Not self-satisfaction, but self-sacrifice, is the order of the day' (Brittain, 1981: 125).

In 'Women and War', the popular versifier Ella Wheeler Wilcox had expressed one sarcastic reaction to the duty of women to teach their sons 'thoughts of love and peace' when men, 'Our self-announced superiors ... go forth to war', and want epics celebrating the heroic deeds of mutilating, starving and killing their fellow-men. But her response was passive: 'What can we do but sit in silent homes, / And wait and suffer?' and negative: 'Why should we women waste our time and words / In talking peace, when men declare for war?' (Wilcox, 1903: 23). Other women, such as Mrs Stobart, were not content to 'smile through their tears' but saw it as the womanly duty of mothers to declare for peace. Margaret Sackville, a convinced pacifist who worked for the Union of Democratic Control, published poetry such as 'Nostra Culpa', denouncing women who betrayed their sons by not speaking out: 'We mothers and we murderers of mankind' (Sackville, 1916). The heroine of Marion Wentworth Craig's protest play, *War Brides*, a pregnant war-widow, commits suicide rather than become a mother to raise yet more cannon fodder (Craig, 1915).

There is some vague echo in Brittain's diary of one feminist view, that men and women may have different attitudes to war since men do not quite understand 'what it means to a woman, who knows the trouble & pain the production of an individual costs, to hear of this light destruction of a human creature' (Brittain, 1981: 305). However, Vera was still only just finding her sexual identity. This was not yet in terms of wife or mother, but as a sweetheart, whose only 'proper' relation to a man was chastely romantic. Unable to maintain her initial opposition to war, she adopted the one relation to men that the drama of war permitted her: the nun-like role of nurse, which ensured 'gallant', 'chivalrous' treatment from men. The intolerable conflict between passive object of desire and independent woman came to a head during Roland's brief week of leave in 1915. Unable to break social conventions to express her passion physically herself, she goaded him into kissing her yet remained unyielding, until finally agreeing to be engaged despite all her scruples against marriage. She did not find her own physical initiative until the very last moment when, in despair, Roland kissed her passionately in public as her train was leaving the station: 'And I kissed him, which I had never done before' (332). That was the last she ever saw of him.

Vera seems to have been completely unaware of the debate that was being fought over the choice of political stance by women, especially mothers, in wartime. In fact, the conflict between her two options, of 'pretty joy' or 'intelligent being in her own right' is perfectly exemplified by an evening early in the War. While she was a student at Oxford, in February 1915, Charles Trevelyan came to speak on 'The Way to Peace'. She remarked to her diary that he was someone 'whom I had not heard about before but seems a famous person'. He had in fact resigned from Asquith's government as a protest against the war with Germany, and was one of the founder members of the Union of Democratic Control. This was the main organisation working for a negotiated peace (Swartz, 1981). Partly in consideration of the lecture, Vera wore a new dress that evening. She did not comment in her diary on the content of the lecture, but was concerned to note that 'I got great satisfaction out of the dress, which seemed to ensure me a pleasant evening' since so many people complimented her on how pretty it was (Brittain, 1981: 185). She had been just as uninvolved in November

1914 when G. K. Chesterton came to speak on 'The War and The Class War': 'I was too interested in trying to draw him to listen much to what he had to say' (152).

Later, her own misery seems to have cut her off from awareness of either the women's peace movement or the 'motherhood-for-militarism' campaign. This was spearheaded by the notorious letter from 'A Little Mother' which was republished as a pamphlet from *The Morning Post* in 1916, and began by identifying with the imperialist view of women's role:

> we play the most important part in the history of the world, for it is we who 'mother the men' who have to uphold the honour and traditions not only of our Empire but of the whole civilized world.

Deliberately opposing Pacifists on behalf of 'mothers of the British race', it then went on to speak of women's 'sacred trust of motherhood . . . We women pass on the human ammunition of "only sons" to fill up the gaps' since women were 'created for the purpose of giving life' as men were created 'to take it'. It concluded triumphantly 'Now we are giving it in a double sense'. A double sense indeed! Graves quoted this sanctimonious, jingoistic letter and the fatuous responses that agreed with its promotion of 'the glorious work' of war, in *Goodbye To All That*. For once he was left speechless.

However, in his play *But It Still Goes On*, Graves did comment on the covert sexuality disguised by the religious rhetoric of the Romance of war. Speaking of the way in which 'a platoon of men will absolutely worship a good-looking young officer', he remarked sardonically: 'it's a very, very strong romantic link'. The attachment is pervertedly 'romantic' though. Instead of picking their officer flowers, they kill him Germans (Graves, 1950: 145–6). In that era when sexuality was so severely restrained and distorted, the sublimated sado-masochism of Christianity acted as a substitute, and decorous religious language became the main expression available for passion. The language of Christianity had been linked to that of Romance and also to warfare through the ideology of the Crusades. The Tales of King Arthur, which formed part of the Victorian cult of medievalism, perpetuated the association by promoting the ideals of chivalry (Girouard, 1981). In a country which boasts as patron saint, St George, who supposedly killed a dragon to save a virgin, the highest reward for public service even now is to be made a Knight of the Garter. It did not therefore seem strange that the public-school ethic fostered the archaic ideals of chivalry. The mutual support of front-line troops was mythified in the consciousness of non-combatants into a 'mystic fellowship' of English soldiers that bears more than a passing resemblance to the legend of the Knights of the Round Table:

> O fellowship whose phantom tread
> Hallows a phantom ground.
> (Newbolt, 'The War Films')

That legend was more than a children's fairy-tale; it provided an enduring frame of moral and spiritual reference. Samuel Smiles's manual, *Self-Help*, first published in 1859, was reprinted several times during the Great War. It defined the 'essence of manly character' in terms of the gentlemanly virtues of chivalry. These were exemplified by the heroic self-denial of Sir Philip Sydney and the discretion exercised by soldiers towards the ladies who nurse them. In 1958 Diana Cooper could still write in her autobiography of the Great War period that 'of all men Ego (Charteris) was the nearest to a knight of chivalry, but there is no echo of laughter from the Round Table, while Ego's humour was a riot of fine flowers and herbs' (Cooper, 1958: 79). Shortly after the War, in 1922, Ernest Raymond ended his novel about the First World War, *Tell England*, by speaking of the death of one of his heroes in the following terms: 'Doe had done a perfect thing at the last, and so grasped the Grail' (Raymond, 1922: 320). (The persistence of cultural mythology is indicated by the fact that that book, a popular gift to schoolboys, was still in print in 1981, 60 years later, having gone through 42 editions.)

This mythical conceptualisation of soldiers and warfare, which implied a passive, bystander role for women, dominated the popular consciousness. Stella, the schoolgirl heroine of *The Ladies' Road*, forms an adolescent infatuation for a Captain Liddell and thinks of him as Sir Galahad. In *The Children's Story of the War* the correspondent Philip Gibbs is quoted describing the wounded returning from battle 'like wounded knights from a tourney' (Parrott, 1917: 53). In 1914 the Archbishop of Canterbury pronounced that it was 'a holy war . . . a sacred cause' and in 1916 the Archdeacon of Ely preached that 'The Christian soldier may be thoroughly chivalrous and may in the course of his duty kill many men whom he does not hate' (Jameson, 1933: 192–7). During a speech made in November 1914, Mrs Pankhurst called upon the male members of her audience to go into battle like a knight of old, who knelt before the altar and vowed he would keep his sword stainless and with absolute honour to his nation (Marwick, 1977: 32). If even a militant feminist like Mrs Pankhurst was speaking in these terms in public, and the popular poet Robert Service was publishing in 1916 such sentiments as 'Over the parapet gleams Romance', one can understand Vera Brittain admiring her brother in her diary as 'fine and knightly' and calling Roland Leighton 'Sir Galahad' because of his 'chevalier's purity and uprightness of heart' (Brittain, 1981: 378). Mrs Leighton assured Vera's parents that Roland's love for Vera was 'essentially of the nature of a romance, chivalrous and loyal'. Echoing Masefield's allusions in *Gallipoli* (1916) to the *Chanson de Roland*, Vera addressed Roland in her poetry as 'Monseigneur: my pure and stainless knight . . . Roland of Roncevalles in modern days' (Brittain, 1934: 13).

Roland Leighton does not appear to have fallen into thinking of Vera as La Belle Dame Sans Merci. For him she remained Lyndall. But the verses addressed by Duff Cooper to his future wife just before the War reveal the nature of the female role in chivalrous conceptions:

> As by enchantment I was back again
> In the far fairy world of chivalry,
> And such a white lost maiden I could see
> Shut up by magic.
>
> (Cooper, 1958: 101–2)

The darker aspect of this image of soldiers as knights who fought to rescue threatened maidens is pointed out by Fraser Harrison in a discussion of Victorian sexuality (Harrison, 1977). He suggests that pushing women back into the role of helpless victim in need of male protection was one response by men to the emancipation women were demanding, and which threatened men's notions of masculine superiority. In an analysis of Frederic Leighton's paintings, particularly that of Perseus and Andromeda, a variation of the theme of St George and the Dragon, Harrison claims that Leighton's idealised vision of woman appeared to confer sublimity while in reality it sought to preserve traditional submissiveness. Harrison's analysis is amply borne out by the illustrations in Mark Girouard's study of Victorian iconography (Girouard, 1981).

Conceptually, the setting up of one field of meaning, chivalry, as dominant, made any reference to modern political or historical reality irrelevant, even unintelligible. A line of women alongside Andromeda or the dragon, holding up political placards, would have been a ridiculous anachronism. In the discourse of that mythical conception of the world it would have been senseless to speak of women's possible assumption of political responsibility. On St George's Day, 23rd April 1916, Vera Brittain sat in Saint Paul's Cathedral near G. F. Watt's picture of Hagar in the Desert. She interpreted the picture to represent the common condition of woman as one of numbed, bewildered endurance: like her, all women of the day were, as merely women, at the mercy of 'an agonising, ruthless fate which it seemed [they] could do nothing to restrain' (Brittain, 1933: 265).

Ignoring the historic context, Brittain identified women's lot as one of passive suffering, caused by an impersonal 'fate' that women were powerless to affect.

For many women the religious aura of chivalry gave some significance to their enforced dependence and to the physical repression and emptiness of a life without young men. Vera unconsciously made her true motivation clear in the diary. Early in 1915 she had written to Leighton about the 'agony and absence of ornamentation' of her present life, of 'its bareness of all but the few great things which are all we have to cling to now – honour and love and heroism and sacrifice'. Then in June 1915, after she had left Oxford to begin nursing, on her first day at the Devonshire Hospital she revealed:

Oh! I love the British Tommy! I shall get so fond of these men, I know. And when I look after any one of them, it is like nursing Roland by proxy. Oh! if only one of them could be the Beloved One! (Brittain, 1981: 270)

The self-image of the Pietá permitted vicarious physical contact with a helpless, 'safe' lover, who was Saint/Knight/Christ, and it made acceptable, even desirable, the fact that Roland would have to be wounded first.

It was the self-deceit of such piousness that earned Sassoon's reproaches in his poem 'Glory of Women': since women believe that 'chivalry redeems / The war's disgrace' and cannot bring themselves to imagine 'that British troops "retire" / When hell's last horror breaks them, and they run, / Trampling the terrible corpses – blind with blood'. Medieval ideals of the spiritual value of war, endorsed by the patriotic verse of inexperienced soldiers, and propaganda about the stalwart British Tommy, were to compensate women for otherwise empty lives, thus willingly embraced. These ideals proved hard to eradicate once rooted in the blood of young men who had apparently died in their belief.

Neither the verse of the *preux chevalier* Rupert Brooke, nor the ideals of chivalry actually proved of much consolation to Vera Brittain as she gradually lost the young men she had known and loved. She quotes Shelley when Leighton dies: 'Why didst thou . . . Dare the unpastured Dragon in his den?' and tries to gain comfort from Rupert Brooke's War Sonnets. She quotes again from Brooke's poetry when other friends, Victor and Geoffrey, are killed in 1917: 'War knows no power'. This line echoes ironically when she reports the death, too, of her only brother, Edward, who was killed in 1918. The ideals of chivalry gave her no means of recognising or understanding the barbarity of modern war, or its political causes. They left her with a maiden's mind, shut up by the magic of poetic propaganda and government flannel.

By the end of the Great War, all those young men with whom she had been intimate in her youth being dead, Vera Brittain confronted an alien world. It was a world which rejected the ideals of chivalry as futile. Her own renunciation now counted for nothing: 'The more fool you!' ('The Lament of the Demobilised', Reilly, 1981: 14). Gradually she regained her sense of purpose, and came to understand, as she put it in *Testament of Experience*, that the real cause of the war had been 'political unconsciousness' (Brittain, 1957: 422). She then finally started on the road leading to pacifism, socialism and internationalism, causes to which she dedicated the rest of her life.

3

'The Magic of Adventure'

Europe as a whole seems to have shared a general euphoria at the declaration of war; yet by 1920 an annual Remembrance Ceremony marked national mourning in Britain. The gradual disenchantment with the War began as early as 1915, but the fighting was continued for another three years. At the beginning, the First World War had lifted the young high on its crest; both young men and young women were impressionable and caught up in the general enthusiasm. As Storm Jameson put it, looking back in 1933:

When the war broke out you and I were young . . . For us and for those who like us were without ballast of experience, the war came as a sudden wave, lifting us high before it threw us under. (Jameson, 1933: 189)

It was also in 1933 that Vera Brittain published her autobiography about the War years. In a chapter headed by a verse about 'the magic of adventure', she expressed what for her was a paradox. Despite the fact that the War was a stupid tragedy which had wasted her youth like everyone else's, betraying her faith, mocking her love and spoiling her career, nevertheless, the year which she spent in Malta in 1916 while the War itself was stagnating, remained in her memory as an interval of glamorous delight:

Come back, magic days! I was sorrowful, anxious, frustrated, lonely – but yet how vividly alive! (Brittain, 1933: 290–1)

She then comments that it is 'this glamour, this magic, this incomparable keying up of the spirit in a time of mortal conflict', which constitute the pacifist's real problem. The glamour of a 'vitalising consciousness of common peril for a common end' allures 'boys and girls who have just reached the age when love and friendship and adventure call more persistently than at any later time'. Pacifism will never be successful until constructive thought achieves 'that element of sanctified loveliness which, like superb sunshine breaking through thunder-clouds, from time to time glorifies war' (291–2).

To present war as an alluring 'adventure' was not simply to label it as a hazardous enterprise; it was to place the events of the Great War on a footing with the deeds of British heroes. These were the men mythicised in the popular imagination by Tennyson, Henty and Newbolt, Kipling and Conan Doyle, as having created the great British Empire by means of 'The Bow' and 'The English Flag', team spirit, and 'The Charge of the Light Brigade'. What Bertrand Russell called 'the whole foul literature of "glory"' extended through poetry, across popular verse to the children's story-books 'with which the minds of children are polluted' (Parker, 1987: 140). The Victorian tradition continued unimpeded through the Great War. If through the books of G. A. Henty the Victorian English child could in imagination fight *At Agincourt* or sail *Under Drake's Flag*, or march *Under Wellington's Command*, or go *With Roberts to Pretoria*, or be *With Clive in India*, now, as that child's children continued to read Captain Frank. H. Shaw, they could sail *With Jellicoe in the North Sea*, or if they read Strang, they could be *With Haig on the Somme* or *Fighting with French*, finally to march *With the Allies to the Rhine* by reading Brereton.

Not merely was it true that 'Adventure stories were the energising myth of empire' which glorified conquest (Green, 1984: 12–13). As Brittain's observation about the 'sanctified loveliness' that 'glorifies war' indicates, the myth such stories promoted implied that the imperial enterprise was divinely sanctioned. As Anne Summers has demonstrated, adventure books combined with evangelical literature to create a 'calendar of Imperial saints', making martyrs of military heroes by endowing them with an 'intense aura of sanctity' (Summers, 1976: 117–18). To join the imperial adventure was to enlist in the advance guard of Christianity. Like the Indian Mutiny, the Great War was presented, as in Kipling's verse, as yet another Holy War against heathenism (Kipling, 1940: 289).

The imperial adventure was not confined to reading by boys. The Duchess of Sutherland wrote in her account of nursing in France during the early weeks of the invasion: 'I felt as if I were actually *living* some book of adventure, such as I had read in my youth' (Gower, 1914: 38). G. M. McDougall gave her war memoirs of nursing at the Front, the resounding subtitle: 'Nursing Adventures in Belgium and France' (McDougall, 1917). In 1915 nurse Violetta Thurstan ended her account of her time spent nursing in Belgium and Russia, with a description of what she called a 'vision of the High Adventure' of war: 'one tastes the joy of comradeship to the full' and 'one could see the poetry of war . . . the zest . . . the delight . . . the keen hunger, the rough food sweetened by the sauce of danger' (Thurstan, 1915: 174–5). She considered it 'a good thing to have had' the vision, despite 'the darkest sides of war', the poignancy and squalor of the dazed, terrified refugees, and the horror of the wounded, to which all the nurses attested.

Nor was the imperial adventure reserved for Sunday School Prizes or Christmas presents alone. Girls, like boys, were subject to stirring patriotism at school too. It was implicit in history and geography text books, and explicitly taught in literature classes (Horn, 1987). A book of *English Patriotic Poetry*, selected by L. Godwin Salt, assistant English mistress at Clapham High School for Girls, was specially compiled in 1911 for the celebrations held in schools on Empire Day. Its object was to 'trace the growth of the Patriotic Note in English Verse' from Spenser, through *Richard II* and *Henry V*, Wordsworth and Swinburne, to Kipling, ending with the National Anthem. It was reprinted in 1912. In 1932 Anthony Haslam compiled an *Anthology of Empire* commencing with 'God Save the King' and containing many more of the same verses but also including some which had not been written in 1911, such as Rupert Brooke's 'The Soldier'. It was not by accident that Vera Brittain's earliest memories were shared with Robert Graves, Diana Manners, and other members of their generation, and that these were of Queen Victoria's Diamond Jubilee and the Boer War (Brittain, 1933: 17; Graves, 1957: 9; Cooper, 1958: 47–8).

Rupert Brooke was the poet who above all expressed the glamour of war for the War Generation, summed up in the imperialist religion of self-sacrifice 'For God, King and Country'. Even in death the British soldier could colonise a corner of a foreign field with the benefits of Englishness, to leave us our heritage of Nobleness, Honour, Holiness, Love and Pain. If 'There was an abyss between combatants and non-combatants' (Hope, 1965: 137), there seems to be a greater abyss between the Great War generation and our own, judging by responses to literature. Brooke's poetry played on what were keynotes of his culture, as displayed, for instance, in the poetry of Tennyson, and Horace A. Vachell's

1905 schoolbook, *The Hill*: the idea of the 'dreariness' and 'petti-ness' of bourgeois life, against which the life of young men was a swift race into the radiance of a heroic death. The distance between that generation and ours may be measured by the satirical effect Anthony Burgess achieves by quotations from Brooke in his novel, *The Wanting Seed* (1962). Yet at Easter, 1915, Dean Inge had eulogised 'The Soldier' from the pulpit in St Paul's. Fifty years later, in 1965, Francis Hope wrote: 'Brooke was both a bad poet and a bad influence, though not an important one' (139). As Blunden mildly observed in 1930:

> [Brooke] did not discern anything more in the case than sacrifice for an ideal, consolation for that sacrifice; what he discerned, that he adorned with a classical manner. Later it became difficult to read his verse. (Brereton, 1930: 14)

Brooke may have been a bad influence. I think he was an important one. His early death in the Dardanelles on St George's Day, 1915, lent itself to his idealisation as both mythical Greek hero and national Christian martyr. In his poetry and in his person he epitomised the glamorous magic of the War. The values he had apparently died for, Honour and Nobleness, had already been established for his generation by their education and childhood reading about 'the adventure of Empire'.

May Wedderburn Cannan was an exact contemporary of Vera Brittain's. In 1976 she published her autobiography, *Grey Ghosts and Voices*, which she called 'a salute to my generation'. In her childhood she had read all the great adventure-writers, such as Scott, Henty, Ballantyne, Strang, as well as the patriotic poets, Wordsworth, Tennyson, Newbolt and Aytoun's Lays: 'so we knew all about the Round Table and the Knights' (Cannan, 1976: 10–11). The emotional influence of this early reading stayed with her. Defending Barrie, despite her acknowledgement that he was 'sentimental, a psychological muddle, and out of date', she asserted that 'It does not always make sense to write the old writers off' (88). She justified this by reporting that a line from *Peter Pan* gave courage to a boy in the trenches at the time of his death: 'To die will be an awfully big adventure'. We may still clap for Tinkerbell, but I cannot imagine anyone nowadays quoting Barrie except in irony. The fact that the boy found something in Barrie, a source of courage to go over the parapet, says more about his culture than about the instrinsic worth of James Barrie's writings.

May Cannan says that during the Great War the taste in poets changed from Masefield and Thompson:

> Our poets were the Rupert Brooke of the *Sonnets*, Charles Sorly, Wilfred Gibson, Grenfell, Baring. The early Sassoon and Robert Graves; Nicholls [sic] and the Mr Kipling of *Not this tide*, *The Trawlers* and *The Children*. (102)

During the War she published her first book of poems, *In War Time*, which makes unabashed allusions to Brooke (for instance: 'And laughter come back to the earth again', Reilly, 1981: 19). She claimed she was lucky to get good reviews and a small fan mail, since after the Somme there was a change of heart among poets. Sassoon declared to the Press that the war was now a war of conquest and without justification, and declared himself to be a conscientious objector. A saying went round: 'Went to the war with Rupert Brooke and came home with Siegfried Sassoon'. May Cannan responded:

> I had much admired some of Sassoon's verse but I was not coming home with him. Someone must go on writing for those who were still convinced of the right of the cause for which they had taken up arms. (113)

As the autobiography makes clear, she remained convinced. Like Vera Brittain, May Cannan lost both a young man she loved, and her fiancé (she had no brother). However, she believed herself fortunate because, although like Vera Brittain she had 'lost everything', yet she 'kept so much':

> I did not believe that the Dead had died for nothing, nor that we should have 'kept out of the war' – The Dead had kept faith, and so, if we did not grudge it, had we. (148)

Part of that 'keeping faith' was being true to her own earlier self and her Edwardian values, established not only by her family environment in Oxford, but by her childhood reading (11, 44–5). Her autobiography was personal and dedicated to her grand-daughter. One never senses in it the gulf that Vera Brittain

establishes in her testament from her generation to their successors, the gap across which she regards the enthusiasms of her
youth from an ironic distance.

One of May Cannan's poems was chosen by Philip Larkin for *The
Oxford Anthology of Twentieth Century Verse* (1978). This is remarkable since very few poems of that war by women were republished
before Catherine Reilly's anthology in 1981. The poem is 'Rouen'.
It is about the adventure of getting to France for four weeks during
the Great War, to help work voluntarily at a Canteen for soldiers
going to the Front. Her autobiography details the background of
that trip, specifically relating the magic of that adventure to the
values expressed by Brooke.

> I suppose it is difficult for anyone to realise now what 'France'
> meant to us. In the second War I met a young man of the Left
> who assured me that Rupert Brooke's verse was of no account,
> phoney, because it was 'impossible that anyone should have
> thought like that'. I turned and rent him, saying that he was
> entitled to his own opinion of Rupert Brooke's verse, but *not*
> entitled to say that no one could have thought like that. How
> could he know how we had thought? – All our hopes and all our
> loves, and God knew, all our fears, were in France; to get to
> France, if only to stand on her soil was something; to share, in
> however small a way, in what was done there was Heart's
> Desire. (89)

It is clear from diaries of the period, such as Vera Brittain's and
Cynthia Asquith's, that May Cannan's admiration for Brooke's
sonnets was general.

Despite what Cannan claims about the change in literary taste
during the War, the general metre of the lines of 'Rouen', breathlessly capturing the excitement of her experience, is similar to that
of Masefield's 'Cargoes' (a poem that relates British trade to the
exotic glories of past empires). Two stanzas out of the 13 will
indicate the character of her verse:

> Can you recall the parcels that we made them for the railroad,
> Crammed and bulging parcels held together by their string,
> And the voices of the sergeants who called the Drafts together,
> And the agony and splendour when they stood to save the King?

. . . When the world slips slow to darkness, when the office fire
   burns lower,
My heart goes out to Rouen, Rouen all the world away;
When other men remember I remember our Adventure
And the trains that go from Rouen at the ending of the day.

The mood of nostalgia, and the questioning, and the cadence of
certain lines ('stretching Eastwards to the sea'), even the title, all
echo, incongruously, Kipling's 'Mandalay' ('looking lazy at the
sea'). It is odd that Larkin should have selected such a derivative
piece, but perhaps he chose it for its sentiments.

May Cannan was not only conservative in her literary style, but
in her views. She was a close family friend of Sir Walter Raleigh,
who was employed to travel to America on British government
propaganda work, and of Sir Arthur Quiller-Couch, who also
supported the government's propaganda campaign. Her father's
firm, the Clarendon Press, for which she worked during the War,
published the propaganda series of Oxford Pamphlets which were
distributed abroad by Wellington House (the government's Propaganda Department). In particular, the Clarendon Press was responsible for publishing Gilbert Murray's *The Foreign Policy of Sir
Edward Grey 1906–15* (1915), which rebutted UDC arguments about
the causes of the War and the desirability of a negotiated settlement. With the co-operation of the Clarendon Press this book was
widely distributed amongst churches, schools and trade unions
(Wright, 1978). Among the crowds celebrating the Armistice in
1918, May Cannan reflected piously on Kipling's 'Recessional'. Yet
she helped her friend Carola Oman to get her wartime poetry *The
Menin Road* (1919) published; this contained the poem 'Ambulance
Train 30' with the exultant last line: '*And the Occupying Army boards
her for Cologne.*' May Cannan's imperialist patriotism is clear in
'Rouen', not only in the mention of the National Anthem, but in
the reference to the Empire: 'And the youth and pride of England
from the ends of all the earth'. Her automatic assumption of
imperialism is even more clear in her elegy, 'Lamplight':

> You and I
> Dreamed greatly of an Empire in those days.
> (Reilly, 1981: 6)

Over 50 years later Cannan's imperialist faith remained unshaken:
'The Dead had saved England, and, if we were wise enough, the

world' (Cannan, 1976: 148). What from, she does not say.

Vera Brittain commenced her autobiography by stating that the Great War came to her unexpectedly, 'as an interruption of the most exasperating kind to my personal plans' (Brittain, 1933: 17). May Cannan had been preparing for the War since she was 18 in 1911; all her (male) friends training as volunteer soldiers, with the Officers' Training Corps or the Special Army Reserve, she decided not to 'lag behind' and enlisted with the women's Voluntary Aid Detachment, training to be a nurse. Her mother was the first Commandant of Oxford's University Detachment and May became the Quartermaster. From 1913, following War Office instructions, their Detachment was prepared to set up a small hospital of 60 beds if mobilised, which, in 1914, they did. In the event it had to be handed over to the Base as an auxiliary: 'It had all come to nothing, the thing that I had worked so hard for and to which I had given my heart . . . The Iliad was over' (Cannan, 1976: 57–79). Instead she helped her father run the Clarendon Press for most of the War, with a few months working for MI5 in Paris to compensate her, and the brief interlude at Rouen where she was 'blissfully happy' (90).

Perhaps Larkin thought May Cannan's writing exemplified what he himself had written about the Edwardian mentality in his often quoted 'MCMXIV': 'Never such innocence again' (Larkin, 1964: 28). But there is a deceit in that idea. The popular fiction published in the years leading up to the First World War presented war as inevitable and ennobling, and writing which opposed this attitude was largely ineffective in the face of the pro-war propaganda engineered by such patriots as Lords Roberts, Baden-Powell, and Northcliffe. An understanding of what industrialised warfare would entail was difficult to bring home to a people bombarded from childhood, at school, at church, and at the hearth, with the glamorous Romance of war. Relying on Bevill Quiller-Couch's epistolary efforts, May Cannan can hardly be blamed for her ignorance of the true conditions of trench warfare, especially so early in the War (for instance, 'This is war and no mistake; and it's grand to be out here' quoted in Cannan, 1976: 104).

Yet there is an evasiveness in her poem as to the destination of the trains going Eastwards. Under whatever conditions, those men were going out to kill other men and to suffer. Vera Brittain intended her *Testament of Youth* to be a memorial to 'those misguided dupes, the boys and girls of the war generation'. Like May Cannan she was 21 in 1914. They were both intelligent women. Brian Bond preferred to qualify what has been called 'the prevailing innocence of mind' of the generation of 1914 'wilful self-delusion' (Bond, 1984: 98). Given May Cannan's connections with the British government's propaganda machine, at least in her case that seems to me a more appropriate epithet. There were poems by women who held no illusions about the waste of war. It is interesting that Larkin did not select any of those.

May Cannan's poem 'Rouen' is subtitled '26 April–25 May 1915'. She apparently experienced no difficulty in crossing the Channel at that time: 'I had a passport'. What she does not mention in her autobiography is that, after months of preparation, the Women's International Peace Conference took place at the Hague from 27 to 30 April 1915 (Wiltsher, 1985: 98). None of the British delegates was permitted to cross the North Sea, the issue of their passports being deliberately delayed until an Admiralty order took effect, closing the North Sea to shipping. Nevertheless over a thousand delegates did attend. The conference passed resolutions concerning universal disarmament and the establishment of a permanent international conference which would have the authority to settle international differences by arbitration and economic pressure, rather than by arms. Many letters of support were received, including one from Gabrielle Dûchene, the President of the Section du Travail du Conseil National des Femmes Françaises, which stated that: '(Women) are strong against war, because not making it they are not intoxicated by the joy of action' (Wiltsher, 1985: 98). Women like May Cannan did help make the War, and were intoxicated by it.

If May Cannan did not know about that conference, she had nevertheless, unlike Vera Brittain, heard about the Union for Democratic Control, since her cousin, the novelist Gilbert Cannan, was amongst the founders. Referring to the colony at Garsington where conscientious objectors could work on the land instead of fighting, she wrote about 'the intellectual élite who stayed there talking of art and verse and genius and pure intellect' (113). Among that 'élite' who May Cannan considered so dilettante, were Bertrand Russell, D. H. Lawrence and Katherine Mansfield

Five years older than May Cannan, Katherine Mansfield also crossed to France early in 1915. Her precise motives in travelling there are not clear, but she did not go in order to help out with any canteen for British Tommies. Using a fabricated letter from false French 'relatives' to obtain a visa, she managed to spend four days with a lover in the French army, in an area of the war zone banned to women. It may have been, as her biographer suggests, that she was getting tired of John Middleton Murry (the man she had been living with for nearly three years and was to marry in 1918 when her divorce came through) and that she really fancied herself in love with the French soldier, Francis Carcot (Alpers, 1980: 173–9). She may, on the other hand, have been using Carcot as an excuse to visit the war zone for herself. Carcot seems to have thought Middleton Murry believed the trip to be 'innocent'; Murry believed it represented Katherine's decision to leave him. Katherine borrowed the money for the trip from her brother, on the pretext that she had a contract for a series of war sketches. She probably had no single, determinate motive.

Born Kathleen Beauchamp, daughter of a businessman who was knighted for services to the Dominion of New Zealand, Katherine Mansfield was personally quite unlike the conventional May Cannan. Cannan was forever anxious to please her father and other paternal gentlemen. Mansfield had escaped from what she regarded as an oppressively bourgeois, patriarchal family-life in the colonies in order to forge her own identity as a writer in London. Like Vera Brittain, although no ardent suffragist (New Zealand had had female suffrage since 1893) she found the expected role of society-wife stultifying. They both wanted to take advantage of the chances offered by the emancipation that feminists were advancing. Yet whereas Vera Brittain had been influenced by a university extension lecturer and looked to a university education to grant her independence, Katherine Mansfield seems to have been inspired by the example of her aunt, the successful author of *Elizabeth and her German Garden*. But writing, for Katherine Mansfield, was not a pastime or a job; it *was* that emancipation from the imposed identity of Kathleen Beauchamp. It enabled her to construct art out of her consciousness, to make her own self into an artist. More courageous than Vera Brittain, and less inhibited sexually, Katherine Mansfield had imbibed Oscar Wilde's views about the duty of self-realisation, and the artist's need of unconventional experience. She paid very dearly for her experience, exchanging the warmth and security of her family for the pain of loneliness, gonorrhoea and an abortion. But it was her confrontation with that suffering, the passion and misery evaded by bourgeois life, which gave depth and complexity to her art (Tomalin, 1987).

Her journal says little about the War before her brother's **death** in uniform, in October 1915, a decisive event in her life. But in January 1915 she mentions discussing 'the war and its horrors' with D. H. Lawrence, and feeling that the war was closing in on her (Stead, 1977: 49). After the War she wrote emphatically in a letter to Murry: 'We have to face our war'. Artists must feel, in the *profoundest* sense, that nothing could ever be the same again. Literature that leaves the war out is 'a lie in the soul'. That did not mean that novels had to be directly about mobilisation and the violation of Belgium, but common things had to be intensified by the tragic knowledge: 'We see death in life' (Murray, 1954: 380, 393). However, that was later. She travelled to Gray in the War Zone in February 1915, when the war was still only a few months old, before the Battles of Loos, Ypres, the Somme, Passchendaele, before the death of her beloved brother. Carcot afterwards portrayed Katherine in his novel *Les Innocents*, as Winnie, 'a predatory huntress out for "copy" ' (Alpers, 1980: 178). Katherine Mansfield's first concern all her adult life was for her art, to which she was 'ruthlessly' dedicated (Gordon, 1971: 32). She produced some short sketches of wartime England (Mansfield, 1915, 1924); Gray, 75 miles behind the trenches, was the nearest she could reach to the battlefront itself.

I have roughed in the inconclusive biographical background to Katherine Mansfield's 1915 visit to the French war zone, to indicate that the short story based on her visit, *An Indiscreet Journey*, should not be confused with confessional autobiography. (Her most complete account of her visit is reprinted in Mansfield, 1954: 74–9.) Mansfield's motivation was not distinct, but that is no guide to the epiphany of her heroine. Like Sassoon's surrogate, the infantry officer who was no poet, the heroine through whose consciousness Mansfield's story is narrated is not a writer, conscientiously committing her experiences immediately to letter-pad and journal as Mansfield herself did. Her heroine is simply borne along by the momentum of her escapade. Furthermore, Mansfield constructed her story with care, selecting events and rewriting her accounts of her sensations, although her original notebook entries were already scrupulously precise. The details of Mansfield's personal relation with Carcot, recorded affectionately in the journal, do not obtrude in her storytelling; the events of the night are left as a blank line on the page. Whether or not Mansfield was deceived by a calculating seducer, as Alpers implies, is not an issue in the story.

An Indiscreet Journey commences with the unlikely phrases: 'She is like St. Anne. Yes, the concierge is the image of St. Anne' and the unnamed thinker then behaves 'like any English lady in any French novel', an *ingénue* abroad (Mansfield, 1924). She buttons on an old borrowed Burberry, which she considers a suitable garment for facing a lion or being rescued from an open boat in mountainous seas. The heroine extravagantly dramatises her situation in ways which combine with the nervousness of her dash to the station and the uncertainty of the nature of her journey to create the suspense and unreality of an adventure-story. Breathlessly excited, her perceptions skim over the surface, lighting upon colours, and unexpectedly finding beauty, first in the prosaic concierge, with a black cloth over her head and whisps of grey hair hanging, and then in the cemeteries which 'flash gay in the sun!' as the train passes by. The levity with which she looks out of the railway window, seeing a soldier 'like a little comic picture waiting for the joke to be written underneath', is undercut by her incredulity: 'Is there really such a thing as war? Are all these laughing voices really going to the war? – have battles been fought in places like these?' Her reactions are gaily superficial; clearly the big wooden sheds 'like rigged-up dancing halls or seaside pavilions' are hospitals for the wounded, just as the 'corn-flowers and poppies and daisies' are not flowers but bunches of ribbons tied on to soldiers' graves. The old woman in black sitting opposite to her is wearing mourning rings and reading a letter from her son, the first she has received for months. The heroine, unconcerned, recalls instead the sensation of childhood journeys to the seaside, and fantasises about drifting in a canal barge 'when the war is over'. Her effervescence refuses to take what she sees to heart.

Throughout the first part of the story there is a constant incongruity between the intoxicated, heedless thoughts of the heroine, and the facts of a society at war, which she flippantly disregards but which impinge on her consciousness nevertheless. There is pathos in details, such as the soldier's coat done up with rusty safety-pins, and the *sabots* tied on another soldier's back with a piece of stout string such as the old woman found requested in the letter from her son. The 'forlorn and desolate' sentries look like a 'comic picture' to the heroine. For her, they are darlings, toy soldiers: their uniforms are ridiculous, with hats out of paper crackers; the colonels have painted cheeks and rolling heads. Brightly coloured, the ubiquitous soldiers are stamped on France like transfers. Nothing is serious. There are severe penalties for her actions but, childlike, her excitement seems to stem precisely from evading warnings and prohibitions. She refuses to heed the concierge, the Nameless Official, the shrewd 'ordinary little woman' on the train. The heroine's conscience is caricatured as a stuffed seagull, camped on the top of the ordinary woman's black velvet toque, 'incredibly surprised'. It responds ironically to her conversation about the militarised zone, where women are not allowed to visit the soldiers. From which it becomes apparent that the heroine has not been honest in her own mind either, imaginatively 'living' her deception. The explanation for the invitation to stay with relatives whose name she cannot remember becomes manifest when she is met at the other end by 'the little corporal'. Despite policemen, absurdly 'thick as violets everywhere', he whisks her off in a carriage to a room in a gay white house. There, once the door is safely closed on them, the heroine tosses her passport in the air and he catches it.

Where is she? The name of the place is never given, it is 'X', reached by changing at 'X.Y.Z'. It is the zone forbidden to women. Her journey there is indiscreet. Is that because she is committing a sexual indiscretion, or because it is rash of her to lie in order to visit the war zone?

The first part of the story, the heroine's trip to X, takes place on a single day, from six o'clock in the morning when the heroine gets up with only just time to catch the train, through one o'clock when she changes trains, to a time of late sunlight when she arrives at the white house in X. The story does not end there, but it then completely changes in tone. There is a gap on the page and the new paragraph begins: 'What an extraordinary thing. We had been there to lunch and to dinner each day; but now in the dusk and alone I could not find it'. No longer does the heroine run, run down, run up, run in and out, dodge or dance. Now she clop-clops in borrowed *sabots* through greasy mud. Now there is no warm sun rosy from rivers, stroking her muff, burning her cheek. Instead there is a 'ragged drifting light and thin rain' and the last breath of day is taken off by some boys swinging by, singing. In this village is no lovely little boy in coloured socks dancing beneath electric lotus buds, but a group of wounded soldiers under a lamp-post, petting a mangy, shivering dog.

She comes across the café. Unlike the noisy, busy buffet where she had changed trains, it is empty and silent: 'really a barn set out with dilapidated tables and chairs'. The heroine has time to contemplate her surroundings. She does not find the bottles in this café make the counter 'beautiful', nor does she like the wallpaper, a creamy paper patterned all over with green and swollen trees, which 'reared their mushroom heads to the ceiling'. Her light-hearted questioning has become sarcastic: it does not seem to her 'beautiful' or 'a gay and lovely thing' always to eat dinner in the middle of such a forest. When she travelled she wore no watch and paid no attention to time passing. In this café a clock is prominent, ticking. On either side of the clock is a coyly romantic picture of two lovers, before and after: the first, *Premier Rencontre*, shows the wooing; the second, *Triomphe d'Amour*, 'amorous confusion'. Unlike her earlier idyllic dream of floating down a canal after the war, she now imagines that 'this is the sort of thing one will do on the very last day of all – sit in an empty café and listen to the clock ticking until – '.

She is dispirited. The sense of tedium, of changeless repetition, is only reinforced by the gradual arrival of other customers. Soldiers, of course. They play cards, voice petty grievances. They ignore the mortification of the waiting-boy at breaking a bottle of liqueur which he will have to pay for. The Madame, unlike the chirrupping madam of the station-buffet, leaves the boy to do all the work, only using her plump hands to note the takings in a red book, and to arrange 'for the hundreth time a frill of lace on her bosom'. She is delighted by the boy's humiliation, but disgusted at the be-haviour of a convalescent soldier who enters. This invalid is troubled by his eyes, which keep watering in the smoky atmos-phere, and he compulsively rocks his body and groans, to the complete indifference of his comrades. The eventual arrival of the tender 'little corporal' does not redeem the sordid circumstances of the din and the suffocating smell of onion soup and boots and damp cloth. The ordinary woman on the train had claimed that the military authorities had to be strict about visits to the war zone: 'You cannot imagine what it would be like otherwise! You know what women are like about soldiers – mad, completely mad'. The heroine does not find it beautiful, or gay and lovely, to be surrounded by a forest of dissatisfied soldiers. But her journey is not over yet.

Later she is finishing her meal with 'the little corporal' and two of his friends, who are 'very drunk'. They wish her to taste a French liqueur, Mirabelle, in order to compare it with whiskey. It is supposed to be finer, sweeter, and not to leave one hungover the morning after like whiskey, but feeling gay. ('Mirabelle' loosely translates as 'glorious' or 'reflecting beauty'.) According to the blue-eyed soldier, 'It is only after the second glass that you really taste it . . . The second glass and then – ah! – then you know'. There being none at that café, they set off for *Café des Amis*, although the clock has struck half-past eight and no soldier is allowed to enter a café after eight o'clock at night. It will be 'worth the risk'. But when they enter, 'a scrag of a woman in a black shawl' screams at them about the time.

In the following moment of silence, as they all listen to the steps of the military police passing by outside, the heroine muses on the appearance of the people already dining. There are about ten of them, seated on two benches at a narrow table. To her they are beautiful, like a family party having supper in the New Testament. At the railway buffet she had noticed an old man in the doorway with a pail of fish – 'like the fish one sees in a glass case, swimming through forests of beautiful pressed sea-weed'. He had looked to her 'as though he had escaped from some holy picture'. The story opened with her reflection on the likeness of the concierge to St Anne, the mother of the Virgin Mary, 'Really very beautiful'. But her journey is no holy visitation. The soldiers are excluded from the peace and solicitude, the timeless sanctity of family life. The angry woman serves them the Mirabelle in 'the dark smelling scullery, full of pans of greasy water, of salad leaves and meat-bones'. 'Ah, at last!' says the blue-eyed soldier. At last, by taking risks, she knows. At last the heroine has arrived at the squalid, profane reality of the war-zone. She realises what it is to take a proper taste of humanity.

In technique and purpose, *An Indiscreet Journey* closely resembles James Joyce's short stories in *Dubliners* (1914), which were designed to reveal the sordid meanness and materialism of Dublin life. In 'After the Race', for instance, the gauche young hero wakes up in the dawn light to an incoherent recognition that the previous day's drunken bonhomie was merely moneygrubbing on the part of his sophisticated acquaintances, and that he has gambled his inheritance away. In 'A Painful Case' Mr Duffy, selfish and puritanical, had 'gnawed the rectitude of his life'. Solitary near a courting couple in a park at the end of the story, he feels obscurely that 'he had been outcast from life's feast'. Both Joyce and Mansfield were influenced by Symbolism in their **attempts to** show the spiritual emptiness at the heart of bourgeois life. Traditional Christian iconography is evoked negatively to reveal what is lacking. Their 'stories' are less narratives with a dénouement than prose poems which develop an image. The author has withdrawn. The words which compose the poem depict the character's consciousness and build up to a moment of emotional apprehension, an ironic epiphany. The reader's insight into what is absent is evoked by a symbol or image, the 'objective correlative' of the awareness. There is no bald statement. In this way Mansfield could avoid the polemical preaching which she found so distasteful in D. H. Lawrence's writing (Hanson, 1981: 17–23). It was also a way of avoiding the strident note of propaganda in dealing with the War.

The central image of *An Indiscreet Journey* is complex, and like any successful imaginative symbol, it does not adequately render up its significance to a discursive analysis. On the surface Mansfield has made use of a traditional narrative form, the journey in a tale of adventure, to express a rite of passage, the initiation into adult reality. Read superficially, her tale might seem to be about the loss of virginity, the post-coital blues that follow the transformation of romance into sexuality. In fact that reading would not do justice to her theme. In Mark Twain's *The Adventures of Huckleberry Finn* a boy accompanies a slave downriver, gradually to penetrate the meaning of slavery. In *Heart of Darkness*, Conrad used the motif of a journey upriver into darkest Africa to penetrate the dark heart of imperialism. In Mansfield's story, the heroine's journey into the military zone to meet a soldier is the account of her encounter with militarism, which breaks men as irreparably as the bottle of liqueur is broken.

It has now become a cliché to point out that war is erotic (Fussell, 1975: 270–2; Brittain, 1940: 52). It arouses men, and it arouses women. The masculinity of men in uniform, the scent of danger, is glamorous to women; there is romance to war. But the idea that war is romantic is as absurd as the idea that military police are like violets. A young girl's innocent, thrilled ideas of the romance of soldiering is a fragile illusion, doomed by the disgusting reality. Mansfield's naive heroine is initially intoxicated by war, like May Sinclair or May Cannan, but a second dose reveals the tedium, the oppression, the exploitation. A sexual adventure is fun, but it is excluded from the enduring value of family solicitude, just as soldiers are. At the heart of Mansfield's story is the image of misery, the convalescent soldier, whose eyes, 'pink as a rabbit's' in his white face, brim and spill, brim and spill. His tears run over the table like the spilled liqueur from the broken bottle, 'as though the table were crying'. He wipes up the mess ineffectually with a wet cloth, like the serving-boy. The heroine now begins to notice eyes: the little corporal 'squeezed up his eyes when he laughed, so that you saw nothing but the long curly lashes'. She is taken by the drunken blue-eyed soldier in search of a liqueur which, unlike the invalid, is not disgusting the morning after; 'it leaves you feeling gay as a rabbit'. Destined for the pot, the lusty, pink-eyed gaiety of a rabbit is short-lived. We know that the brief, intoxicating effect of alcohol is a poor substitute for what the old mother on the train sips and savours from her son's letter.

Indiscreetly transgressing social rules, the heroine has discovered the reality of war. She has adventured beyond the sphere of virgin ignorance, into the forbidden zone of masculine knowledge.

Although it seems to have been written while Mansfield was staying in Carcot's Paris flat, in March 1915, *An Indiscreet Journey* was not published until after her death. Murry included it in *Something Childish and Other Stories* in 1924, with no explanation as to why it had not been published previously. Yet it played an important part in her artistic development, thematically and structurally. Not only does it mark the point in her work at which the family is seen as having a positive value, a key to her later portrayal of her childhood in New Zealand; in its use of symbolism and cross reference, and in the scope of its implications, 'An Indiscreet Journey' was technically more sophisticated than her other writing to date, or than pieces which followed and were published in *Bliss, and Other Stories* (1920).

Her first collection of short stories, entitled *In a German Pension*, had been published in 1911. Although some of these stories were based on her experiences in New Zealand, they were given a German setting, relying on a short spell Mansfield had spent at a German spa in 1909. They had first appeared in *The New Age* and their republication was clearly related to the climate of hostility between Germany and England, that increased in the years just before the First World War. According to Murry she refused to allow them to be republished again during the War, calling the book unworthy. She considered it unworthy partly because it was juvenile, but also because 'it's a lie' (Mansfield, 1926: introduction). The opening pieces, which play hardest on anti-German prejudice, are the least worthy. Presenting the Germans as piggish and soulless, these sketches conformed to the pre-war xenophobia that made British wartime propaganda credible. Criticising German snobbery, the sketches themselves reveal a parallel snobbery, for instance, in the nice distinction between the narrator's own use of the term 'napkin' and the genteelism 'serviette' attributed to her hosts.

The opening story is the most blatant. (The very title 'Germans at Meat' instead of 'at Table' relates the diners to animals.) Trying to forestall expected indelicacies in the conversation, the prim narrator details the decidedly unrestrained table-manners and eating habits of her fellow guests at the Pension, from Herr Rat, who blows on his soup, and Herr Hoffmann, who wipes soup drippings from his coat and waistcoat, to the Widow, who picks her teeth with a hairpin while speaking. Herr Hoffmann, prompted by his declaration that beer makes him sweat so, 'wiped his neck and face with his dinner napkin and carefully cleaned his ears'. They do not disguise either their hearty appetites or their contempt for the English. The conversation moves on to a view expressed by the Traveller, that the English are frightened of invasion. However, Herr Hoffmann claims that 'we don't want England. If we did we would have had her long ago'. The heroine makes it quite clear that 'we certainly do not want Germany'.

It was only a short step from this antagonism to the cruder prejudice of wartime writings, such as Herbert Strang's *With Haig on the Somme*. (This was first published in 1917 and was still being reprinted in 1934.) In this book for boys a German agent betrays himself by his eating habits, 'dead to the graces of the table'. In a 'repellent scene' of 'disgusting gormandising' two gluttons, 'gorging' and 'guzzling' with 'piggish noises', speak with their mouths full and grunt in lieu of conversation (Strang, 1917: 224–7). The English heroes are appalled at such 'hoggishness'. The inability of Germans to control their bestial instincts was linked in adult literature to the depravity of their sexual appetites. Visual propaganda, for instance, in the form of posters for the British Empire Union, exhorted the public to boycott German goods rather than buy from this 'Robber, Ravisher and Murderer' who was depicted bayonetting a baby, shooting a Red Cross nurse, and about to force a fate worse than death on a young woman (Darracott, 1981: 60). As Cooperman demonstrates, 'the atrocities reported by the enormous propaganda machine of the British ...

resulted in the portrait of a racially depraved, sexually perverted Teutonic Beast' (Cooperman, 1967: 101).

The effectiveness of this psychological warfare is well attested. Much of the popular literature of the War period feeds hatred for the cruelty of Germans caricatured in this way. Even Mansfield's aunt, now Elizabeth Russell, did her bit for the allied war effort with the pseudonymous publication of *Christine*, in which the innocent young heroine, an English music student, dies while trying to escape from Germany after Britain declares war. In 1917, when assigned to a ward for German prisoners in a base hospital in Étaples, Vera Brittain remembered how Huns were supposed to have 'subjected pure and stainless females to unmentionable "atrocities"' and 'half expected that one or two of the patients would get out of bed and try to rape me' (Brittain, 1933: 374).

Placed within the context of other writing about the war, the originality of *An Indiscreet Journey* is marked. It not only avoids the commonplaces and sensationalism of contemporary popular literature. Ironically querying the seeming objectivity of picturesque descriptions, the beauty of appearances, it reveals the actual self-centredness of individual consciousness. By using allusion and symbol to uncover what the wartime propaganda about the excitement and heroic 'manliness' of war concealed, it also depicts the mental evasiveness on which propaganda relies. Unlike her more popular stories, such as *The Little Governess* or *The Doll's House*, this story by Katherine Mansfield does not pander to the reader's sense of superiority or to nostalgia for lost innocence.

Difficult though it was to visit the militarised zone, Katherine Mansfield was not the only woman to write at first hand about the experience of life under martial law. Ellen La Motte was an American nurse who had graduated from hospital training school in 1902. Specialising in tuberculosis she had gone to work in Paris in 1913 and from 1915 she worked in a French military field hospital, ten kilometres behind the lines in Belgium, not far from Ypres. Her prose sketches of that life were written between April 1915 and June 1916. 'Heroes' first appeared in *Atlantic Monthly* 1915. It was republished together with the other stories in a volume entitled *The Backwash of War*. After its first appearance in the autumn of 1916, this book went into several impressions. (A copy of the first edition was deposited in the British Library.)

It was re-issued in 1934 with an explanatory introduction by the author:

> *The Backwash of War* was first published in the autumn of 1916, and was suppressed in the summer of 1918. Until this happened it went through several printings, but the pictures presented – back of the scenes, so to speak – were considered damaging to the morale. In the flood of war propaganda pouring over the country, these dozen short sketches were considered undesirable. / From its first appearance, this small book was kept out of England and France. But it did very well in the United States, until we entered the War. Even then, by some oversight, it continued to be sold, although suppression and censorship held full sway. Then in the summer of 1918, however, something happened. (La Motte, 1934: introductory note)

The author received no official notification that her book was banned, but recommendations of it in print began to be inked out by the censor. The publishers finally informed her, in response to an enquiry, that the government 'did not care for the book'.

La Motte's reference to 'back of the scenes' is a clear allusion to the theatrical nature of much pro-war writing, such as Ian Hay's, which gave front-of-stage starring roles to soldiers at the battle-front, and relegated women to anonymous jobs out of sight. It also indirectly recalls the title of one of the earliest works of British propaganda, Phyllis Campbell's *Back of the Front: Experiences of a Nurse* (1915). Campbell had been a student in Germany but at the outbreak of war she had escaped to a country-house near Paris. When France mobilised she apparently took a crash course in nursing, helped at a dressing-station, and then published her experiences as a 'Nurse'. According to David Mitchell her book was ghost-written to help substantiate the Bryce Report on German Atrocities (Mitchell, 1966: 42–5). It is a strange hash designed to arouse the reader's horror and sentimentality. One of the Belgian refugees she describes was 'a naked girl of about 23', the front of whose body was covered with a piece of her sister's undergarment, 'saturated with blood from her cut-off breasts' (Campbell, 1915: 126). Alongside this description Campbell places the account of a kitten which had been tied to a tree and tortured:

> I sat down and bandaged the little black hand [sic]. Of all the devilish cruelties I had seen, none so brought home to me the

utter depravity of the German soul . . . It seemed to me that all the wickedness, all the fear and filthiness unimaginable that exists can be summed up in one word: GERMAN. (126)

But she has a vision of France, apparently so corrupt and degenerate, wiping the stain of invasion away through victory: 'France was suddenly stripped bare to the soul, and behold! that soul was a pure white light of knightly splendour' (126).

The title of Ellen La Motte's book of sketches played on the common idea of 'the sea of war', war perceived as an uncontrollable natural phenomenon like a tidal wave. She subtitled her book: 'The Human Wreckage of the Battlefield as Witnessed by an American Hospital Nurse'. Like Mansfield, La Motte emphasises not glorious deeds of valour, the heroic pageantry of warfare, but the boredom of a war where the deadlocked lines have not moved for months. She is concerned with the stagnant place behind the Front, the slime in the shallows stirred up by the current of progress, the repellent little lives churned up in the wake of war. 'There is a dirty sediment at the bottom of most souls' (La Motte, 1916: 105). Her aim is to counter the view expressed in propaganda such as Phyllis Campbell's that war is 'a filtering process, by which men and nations may be purified'. (The English scholar, Sir Edmund Gosse, had converted this Victorian piety into a veritable advertisement for war: 'It is the sovereign disinfectant, and its red stream of blood is the Condy's Fluid that cleans out the stagnant pools and clotted channels of the intellect' (Gosse, 1916: 3).

While there are many people promoting 'the noble side, the heroic side, the exalted side of war' La Motte writes of what she has seen, 'the other side, the backwash' (La Motte, 1916: 105). The men she nurses have fought for ideals of freedom and patriotism, but they remain selfish and filthy-minded. This she explains by supposing that the fine ideals have been compulsorily imposed from without, a state of mind which was not in these ignoble, petty, commonplace men, of themselves. They are 'base metal, gilded'. And always she implies that the Germans are no different. The French have been harnessed to a Juggernaut, and all that is really demanded of them is their collective physical strength; mentally they are in the same position as their opponents: 'when we captured that German battery a few days ago, we found the gunners chained to their guns' (12–13).

She points out that to the men in the war zone, 'all the glories and heroisms of war seemed of less interest, as a factor in life' than their wives. Like Mansfield, La Motte agrees with Sassoon's mundane image of soldiers as 'mocked by hopeless longing'. Although they are sworn to action, heroically to risk their lives at a moment of destiny,

> Soldiers are dreamers; when the guns begin
> They think of firelit homes, clean beds and wives.
> (Sassoon, 'Dreamers' in Black, 1970: 60)

But the wives are not allowed near the Front. 'So for long weary months men must remain at the Front, on active inactivity, and their wives cannot come to see them'. Neatly juxtaposing her clear, simple statements of fact, she sends up the martial law with its fine distinctions. 'Women can come into the war Zone, on various pretexts, but wives cannot' ... 'Only other people's wives may come' (70). There may seem no difference, but she goes on to explain the significance of that distinction, for there are always 'plenty of women' at the Front. Wives mean responsibility, they establish a link between the soldier and his home, the life he has been compelled to resign. But 'just women' mean distraction and amusement, like food and wine.

She describes in detail the suffering and death from gas gangrene of one man, Rochard, 'an interesting case'. He had been decorated with the *Médaille Militaire* as he left the operating table. But he meant nothing to anyone there. He was a dying man in a field hospital, that was all, 'a stranger among strangers. And there were many people there to wait upon him, but there was no one there to love him' and to forget about the vile gangrene smell: 'His was a filthy death. He died after three days' cursing and raving' (31). He died alone, behind screens, while the two orderlies sat at the other end of the ward, drinking wine.

Despite the ban on wives, there are, La Motte points out, plenty of Belgian women living in the military zone. This does not only include the wife of the *estaminet* owner, who is braving the danger from shells, in order to make money out of selling drink to English soldiers. All the men who work at the hospital have a girl in the village. There is, for instance, the little girl of 14, who is regularly visited by the old doctor, who is 64 and has grandchildren. They were decent girls at the start. 'Of course the professional prostitutes from Paris aren't admitted to the War Zone, but the Belgian girls made such fools of themselves, the others weren't needed'. Sarcastically she repeats the anti-German propaganda about what exceptional brutes the Huns are. Behind the German lines it is different. 'Over there, in the invaded districts, the Germans forced those girls. Here, on this side, the girls cajoled the men till they gave in'. And of course some of the girls are dangerous spies. It seems that two girls were discovered to have elicited information for the Germans from their customers, allied officers. The Germans were holding their families hostage. 'Wasn't it beastly! Making these girls prostitutes and spies, upon pain of reprisals upon their families'. Encouragingly, she agrees that the Germans are vile: 'The curious thing is, how well they understand how to bait a trap for their enemies. In spite of having nothing in common with them, how well they understand the nature of those who are fighting in the name of Justice, Liberty and Civilisation' (111).

La Motte not only opposed the chivalric conception of the pageantry of war, that represented all allied soldiers as Christian heroes by contrast with those 'devilish beasts', the Germans. She found a new vocabulary, a new code by which to depict the inhuman mechanisation of industrialised warfare. And she related this to a political indictment of the type of society that was indifferent to such inhumanity.

Her book commences with a sardonic sketch entitled 'Heroes', about the attitude in the hospital to a soldier who 'could stand it no longer' but bungled his suicide attempt. It was a pleasure to nurse back to health either those who were to be returned to their homes, mutilated for life, or those who could march again and 'be torn to pieces in the firing-line'. But to nurse back to health a deserter who was to be court-martialled and shot, 'truly that seemed a dead-end occupation' (7). That pun is typical of the satire by which women found a weapon against the militaristic society which depersonalised both men and women. Richard Aldington complained on behalf of many soldiers that to the military machine a soldier was 'merely a unit, a murder robot, a wisp of cannon fodder' (Aldington, 1965: 228). The reduction of human beings to inert objects in the factory system of a field hospital after a battle was expressed by La Motte in a strikingly modern prose of flat repetition:

From the operating room they are brought into the wards, these bandaged heaps from the operating tables, these heaps that once were men. The clean beds of the ward are turned back to receive them, to receive the motionless, bandaged heaps that are lifted, shoved, or rolled from the stretchers to the beds. (83–4)

The emotionless repetition of the sentences is the correlative of the mechanical process they describe. The soldiers are no longer men. They are heaps, wrecks to be recycled like the scrap metal of wrecked cars.

Ellen La Motte was not the only woman writer forging a new literary code to cope with the reality of war. At the same time as La Motte was writing *Backwash*, another American nurse was setting aside poetry and sketches about her war experiences in a French field hospital. Mary Borden, a millionaire from Baltimore had set up a hospital unit in which she worked at the Front from 1914 to 1918, but she did not publish her account of those years until 1929, when she also included five stories which she had only written much later. The early pieces are barren pictures of the dreary life behind the lines; the stories added after concern her own reactions to events in the hospital. (Amongst this later work was *Blind*, which seems to me to be one of the most significant pieces of literature to have come out of that War.)

Borden called her collection of fragments *The Forbidden Zone* after the strip of land immediately behind the firing-line where the hospital unit was stationed. Her unit was moved up and down inside it, from Flanders to the Somme, to Champagne and then back to Belgium, but they never left 'La Zone Interdite'. That title comes to stand for not simply a stretch of land but an emotional space as significant as No-Man's-Land; it was the area where common human feeling was banned, where the agony was too great to respond to as an ordinary woman without breaking down. The unit dealt with the wounded straight from the battlefront: ' "We will send you the dying, the desperate, the moribund," the Inspector-General had said. "You must expect a thirty per cent. mortality." ' (147). Borden's writings try to deal with the enormity, the incredibility of that bald statement. The military mind was practised in reducing facts to simple numerical statements, bare 'objective' accounts which omitted individual suffering. As the anonymous letter complained to *The Nation* in 1916, away from the Front battles were treated like calculations of profit or loss, 'as though the unspeakable agonies of the Somme were an item in a commercial proposition'. Women tried to humanise that profane world.

Like La Motte, Borden also commences with a rejoinder to war-time propaganda. Identifying Belgium to an astonished stranger she points out what remains of 'plucky little Belgium's heroic army'. The uncouth, dishevelled, dirty men lolling between a pigsty and a graveyard in all that remains of a village are soldiers, stale with despair. Having nowhere further to retreat to, they have nowhere to go to and nothing to do now: 'how boring it is to be a hero' (2).

Borden locates another sketch at a beach-resort, pointing up the incongruity between the loveliness of a young woman sitting there on the sand, and the war-cripple in a wheelchair beside her. The weather is perfect and the woman is glad to be alive. He takes his revenge on the war in reminding her of his suffering, and the inhuman suffering of other men like him, jealously infecting her with his own disgust. She can hardly leave him, although he now seems a stranger to her. This vignette of a cruel psychological tie is as grotesque as the absurdist theatre of Beckett and Arrabal, writing in the aftermath of the next war. The ugly horror depicted goes far beyond ordinary compassion to encompass.

The cripple is being treated at a nearby hospital, a converted casino. Such an incongruous use of a casino was commented on in several war-diaries, for instance Kate Finzi's: 'the Casino's spacious gaming rooms make wonderful cheerful wards' (Finzi, 1916: 104). Even she was not immune to the irony of a concert-party's performance in one of these wards:

> 'Messieurs, faites vos jeux, le jeu est fait!' Over and over again the suave voice of the croupier seemed to ring in my ears – as it had so often rung in this very room in peace time. 'Faites vos jeux.' What an awful thing this new game of War is, only those who have seen can grasp.
>
> 'Le jeu est fait!' – and here in this gilded hall, that once witnessed such a different game, we see the results. (113)

But her diary was published as part of the facile war-propaganda reminding those at home of 'the awful sufferings that our gallant defenders have had to undergo in doing their duty, in the service of their King and country, for the honour and integrity of the Empire, and for the safety and protection of the people in this country in this great war of liberation' (xvii). Finzi's response to 'the awful sufferings' in 'this new game of War' was to claim that

'One's heart goes out to these men, especially the wounded ones' (104).

The hollow mockery of this stock phrasing reverberates against the exasperated voice of the cripple in Borden's sketch. Ironically playing on the colloquial meaning of expressions like 'gone to pieces' and 'faceless', he satirises the desperation of the anonymous wounded after a battle:

> They've a gala night in our casino whenever there's a battle . . . You never saw such a crowd. They all rush here from the front you know – Still, our crowd here aren't precisely wasters. Gamblers, of course, down and outs, wrecks – all gone to pieces, parts of 'em missing, you know, tops of the heads gone, or one of their legs . . . Come closer, I'll whisper it. Some of them have no faces. / Little things like that don't keep us away. If we can't walk in we get carried in. All that's needed is a ticket. It's tied to you like a luggage label. It has your name on it in case you don't remember your name. You needn't have a face, but a ticket you must have to get into our casino. (46–7)

Confronted by that despair his wife's helpless efforts to comfort him by recalling their past love are as futile as the bell-buoy far away ringing against the sounds of a battle at sea.

Borden elaborates the idea of the anonymity of the wounded washed up by the seas of war in her sketch 'The City in the Desert'. The village she used to know has been engulfed, and now she is lost. In this secret place where there's not a tree to be seen, nothing but mud, 'some strange industry, some dreadful trade is evidently being carried out'. The workers might be smugglers of 'some shameful merchandise', 'gangs of beachcombers, bringing up bundles of wreckage' from the backwash. But those bundles, 'those inert lumps' are men:

> Bundled into vans they were, all mangled and broken, carried back over the sliding mud . . . to be saved. To be hauled about and man-handled, to have their broken, bleeding nakedness uncovered, to have their bodies cut again with knives and their deep wounds probed with pincers, and to have the breath choked back in their sobbing lungs again, so that they may be saved for this world. (116)

In their helplessness they are violated and recycled. In 'Conspiracy' she explores the madness of this impersonal treatment of human bodies, all 'carefully arranged' with commercial efficiency:

> Just as you send your clothes to the laundry and mend them when they come back, so we send our men to the trenches and mend them when they come back again. You send your socks and your shirts again and again to the laundry, and you sew up the tears and clip the ravelled edges again and again just as many times as they will stand it. And then you throw them away. And we send our men to the war again and again, just as long as they will stand it; just until they are dead, and then we throw them into the ground. (117)

Men are as expendable and disposable as any other commodity. They are as lacking in personal identity as the items on a conveyor belt. Lying on their backs on stretchers, they are 'pulled out of the ambulances as loaves of bread are pulled out of the oven' (118).

In 'Paraphernalia' she chides the fussy busying about of the professional nurse in the hospital, 'You show off the skilled movements of your hands beside the erratic jerkings of his terrible limbs', crowding up the place of death: 'Why do you crowd all these things up to the edge of the great emptiness?' Re-asserting the value of the sacred in the midst of this profane industry she reminds the nurse 'There is no time for all this business. There is only one moment between this man and eternity' (124).

Borden and La Motte speak a similar ironic language to convey the dehumanisation of the wounded. Using the same blank, monotonous repetition – 'It is always the same on the road. It is always the same' – their very sentence structure typifies the routine process of the war-machine. But where Borden is bewildered and finally prayerful, La Motte is angry. She finds the injustice of a tyrannical political system to blame. La Motte agrees with Mildred Aldrich that this is the Nation's war, and since France is democratic all the men of the nation are serving, regardless of rank. However, with Orwellian-style logic, some serve in better places than others. The trenches are mostly reserved for men of the working-class, which is 'reasonable' as there are more of them. The *infirmiers* and *brancardiers* (stretcher-bearers) have 'had a snap'. They had powerful friends, or were a friend of a friend of a deputy. They might be young and strong, but they are doing 'a woman's task' in safety.

Others have to die for 'La Patrie'. 'Freely' giving their lives, they earn a medal. Or rather their captain wins it for them. He makes them brave with a revolver in his hand.

La Motte's book concludes with 'An Incident', a sketch with far-reaching political implications. It concerns the indifference of an army officer to a road accident in Paris. His cab runs down a young lad, the horse stepping squarely on the boy's face. Bored, annoyed at the delay in his journey to the War Office, the officer gazes at the sky, 'one arm lying negligently along the back of the seat, the fingers of the other hand caressing the Cross of the Legion of Honour, upon his breast'. Women crowd round. Was he one of the *embusqués*, one of the shirkers in a soft place at the rear, or had he grown callous in command at the Front? 'Was this his attitude to all suffering? Was this the Nation's attitude to the suffering of their sons?' It is not surprising that neither the British nor the American government cared much for *The Backwash of War*.

While some women, such as May Cannan and Vera Brittain, saw the Great War as part of the Imperial Christian Adventure by which Britain was civilising the world, 'The Holy War – 1917' as Kipling called it, 'outsiders' like the New Zealander, Katherine Mansfield, and the Americans, Ellen La Motte and Mary Borden, were less likely to be taken in by this imperial myth. They challenged it. In order to oppose the rhetoric of the purifying crusade, they had to find a new linguistic mode and narrative technique. One technique which they shared was devised to replace the imagery of 'heroes' as active adventurers courageously setting forth to brave the evil of bestial savagery. Instead these women writers chose a repetitive style that displayed soldiers as passive victims of an uncontrollable, inhuman, mechanical social system. Their new tone used the traditional women's weapons of sarcasm and irony to show contempt for patriarchal eyewash. Absurdity and bathos implicity undermined the emblem of triumphant Christianity: St George defeating the dragon – Germany. Mundane characters, sordid events and colloquial language deflated the rarified imagery of medieval chivalry and gallant deeds. Breaking the rules of 'good taste' they openly alluded to the financial aspects of the War, indicating the greed that underlay imperial rivalry. And they made quite clear that the armies were far from pure sexually.

4

'Despised and Rejected'

CENSORSHIP AND WOMEN'S PACIFIST NOVELS OF THE
FIRST WORLD WAR, 1916–18

During the First World War men fighting in the trenches had little
opportunity to compose poetry, let alone write novels, and few
civilian writers cut through the political smokescreen on their
behalf. Joseph Conrad did not deal directly with the War, and even
an astute author like Henry James fell into the propaganda trap.
'Men of Letters' such as Galsworthy, Bennet and Conan Doyle
simply scribbled puff for the government's case (Wright, 1978).
Dorothy Richardson continued writing her solipsistic *Pilgrimage*
throughout the war years and only concluded the final volume in
1938 at the fictional point where the Great War was about to be
declared. Joyce stagnated at Bloom's Day, 16 June 1904. Neither
Virginia Woolf nor D. H. Lawrence confronted the effects of the
War in a novel until some years after the Armistice.

Less original writers and thinkers did try to make novels out of
the War, revealing the poverty of the Victorian and Edwardian
models. Their failure was not due to ignorance. Leaders of
women's opinion like Mrs Humphry Ward, May Sinclair and Edith
Wharton all had first-hand experience of conditions in the
war-zone. They wrote chivalric romances about it such as May
Sinclair's *Tasker Jevons* (1916), Mrs Ward's *'Missing'* (1917) and
Edith Wharton's *The Marne* (1918). Where they failed, the failures
of the second-rate are even more conspicuous. Elizabeth Robins,
first president of the Women Writers Suffrage League, a militant
supporter of Mrs Pankhurst and one of the four committee-
members running the war-time WSPU, had written a successful if
melodramatic play about women's suffrage, *Votes for Women!*
(1907). With *The Messenger* (1919) she reduced the War to a
sensational adventure story about German spies and British
aristocrats, including an island and a shipwreck, which makes
John Buchan's *Thirty-nine Steps* look probable. This was only one of
many war spy-tales by popular writers continuing the pre-war

precedent, such as Mrs Belloc Lowndes' *Good Old Anna* (1915) and *Out of the War?* (1918). They bear out what John Sutherland has said about the 'ineradicable nastiness at the genre's core': 'From its earliest evolution the fiction of espionage has served as the receptacle of race hatred and nationalist excess' (Sutherland, 1987). Typical of the paranoid vision of espionage fiction, the British characters were impossibly heroic and the Germans bestial.

Beatrice Harraden, another militant suffragette and founder of the WWSL, continued along a third strand of Victorian popular fiction – the ethical-didactic tradition. In 1893 she had published the best-selling, most widely read novel of the year: *Ships That Pass in the Night*. In 1918, spiced with the ingredients of melodrama (a dead baby, a mad girl, a spy with a false hand), her novel *Where Your Treasure Is* preached the ethical value of war. The moral of her story was that financial transactions were not the most valuable of human relationships; avarice could be replaced by generosity. On a personal level, the plight of war refugees served the spiritual purpose of converting the heroine to the Christian virtue of financial charity. Furthermore, at the public level, despite the 'murderous brutality' called for by war it had also called forth splendid courage and patriotic devotion from both men and women.

These women writers were all aged over 50 at the beginning of the War. They all seem to have held the high Victorian belief that war would revitalise a society in danger of decadence, replacing materialist values with spiritual. Mrs Humphry Ward expressed it plainly in *Towards the Goal* (1917), a series of letters to the American people written at the instigation of the British Bureau of Propaganda: 'As in America, so in England, a surfeit of materialism had produced a lack of high spiritual purpose'. Conservatives such as Mrs Ward and Edith Wharton glorified the opportunity for heroism offered to young men. And as F. Tennyson Jesse asked in *The Sword of Deborah* (1919), an account of women's war-work written for the Ministry of Information, 'How could we bear to do nothing when the men are doing the most wonderful thing that has ever been done in the world?' (Jesse, 1919: 135). According to the suffragette propaganda, on the public level the war had also brought about the essential 'changes in outlook and custom and tradition which would not have been thought possible in England at the outset of the war' that enabled young women to show their gallantry, too (Harraden, 1918: 152). The enthusiasm for the War shown by elderly feminists such as Sinclair and Harraden is explained by characters in Harraden's novel. One young woman justifies her refusal to give up her war-time work with the Ambulance Section of the First Aid Nursing Yeomanry Corps to get married and take up 'domestic life', by telling her fiancé that her 'outside life is so thrilling and interesting, and one's being useful too – and wanted' (136). When he calls on his mother to take his side, Mrs Thornton says that on the contrary were she young she would want to be off to the Front too, for

in a sense she had always felt chained up, and that she, even as many other women of her generation, inarticulate, in a back-water of life, without initiative, and drilled by tradition in an unnecessary and unwholesome and very dull sacrifice of self, had nevertheless longed at times to seek a path for herself, but was now at least experiencing the joy, almost the personal triumph of seeing her own vague dreams realized by this generation of young women. (139)

Judging by autobiographies and diaries published after the War, the actual realisation of these 'vague dreams' was nearly as traumatic for young women as it was for some young soldiers. The unwholesome nature of outside life at the Front is revealed in the diaries of one of the pioneer ambulance drivers, that Heroine of Pervyse, Mairi Chisholm:

Taking wounded to hospital fifteen miles back at night was a very real strain – no lights, shell-pocked pavie roads mud-covered, often under fire, men and guns coming up to relieve the trenches, total darkness, yells to mind one's self and get out of the way, meaning a sickening slide off the pavie into deep mud – screams from the stretchers behind one and thumps in the back through the canvas – then an appeal to passing soldiers to shoulder the ambulance back on the pavie. Two or three of these journeys by night and one's eyes were on stalks, bloodshot and strained. (Marwick, 1977: 107)

It proved to be self-sacrifice in a different guise after March 1918 when a mustard-and-arsenic-gas shell exploded near her sleeping quarters. The long-term after-effects brought the adventure to a close.

The lives and writings of the women of the older generation, the generation which Elaine Showalter characterised as the fourth generation of 19th-century women novelists, reveal that for them romance and melodrama were not merely literary forms, clearly recognised to be fictional or fantastic (Showalter, 1977: chapter 1). Their understanding of the world was constructed out of the themes and ideas of romance, on the basis of the moral values of melodrama. For them war justified the extravagantly emotional conventions they had inherited, of larger-than-life heroism, the nobility of love, fiendish foreigners, spectacular panoramas and, perhaps the most inappropriate of all, lugubrious death-bed scenes. Thus, unlike Herbert Asquith, who was aware of a sharp feeling of irony at complacent, prim 'bathing-machines letting the light of day through their gaping wounds' on former pleasure beaches (Asquith, 1937: 217), to May Sinclair there was no oddity in the fact of bathing machines being used to house refugees at Ostend. Refugees sheltering in an exhibition hall became an opportunity for her to compare them sadly with the vivid, exotic flowers they had replaced, rather than to consider what it does to people to find themselves wrenched up by their roots (Sinclair, 1915: 168–9). Beatrice Harraden unself-consciously concurs with May Sinclair in finding the sight of the thousands of tents of the Bergen-op-Zoom refugee camp 'very picturesque'; it was not only a 'curious and interesting sight', it was 'exactly like a scene from a play' (Harraden, 1918: 80). Similarly, on the Eastern Front, the professional nurse Violetta Thurstan found no incongruity in making a 'suitable hospital' out of a private theatre where

> The scenery had never been taken down after the last dramatic performance played in the theatre, and wounded men lay everywhere between the wings and the drop scenes. (Thurstan, 1915: 152–3)

Writers who were less ambitious and restricted their writings to the unadventurous happenings of the home front tended to produce pale reminders of *Cranford*, such as Mrs George Norman's ingenuous *Just Ourselves* (1916) or Mrs J. E. Buckrose's *War-Time in Our Street* (1917). Other novels about the home-front were less superficial. Of these the satire in E. M. Delafield's *The War-Workers* (1918) has endured well. (This was Edmée de la Pasture's first novel, based on her own experiences as a VAD.) Gladys Bronwyn

Stern's witty anatomy of the problems for Jews in an England at war, *Children of No Man's Land* (1919), is still of interest. Sheila Kaye-Smith's *Little England* (1918) was popular at the time, although not much more can now be said for it than Frank Swinnerton said of her other novels: 'while they have neither brilliance nor humour, they have great sincerity' (Swinnerton, 1938: 216). What she owed to the English Romantic tradition, that had its last flowering in the verse of Hardy and Kipling, and went to seed in Brooke's sonnets, is clear from the following extract:

> They had not died for England – what did they know of England and the British Empire? They had died for a little corner of ground which was England to them. (Kaye-Smith, 1918: 293)

There were numberless books composed of letters, such as E. Pennel's *The Lovers* (1917) or *The Letters of Tomasina Atkins* (1918). They were usually 'gushing' to quote *The Times Literary Supplement* (1916: 295).

According to Mary Hamilton's autobiography, even people who had not left Britain could not for long have remained in ignorance of what the War entailed:

> Within weeks, horror was fully upon us. That war means the massive, selective slaughter, the killing, maiming, blinding, shell-shocking of men was a fact no one could refuse to see. Daily vast convoys of wounded arrived; the hospitals were crowded; the casualty lists filled columns of small print, as the flower of our young manhood was annihilated. (Hamilton, 1944: 71)

Nevertheless, in 1916 the majority of writers were still refusing to contemplate what they saw. The existence of the War was taken-for-granted. Its 'horror' was still so unassimilated, its political antecedents and consequences were so unquestioned, and the moral preconceptions about war remained so unshaken, that the *TLS* reviewer was moved to point out that 'War has become as much the stock-in-trade of the novelist as are treasure islands, pirate schooners or the Great North road' (1916: 416). War simply provided part of the larder for cooking up more sensationalist, romantic or edifying goodies.

Against this background of 'fiction as usual' several novels by younger women stand out in their attempts to twist the conventional romantic-love plot, with its potential for social criticism and moral edification, into a vehicle for serious cultural comment. Mary Agnes Hamilton, Rose Macaulay and Rose Allatini all published pacifist novels. Bringing into central focus their consciousness of the suffering entailed by war, they each attacked both political complacency and jingoism. Hamilton's novel is by far the longest of the three, and the widest-ranging. The gaze of Rose Macaulay's is the most concentrated, her narrative the neatest, her dissection probes nearest the bone, but her dry style was not congenial to reviewers. It was even claimed that her careful elimination of sentimentality actually achieved the 'impossible' effect of *exaggerating* the 'misery and horror of these times' (*TLS*, 1916: 416). It is just her emotional understatement which marks her writing as modern and leaves her novel, of the three, the most approachable by later readers. But all three are firmly tied to issues which still confront us. Their explicit committedness, whilst nagging the reader, nevertheless shows up the ideological furtiveness of most writing of our own time.

Mary Hamilton's *Dead Yesterday* (Duckworth, 1916) was the first of these serious war-novels by younger women to appear. It was reviewed favourably by *The Times* and *The Nation*, and the *Westminster Gazette* summed up the general impression of the critics that, although slightly beyond the author's powers, it made 'a real contribution to ... English history' so that the future social historian might trust it as a document of London life and opinions (*TLS*, 1916: 236). Only the *Punch* 'Booking Office' demurred, finding it to be a thinly disguised pacifist tract, made yet more objectionable by being precociously feminist (*Punch*, 1916: 212).

Mary Hamilton, born the daughter of a professor of logic in 1883, and reared in two centres of political radicalism, Manchester and Glasgow, was not only a feminist and a suffragist, but an active, lifelong socialist. Having read history at Newnham, she studied in Germany for a year and then worked*in London from 1905 as a professional writer. She was a founding member of the Union for the Democratic Control of Foreign Policy ('UDC'), the main body working for a negotiated settlement to the War (Carsten, 1982). In 1919 Virginia Woolf counted her among her friends, 'the set distinguished by their social and political character' (Woolf, 1977: 234), but considered that 'The truth is that Molly Hamilton with all her ability to think like a man, & her strong serviceable mind, & her independent, self-respecting life is not a writer' (255). Hamilton claims in her autobiography, that the group of young people she described at the beginning of *Dead Yesterday* were 'very much like' the set of young people she belonged to in 1914: 'earnest, politically minded, but invincibly ignorant' and so dumbfounded by the War (Hamilton, 1944: 64). Out of that group the course of one man is followed, and the selfish nature of his ignorance is exposed.

The novel, which opens in 1912, concerns four main characters: a 37-year-old journalist named Nigel Strode, who works for a journal called *The New World*; a civil servant, Hugh Infield, with whom he shares rooms in the Temple; Mrs Aurelia Leonard, a widow who lives in Italy, near Florence; and her daughter Daphne, just graduating from Newnham. When Daphne was a child Mrs Leonard had deserted her husband, an army colonel, because of his sexual promiscuity. He was later killed in South Africa. Towards the end of the novel we learn that Hugh Infield, although in love with her at the time, had failed to give her any moral support in her decision to leave her husband, and this is one example of the selfish moral cowardice which the novel argues against. Inner strength is necessary to counteract such evils as war, and pacifism is not mere running away. It requires the kind of independent determination that Mrs Leonard managed to display in countering public opinion. Nigel is briefly captivated by Mrs Leonard before meeting Daphne, to whom he becomes engaged. The plot of the novel follows the story of their engagement which is tested by their differing reactions to the War.

Mrs Leonard, apparently based on the philosopher and writer 'Vernon Lee' (Violet Paget, 1856–1935), is a kind of sage, whose faith in International Socialism puts Nigel's political insularity and mental laziness to shame. Her steadfastness is also a reproach to the indecision and moral cowardice of Hugh and of Jimmy, one of Nigel's friends. Jimmy's suicide is one of the few melodramatic incidents (along with the thunderstorm that heightens Nigel's first meeting with Mrs Leonard) which betray the Victorian tradition of theatrical exaggeration to which the novel belongs. Daphne, a more intuitive, less intellectual person than her mother, nevertheless finally manifests the same moral strength by breaking her engagement to Nigel. She asked him 'to feel war as a horror' as she herself gradually comes to do through her personal encounter with the distress of widows and orphans; but he could not. What Nigel feels instead is thrilling exaltation, together with crowds of other people who 'in an awful way' enjoy the war. 'To thousands war was still a great external pageant, absorbing as no cinematograph or theatre had ever been' (314).

The salient purpose of Hamilton's book is to oppose the construction of war as justifiedly thrilling, and to bring home to the reader just how grim and dull war is, and what it means to women and children in particular. She handles this aspect with quiet restraint. Underlying this aim is an intellectual argument about the costs of a belligerent foreign policy, at the mercy of which lie the social reforms that the country is in urgent need of. However, the importance Mrs Leonard claims for a knowledge of international affairs, and which Hamilton herself believed in, is not developed far in the novel and an acquaintance with the necessary social reforms is taken for granted. (The titles of classical documents of social investigation are mentioned – *Minority Report of the Poor Law Commission*, *The Condition of England*, and *Poverty, a Study of Town Life* – but there is no demonstration at first hand that 'the condition of labour is bad'.) The novel relies instead on emotive techniques to strengthen the appeal of Mrs Leonard as the author's spokesperson, and this, considering its criticism of emotionalism, is the source of the novel's weakness. It is the authoritative moral didacticism of the novel, together with the idealised presentation of the saintly Mrs Leonard which make the novel now seem so Victorian:

> It was sheer pleasure to listen to her voice, if only he might listen to the sound without being asked to take in what she said, and to watch her as the moving light of the gradually sinking sun played over her pale face and wonderful hands. (21)

The pacifism Mrs Leonard preaches is not merely 'the negation of war'; it is a state of self-control and endurance, both in the individual as in the general society. Nigel, by contrast, craves, thrills, excitement, 'self-realisation'. It is his egoistical sense of ennui, of boredom, that nothing matters, which makes him respond to the 'big common impulse' of patriotism and war. He cannot distinguish the ghoulish gloating over the horrors of war, which satisfies his desire for excitement, from the genuine compassion that moves Daphne. The joy that he finds in his exalted feelings as one of a crowd is sanctioned and ennobled, given 'an almost sacred tinge' by the language of propaganda – the language that speaks of 'honour' and of 'spiritual value' as against 'brute force' and 'Prussianism'.

Hamilton was a good friend of Irene Cooper Willis, Violet Paget's secretary. During the War, as part of her work for pacifism, Cooper Willis made a study of the propaganda techniques of Liberal newspapers (Cooper Willis, 1928). *Dead Yesterday* provides a disturbing analysis of just how such propaganda worked, and a diagnosis of the state of mind of those on whom it was effective. Although Hamilton's novel is cast in the same mould of spiritual uplift as the propaganda writing she was explicitly opposing, making it appear nearly as unctuous to the modern reader, her analysis and diagnosis still stand.

At the outbreak of war Mary Hamilton was working on *The Economist*. During the War she followed the editor, Francis Hirst, to *Common Sense* and many of her close friends were journalists and writers. It is pertinent to discover that previously she had worked for some years editing the *Review of Reviews* with Philip Gibbs, the war-correspondent who was knighted for his services to war-time propaganda. What Hamilton says about the difference between true compassion and the mere indulgence of sensation provides an insightful reading of his war-time reports from the battlefront. In one of the best scenes in the book, set at a party, Hamilton contrasts Nigel Stroud's colourful ideas of the war with the 'dry and unsentimental' stories which he elicits from a professional soldier, Captain Herbert Toller, who is home on leave from the Front. 'War as it emerged from his laconic utterances was a dreary routine of continuous discomfort', 'singularly unpictorial' and yet more grim than 'any decorated tale of horror' (308). He dismisses any idea of the virtues to be gained from warfare, especially the view that it might improve the race: 'Killing does nobody any good'. When Nigel suggests that Toller may have been too close and that those at home might have a better sense of proportion, he tersely rejoins:

> Twenty kilometres of corpses, burning like dead leaves, does rather put one out of focus, I dare say. (309)

Mary Hamilton's account in *Dead Yesterday* of the events in London at the beginning of August 1914, based on her own experiences among the crowds in the streets at the time, has a direct vividness quite unlike the eye-witness reporting of the older writers such as May Sinclair. It makes an interesting comparison with Sylvia Pankhurst's description of returning to England on the ferry from Dublin during the same period, kept awake by the noisy revelry of drunken soldiers: 'yelling of tuneless choruses, shouting of mirthless laughter, hideous to the sensitive ear, poignantly sorrowful to deeper thought' and the sound of the ferry: 'our ship's siren screamed and hooted monstrously, and every ship in sight raked the still air with strident echoes, like demon bellowing of the ghouls of war' (Pankhurst, 1932: 13–15). Hamilton characterises the London-crowd as at first simply waiting, 'like people at a theatre', 'infinitely capable of suggestion or response'. Once war is declared, this 'one blind, dumb organism' becomes 'a mob of people and an indescribable inferno of sound ... the seething, hideously shouting mass, all crying, as with one hungry blood-hound throat – "War. War. War" ' (234). She opposes a nightmare of cacophony to the conventional, visual idea of the heroic pageantry of war: war brutalises rather than ennobles.

In order to reinforce the unreality of attitudes to the 'theatre of war', which don't consider 'people as real at all, or what it means for men to go and kill and want to kill' (179), Hamilton develops this image of grotesque mindlessness with a satirical portrait of a playwright, Royal Carrington. Carrington envisages the war as 'a tremendous artistic opportunity'. Planning to 'put modern war on the stage', he discusses which military campaign would be 'the most pictorial' to commence with and decides that riots in Hungary 'would be a splendid scene' to follow (254). He demonstrates that there is little difference between seeing the war as a moral spectacle of British manhood or as a great military display of British might, and sentimentally speaking of the war as a tragedy. Thinking along similar lines to Hamilton, Rose Macaulay chose as an epigraph to her novel, *Non-Combatants and Others* (1916), a poem by Walter de la Mare, *The Marionettes*, where the Devil is among the Spectators applauding 'the frenzied show' of war and deafening the rest of the audience with his jingoistic hooting: 'the Cause!' In de la Mare's poem, 'we' come to realise that it is not sawdust being bled, that the agony of the 'foul scene' is true. The protagonist of Macaulay's novel also tries at first to treat the nightmare of war as merely an illusion, but gradually recognises that it is real.

Rose Macaulay's war-novel, *Non-Combatants and Others*, appeared a few months later than Mary Hamilton's. Whereas *Dead Yesterday* was only Hamilton's third novel, Rose Macaulay was already a novelist of some note. By 1914 she had published seven novels, and one of these, *The Lee Shore* (1912), had won a major literary prize. A year older than Hamilton, Macaulay had also read History, but at Somerville, and she too came from an academic background. Her father, having held the chair in English at Aberystwyth, became a lecturer at Cambridge in 1906 (Babington Smith, 1972). However, there the similarity ceases.

Hamilton had married in 1905. The marriage collapsed within a few months, and she worked as a writer in order to earn her own living. She was a socialist and a feminist. Macaulay, after a break-down at university, had conformed to the role of the unmarried daughter and was still living at home with her parents at the beginning of the War, jobless. (Her two brothers and three sisters had all left home by that time.) Her domineering mother was a strict Anglican and, despite an unconventional childhood in Italy, Rose Macaulay was a member of an extremely conventional family which had ties with the heart of the English establishment. It was Liberal, 'the sort of Liberal one felt would never, however changed the circumstances, become Conservative' as she described another Cambridge family in *The Making of a Bigot* (1914). To continue the quotation is to show why she herself was the sort of Liberal who would never become a Socialist either: '(they were) a valuable type, representing breeding and conscience in a rough-and-tumble world'; Liberals of her type believed in 'bettering the poor', and were 'in brief, gentlemen and ladies' (Macaulay, 1914: 173–4). Identifying herself as a 'Cambridge provincial' she may have found such inflexibility and resistance to 'wide-awake ideas' amusing but they were the features of her own mentality which prevented her from ever confronting the political grounds of the War. In 1923 she wrote that the majority of people had responded to the War, 'that nightmare and chaos and the abomination of desolation', as if it were 'merely a catastrophe like an earthquake, to be gone through blindly, until better might be' (Macaulay, 1923: 290–1). It was that blindness and closed-mindedness that she tried to confront in *Non-Combatants and Others*.

Non-Combatants and Others is a shorter, sparer work than *Dead Yesterday*, although its main purpose is identical: to show how it must not be ignored that the War is hurting people, and that it is no good pretending otherwise. Where Hamilton's book is compli-cated by having the several viewpoints of four main characters, only one of whom is consistently clearsighted and morally correct,

Macaulay concentrates on the point of view of her 25-year-old protagonist, Alix Sandomir, and even at the end of the novel is not adamant that Alix has taken the right moral decision. It is the moral uncertainty of the work, the author's refusal to dictate a position, which marks it as totally unVictorian. And, since there is no moral/ religious authority to glamorise and there are no saints or villains in Macaulay's world, there is no need for the melodramatic atmospherics or over-ripe prose of the Victorian novel either. This marks a decisive break with the influence of Mrs Humphry Ward manifested in her earlier novels.

What is particularly interesting about the chief character, an art student, is that this is Macaulay's first female protagonist, and she is crippled; having had a diseased hip-joint as a child, Alix Sandomir walks with a stick. Ever since Frederick J. Hoffman observed that a 'sense of violation is present in each of the principal works of American war literature' it has been common to talk of the 'psychic wound' of the First World War veterans, of the sexual impotence that resulted from their sense of the powerlessness entailed by modern war (Hoffman, 1949: 57; Cooperman, 1967: 64). Alix's crippled body manifests the incapacity of her nature to meet the demands of war-time society. This incapacity stems partly from the fact that she is the 'wrong sex' – women are not allowed to perform physical combat for their country. Alix claims: 'Oh I do so want to go and fight . . . But I want to go and help to end it . . . Oh, it's rotten not being able to; simply rotten . . . Why *shouldn't* girls?' (141). Like Imogen, a character in Macaulay's post-war novel, *Told By an Idiot* (1923), 'she had never before so completely realized that she was not, in point of fact, a young man' (Macaulay, 1923: 295). Nor, being serious and intelligent, is Alix even the stereotypically 'feminine' woman of 'dainty fluffiness' that militarised men call for in war-time, so that she is a double failure sexually. Her incapacity also stems from her imagination and hypersensitivity, qualities which make her 'a broken, nerve-wracked, frightened child' (Macaulay, 1916: 129) and which prevent her from carrying out the war-time role that is specifically women's: that of efficiently tending the wounded. On the other hand, these are precisely the qualities that enable her to empathise with her younger brother, no soldier by nature either, who 'funks' and shoots himself in the trenches. There is some comfort to be gained for her unsuitedness to fighting which most women would hate and be hopeless at, from a soldier's statement that 'Plenty of men hate it and are hopeless, if you come to that' (121). As the male combatants are wounded, physically and psychologically, so Alix's limp and nausea link her nature to theirs in a common vulnerability.

Non-Combatants and Others was dedicated 'To my brother and other combatants'. One of Rose Macaulay's younger brothers, Willie, who had emigrated to Canada as a farmer some years previously, had volunteered as an officer in the King's Royal Rifles. (He survived the War, but was wounded, losing a lung and the use of one arm.) The other brother, Aulay, had enlisted in the Royal Engineers in 1906 and had been murdered in 1909 while serving on the North West Frontier. His violent death devastated the family, and Rose was 'sadly broken' and remained depressed for some months. Under the stress of this emotional crisis she dropped the agnosticism she had inwardly adopted since her teens, and gradually became a devout Christian. It was as she was pulling out of the depression that she began work on her fourth novel, *The Valley Captives* (1911). In *The Valley Captives* a young man without physical courage becomes morally degraded as a result of being bullied, but he redeems himself by a heroic act in which he dies saving a woman's life. This act inspires other people like 'an illuminating flame' (Newbolt would have approved): his ineffective life suddenly 'plunges among the swords, is drenched in blood' and achieves fruition. In a speech made, appropriately, by his grandfather, who came of an army family, the explicitly Christian consolation for his death is expressed in a rhetoric worthy of the National Service League:

Isn't that the secret of Christianity – the last desperate adventure of sacrifice – sacrifice which means freedom, Life through death – the violent breaking of prison walls. Doesn't it give life new values, that desperate death dared and stormed? Isn't it that which lights the world – the power of such daring – lights it and lifts it to the heroic plane? (Macaulay, 1911: 327)

By the time Rose Macaulay came to write *Non-Combatants and Others* she had fundamentally changed her attitude to 'the last desperate adventure of sacrifice'.

At the beginning of the War one of Rose Macaulay's sisters was a missionary in India and another was a nun. The third, Jean, went to France as a Red Cross nurse. After the death of Rupert Brooke in

April 1915 (he was a close family friend and especially dear to Rose), Rose still continued to live at home in Cambridge but volunteered to help at a local hospital for military convalescents which opened nearby in May. According to Jean this was in order to keep her thoughts off the War but was a mad choice since Rose was 'hyper-sensitive to physical pain and also uncontrollably squeamish; she tended to vomit or faint at the sight of blood or the mere mention of horrors' (Babington Smith, 78). It was a reaction Rose shared with Alix Sandomir, the chief character of the novel which she was writing at this time. By February 1916 she had given up the drudgery at the hospital to become a land-girl on a local farm instead, and the novel was completed that year.

Non-Combatants and Others covers a period from late April to New Year's Eve, 1915, during which time Alix, 'the Girl who isn't doing her bit', tries to shut her eyes to the 'horror beyond speech' which other people have endured in the War. The plot of the novel, which concerns Alix's facing up to the War, is linked to the development of a romantic attachment between Alix and another art student, Basil Doye. The novel follows Alix's psychological flight from the pain of war, trying refuge after refuge. The refuges, at the homes of various relatives, all fail her. Eventually she has to face up to the War, just as she has to recognise that Basil prefers someone else. When Alix's energetic mother, Daphne, returns from a peace mission abroad Alix moves back to live with her. Daphne very forcibly criticises her for selfishness in behaving like an ostrich. Discovering that she cannot keep her eyes closed, Alix decides to fight against the War by joining her mother's society, which is working to promote peace, and by becoming a Christian, two courses which she claims to be equivalent (while recognising that others might not). Since it is not the Society of Friends that she is considering joining, but the Church of England, her equation of Christianity with pacifism ignores the way in which the Church of England was actually supporting the War, with bishops pronouncing it a holy crusade and blessing flags. This posed a problem for many Christians who believed that Christianity taught against taking life, and (as Mary Hamilton pointed out in her novel) one of the chief intentions of the government's war propaganda was to divert attention from the fact that soldiers had to kill other human beings, other Christians.

The evasion of the Anglican Church's complicity in the government's war aims is an indication of the political obscurity which

Alix blunders around in and which the author does nothing to dispel. She concentrates instead on the 'essentially romantic and adventurous and mystical force' of religion (111). In fact, West, an Anglican clergyman whom Alix admires and who publicly defends the UDC, is scolded by his vicar for taking part in political movements, and the authorial voice decides that the reasons for Alix's mother, Daphne, not being a member of the UDC 'need not here be detailed' (14). Instead, Macaulay dreams up an imaginary pacifist organisation which will have no taint of either feminism or socialism (despite its identity being strongly dependent on both Quaker activity and the women's international peace movement). Although Alix agrees with her mother in what appears to be the main message of the novel, that what is needed is 'clear thinking', Macaulay never clearly confronts the arguments about the political grounds of the War or the possibility of political solutions to it. In fact she obfuscates the matter by linking 'all the heterogeneous crowd of humanity' in one desire for peace, as if all the groups she lists, such as the Anti-German League and conscientious objectors, had no conflict of interest in the way in which peace was to be achieved or what that peace would consist of. Despite the novel's surface message of pacifism, and Macaulay's own friendship with such early committed UDC members as Gilbert Cannan and Mary Hamilton, one can see why Mary Hamilton stated unequivocally in her memoir that 'Rose Macaulay was not a pacifist in 1914 . . . she was an artist' (Hamilton, 1944: 139). The problem that political commitment presents for an artist Hamilton did not go into.

At first Alix held on to the belief that the 'unspeakable things' of war were really only evil dreams and underneath are all the time 'the real things' such as music and loveliness (10), but as she gradually faces up to the evil dreams, this aesthetic idealism ceases to be any protection against unbearable reality. The evil dream of war first impinges when she witnesses her convalescent cousin having a nightmare. She listens to him talking in his sleep, reliving being shelled in the trenches:

> Minnie coming along to blow the whole trench inside out . . . legs and arms and bits of men flying through the air . . . the rest of them buried deep in choking earth . . . perhaps to be dug out alive, perhaps dead . . . the leg of a friend . . . pulling it out of the chaos of earth and mud and stones which had been a trench . . . thinking it led to the entire friend, finding it didn't, was a detached bit. (21)

Wondering what sort of pictures one would paint at the Front, Alix decides that 'painting and war don't go together'. The relation between war and literature is also problematic. Linguistic pictures such as: 'She drew till the green light became green gloom, lit by a golden star that peered down between the pines' (3) seem otiose when Alix turns 'the greenish pallor of pale, ageing cheese' at the thought of the Front (21).

During a conversation with Alix, her brother Nicholas quotes from a book he is reviewing on *The Effects of the War on Literature*, which suggests that before the War literature and life had degenerated into sordidness and triviality; but the War had returned heroism to literature and life: 'we have been made great' and 'may expect a renascence of beauty worthy to rank with the Romantic Revival' (44). Nicholas considers on the contrary that the War has swept a flood of cheap heroics and commonplace patriotic claptrap 'slobbering all over us'. It is this sort of glamorising claptrap that Alix's cousin, Mrs Frampton, comes out with to comfort Alix for the death of her other brother, Paul: 'The poor dear boy has died doing his duty and serving his country . . . a noble end, dearie . . . not a wasted life . . . He died a noble death, serving his country in her need'. Alix echoes the words 'mechanically, as if it was a foreign language' (69). She rejects the news and the comfort as a lie: Paul had gone into the army straight from school at the age of 18, 'but he hadn't lived yet . . .' (70).

However, alternating between cynicism and religiosity, Rose Macaulay found no new mental framework, no new literary language, to replace the old ones from which she was now alienated.

Alix Sandomir rejects the Victorian rhetoric of the nobility of patriotic sacrifice, and she also finds the cultural tradition of pastoral beauty untenable in the hideous face of war. Yet at the end of the novel Alix returns to a tranquil rural scene centring on 'a little grey church with a Norman door' as her image of peace. There is no final recognition in the novel that the pastoral mode is a backtracking anachronism. Rose Macaulay's own state of mind is eloquently depicted in a poem she published during the War, *Picnic, July 1917*:

> We are shut about by guarding walls:
> (We have built them lest we run
> Mad from dreaming of naked fear
> And of black things done).

We are ringed about by guarding walls,
　So high, they shut the view.
Not all the guns that shatter the world
　Can quite break through.
(Reilly, 1981: 66–7)

The poem ends on a determination to lie quite still, without listening or looking, 'Lest, battered too long, our walls and we / Should break'. The prospect of a breakdown was a real one for Rose Macaulay, and she did suffer another in 1919. The fictional solution of non-political, Anglican pacifism had proved to be no crutch in real life either.

By 1917 she was working ten hours a day for the Civil Service, and spending three hours a day travelling. Perhaps for her as for her character Imogen, 'daily work in an office, so cheerful, so fruitless, so absurd, was an anodyne' (Macaulay, 1923: 298). She presumably needed to be encased in the same 'armour of easy cynicism' that Imogen wore. The job began in the Ministry of War, dealing with conscientious objectors, and then early in 1918 she moved to the Ministry of Information, working under Lord Northcliffe in the Italian section of the Department of Propaganda in Enemy Countries. After the War she satirised both the journalism of the Northcliffe press and the books of propaganda promoted by the Ministry of Information, in *Potterism* (1920). In 1926 in *Catchwords and Claptrap*, Macaulay warned about the importance of a careful use of language, since the facile repetition of tags and slogans places one helplessly in the hands of propagandists and manipulators. If anyone knew about patriotic, religious and political claptrap by that time, it must have been Rose Macaulay.

Mary Hamilton and Rose Macaulay were writing their novels in 1915, before military service was made compulsory. The Military Service Act was introduced in January 1916, conscripting all unmarried men between the ages of 18 and 41. Conscription was extended to married men in May. There was a clumsily enforced provision for objectors, who might gain exemption by stating their reasons before a tribunal. About 7000 objectors agreed to perform non-combatant service, mainly in ambulance work. But there were some 1500 'absolutists' who refused to play any part whatever in the War. They were imprisoned and treated savagely, Lloyd George publicly taking the lead in harrying them: 'I will make their path as hard as I can'. The No Conscription Fellowship had been set up in November 1915 to help conscientious objectors who refused 'to kill and be killed for the state'. Founded by socialists, most of its members were religious pacifists, mainly Quakers, who were also members of the Independent Labour Party. At one point about half of the 12 000 membership was in prison, where objectors were subjected to physical and mental torture. Several committed suicide. The Fellowship continued to be run by its women members, such as Irene Cooper Willis and Catherine Marshall, who were harrassed by the police and prosecuted under the Defence of the Realm Act, 'DORA' (Hopkin, 1970; Pankhurst, 1932: 36). After 1916 the pacifist movement in general became more urgent in its public statements; these became more difficult to get heard or published as DORA was enforced more strenuously.

There had been censorship of books before the First World War, when the mere word of a bishop or a visit from a police-officer was sufficient to restrict the circulation of a novel. Legislation was available under the Obscene Publications Act of 1857, and sexual or religious indiscretion was used as grounds to prosecute booksellers or printers for political reasons (Hynes, 1968: chapter 8). A fine or imprisonment might follow. During the War, the sanctions under section 42 of DORA were more severe, including the possibility of six months' hard labour and the forfeit of the printer's machinery; if the case were heard by court martial the sentence could be life-imprisonment. The general wording of the regulation, which referred to 'the spread of reports likely to cause disaffection or alarm' either among the forces or the civilian population, was vague enough for the police to use it to intimidate the less politically desperate. Threats or raids were usually sufficient. The government was anxious not to tarnish the British reputation for permitting freedom of speech, especially by court cases which in any case gave free publicity to dissidents. However, it is an indication of the strength and seriousness of the opposition to the government's war policies that both sides were prepared to risk open confrontation on occasion.

In *Non-Combatants and Others*, Nicholas cynically predicts that the despotism of the (Liberal) government would continue after the War: 'After all this Defending of the Realm, and cancelling of scraps of paper such as Magna Carta and Habeas Corpus, and ordering the press, and controlling industries and finance and food and drink, and saying, "Let there be darkness" (and there was darkness) . . . the realm will go on being defended long after it's weathered this storm' (184). Rose Macaulay's second novel to be written out of her war experiences, *What Not: A Prophetic Comedy*, an anti-utopian satire which ridiculed wartime bureaucracy and government measures for the enforcement of its policies, itself suffered difficulties with DORA. The novel was announced by the publishers as due out in the autumn of 1918; it did not appear until spring 1919 when the War was over. A note by the author explained that after the book was ready for publication, 'a slight alteration in the text was essential, to safeguard it against one of the laws of the realm'.

Another novel which did appear in 1918 was banned altogether. *Despised and Rejected* by 'A. T. Fitzroy' was announced in April 1918 and was given a brief review in the *TLS* on 6 June. A thousand copies were printed, over half of which were sold. On 27 September 1918 the publisher, C. W. Daniel, was successfully prosecuted for sedition under the regulations of DORA, and the book was banned as 'likely to prejudice the recruiting, training and discipline of persons in his Majesty's forces'. Its seditious moral was identified as the statement made by one of the characters that 'lasting peace can never be achieved by war, because war only breeds war' (*TLS*, 27 September 1918: 3; 11 October 1918: 5). During the month before the Armistice all available copies of the novel were destroyed. The only originals I have been able to trace are at the Universities of Reading, Illinois and Yale. There is no mention of it in the British Library Catalogue.

The publisher's announcement described the book as 'a vigorous and original story, dealing in an illuminating way with two classes of people who are very commonly misunderstood – conscientious objectors who refuse Military Service and the so-called Uranians whose domestic attachments are more in the way of friendship than of ordinary marriage'. The *TLS* reviewer called it 'a well-written novel – evidently the work of a woman – on the subjects of pacifism and of abnormality in the affections... As a frank and sympathetic study of certain types of mind and character, it is of interest; but it is not to be recommended for general reading' (6 June 1918: 266). The novel *was* the work of a woman, Rose Laure Allatini, about whom little seems to have been recorded, although she is mentioned in Virginia Woolf's letters and diaries as an acquaintance of Ottoline Morrell. Apparently she was born in 1890, which makes her several years younger than either Macaulay or Hamilton. She studied music in Vienna and married the composer Cyril Scott in 1919. While I would not go so far as the publisher and call her novel 'a great work of art', *Despised and Rejected* is certainly of great cultural interest.

The title, of course, refers to the biblical description of Christ familiar from Handel's *Messiah* (Isaiah 58:3), and the novel provocatively applies the Great War cliché of 'Greater Love' to two male homosexuals who, out of love for the patient boy-heroes on both sides that go joking to their deaths, are ready to suffer and 'lay down their life' as objectors to the War rather than be forced to kill their brother man. However, this major theme of the novel is not apparent at the beginning.

The first part of the book resembles the light social comedy of the conventional love-stories Rose Allatini had written previously, under titles like *Happy Ever After* (which was published by Mills and Boon in 1914). The story of *Despised and Rejected* opens in a holiday hotel during the summer of 1914, and until a hundred pages further on seems set to follow a romance between the dynamic, assertive young heroine, Antoinette de Courcy, and the hero, a 24-year-old composer called Dennis Blackwood. Dennis is on a walking-tour of Devon with a male friend, writing daily to Antoinette, when he meets a young and ardent socialist, Alan Rutherford, and falls in love with him. Not that he immediately reveals this love. Dennis loathes himself for having been given by nature 'the soul of a woman in the body of a man'. He feels 'abnormal – perverted – against nature' and believes that he deserves to be an outcast, despised and mocked because he is different from others. But what he must not tell Alan in words he utters in music, 'music that was as virile and splendid as the one who had inspired it'. He gives this music to the young man by whom he is so 'oddly stimulated, oddly excited' and runs away from 'that which all his life long he had sought and from which he must now flee, in order that it might not become shameful' (106–8). His letters to Antoinette cease.

In Part II war intervenes, but Dennis refuses to enlist. He bumps into Antoinette again in London and his anti-conscription stand brings them both into contact with Alan. In 1916 Alan refuses any form of military service on political grounds and he is arrested and imprisoned. Certain hints from earlier in the novel are now drawn together, and it becomes plain that for Antoinette men are just as 'devoid of that stimulus for which she craved' as women are for Dennis. She comes to understand what Dennis and Alan feel for each other by analogy with her own adolescent crushes on teachers at school, or with her responses to an older woman who motivated in Antoinette's whole person an 'air of tense vitality'. As Dennis explains to her, 'because there's a certain amount of the masculine element in you, and of the feminine element in me, we both have to suffer in the same way' (220).

Part III is the shortest. It consists mainly of Dennis's tribunal, at which he takes advantage of his opportunity to explain and argue for the political position he shares with Alan, and in which Antoinette supports him: 'There is no such thing as a "war to end war"; the solution of international disputes should be sought in arbitration and diplomacy, rather than in bloodshed' (331). He is sentenced to stone breaking, which ruins his hands for playing the piano.

By the end of her novel Allatini has attacked head-on two fundamental issues that Rose Macaulay and Mary Hamilton only skirted around: what it means for men to go and kill, and want to kill, to desire suffering and death for other men; and why it should be considered shameful for a man to refuse to do what in other circumstances would itself be regarded as a shameful act of murder. The nearest Rose Macaulay came to considering bloodlust was with the phrase 'the black things done'. Mary Hamilton drew attention to similar euphemisms – 'having a whack at Berlin', 'being ready to take anyone on', 'destroying a wasps' nest', – as being used to disguise the desire to kill. Macaulay gestured in the same direction as Rose Allatini, when she equated Alix's shameful, unfeminine behaviour in revealing her love to a man before he made any declaration to her, with Paul's shameful, unmanly act of cowardice in the trenches. These things were perhaps 'mere conventions, after all' but to challenge the sexual conventions seems for Macaulay to have been another step back into the moral chaos and savagery that she so dreaded. Allatini boldly confronts them.

The publisher's blurb for *Despised and Rejected* makes it sound as if the two issues of conscientious objection and what it calls 'Uranians' were only tangentially related, whereas it is part of Allatini's thesis that belligerence had been bound into the very definition of masculinity, and that homosexuality and the refusal to kill were intimately related in their defiance of the established notions of manhood. (Although she was clearly influenced by the ideas of Edward Carpenter, as the publisher's reference to Uranism indicates, Allatini's male characters are not like the slightly fay 'darkling ... strange' 'Child of Uranus' that Carpenter depicted in *Towards Democracy* (1883–1902) (Pearsall, 1969: chapter 10; Hynes, 1968: chapter 5; Fussell, 1975: chapter 8). Dennis and Alan are articulate and forceful.) Allatini links her analysis of 'manliness' to the current cultural debate about the degeneracy of the British race and the decadence of English culture. Dennis's father believes that 'Nations that have had no wars have become degenerate, and gone to the wall'. Criticising Dennis for being a 'spoilt namby-pamby' he claims that human nature is unalterable and man is a fighting animal by instinct, 'if a man's got no fight in him, he's unnatural' (194). Dennis on the contrary thinks that the war-instinct is 'nothing but a hindrance to civilisation and progress'. Turning the argument based on Darwinian evolutionary theory back onto itself, Allatini's spokesperson – Barnaby – claims that homosexuals, far from being degenerate, are actually 'the advance-guard of a more enlightened civilisation... From them a new humanity is being evolved' (348).

In the late 19th century, scientists in various fields had tried to find physical bases for gender distinctions which are nowadays generally regarded as culturally constructed. In so doing they revealed their bias towards maintaining the *status quo* that kept women in subjection to men, interpreting biological facts as evidence for the 'naturalness' of female submissiveness to male superiority. Of supreme influence in this cultural debate was Charles Darwin's *The Descent of Man and Selection in Relation to Sex* (1871). Using the difference between bulls and cows as a guide, Darwin had claimed that there were inherent differences between men and women: 'Man is more courageous, pugnacious and energetic than woman'; woman had more tenderness and less selfishness than man. Although the powers of intuition, perception and imitation were stronger in woman than in man, these were also the characteristics of lower races, of past and lower states of civilisation. The conclusion drawn from such an expert was that a man who was not courageous or pugnacious was effeminate, and like his racial inferiors.

Conservative apologists for imperialism combined Darwin's biological theories with the social philosophy of Herbert Spencer's *Principles of Sociology* (1876–96) to justify the view that if 'effeminate' men predominated in a culture, the civilisation was either not yet properly evolved, or was past its prime and on the way to extinction. Military supremacy was made its own *raison d'être*. To promote courageous, aggressive manliness was therefore seen as essential for the maintenance of the British Empire. Furthermore, women must unselfishly submit to breeding the 'masculine' type of man, who would ensure the stability and growth of British civilisation. On this depended the world's moral progress out of savagery (Davin, 1978; Harrison, 1977: chapter 6).

It was crucial for feminists to oppose such arguments, although they had not yet seen that the very grounds of the debate needed to be changed. Consequently Olive Schreiner's *Women and Labour* (1911), the 'Bible of the Women's Movement', tried to demonstrate that the idea of inherent sexual characteristics was logically in contradiction with the idea of evolution. As environmental circumstances changed with economic development, there was every reason to suppose that men and women would change too. Furthermore, one should not argue from the average to the particular: individual men might be far more imaginative than the average woman, and certain women might make better leaders than any man. However, Schreiner's own arguments were caught up in *non sequiturs* since she believed that women were naturally more 'maternal' and tender than men, although she had faith that men might become caring. Having been raised a white in 19th-century South Africa, her racist background was a further restriction on her vision. But the boldness of her challenge to rigid definitions of sexuality was fruitful for other women, and for men, too, and was the foundation of her encouragement to pacifists. It was not necessarily more masculine or more advanced to be militaristic.

However, the general acceptance of Darwinian ideas and the reactionary effect the War had on many pre-war feminists can be seen from May Sinclair's novel *The Romantic* (1920). There a man's cowardice in the war-zone is explained by his sexual impotence, and 'degenerate' is used as a synonym for 'emasculated'. The heroine, a New Woman, proves to be more courageous. (The novel is nevertheless surprisingly insightful with regard to the erotic excitement of war, at a time when virility was defined in terms of active assault. Sinclair's equation of the dejectedness of a retreating army with the anti-climax of sexual failure is imaginatively powerful.) This illuminates the kind of strain imposed on men to conceal their instinctive responses, when fear or hesitation might reveal them to be not merely cowards but not even 'real' men. Fear was then a sign for a man to be ashamed of in himself, even to despise himself as he might a member of an 'inferior race', or a girl.

Presumably because she had no sense of inferiority to men, unlike Rose Macaulay, Rose Allatini paid little more attention than Mary Hamilton did to the opportunities the war-time state offered for women to take initiative and demonstrate physical courage. She was perhaps more honest about women's belligerence than Hamilton, and would have agreed with Macaulay that it was 'sentimental rubbish [to say] that women are the guardians of life and therefore mind war more than men do'. And whereas Hamilton's warmongers are all men, despite the blatant public examples of Mrs Pankhurst, Mrs Ward and Baroness Orczy, Allatini is more balanced. She demonstrates the kind of pressures some older women brought to bear on men who would not fight, and the fantastic envy that motivated some of the younger women: 'Oh, if only I were a man! I'd give anything to lead a fine cavalry charge . . .' but she also illustrates the dilemma for mothers, in her sensitive picture of the relationship between Dennis and Mrs Blackwood. However, her main concern was not with what was womanly, or manly, but with what was 'humanly'. Dennis and Alan are the forerunners of a new humanity being evolved: 'the human soul complete in itself, perfectly balanced, not limited by the psychological bounds of one sex . . . a dual nature, possessing the extended range, the attributes of both sides, and therefore loving and beloved of both alike' (349).

The sage in Allatini's novel is not a woman as in Hamilton's, but Barnaby, a cripple who is congenitally deformed. Yet (unlike Alix Sandomir) this reinforces his spiritual strength. He is more civilised in his outlook than Dennis's father, and no more to be despised or rejected than Dennis. (The bold generosity of the novel's characterisation and treatment of Jews, Irish nationalists, the disabled, a German girl and a coward, is one way in which it practices the socialism Dennis preaches.) Barnaby's physical disability is linked to a central, recurrent image which condenses the argument of the novel. The conscientious objectors meet in a basement tea-shop off the Strand. From her table Antoinette can see through a small barred window near the ceiling, which is on a level with the street, the legs and feet of the continual passers-by. They are legs and feet without visible bodies or heads. Several conversations are punctuated by glimpses of these 'strange bodiless legs'. It is a reminder of the war-crippled, and of the wounded in the hospitals:

being tended and mended, so that they might be sent out again, and broken again . . . And already one saw those who could not be sent out again: armless, legless, blind; wreckage that could not be utilised either on the field of battle, or on any other. (157)

In Barnaby's opinion it is better to write music that will live than to fill the world with 'things' like that, like himself.

Allatini's angry horror at the war's mechanical dehumanisation of young men speaks to us with the same voice as Ellen La Motte's and Mary Borden's and Katherine Mansfield's (women who could not have read each other's work at the time they were writing [Tylee, 1988]). It is the voice of women contemptuous of the patriarchal political system, and it is an international voice which is to be heard over and over in women's writings about the War.

However, Rose Allatini and Mary Hamilton do not share Rose Macaulay's despair. Taking a walk in the country, Dennis lies at full length on a ridge looking out over a spread, misty landscape, and compares this peaceful view with a Europe at war, where frontiers sever the connection between one country and another. He is determined that the roads and railways should link the countries of Europe together again and 'the barriers of racial hatred and racial envy be swept away'; the thought of this new civilisation translates itself into music, an international symphony to replace the tortured nightmare-music of war. It determines him to act on his beliefs for the sake of the generations to come. And Mary Hamilton likewise asssured her readers that 'to the eyes of any one generation all might seem to be lost; but it was not. Beyond their winter the spring brooded, invisible, but sure' (407).

Most of the popular fiction published during the war consisted either of tales about spies, or romantic love stories. Many books managed to combine both genres. Very few creative writers create new literary forms; most authors with a serious purpose tend to choose popular genres and then subvert them. Hamilton, Macaulay and Allatini all chose to present their novels in the initial guise of stories of romantic love, but departed from the conventions of this genre: their heroines do not finally marry the man of their choice. It is a genre with very rigid rules and generally the reader's pleasure stems from the fulfilment of the expectation that the rules will be kept. There is a formulaic certainty that no matter how complicated the plot, at the end the reciprocal love between the heroine and her lover will result in their vows of mutual commitment, declared for all time (Worple, 1984: chapter 3). The genre reinforces heterosexual stereotypes and social conventions, and all difficulties that these present are (magically) resolved. By refusing to satisfy the reader in this way, Hamilton, Macaulay and Allatini all challenge the cultural security on which the literary conventions rest and which they reinforce. Their novels are subversive not merely of the literary genre but of the social order. By questioning the heterosexual stereotypes, and denying the reward for 'playing the game', they reveal the way in which the prosecution of the War depended upon the reinforcement of moral values and gender-definitions which it covertly made impossible. Perhaps the biggest lie of that dehumanising war was: 'I'll make a man of any one of you!' They each reveal the sham of the war-time propaganda about the noble heroism of war, and ridicule the idea that war is glorious.

In 1930 Cyril Falls failed to list either Mary Hamilton's *Dead Yesterday*, or Rose Macaulay's *Non-Combatants and Others*, or Rose Allatini's *Despised and Rejected* in his annotated *War Books: A Critical Guide*. By 1931 they had so totally fallen from mind that an article in *The Bookman* on 'War Books and Propaganda' could state categorically that 'In England there have been few pacifist war novels – and those few pacifist rather by implication than by design', and proceed without mentioning the books by Hamilton, Macaulay or Allatini at all (Hindle, 1931). That oblivion has continued. In view of the suppression of *Despised and Rejected* and the constant vigilance of the police against pacifist and UDC publications of all kinds in the enforcement of DORA, some remarks by John Sutherland may suggest an explanation for the war-time popularity of that other best-selling genre, spy fiction: 'Probably the most valuable myth spy fiction promotes is that the nation's security service is wholly directed against foreigners and traitors, rather than against its own dissident population' (Sutherland, 1987: 1001).

Pro-war propaganda is made effective by excluding dissident voices. In common with spy fiction, the persistant critical attention focussed on the poetry and memoirs of First World War veterans has the paradoxical effects of glamorising armed hostility and perpetuating the attitude that war is a normal, inevitable mode of international relations. From 1914 to 1918 propaganda and censorship wedged a mythical rift between 'Those Who Were There' on the Western Front and the 'Other Nation' on the home-front, alienating young men from young women. Later literary history has ignored the imaginative hands women stretched over that gulf, despite prohibitions.

5

Best-Sellers

There may have been no such thing as 'blockbusters' before the arrival of paperbacks, but from the time that there were first books there were best-sellers. Among the books which Claude Cockburn considered in *Bestseller: The Books that Everyone Read 1900–1939* (1972) was Ian Hay's Great War comedy about Kitchener's Army, *The First Hundred Thousand*, first published in 1915. Best-sellers are, in Cockburn's view, a rich source of information about attitudes and prejudices, and from *The First Hundred Thousand* we can discover views about war prevalent during the First World War. Although with hindsight we may regard it as pathetically naïve, Hay's book reveals that the middle-class saw an international war with 'the Boche' as a blessed escape from the class war at home. The author's spokesman, Major Wagstaffe, suggests that the War is a tonic for the country, which will lead to the miraculous cessation of class conflict altogether. (Similar sentiments were propounded in children's fiction of the time, such as H. Strang's *Fighting With French*.) However, whereas the political notions of a period are often made explicit like this in popular fiction, Cockburn found that 'the situation on the "private sector", including the status of women, is often taken more or less for granted, as being part of a settled order of things requiring no exposition' (Cockburn, 1972: 14).

In fact the status of women is explicitly discussed in Hay's book, briefly. According to Wagstaffe, one of the things to recommend the War is that it wipes out 'all the small nuisances of peace-time' such as Suffragettes, Bernard Shaw, and party politics, so that 'the things that are really big get viewed in their proper perspective'. Although 'the War has bucked up the nation' so that even girls have taken to nursing, 'One Nightingale doesn't make a base hospital'. There are women who are prepared to undergo the drudgery and discomfort of hospital training, but most girls only want to play the angel-of-mercy game in order to flirt with officers.

130

In general 'Women are the most extraordinary creatures' – a view with which that other Great War best-selling author, John Buchan, would certainly have concurred. Hay's message is delivered succinctly by Major Kemp: boys may wish for a strictly personal relationship with one particular girl, but 'Women in war-time are best left at home' (Hay, 1916: 84). (The swinging between the terms 'girl' and 'woman' is left unexplained, but 'girls' seem to be nubile and ridiculous; 'women' are apparently not on the marriage market.) Disturbingly, Hay's book was not only a war-time best-seller with regard to the volume of copies sold, and the pace at which they sold. His book is still in print, in a paperback edition, three-quarters of a century later. It seems that some attitudes remain unchanged.

Cockburn did not discuss any best-selling books about the First World War written by women, perhaps because, as he said, 'anyone who, with the utmost goodwill towards the authors, has tried to plough through numbers of other once-popular and now forgotten novels using the First World War as background has to admit that even that background is not in itself sufficiently dramatic, lurid, or tragic to enable a writer without high skill to construct a readable book' (Cockburn, 1972: 8). Certainly some popular war-books by women were ephemeral; E. M. Delafield's skilful novels were reprinted, whereas Mrs Belloc Lowndes and Berta Ruck did not require DORA to achieve the bliss of oblivion. Neither did Mrs Humphry Ward. May Sinclair's second war-time novel, *The Tree of Heaven*, which appeared in the late autumn of 1917 and was a best-seller in 1918, also disappeared after the War. The very reason for its wartime success, its idealistic patriotism, may have been sufficient reason for it also to be forgotten.

Like Ian Hay, Sinclair believed that the War was inaugurating a new era of selfless co-operation among all classes of English society. Through the courage to achieve 'Victory' (the title of Part 3 of her novel, which deals with the War), society would develop out of the violent period of 1910–14 (which she covers in Part 2, 'The Vortex'), and through to a peace based on the family virtues of self-sacrifice and mutual loyalty, which had contributed to the security of the years from 1895 to 1910 (that she had dealt with in Part 1, 'Peace'). The popular form Sinclair adopted for this book, that of a family saga, is an indication of its slipperiness. Sagas are the fictional form of chronicles. They tend to slide over misery and to lack a grip on historical explanation in much the same way that pageants do. Thus, although she recreated the pre-war excitement of the suffragette movement and sensitively delineated the frustrated lives of three maiden aunts, Sinclair's novel does not explore the class conflict that the War was supposed to resolve. (Indeed, judging by her earlier war novel, *Tasker Jevons* [1916], one might suppose that the reason for class struggle was simply snobbery, a matter of lacking the correct social graces.) The basic analogy between society and the family, implicit in the argument of the book, evades both the squalid wretchedness of the poor and the racial subjugation which led to such conflict as the Easter Uprising in 1916.

By 1917 the sordidness of trench warfare was common knowledge, yet Sinclair continued to preach the Victorian message of the spiritual value of war. Drawing on her own brief experience of the war-zone (but ignoring the despair of war refugees), May Sinclair interpreted the sense of ecstasy felt at intense danger as an awareness of the nearness of God, through which 'you lay hold on eternal life' (Sinclair, 1917: 347). She deliberately opposed this view of war as beneficial, to the profane version of war pioneered in print by Barbusse in *Le Feu: Journal d'une escouade*. (*Le Feu* first appeared in French in 1916, and was published in Fitzwater Wray's English translation as *Under Fire: the story of a squad*, in 1917.) In Sinclair's novel, the letters written home from the Front by a young poet, Michael Harrison, speak of 'a Frenchman who has told the truth, piling up all the horrors, faithfully, remorselessly, magnificently' in order to deter governments from ever starting another war; but Harrison claims that besides the material reality there is also the sacred truth about war, which is 'our glory, our spiritual compensation for the physical torture and there would be a sort of infamy in trying to take it from us' (348). The divine grace which enables people to sacrifice themselves that others may live in harmony with one another is symbolised by the tree which grows in Michael's mother's garden. While her husband sceptically calls it an 'ash tree', signifying that the force of such faith has burned out, Mrs Harrison insists that it is a 'tree of heaven'.

Sinclair's character of Michael Harrison was probably based on the poet Richard Aldington, whom she knew well at the beginning of the War. It seems likely that he would have dismissed her ideas about the 'sacred truth' of the glory of war, as part of the 'bunk', the 'sickening putrid cant' which he denounced in *Death of a Hero*, where he described the War itself as 'the supreme and tragic climax of Victorian Cant' (Adlington, 1965: 35, 223).

Although the *TLS* reviewer in 1917 considered that Miss Sinclair's imagination worked 'at its finest and fullest' when exercised with the War, 60 years later contemporary criticism has found the first two sections of the novel 'the best parts' (Zegger, 1976: 90). This is because of the 'interesting social history' about the suffrage movement and developments in the arts, two fields about which May Sinclair knew from personal experience. But the main thesis of the novel, which governs its overall shape, depends upon the final section and its appraisal of War. It was precisely because it was her intellectual fantasy rather than her imagination which was at full stretch when dealing with the experience of the battlefront that her novel seems sheer romancing to a later generation which has heard from the men themselves. She concentrated on the immediate sensations of excitement such as she herself had briefly felt as a non-combatant, without fathoming the drawn-out strain that front-line soldiers had to endure, or the deep trauma of killing. Her claims about the value of self-sacrifice appear not merely callous with regard to physical suffering, but fatuous in their evasion of conscription.

Like Baden-Powell and other Victorians (*supra* 45), Sinclair suggested that international war over-rode all other social and political considerations, reducing them to their true relative insignificance compared with 'the freedom of the world' being achieved by 'the Great War of Redemption'. Her character Dorothy Harrison, a graduate of Newnham, voices one aspect of this scale of values. Before the War Dorothy had been jailed for four weeks as a result of her participation in public political action for women's suffrage, although she had not actually joined the Women's Social and Political Union because of the dictatorial methods of its leaders. When her lover is killed at Mons, she regrets the time she now believes she wasted in asserting her independence and trying to achieve the vote: 'All those years – like a fool – over that silly suffrage' (276).

It was not until the men returned after the War and Sinclair saw their treatment and the treatment of Germany's starving children that she became disillusioned with her belief in the political and spiritual benefits of war.

At first sight it looks as if another successful writer, Cicely Hamilton, agreed with Ian Hay and May Sinclair about the over-riding importance of an international war as compared with conflicts within the nation. Although an active suffragist before the

War, even after it was over she too contrasted the minor pre-war efforts of the suffragettes with the major significance of international war.

Her novel *William – An Englishman*, which was published in 1919, won the first Femina Vie Heureuse prize. The book tells the story of the way in which an ordinary little man is affected by his experiences of the German invasion of Belgium (which occurs while he is on honeymoon in the Belgian Ardennes). Abandoning his pre-war beliefs in pacifism, socialism and internationalism, he is converted into an ardent patriot. On the surface this seems to be a typically propagandist war-novel, the tale of how, through war, William becomes 'an Englishman', thinking of himself as 'a man of the English race'. Philip Hager's bibliography describes it as 'somewhat of an after-the-fact propaganda piece that attempts to show the weakness of the socialist/pacifist ideology in the face of the ruthless terror of war' (Hager, 1981: 123). Yet according to Cicely Hamilton's autobiography, *Life Errant* (1935), the story had its genesis in an idea that occurred to her before the War. In a chapter about her activities in the suffrage movement, entitled 'Women on the Warpath', she explains that *William* only dealt with 1914 accidentally: 'It was really a "suffrage" novel; its ouline had taken shape in my thoughts before there was any suspicion of the war to come, and its beginnings I date from a gathering where I heard certain members of the militant section hold forth on the subject of their "war" '. She claimed to have had little understanding of what modern warfare would mean, but expected that it would be 'something more dangerous to life and limb than rough-and-tumbles round the Houses of Parliament' (Hamilton, 1935: 84). Here was the material for her story: 'a young man and woman, enthusiastic, ignorant, who had thought of their political scuffles as war and who stumbled accidentally into the other kind of war – of bullets and blood and high explosives' (85).

In fact the novel has little connection with 'modern warfare', although it illuminates why many pre-War feminists became war-time jingoists.

Aged 42 in 1914 Cicely Hamilton served in France during the First World War. She acted first as a clerk with one of Dr Elsie Inglis's NUWSS Scottish Women's Hosptials at Royaumont, some 30 miles behind the trenches. Then after two and a half years, she worked from 1917 to 1919 as an entertainer to the troops with Lena Ashwell's organisation, which, under the auspices of the YMCA, gave 'Concerts at the Front'. It was centred first at Abbeville, later near Cambrai and 'the Devastated Area', and finally in Cologne. Yet Hamilton's novel draws directly on none of that experience. Taking off from a contrast between the treatment of war-hostages by German soldiers, and the way in which suffragettes 'enjoyed' their 'scuffle' with the police on a Pankhurst demonstration, her book is an excuse to release an extraordinary aggression towards the representative suffragette who becomes William's wife, an aggression which is then diverted into the currently acceptable form: hatred for Germans.

Cicely Hamilton was about ten years younger than Elizabeth Robins, Beatrice Harraden or May Sinclair (and 20 years younger than Mrs Humphry Ward). She had helped to found the democratic Women's Freedom League which, under Charlotte Despard's leadership, broke away from Mrs Pankhurst's autocratic handling of the WSPU in 1907. (Cicely Hamilton was not, however, a committed marxist or pacifist like Charlotte Despard.) Following the WFL's aim of directing its militant action only against the government, Hamilton took part in the boycott of the 1911 census and was an active member of the Women's Tax Resistance League. However, as she admitted on several occasions, she had little physical courage and, although she spoke in public in favour of women's suffrage, she never committed any actions that resulted in her imprisonment: 'I am not the stuff whereof martyrs are made, and I much preferred that my knowledge of Holloway should be from the outside only' (Hamilton, 1935: 91). Thus she did not risk the forced-feeding that many WSPU members underwent in prison, and which their publicity represented as a violation of a woman's body akin to rape. Nor did she experience the humiliation and brutality used against women publicly demonstrating for the vote.

In 1908 she joined the Actresses' Franchise League, which she had helped Elizabeth Robins to establish. She also helped to set up the Women Writers' Suffrage League as an auxiliary to the NUWSS, with the express aim of working for women's suffrage by 'using methods proper to writers'. It was in accordance with that aim that Cicely Hamilton authored the famous spectacular, *A Pageant of Great Women*, and a political pamphlet which was published by the WWSL. With the help of her close friend, Christabel Marshall ('Christopher St John'), Hamilton adapted the pamphlet into a play that became a smash-hit in 1909 – *How the*

Vote Was Won. She also wrote for the early suffragist paper *The Women's Franchise*, criticising what she called 'the Noah's Ark Principle': that 'all human beings naturally ... pair off and beget children'. Hamilton stated that marriage was not the only career for women, many of whom, like herself, had no vocation for motherhood. The word 'woman' should not be synonymous with 'mother'. She developed these ideas in the influential work *Marriage as a Trade* (1909), which was both an analysis of women's economic exploitation and a proposal for women to achieve economic and psychological independence.

In her autobiography, she carefully distinguishes between suffragists, even the militant suffragists of the WFL, and the suffragettes who formed part of Mrs Pankhurst's 'army'. Cicely Hamilton shared with May Sinclair and other women a dislike for Mrs Pankhurst's demand for military-style obedience from members of the WSPU, calling her 'a magnificent demagogue' and a dictator, 'a forerunner of Lenin, Hitler and Mussolini – the leader whose fiat must not be questioned'. Hamilton's objections to the WSPU itself seem to have stemmed partly from her horror of suffragette violence, which, like May Sinclair, she saw as mob-rule, 'brutal and crazy', and partly from her resistance to the suffragette 'insistence on the feminine note ... all suggestion of the masculine was carefully avoided'. Cicely Hamilton herself wore the severe tailored coat and skirt which the suffragettes disfavoured, and she clearly disliked the 'picture-hats' which they adopted as their camouflage for militant raids. She pointed out that although Mrs Pankhurst encouraged the legend about herself that she was 'sweet-womanly', Mrs Pankhurst's main public characteristic was a stubborn forcefulness 'not usually associated with women one describes as "so feminine"!' (Hamilton, 1935: 75–7). Hamilton was at pains to make clear in her autobiography that her personal revolt was feminist rather than suffragist. What she rebelled against was the dependence implied in the idea of 'destined' marriage, 'destined' motherhood, 'the artificial concentration of the hopes of girlhood on sexual attraction and maternity'.

The oldest of the four children of an army-officer, Cicely Hamilton had felt responsible for her younger sister and brothers when they were 'farmed out' on foster parents while their father was serving abroad. (The loss of her much-loved mother is left unexplained. I assume she died in child-birth.) Later, having to earn her own living and determined to provide a home at last for herself and her sister, Cicely Hamilton saw hardship and knew social helplessness. She records that, while working as an actress, 'Twice in the course of my life on tour I was thrown out of work to make room for a manager's mistress . . . how bitterly I raged in my heart at the injustice; for on each occasion, when the blow fell, times had been hard and there was very little in the savings bank'. The kind of strength required by such a feminist as Hamilton was not shown in public boldness during brief skirmishes with London policemen, supported by a crowd of other women. That kind of flamboyance was an egotistical misconception of what the women's struggle for independence necessitated. As her auto-biography shows, although self-supporting women were fighting what in one of her plays Hamilton called the same 'battle of life' as men, women were at a disadvantage. The single woman was at the mercy of men, and the strength a feminist needed was the unobtrusive courage of endurance. Cicely Hamilton was utterly contemptuous and frightened of femininity in as far as it implied weak helplessness. Men were exploiters of frailty rather than chivalrous protectors. A woman's sexuality put her body at risk from men, the risk of rape, of childbirth, and of VD. Hamilton's analysis followed that of the great Victorian campaigners for women's emancipation, such as Josephine Butler.

Yet in the Great War, women were forced into dependence on the male army for their defence against invasion. About ten years older than Rose Macaulay, in 1916 Cicely Hamilton voiced in poetry a similar sense of shameful uselessness at being a non-combatant during the War: ' – an idle, useless mouth, / As cumbrous – nay, more cumbrous – than the dead,'

> That is my hurt – my burning, beating wound;
> That is the spear-thrust driven through my pride!
>
> Let me endure it then – I give my pride
> Where others give a life.
>
> (Reilly, 1981: 46)

The heroine of her novel, *William – An Englishman*, is called Griselda, like the 'ideal' wife in the tale told by the Clerk of Oxford in Chaucer's *Canterbury Tales*, Grisilde, who is the epitome of submissive, long-suffering womanhood. Hamilton's Griselda is 'a piece of blank-minded, suburban young womanhood' who is ideally matched with her 28-year-old husband, the mild-mannered

William, being 'his exact counterpart in petticoats'. At the beginning of *William*, the authorial voice is scornful of both William and Griselda. They are both 'cocksure, contemptuous, intolerant' and although they proclaim themselves internationalists and pacifists, they are 'unconscious little humbugs'. They support the votes-for-women campaign, and Griselda wears a suffragette badge to show she has 'suffered for the Cause in Holloway', but according to the narrator they have no idea of real suffering and their historical ignorance is so profound that they 'look on the strife of nations as a glorified scuffle on the lines of a Pankhurst demonstration' (Hamilton, 1919: 83).

Humiliated and incredulous, they find themselves caught up in the German invasion of Belgium, watching the shooting of hostages and the bombing of civilians. William begins to feel 'a vague, unreasoning, natural longing for home'. 'In the clutch of brute force', he is subjected to forced labour, and Griselda, helpless against 'licentious soldiery', is raped by a German soldier and then knocked down and fatally injured by a German army motor-cyclist.

Following only William's consciousness once the couple are separated, the reader does not witness Griselda's rape, except through William's suddenly vivid imagination. Her vulnerability changes her from a comrade into a cumbrous burden for William. They escape behind the lines with other refugees, and as they travel through the Forest of Arden William's mind wanders off into a vague recollection of the tale of 'a knightly lover who had carried his mistress long miles through a forest in his arms'. Then he imagines himself as a starving fugitive during 'the Great Civil War', who had seen other men 'dismembered and done to death' in a war which was not 'civil'. Meanwhile, the pitiful, violated Griselda has 'died very quietly' in the straw at the bottom of the cart. The authorial voice begins to speak more approvingly of William, as he gradually becomes determined to help stop such things.

William returns alone to England, where he is helped by a calm woman, Edith Haynes: 'a kindly and capable good comrade'. Her brother having been killed in France, Edith runs the family farm and supports her elderly mother in his place. William, changed by his experience, now regards pacifism as 'child's talk – ridiculous babble'. Dreaming of heroism, he joins the army, but he is given non-combatant work as a clerk. Disillusioned by the military machine, and weary of war, he nevertheless keeps 'a smoulder of hatred' at the bottom of his heart: 'He was still in his heart a soldier'. It has become a matter of fundamental faith to him that pacifism is wrong, that 'that devilry' has got to be stopped, so 'all the moral strength he possessed went into the effort not to shrink, to be master of his body, to behave decently and endure' (245). He is finally killed in an air-raid. The capable Edith survives the War.

Despite the fact that it dates from 1919, this image of war is of a piece with the propaganda writing from early on in the First World War, such as the fantastic book by Phyllis Campbell and the fictitious Bryce Report, tales of atrocities which played on the primitive fear of rape and encouraged the superstition about the cruel sadism of Prussian Uhlans (the German cavalry, whom Mildred Aldrich found surprisingly courteous). Pressing examples such as the execution of Nurse Edith Cavell, the British propaganda aimed at civilians misrepresented German martial law as brutal anarchy. This reinforced the paranoia that had been encouraged by Northcliffe and Roberts before the War. When Cicely Hamilton talks about a time 'before there was any suspicion of the war to come', she would have to be referring to a time before her birth, judging by what I. F. Clarke had dredged up about the prevalence of prophecies of war in popular fiction from 1870 onwards. Hamilton's images of what war is, what war means, are to do with the fears of invasion created by such works as *The Great War in England in 1870*. They have nothing to do with a war between opposing armies. They are primarily concerned with what happens away from the battlefront. Her images may have some connection with her actual experience of refugees and wounded soldiers behind the lines, but not much. She repeats the old cliché that 'war's hell' with very little to fill it out beyond the pre-war clichés of rape and the shooting of hostages.

Nothing appears in her book of the specific hell of the Great War, as a technological war of attrition, which has been vividly recreated for us in the writings of ambulance-drivers, and nurses and doctors at casualty clearing stations, as well as by soldiers. They depicted an inflexible military machine, indifferent to the price paid for victory in terms of innumerable dead and of immeasurable human suffering, both physical and mental, that continued long after the Armistice. What is to be found in most of the Great War memoirs, an allocation of the responsibility for the suffering to the older male generation and their Victorian military ethos, rather than to the Germans, finds no place in Hamilton's novel. For Hamilton the enemy is *Male Outsiders*, and what is being defended is *Home*. Her protagonist is a non-combatant in uniform, on the home-front, rather than a soldier in the trenches.

A non-combatant in uniform herself, Cicely Hamilton's novel can be read as a woman's picture of the divided self. It is then about the suppression of the shameful, weaker aspect of her nature, just as Conrad's *The Secret Sharer* is a man's representation of the suppression of cowardice. *William* is a war-novel, although not exactly a novel about the Great War; it is a myth about what Cicely Hamilton had called 'the battle of life' for the independent woman at the time of the First World War. William and Griselda are male and female counterparts, whose 'two hearts beat as one', the masculine and feminine aspects of a single, female self.

The central event of the book, the flight through the Forest, is not based on the Belgian Ardennes, but on Shakespeare's Forest of Arden in *As You Like It*. Shakespeare's story of Rosalind and Celia was a powerful myth for women at the time of the Great War (Holtby, 1938: *passim*). In their flight from male tyranny, in the mirror-reverse world of the greenwood, Rosalind, dressed as a man, supports her physically weaker relative, Celia, who was previously the dominant partner in the relationship. Celia becomes a passive spectator as Rosalind, through her masculine masquerade, explores both male and female psyches, gaining new powers of self-assertion. During the Great War many women were able to trespass on the previously male preserve, wearing male-style uniforms in company with comrades and using their own initiative to carry out what had been previously men's jobs.

In Cicely Hamilton's novel, William imagines himself first as a knight errant, supporting his frail damsel, and secondly as a fugitive during the Civil War. As is clear from her autobiography, *Life Errant*, Cicely Hamilton saw herself partly as the 'Juif Errant', the homeless Wandering Jew, and partly as a knight errant, performing chivalrous acts on behalf of less fortunate women. She knew herself to be too physically and psychologically vulnerable to male bullying to take part in the militant suffragette fight, a civil war where female prisoners were symbolically 'raped' by prison doctors. That shameful, feminine side of herself had to die off, painful as the loss might be, if she were to survive. The threat to her identity came from masculine brutality. War had been depicted in feminist writing as masculinity taken to extremes, 'maleness run riot' (Stobart, 1916: vii), and in British propaganda German soldiers represented the worst of masculine bestiality. In 1915 Mrs Pankhurst had talked of brutal 'male' Germany having raped gentle 'female' Belgium (Wiltsher, 1985: 41). The aggression which Hamilton felt at the wound to her sense of her own worth, when the 'You' in the message 'Your Country Needs You' did not mean women, she deflected onto the archetypally male threat, the Hun. Not all men were heroes-at-arms. She might do at least as well as the men not at the battle-front, enduring the same dangers that they did. She would be 'master of her own body'. By the end of the War, with the vote largely won, the suffrage struggle was over. By the end of the War William, too, is dead. The survivor is the capable, unbelligerent Edith, who took over the male role of keeping the country running.

Nichola Beauman recently described *William – An Englishman* as 'wonderful, incomparable ... this masterpiece' (Beauman, 1983: 28). Yet, like *The Tree of Heaven*, for all its success at the time of publication *William* has been out of print for half a century.

But there were books written by women, that relied on a First World War background for their impact, which have been found sufficiently readable (at least by women) to have remained in print after their first appearance and to have gone on selling steadily ever since.

Three of these, by writers whose names are almost household words, Rebecca West's *The Return of the Soldier* (1918), Virginia Woolf's *Mrs Dalloway* (1925) and Radclyffe Hall's *The Well of Loneliness* (1928), were not 'war books' at all as Cyril Falls used the category. Their main interest is not in their attempts to 'mirror' British society during the actual period between 1914 and 1918, as Mary Hamilton, Rose Macaulay and Rose Allatini tried to do. Nor do they try to imagine what it was like for soldiers to be fighting for their lives. We would not read the works of West, Woolf or Hall in order to gain any knowledge of conditions on the Western Front or the responses of the 'Other Nation' to those conditions. Rather, their novels take for granted a common fund of images of the war-zone and of home-front reactions to it. I think these novels have continued to be of interest precisely because of their reliance on generally accepted ideas about the Great War, and the use they make of these ideas in their analysis of women's gender identity, especially as it is defined in relation to men. Myths about the Great War are here given wider cultural significance, to inform women's imagined sense of their own being. These novels are every bit as important to an understanding of modern consciousness as are, for instance, Richard Aldington's *Death of a Hero* or the verse of Siegfried Sassoon – *women's* consciousness, that is.

As Cockburn pointed out, the responses of literary critics – whether fatuous or serious – are no sure clue to the cultural impact of books. In May 1918 the *Times Literary Supplement* did not rate Rebecca West's *The Return of the Soldier* as worth more than a brief mention in a list, since the situation developed in the novel did not 'vindicate itself as real or even possible'. The reviewer conceded that 'the story . . . can, no doubt, be enjoyed by lovers of sentiment' (*TLS*, 1918: 255). Over half a century later, the *TLS* covering the umpteenth reprint of the novel in 1973, could still find nothing more constructive to say about it than that it was 'a woman's war novel' (*TLS*, 1973: 1553). In the meantime, what had originally started life as a magazine serial had been turned into a play and chosen for the *Daily Express* book club. Reprinted and reprinted, in 1981 it was made into a film with an all-star cast including Julie Christie, Glenda Jackson, Ian Holm and Oliver Reed, a film which was later televised at peak viewing-time over Christmas in 1986. Perhaps G. B. Shaw's verdict on the book, quoted in the publisher's advertisement in June 1918, that *The Return of the Soldier* was 'one of the best stories in the language', is not quite the hyperbole that it may have seemed at the time. In view of Max Beerbohm's characterisation of Rebecca West's writing as itself 'very Shavian – cool, frank, breezy, trenchant' it is odd that the *TLS* critics were so dismissive.

The Return of the Soldier was Rebecca West's first novel, but she was already a well-known journalist and in 1916 had published a critical study of Henry James. Her articles in the socialist paper *The Clarion* from 1912 were indeed 'Shavian', and the amalgam of feminism and socialism which they display is illuminating with regard to the characters in her fiction. In her journalism, she developed an idea of the 'parasitic woman' which is indebted to Olive Schreiner and indicates that the inspiration for the novel did not only stem from the more obvious influence of May Sinclair, a novelist for whom West had a great admiration. In fact the mystical idealism which derives from Sinclair's philosophy sits rather oddly with the Jamesian social analysis, but it seems to be what makes the story palatable; the conflict between the two attitudes keeps the book rankling in the mind despite the pat ending, which is a classic example of the way in which popular literature attempts to reconcile the implicit contradictions of false consciousness.

The Return of the Soldier is narrated in the first person by Jenny who recounts the story of her cousin Chris Baldry. Chris is a war-time army-officer invalided home from the Western Front suffering from 'shellshock'. As the result of (an unspecified) shock, Chris has lost his memory of the previous 15 years. He has forgotten being married to Kitty, and has regressed to the time of his young manhood when he was in love with a girl called Margaret. Chris comes of a wealthy family and supports both Jenny and Kitty at Baldry Court, the family estate at Harrow Weald; Margaret, the daughter of a publican, married a sick man much further down the social scale and now lives in respectable suburban poverty in Wealdstone. It is to Margaret that Chris writes from hospital, having forgotten the misunderstanding that led to their estrangement and separate marriages. He totally fails to recognise his glamorous wife, who is mortified at his preference for such a 'dowd' (that is, 'a slut'). Jenny too is jealous of his simple contentment with Margaret. Eventually Kitty calls in a psychiatrist. Persuaded by this doctor that Chris cannot remain a psychological adolescent forever, despite the fact that recovery will mean return to the Front, Margaret brings about the recall of Chris's memory. Along with his memory returns an awareness of present reality, and he squares up to both his loveless marriage and the War like a man, in fact 'like a soldier'. Hence the ambiguous resonance of the title.

Although Rebecca West uses the Jamesian technique of presenting the story through the percipient but limited point of view of one of the characters, she does not put this to the sophisticated effect that James achieves in, say, *The Turn of the Screw*. The reader soon recognises that Jenny is in love with her cousin. Despite her jealousy she manages to be fairer to Margaret than Kitty is, and to achieve sympathy for Kitty, too, but in the process she reveals the same regard for material objects and the same snobbish contempt for poverty that Kitty shows more openly: Margaret's vulgarity is 'a spreading stain on the fabric of our lives'. There is some irony in this presentation of social injustice in aesthetic terms which twist the moral blame, since the aesthetics are shown to be superificially artificial in a way that also reveals the cattiness of Jenny: she describes Kitty's loveliness as so artful that 'one expected to find a large '7d.' somewhere attached to her person' as if she were on a magazine cover. Similarly, Baldry Court is described as having been manicured knowingly by the architects, and 'massaged' for more magazine photos. Yet Jennie becomes a mouthpiece for the author by justifying Kitty's existence: 'there is, you know, really room for all of us; we each have our peculiar use'. With the outcome of the story, Chris's return to his manifestly empty marriage, the book finally appears to endorse Jenny's views and the snobbery and vanity that destroyed Chris's inner peace.

The doubtful moral of the story is that there is dignified sanity in returning to the No-Man's-Land of marriage to a possessive, selfish woman, for 'The truth's the truth'. To continue the fight is to be a man. Although the doctor doesn't see 'the urgency' himself, the three women are agreed that Chris must be made 'normal' and 'ordinary' again. This is presented by Jenny as a sacrament, a sacred communion with reality, for it is the return of the 'divine essential of his soul'. (The holy insight that Jenny and Margaret supposedly attain far surpasses the vision, not only of the mere psychiatrist, but also of the rather limited Anglican padre who visited Chris in hospital.) Although there might be irony in the final words of the novel, that Chris is 'cured' when he walks like a soldier again, the religious language has pre-empted that dimension. Any gap that might have appeared between the values of the author and the point of view of her narrator has decisively closed.

This is not at all the novel one might have expected from Rebecca West's journalism. The assumption of religious language conceals the same kind of dilemma which she faced in her personal life at this time over her adulterous relationship with H. G. Wells. The resolution of the plot relies on the classism inherent in the suffragette support for the War, which is in fact implicit in West's war-time journalism for all its avowal of socialism. Originally a magazine story, *The Return of the Soldier* goes beyond the mere 'compromises' with the conventions of popular fiction which Harold Orel identifies, such as the painlessness of traumatic events (Orel, 1986: 125). The magical disguising of the contradiction at the heart of the novel is of the essence of popular fiction, especially as it is to be found in women's magazines, and is, I think, precisely what is responsible for the novel's continued popularity. The romantic love between Chris and Margaret, which over-rides physical appearance and class difference, is presented as not only sane and real, but – in the florid language which Harold Orel finds typical of the genre – as solemn and beatified. Margaret, despite

3. Mrs St Clair Stobart

2. 'The Heroines of Pervyse' – Mairi Chisholm and Mrs Knocker (Baroness T'Serclaes) war-worn in the street of Pervyse, displaying their Belgian decoration as 'Chevaliers of the Order of Leopold'

1. Sergeant Flora Sandes in Salonika 1916, convalescing from the battle wound for which she was awarded the 'Kara George Star'

5. John Everett Millais, *Knight Errant*, 1870

4. Frederick Leighton, *Perseus and Andromeda*, 1891

7. David Wilson, 'Once a German – Always a German!', 1918

6. A. E. Foringer, *The Greatest Mother in the World*, 1918

8. May Sinclair (centre) as a suffragist in 1910

9. Mrs Humphry Ward visits the Western Front in 1916

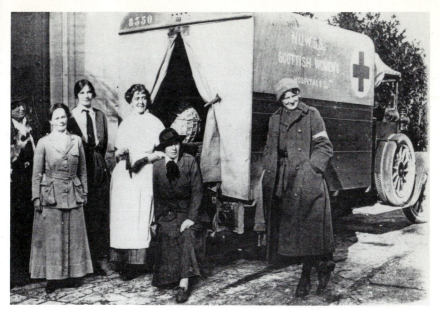

10. Cicely Hamilton (seated) working for the NUWSS Scottish Women's Hospitals at Royaumont Hospital, 1916

11. Toupie Lowther (second left, middle row) with her all women's ambulance unit, 1918

12. Sylvia Pankhurst with a deputation of Old Aged Pensioners from the East End in 1915

13. (*left*) Vera Brittain as a pre-War Lady, with hat, gloves and parasol

14. (*above*) Lady Cynthia Asquith

15. (*above*) Richard Aldington (2nd from right) as a poet amongst poets in 1914

16. (*left*) Richard Aldington as an army officer in 1917

17. The Monument to Nurse Edith Cavell: 'PATRIOTISM IS NOT ENOUGH'

her dreary poverty, is seen by Jenny as the Virgin Mother, one of those 'women who could bring God into the world by the passion of their motherhood' (West, 1918: 172), with a mystic sense of life which assures peace and security. It is typical of romantic fiction that unspoilt nature is the setting for the sanctified reality of romantic love. However, this supernatural reality becomes a dream that totters and dissolves into the unnatural nightmare of No-Man's-Land, the harsh reality that Chris must return to:

a hateful world where barbed-wire entanglements showed impish knots against a livid sky full of booming noise and splashes of fire and wails for water. (86)

West has given a clear exposition of the empty materialism and class antagonism of the society to which the artificial Kitty and Jenny belong, 'the whole truth about us lies in our material seeming', and of the need for the healthy, essential values exemplified by the generosity and candour of Margaret, who is 'saner than the rest of us', since 'if humanity forgets these attitudes there is an end to the world'. Nevertheless Chris's return to sanity is a resumption of the materialist values of the bourgeois marriage, which have never really been at risk. Margaret also accepts those values. The war is never questioned, and neither is the social inequality on which the novel is founded. In fact to question them would be, in the terms of the novel, not merely eccentric but adolescent.

Despite Rebecca West's criticism of Henry James for his failure 'to dramatize in his imagination anything concerning women save their failures and successes as sexual beings' the entire existence of Jenny, Kitty and Margaret revolves around their relation to Chris. There is no indication in the novel that women might find some purpose to their lives apart from domesticity; no indication that there might exist those adventurous-minded young women of whom West wrote in 1912, that they might, for instance, wish to be wireless operators on board ship in order 'to see over the edge of the world'. In fact the novel even presents a justification for the parasitic women of Kitty's class that West had so objected to before the War. She had argued that 'the parasite woman costs money' and that if non-productive middle-class women were to remain parasites, then the four-fifths of the population who were manual workers would have to remain at the subsistence level in order to support them. West had also held such women actually responsible for the white slave trade of prostitution: 'The passion which these parasite women inspire, being based on no pretence of comradeship or equality, is not such as commands faithful waiting, so men visit the vagrant passion of their youth on the daughters of the poor'. But Jenny claims that even Kitty has a use, since her beauty over-rules class distinction; it is her 'civilizing mission to flash the jewel of (her) beauty before all men, so that they shall desire it and work to get the wealth to buy it, and thus be seduced by a present appetite to a tilling of the earth that serves the future' (154). But, true to the conventions of romantic fiction, that Margaret's unseductive hands are the price of Kitty's glamour is a point the novel does not make.

Pace Elaine Showalter, this is not the first English novel to deal with shell-shock, and a brief comparison with Rose Macaulay's *Non-Combatants and Others* reveals how the distressing details of shell-shock are glanced over by West. Nor is this the first novel to deal with the main symptom of shell-shock that West's novel relies on – amnesia. Loss of memory had been one of the ingredients of popular ('gothic') fiction for at least half a century. Several novels of the war-period besides West's made use of this device. They either created a moral drama out of the dilemma for a woman whose lover or husband unexpectedly reappears after having been listed as 'missing believed dead' while suffering from a loss of memory, or they created a psychological thriller out of the veteran who commits murder while suffering from a recurrence of shell-shock. Before *The Return of the Soldier* was published, the case of the amnesiac husband was exploited by Mrs Belloc Lowndes (in *Lilla: A Part of her Life* [1916]), by 'Charles de Crespigny' (Charles and Alice Williamson, in The War Wedding [1916]) and by Mrs Humphry Ward (in *Missing* [1917]), all to good melodramatic effect. The idea still had enough steam to motivate Sylvia Thompson's post-war best-seller, *The Hounds of Spring* (1926). A. M. N. Jenkin's *The End of a Dream* (1919) seems to have been the first novel in which the delusion of being still in the trenches leads to murder, but it was not the last. Vera Brittain used the same motif in *Account Rendered* in 1945, and in 1950 C. S. Forester made use of it in *Randall and the River of Time*, a book which was republished several times and was still in print in 1968.

However, it is not in the exploitation of a potentially sensational plot that the significance of West's novel lies. There is, in fact, very little incident or story, and what plot there is relies on a psychological ploy which at first appears to be sentimental and irrelevant: Chris's 'cure' is effected by a trick as banal as the trick of hypnotism which the novel condemns. The likelihood of a shocked reaction to such an attempted cure is evaded by the method of narration; the scene takes place out of Jenny's sight or hearing. In this way Chris's recognition of 'reality' is rendered unproblematical, and the possibility of his facing up to the mutually incompatible wishes which are the cause of his fugue, or of finding any method of bridging the two contradictory realities, is avoided.

The novel offers no solution to its problematic of combining a desire for adventure with the need for humanity, the selfish acquisitive urge which leads to towns, classes and 'civilisation' (personified by Kitty), with the need for non-material values such as beauty and peace, which require unselfish generosity (personi- fied in Margaret). Indeed, Chris is shocked back to 'normality' by the recognition that his hopes for the future, his son, 'had only half a life' and had died, like Margaret's, while still in infancy; in a symbolic sense, the fact that Kitty cannot bear another baby is a sign not only of the sterility of his marriage, but of his society. And Margaret's generosity only serves to reinforce Kitty's aggressive selfishness. In that sense I think that Elaine Showalter is right, that West incoherently grasped 'the connections between male hysteria and a whole range of male social obligations' and that the treatment that 'cures' Chris Baldry 'sends him back into a normality that is [drab,] unfeeling, and unreal' (Showalter, 1987: 191, 241). But the novel suggests that a state of hostility is, however undesirable, natural; indeed, 'reasonable'. To that extent the novel endorses the main pre-war theme of Tory-dominated fiction: war is inevitable. Far from the socialist pacifism of Rose Allatini or Mary Hamilton, West predicts no new future. Chris's 'cure' is the eradication of an un*real*isable dream. From the point of view of the modern, materialist world, the 'sacred' dream of peace relies on a belief in magic.

What I find of particular interest is the images West uses to present this political position. To contrast the two worlds, the false, hostile world of a bourgeois marriage and the sacred sim- plicity of common humanity, West chooses two zones: No-Man's- Land, and the support-area just behind the Firing Line (not the trenches, but a bombed village). Both only appear to us in the novel through the imagination of Jenny, based on war-films she has seen; neither of them is a place she has actually visited, but they are ideas of places which she uses to form a conception of Chris's mental states. West's book elaborates on a simple analogy first archly propounded by Hay:

> The firing-trench is our place of business – our office in the city, so to speak. The supporting trench is our suburban residence, whither the weary toiler may take himself periodically. (Hay, 1916: 97)

The book opens with Jenny's anxiety about Chris: 'I wanted to snatch my cousin Chris from the wars' (13). It is an anxiety she shares with 'most Englishwomen' apart from Kitty. 'The wars' she wants to rescue him from are not scenes of fighting, but scenes 'packed full of horror', a horror she imagines in two ways, visual and auditory. The visual horror is a nightmare of Chris 'running across the brown rottenness of No Man's Land, starting back here because he trod upon a hand, not even looking there because of the awfulness of an unburied head' (13). The audible horror is a story told in the flattened but indomitable tones of the modern subaltern:

> We were all of us in a barn one night, and a shell came along. My pal sang out, *'Help me, old man, I've got no legs!'* and I had to answer, *'I can't, old man, I've got no hands!'* (14)

And at the very end of the book Jenny sees Chris looking up at the house which is his home, 'as though it were a hated place to which, against all his hopes, business had forced him to return'. Worse than the marriage 'yoke' that makes him walk like a soldier, with 'a dreadful decent smile', is the fact that he must also return to 'that flooded trench in Flanders under that sky more full of flying death than clouds, to that No Man's Land where bullets fall like rain on the rotting faces of the dead . . .' (187). These horrors have been 'brought forth' by the unnatural changes of modern life brought about by 'adventurous men' (63).

Set against these horrors is Monkey Island, where Chris first met his adolescent love, not so much a place as a 'magic state' of healing and liquid loveliness (102–3). Margaret is essentially pitying and protective, but Chris lost her partly because of an argument about class differences, and partly because of his family's firm and its foreign investment. She represents safety, and is to Jenny like 'one carrying a wounded man from under fire' (122). The magic state of security from hositility, which the saintly Margaret represents, is contrasted with the malice and financial burden of Kitty, who is likened to a mean speculator, and with the irrelevance of doctors, who are likened to inquisitive commercial travellers. In other words, within the metaphorical language of the book, Margaret is opposed to the world of business ventures (including marriage as a financial contract), which thus becomes identified with No-Man's-Land.

The two sets of value (materialist and spiritual, Kitty and Margaret) are represented in Jenny's mind by crystal spheres. In a place behind the lines Chris chooses between them, and in this zone he chooses Margaret, who appears transfigured in the light of eternity. The place where eternal values become clear is a hideous, dirty, ruined village, alive with flies. It is the 'forbidden zone' – the area where all people are equal, all equally defenceless, and nothing is to be gained by physical attractiveness or social prestige, where neither sexual nor financial matters count, only compassion. That compassion is essentially feminine.

Margaret's selflessness might be preferable, all things being equal. But all things not being equal, women must see themselves as desirable commodities and sell to the highest bidder. Men have created a civilisation that excludes the feminine generosity they need. The equal companion, the playmate, the pal – Jenny – counts for nothing in this scheme of things. Unmarried women are also parasites. Like the lower-class man (represented by Margaret's husband, William), the single woman is neutralised. Seen only as individuals, Jenny and William lack the potential political power that in real historical time threatened the whole bourgeois system when women and working-class men, formed social and political unions to campaign for their own interests and gain themselves the vote, which had formerly been the prerogative of men of Chris's class. (1918, the year when *The Return of the Soldier* first appeared, was the year when suffrage was extended to working men and to women over the age of 30; it was also the year following the Russian Revolution.)

In fact Rebecca West has used the First World War setting to produce a myth about personal relations which over-rides historical circumstances. It is a myth which presents certain contingent facts that depend upon a particular social system, as inevitable and independently 'real'. In doing so she has used two very powerful metaphors with a deep inner logic. No-Man's-Land, the emotion-less zone of inherent, inevitable hostility, creates, and requires for its continued existence, a conflict-free support zone where basic human needs are met out of simple common humanity. In male mythology that area is the trenches, the area where class and money are irrelevant and all men are brothers. The comradeship and spirit of the trenches has become proverbial in British consciousness. But in female mythology that support-area is the 'Forbidden Zone', the area where wives are prohibited but men's basic needs are met by free women – either asexual nurses and ambulance-drivers, or women who have challenged and broken the sexual rules, who provide the compassion without which human life cannot continue.

The obvious difference between the myths is that in the male myth men can be all-sufficient to each other; in the female version women are necessary to men, who are helpless to live without them.

Whereas in *The Return of the Soldier* 'shell-shock' was an abstract device to expose the true nature of bourgeois marriage, the visionary madness of a war-shocked soldier is itself part of the collective consciousness which constitutes the reality of *Mrs Dalloway*. Drawing on her own experience of derangement to convey the pained mind of Septimus Warren Smith, Virginia Woolf places his subjectivity within a network that connects him with a society-lady, Mrs Dalloway. The novel plots their mutual con-straint by the values of an imperial political system. This was Woolf's second attempt to deal with the Great War in fiction. Like her other books, it was not an immediate best-seller, yet more copies of it are now sold annually than were read during the whole of her lifetime. *Mrs Dalloway*, first published in 1925, has become one of the classics of modern literature.

It may seem odd to classify *Mrs Dalloway* as a novel to do with the First World War at all, since it specifically covers events in London on a day in mid-June in 1923, when 'the War was over'. However, the novel climaxes on the delayed shock of the War which cannot be forgotten: 'this late age of world's experience had bred in them all, all men and women, a well of tears', sorrow, together with the stoicism to endure it (Woolf, 1925: 12). The novel, while examining that 'stoical bearing', is pervaded with the awareness of time passing and the irrevocability of death, as those who are left grow old. The day is punctuated by the chiming of Big Ben, the tolling that links different individual consciousnesses in a common remembrance that 'in the midst of life we are in death'; and as the death of any particular person diminishes all the rest, so Septimus Warren's suicide impinges deeply on Clarissa Dalloway, although they had never met.

Big Ben is not only a reminder of time passing; it is also an insistent reminder of masculine authority, an authority headed by the Prime Minister in the Parliament at Westminster, whose powerful influence spreads out over society deadening the anarchic spontaneity of life. It is contrasted with the bell of St Margaret's, the queenly voice of the hostess, 'reluctant to inflict its individuality' (56), which expresses grief, concern, delight, celebrating the life of the spirit. Beaten and broken up by assault and brutality, feminine power lollops in the wake of the vigorous, inconsiderate, masculine stroke which lays down the law. Whereas the masculine desire to dominate drugs the soul into a stiff corpse, violating it (as the central allusion to Richardson's novel, *Clarissa*, recalls), it is the apparently trivial, feminine carnival of partying which enables the soul to brave itself to endure the perpetual threat of loss and death. Men's aggression destroys the very joy of life; invitingly, women welcome people in to share each other's company.

The structure of Woolf's novel, governed by one June day in a capital city where the paths of two main characters cross, and her method of narration, concerned with displaying the contents of people's consciousnesses rather than recounting a story, are clearly influenced by that other landmark of modernist fiction which Woolf was reading while she composed *Mrs Dalloway*: James Joyce's *Ulysses*. However, whereas Joyce used mock-epic parallels to present Bloom on Bloomsday in Dublin as a timeless type of vulgar Everyman, Woolf's lyrical pattern of allusion and metaphor creates, through the portrait of a worldly, middle-aged lady, a picture of irrepressible feminine creativity, the power to bring people together and facilitate happiness. To place *Mrs Dalloway* against the two other modernist works which it parallels, Joyce's 'The Dead' and Mansfield's 'The Garden Party', is to become aware of what distinguishes Woolf's work: her ruthless wit which slices through surfaces. Joyce and Mansfield are also comic writers, ironically delighting in absurdity. But Woolf's metaphors modulate into a caricature which is cutting in its hatred for human brutality, and by which her compassion defends the weak and the apparently frivolous. Owing much, ultimately, to Conrad, *Mrs Dalloway* is a penetrating indictment of British imperialism, the 'tolerable show' which covers over a hollow heart, the 'damnable humbug' that reduces to 'stuffing and bunkum' what is owed to the young and the war-dead.

Her novel is an example of the type of fiction which Virginia Woolf defined in *Women and Fiction* (1929) as specific to the liberated woman writer: less an analysis of individual lives than a criticism of society. And, as Woolf predicted, her wish to alter established values, 'to make serious what appears trivial to a man, and trivial what to him is important' was indeed judged by male critics to be itself weak and trivial. Although Winifred Holtby ranked Virginia Woolf's writing 'beside the work of the great masters' (Holtby, 1932: 201–2), she was rated 'adolescent', 'naïve' and 'a minor talent' by Frank W. Bradbrook in *The Pelican Guide to English Literature* in 1961. He saw no reason to change this opinion when the Guide was revised in 1983. In the meantime Virginia Woolf was being reclaimed as a 'literary mother' by American feminist critics, who described her writing as 'an active political effort of committed socialist feminism' (Marcus, 1981: xiv). This was despite Leonard Woolf's often quoted assertion that 'she was the least political animal that has lived since Aristotle invented the definition' (Woolf, 1979: xviii). Of course, as Lee R. Edwards ironically remarked, that all depends on what you mean by 'political' – which confirms Virginia Woolf's point (Edwards, 1977: 160).

To take an example: while she was writing *Mrs Dalloway*, Virginia Woolf spent an afternoon with Mary Sheepshanks. Leonard Woolf included her account of this visit when he edited *A Writer's Diary* (Woolf, 1953: 62), but he did not consider it worth-while listing Sheepshanks in the index. Ten years older than Virginia Woolf, Mary Sheepshanks was the rebellious daughter of a bishop. She had studied at Newnham (where Virginia's aunt had been principal), and then worked in a settlement in Southwark. After she became Principal of Morley College, she persuaded Virginia to give evening-classes to working-people, a task Virginia took seriously. During the First World War, Mary Sheepshanks was an active member of the UDC. She continued to edit *Jus Suffragii*, the newspaper of the International Woman Suffrage

Alliance, maintaining a non-belligerent stance by publishing international news and pacifist letters from abroad. Amongst these was the letter from Dutch suffragists which led to the staging of the Women's International Congress at The Hague in 1915. Sheepshanks was one of many socialist-feminist friends, such as Margaret Llewellyn-Davies and Ethel Smyth, with whom Virginia Woolf continued to 'beat up the waters of talk'. They formed part of the supportive political base which underlay such books as *Three Guineas*, *A Room of One's Own* and *Mrs Dalloway*.

Since *Mrs Dalloway* concentrates particularly on the inner life of individuals, and on their society's repression of feelings which nevertheless continue to affect them powerfully, it is hard to judge how far Virginia Woolf was herself in conscious control of the patterns of evasion and allusion which she depicts. She herself disclaimed conscious direction in the plan of the book, abandoning early attempts at 'forecast', but, as Reuben Arthur Brower has demonstrated, when the writer's vision is in action the integrity of the imagination pressures a design (Brower, 1951: 202). Recently, assessment of Virginia Woolf's fiction has been bound up with new biographical interpretations of her mental breakdowns. However, I take A. D. Moody's point that: 'her actual life and experience did not enter directly into her art, but was only its raw material' (Moody, 1963: 2). My interest is not primarily in Virginia Woolf's life. Rather, it lies in the novel, *Mrs Dalloway*, as publicly published for a wide readership of people not intimately acquainted with her. How does the novel's field of force relate the suicide of a First World War veteran, a shabby, insignificant clerk, to a lady of high society, in such a way that her private response to that suicide forms the climax to the novel? What is the visionary design created by the iterated imagery?

Mary Hamilton recorded that right from 1914 shell-shocked soldiers were recognisable among the casualties brought home from the Front. And, as we see from Rose Macaulay's writing, their anguished behaviour was deeply distressing to other people. Some soldiers went incurably mad. The poet, Ivor Gurney, was one. Others, with kind and sympathetic treatment, recovered. Cynthia Asquith describes in her diary how she tried to understand her husband's 'unhinged' reaction to the strain of artillery work at the Front, which took the form of violently smashing ugly things and 'talking with tremendous feeling, even tears, of the sufferings and gallantry of the men and officers . . . he has a sense that the beauty of their heroism is not appreciated' (Asquith, 1968: 80). His own father, then Prime Minister, was unable to talk to his sons about their war experience and never mentioned it: 'He likes to blink facts and avoid being confronted by anything unpleasant . . . Beb [her husband] rather feels it, as it is always soothing – at least it generally is – to talk about one's experiences' (391).

However, poets wrote about it, notably Siegfried Sassoon and Wilfred Owen. Virginia Woolf was by conviction a pacifist, and it was through her pacifist connections that she was persuaded to review a volume of Sassoon's poetry for the *TLS* in May, 1917. She found that

> What Mr Sassoon has felt to be the most sordid and horrible experiences in the world he makes us feel to be so . . . we say to ourselves 'Yes, this is going on; and we are sitting here watching it,' with a new shock of surprise, with an uneasy desire to leave our place in the audience.

This suggests that she thought it right for literature to have a political effect, to jolt people out of passively regarding the War as a spectacle, although she herself undertook no overt action either for or against it. Her brother-in-law, Clive Bell, had quickly responded in writing. In the Spring of 1915 he published a pacifist pamphlet, *Peace at Once*, urging a negotiated settlement. The pamphlet was just as speedily destroyed in the summer of 1915, by order of the Lord Mayor of London.

Reviewing a novel in 1917, Virginia Woolf suggested that the War was towering too closely and tremendously to be worked into fiction yet (*TLS*, 1917: 104). She herself did not gain the necessary perspective until 1920, when she began what Winifred Holtby called 'her war book', *Jacob's Room*. This was an attempt to ascertain just what her society had lost in the deaths of so many young men like Rupert Brooke, or Charles Sorley, not fully formed yet. *Jacob's Room* is scathing about the impassive attitude of 'the men in clubs and cabinets' to the smooth accuracy by which, equally, youths are killed or traffic conducted. By such clubmen and Cabinet Ministers, she meant people like her uncle, Herbert Fisher, who was 'in the very centre of the very centre' at Downing Street during the War (Woolf, 1977: 204). It was not until a couple of years later still that Virginia Woolf found a way of displaying the personal consequences of that impassive discipline and its 'manful' determination to control the course of history. It was also a way of conveying to the alien masculine consciousness what lay behind apparent feminine passionlessness. Through it she achieved what she had apparently despaired of, a way of elucidating her own mental breakdowns.

By the time Virginia Woolf came to write *Mrs Dalloway* there had been a great deal of public interest in 'shell-shock'. Public discussion of the question had included not only poetry but learned articles and books on the subject, even a Parliamentary Report. The Committee's terms of reference were 'To consider the different types of hysteria and traumatic neurosis, commonly called "shell-shock"; . . . and to advise whether by military training or education, some scientific method of guarding against its occurrence can be devised'.

It is that official attitude, that Parliament, through the law, could deal with 'the most dejected of miseries', which Clarissa Dalloway is scornful of from the moment we first encounter her, loving life 'with an absurd and faithful passion'. This love of life, which she has in common with even 'the veriest frumps', is what she celebrates in her parties: despite all objective differences of class and money, she subjectively shares a common humanity with the down and out. And it is his repeated attempts, in the midst of his hypersensitive ecstasy, to try to be scientific, which accentuate the particular desperation of Septimus Warren Smith: 'for one must be scientific above all things' (Woolf, 1925: 76). The logical impossibility of objectively 'proving' such revelations as that 'heaven was divinely merciful, infinitely benignant' or 'Beauty, the world seemed to say', prevents either his 'madness', or his soul, from being scientifically intelligible. Yet, however frivolous and empty-headed Clarissa may be, however prudish and snobbish, she recognises the objective, scientific attitude to the life of the spirit to be 'obscurely evil' (204). It is her recognition of that evil at the heart of her society, that it can make life *in*tolerable, and her empathy with the young man's determination to preserve his inner life against the scientific violation of his soul, that forms the epiphany of *Mrs Dalloway*.

The society which Virginia Woolf describes in *Mrs Dalloway* is one which suppresses emotion, especially grief ('The War was over, except for . . . Lady Bexborough who opened a bazaar, they said, with the telegram in her hand, John, her favourite, killed'). In her critical book, *The Common Reader* (1925), which she was working on at the same time as composing *Mrs Dalloway*, Virginia Woolf judged the European War to have been such a vast catastrophe that confrontation with the horror and suffering would have been intolerable. Direct emotional response to it would have blinded and bewildered (Woolf, 1925, B: 43). Grief for the dead could only be expressed indirectly, as through the satiric poetry of Siegfried Sassoon or Wilfred Owen. What she valued in Sassoon's poetry was that he managed to awaken his readers to what he himself had felt. Behind his jaunty statements were loathing and hatred, emotions which are usually firmly prohibited. She had noticed at the time how the young soldiers she encountered on leave or convalescing seemed indifferent to their shocking experiences, and yet Sassoon voiced very powerful emotions on their behalf. For instance, in December 1917 when Philip Woolf, her brother-in-law, was recovering from injuries that he had received from a shell-burst which killed his brother Cecil, she noted in her diary: 'To me, Philip looked well; though there was that absentmindedness which one sees in Nick [Bagenal]. I suppose to Philip these days pass in a dream from which he feels himself detached. I can imagine he is puzzled why he doesn't feel more' (Woolf, 1977: 92). The medical papers published on shell-shock suggested that hysteria was caused by the repression of powerful experiences, and then the repression of that repression – a theory of Freud's which we now take for granted but which was still being established at that time. What soldiers were diagnosed as particularly repressing were fear and grief. It is fear which haunts the thoughts of Clarissa Dalloway.

Running through her mind on the midsummer's day in 1923 is the beginning of the dirge from *Cymbeline*, spoken over the body of the perfect wife, Imogen, who, although lifeless, is not actually dead:

> Fear no more the heat o' the sun
> Nor the furious winter's rages.

But Clarissa is not actually dead either, and she is afraid. She fears the plunge into experience, which may mean grief and pain; but she also fears the absence of emotion, the numbness that will signify the death of the spirit. She resents other people forcing their emotions on her to gain her emotional response; but she is equally frightened of emotional isolation. She enjoys the impersonal uproar of London, but avoids close personal involvement. She is terrified of life and of death: 'How unbelievable death was!' (Woolf, 1925: 135).

On the day of the novel, the day she is to give a party, both Clarissa Dalloway and Peter Walsh are obsessed with the events of 30 years before. They are both still struggling with the question of why Clarissa refused Peter and married Richard Dalloway instead. Peter was clearly passionately in love with her, and 'she had borne about her for years like an arrow sticking in her heart the grief, the anguish' of having rejected him. In fact, despite all the references to Darwin, to breeding and refinement, to the advantages of an advanced civilisation, Clarissa feels primitive emotions such as hatred and love very violently. On that day, after five years away in India, Peter comes to visit her. He quickly disturbs her hard-won tranquillity: 'thrown by uncontrollable forces, thrown through the air, he burst into tears' and she responds by taking his hand and kissing him, experiencing 'the brandishing of silver-flashing plumes like pampas grass in a tropic gale in her breast' (52). However, they regain their composure.

Shortly afterwards in Regent's Park, Peter, who had not 'the ghost of a notion what anyone else was feeling' (52), reflects that there was always something cold about Clarissa, a sort of timidity which had become conventionality; she was timid, hard, arrogant, prudish. He diagnoses this as 'the death of the soul'. He had felt in her a profound coldness, a woodenness, an impenetrability, which made him call her 'the perfect hostess' in order to wound her, which it did. He concludes that women 'don't know what passion is. They don't know the meaning of it to men' (89). His thoughts are interrupted by the sound of a battered old woman singing. She is standing in the gutter and voicing an ageless, wordless, primeval lament for a long-dead lover, a song of ever-prevailing love:

ee um fah um so
foo swee too eem oo.

It is the sound of an ancient spring, an old bubbling, burbling song which spouts from the earth, cheerfully imploring: 'Look in my eyes with thy sweet eyes intently, give me your hand and let me press it gently, and if someone should see, what matter they?' (90–3). This is the abandoned, enigmatic expression of woman's passion, a soft entreaty. Peter, of course, does not recognise any connection between such a frump and Clarissa. He merely hands the woman a coin.

Earlier Clarissa had been pondering on the fact that, although a virginity clung to her, she did undoubtedly feel at times what men felt: she fell in love with women. And she recollects clearly the feeling that she felt the summer she refused Peter, a feeling for her friend, Sally Seton. But it had purity and integrity, and a quality that she thought could only exist between women, which sprang from a sense of their being in league together: it was disinterested and protective, in fact 'chivalrous' (39). The most exquisite moment in her whole life had come when Sally kissed her on the lips, but she was shocked by what she felt as Peter's sneering hostility to this, his jealousy, his determination to break up their companionship.

Although Clarissa claims purity for her feelings, which is expressed through the harmless passivity of flowers, women's emotions are in fact physically arousing like men's. It was extremely difficult for Virginia Woolf to find a way of indicating this, partly because of the law about obscenity (which censored both Joyce's and D. H. Lawrence's portrayals of the physicality of human emotion), but also because the taboo about women, or rather 'ladies', even having any physical awareness not only prevented women from displaying themselves physically but extended to the written expression of female feelings. There were matters it was indecent for a woman to be conscious of, let alone to mention in print. 'A lady is known by her gloves' (13) and she must wear them not only in public but even in the privacy of her own mind. The consciousness of such rules of feminine decorum was caricatured by Virginia Woolf as 'The Angel in the House' in her talk *Professions for Women* (1931). There she identified the first part of the occupation of a woman writer to be 'Killing the Angel in the House'. That done, the second difficult task she faced was in telling the truths about her own experiences as a body, about the passions, which it would be thought by men to be 'unfitting', 'shocking', for her to write.

Virginia Woolf found certain strategies to express what her society insisted on keeping hidden. Clothes, blinds and curtains were the outward sign of its propriety. So in her novel doors and windows are the access to sensuous experience; a pink face appearing at a window is flushingly registering that experience. Tears betray emotion. In the space behind the window is the secret self. The hand that draws a blind down is decorously gloved; but the wind that makes the blind flap is the breath of spontaneous life. To indicate the physicality of emotions and to convey the nature of private mental experience Woolf developed these basic signs through a range of associated metaphors and symbolism. (This is to some extent the same strategy by which, according to Freud, the unconscious disguises itself and may be read.) It gives her work a resonant vibrancy akin to Shakespeare's later poetry.

Her depiction of Septimus's mind is partly an exploration of the poetic imagination diving into the unconscious 'well of tears' of emotional memory, which is symbolised by water, and striving for inspiration in words to express this experience, using the sky as a symbol of the intellectual imagination. The 'seas' of emotion may drown one, or leave one dry and exhaustedly exposed in the effort to conquer them. At a simple level she uses imagery about birds and animals to indicate people's current emotional life. The uninhibited behaviour of dogs expresses bold, public displays of spontaneous affection and aggression, 'busy with the railings, busy with each other' (30); the more timid behaviour of birds expresses vulnerability. Ducks can swim happily, dive and fly, like gulls, but often birds crouch or perch apprehensively. Metaphors and similes to do with birds, swimming and flying, 'plunging', recur constantly throughout the novel. By contrast, the epithet 'dogged' makes Richard and Doris Kilman sound earthbound and prosaic.

Certain other symbols are present in the concrete reality that the novel depicts. Thus Peter continually plays with his pocket-knife, exhibiting 'bad manners' as he does so, by drawing attention to his body. The knife, by metaphor, stands for his wounding behaviour, his sharp insights and cutting language. It also stands for the undisciplined masculinity of this behaviour, which should be kept hidden in his trousers, like other obtrusive reminders of his nature. The other symbol which expresses Peter's lack of emotional control is the fountain with a leaky spout that dribbles incessantly like the tears that run down Peter's face. This fountain, a source of green fertility, hidden from the house by shrubs, is clearly phallic. Once that is grasped (in a manner of speaking) then the likening of the ancient singer to a funnel, a pump, her mouth to a 'hole in the [green] earth, muddy too, matted with root fibres' through which her song soaks, can be identified as vaginal imagery. Street women like her may be restrained by the police from throwing flowers, but the law cannot finally quell the passion which they voice. Her whole yearning body makes visible what Clarissa senses to be unseen, unknown about herself.

Clarissa insists she was right to marry Richard because, unlike Peter, who tried to force her to reveal her emotions, Richard respects her inner privacy, her right to be herself:

> And there is a dignity in people; a solitude; even between husband and wife a gulf; and that one must respect ... for one would not part with it oneself, or take it, against his will, from one's husband, without losing one's independence, one's self-respect – something, after all, priceless. (132–3)

> But with Peter everything had to be shared; everything gone into. And it was intolerable. (10)

Richard wishes to give, not to take or dominate. He bandages her wounded dog and offers her flowers, the fragile symbol of fleeting happiness. Flowers stand for the way life-enhancing emotional experiences are stowed in the memory like seeds, to be nurtured and flourish with beauty later. Thus cherished, Clarissa remains psychically inviolate like a nun. Attempts to disturb her cool, inner peace she repels, in retreat from passion. But the sterile emotional loneliness of this state is indicated by the green linoleum and dripping tap in the bathroom, and by the tight narrow bed in her attic-bedroom. Richard takes a hot-water bottle to his solitary bed.

Although Clarissa is attracted to women as well as men, she fights off her awareness of female physicality and fleshly needs. These are made manifest in the grotesque figure of her daughter's history tutor, Doris Kilman, who perspires heavily in a green mac. Clarissa's ambition for social success, to be envied as a refined and charming hostess, is precisely what marks out Doris Kilman as an undesirable failure. The exact antithesis of Clarissa, frustrated and graceless, poor and a spinster, intellectual and politically conscious, Kilman has made the War into a personal grievance that stands for all her bitterness against life. Her very existence reveals the vanity and self-love on which Clarissa's contentment is founded, as Clarissa is resentfully aware. Clarissa finds Kilman's envious, voracious lust to dominate and humiliate her even more threatening than Peter's egocentric rapacity.

Such egotism is evinced in an animal greediness for food, which selfishly disregards the wishes of others. It is a sense of self-importance, shared by Hugh Whitbread and Miss Kilman, which tries to force others to submit. Even domineering women of high rank like Lady Bruton finally feel inferior enough to defer to male authority. That is the public pattern required by the State: disciplined submission to authority. It is also the pattern imposed privately: women like Evelyn Whitbread and Lady Bradshaw weakly surrender to their husband's will, losing their own identity as separate individuals. They become little better than acquisitions, possessed through marriage so that no other man may have them. This is the death that Clarissa fears. That through the extreme heat of passion, or the cold of emotional deprivation, she would be coerced into the submission of her own identity. Not sharing Sally's reckless self-confidence, Clarissa protects her emotional autonomy.

The novel as a whole can be seen to lay out patterns of behaviour, patterns of social relationship, both public and private, which display the evil of a greed for power, and the forms of resistance to it. The overall effect of *Mrs Dalloway* is to demystify social prestige and the blind religious respect by which it is maintained. The enduring symbol of power is the discreet 'car' which forces its way through, up 'Brook Street', burning, throbbing with a pulse that drums through the entire body. Hidden behind the civilised veneer lies physical desire converted into the ambition for social success. Society's pressure to conform to the conventions of the pack, enforces the surrender of personal integrity. The concomitant concern about 'what people will think' exerts a deadly price. Clarissa's horrified determination to preserve her own identity and to respect the dignity of other people's individuality is weak indeed against the danger that Septimus fears. The pistol-shot and the whip-lash which they hear are the signs of society's threat against non-conformity. It could mean prison or the lunatic asylum. Or the water-cure for lesbianism, which Katherine Mansfield was forced to endure (Alpers, 1980: 96). The price of inner freedom is outward conformity. But the self-control required by society may lead to inward rigor, too. The novel constantly mocks pompous solemnity but reveals it as menacing, even to the simple delight in being alive.

The novel posits an attracting antagonism between the values of Clarissa and those of Peter Walsh. His key-ideas of 'civilization' (which he admires) and 'sentimentality' (which he despises) are exposed by the novel as not merely complacent shams, but deadening. What he identifies as 'one of the triumphs of civilization', an example of 'the communal spirit of London' (167), is the ambulance carrying off the mangled body of Septimus. The imperial civilisation which Peter as a third-generation Anglo-Indian both represents and upholds, imposes a religion of duty and self-sacrifice, stamped 'indelibly in the sanctuaries of others' (113). This code of self-discipline is promoted by public-schools and epitomised in imperial heroes such as Gordon. It is a discipline that mechanically represses any spontaneous emotional response to life as 'sentiment' and substitutes the artificial thrill of patriotism, felt in the thighs. The result is the effigy of a man, a statue, an 'empty tomb' (57). The 'self' has been dutifully 'sacrificed'.

Living flowers become a wreath. The conventions of this society require a rigid 'manliness' or 'gentlemanliness' and an upright 'ladylike' posture combined with 'feminine' charm, which have refined and deadened the 'miracle of life' into the efficient decisiveness of the humbug, Sir William Bradshaw, the punctiliousness of that lackey, Hugh Whitbread, and the polished entertaining of artificial Mayfair hostesses. There is a 'grand deception' practised by such citizens; the 'profound illusion' they generate is that the smooth operation of their civilisation functions 'voluntarily' and is 'not paid for' (115). The society Peter Walsh respects rests on a deceit which, for all the celebration of the Unknown Warrior, masks what is finally paid for it in war, by 'those thousands of poor chaps, with all their lives before them, shovelled together' (128). The system of authority which supports this sham – judges, doctors, police – relies on the power to shut people up. The state can force people to live or force them to die. Using ideas of 'religion' or 'love', it has the power to coerce an inner conformity, which is the real death of the soul. When the anarchic Sally Seton claims at Clarissa's party that one must say simply what one feels, poor Peter Walsh, in late middle-age, responds that he does not know what he feels.

Lacking any passionate emotional involvement, Clarissa finds that there is an 'emptiness about the heart of life' (35). The ominous lines 'Fear no more ...' also pass through Septimus Warren's mind. He too suffers from isolation in marriage, but is less able to deceive himself about the cause.

Septimus came to London to be a poet, and volunteered in the War to defend an England that consisted largely of Shakespeare and of his romantic love for the woman who taught him about poetry. Isabel Pole introduced him to *Antony and Cleopatra*. This play about extra-marital passion and empty, diplomatic marriage reveals what is wrong with the marriages of both Clarissa and

Septimus. The appreciation of Shakespeare, the national poet, is a key to the values of the British 'governing-class'. Lady Bruton has a patriotic ability to misremember bits of *Richard II*, but Dalloway solemnly believes that no decent man ought to read Shakespeare's sonnets. Like Shakespeare, and like Clarissa, Septimus is what is crudely called bi-sexual; that is, he is capable of loving both men and women. During the war he loved an officer called Evans; their mutual affection is described in terms of the spontaneity of dogs playing good-temperedly together. When Evans was killed, Septimus showed no emotional reaction. In the army he had learned 'manliness', the self-discipline of not betraying what he feels. But he disguises his feelings from himself too and begins to believe that he actually feels nothing. In this state of emotional numbness the world loses significance for him, but he continues to do what is expected of him as a 'normal' man, and marries a young, emotional Italian girl. Like other shell-shocked soldiers who repressed their grief, he begins to see the dead in the living. (Graves describes such an event in *Goodbye to All That*.) When Rezia presses him to have children and cries at his lack of response, he can maintain the charade no longer.

In this there is also something like Clarissa. She never recalls to mind witnessing the sudden death of her sister, Sylvia, caused by her father's carelessness; but Peter remembers the event and attributes her coldness to her idea then that behaving like a lady somehow shielded her from bitterness. 'Ladylike' behaviour has much in common with 'manliness'. In Septimus's case his wife is unable to defend him from the consequences of his despair. Once he speaks of committing suicide the law is invoked to prevent him. The psychiatrist, Sir William Bradshaw, a 'priest of science' who knows nothing about the human soul, threatens to restore his 'normality' – forcibly converting him to a disciplined sense of proportion. At the idea that he is to be imprisoned and subjected to a force which will violate his very self, Septimus plunges to his death.

Septimus saw himself as a sacrificial scapegoat. That soldiers were sacrificing themselves for their country was a common platitude during the First World War. It was a platitude that was subverted by young poets. The idea that young men were being wilfully sacrificed by their callous fathers was the satirical theme of such poems as Osbert Sitwell's 'Arm-chair' and 'Abraham' and Wilfred Owen's 'The Parable of the Old Man and the Young'. In his poem 'Insensibility', Owen called soldiers happy, if, like Septimus, their emotions had been cauterised by the War, but he cursed those who, never having been at the Front, had no feelings of compassion to stir. Septimus is the scapegoat for his society's denial of humanity. The society that Peter Walsh finds a tolerable show, is fundamentally militaristic. Despite the fact that 'the War is over', young men are still being trained to repress their vital spontaneity, to keep in step, carrying guns. They have imperialist values drummed into their very thoughts: 'duty, gratitude, fidelity, love of England' (57). A respect for these values is conditioned into them, just as sexual propriety is part of the conditioning of young ladies. Soldiers manifest the extreme form of social control, their rigid behaviour caricaturing the unfeeling impersonality that is expected of them, so that they hardly know what irreticent, sensuous pleasure they have renounced. When Septimus chose to kill himself, he grabbed the only freedom left him. By throwing himself through a window, he made public his inward defiance of the idea of duty. During the War young soldiers shot themselves in the trenches to escape 'the hell where youth and laughter go'. Civilian society is a worse inferno.

During the War, under the editorship of Mary Sheepshanks *Jus Suffragii* published various articles on women and war jointly authored by Mary Sargant Florence and C. K. Ogden. These were to form part of the (anonymous) pamphlet, *Militarism versus Feminism*, published by Allen & Unwin in 1915, which received reviews in respectable journals such as the *TLS*. The main thesis of this widely researched pamphlet was to show the connection between militarism and the position of women in society. Florence and Ogden argued that militarism by its very nature implied the subservience of women. They corroborated this thesis by a mass of empirical evidence. (One of the matters referred to was the revelation by two American women in 1899 of the British Army regulations regarding the provision of prostitutes for the 'benefit' of British soldiers in India.)

This was one of many wartime publications which discussed the nature of gender definitions and their effect on the role of women, taking up the current debate on the political capability of women and relating it to the vital question of a society based on war and military repression. For instance, Catherine Marshall (later to be secretary to the No Conscription Fellowship) published two articles concerning women and militarism: one in *Common Cause: Organ of the National Union of Women's Suffrage Societies* in 1915, the other in the *Labour Year Book* for 1916. She defined militarism as 'a belief in the supremacy of force'. It is the desire to dominate rather than co-operate. A militarist is one who justifies the use of power to compel submission to his desires, without any further sanction than his own conviction that those desires are reasonable. Militarism favours those in possession of power of whatever kind, enabling them to impose their will on others. A monopoly of power can be used to exploit the weak, whether they be small nations, workers, or women, thus reducing human beings to ciphers.

Virginia Woolf was drawing on this political background when she connected Clarissa Dalloway's emotional frigidity with the suicide of a mad veteran. Both characters suffer from the emotional restraint inculcated by the Victorian values of the British Empire, which relied on military discipline for its maintenance. In order to protect himself from violation, from an interfering investigation of his unorthodox sexuality, Septimus literally kills himself to escape from Dr *Holmes*. Septimus was a war-hero. His reaction is not due to 'funk' but to despair. In a parallel situation where Peter, like Holmes, barges in on Clarissa's sanctuary, she too moves to protect her privacy. Outraged, 'like a virgin protecting chastity', she summons up her marriage 'to beat off the enemy' (45–50). To defend herself from Peter's emotional interference, his bullying demand to know the truth, she has committed an emotional suicide by marrying Richard. As a married lady she is 'safe', but her snobbery and her fear of passion have cut her off from the two people who really matter to her: Sally and Peter.

She has 'wreathed about' her dormant passion. The romantic flowers of memory which she falsely offers to Kilman instead, the poor woman squashes. Kilman needs human communion, not token substitutes. Frustrated, she becomes desperate, unable to feed or kill her physical desire. Nor can Clarissa ignore it. As Virginia Woolf makes clear at the beginning of the novel, Kilman is Clarissa's secret self, the physical monstrous self which 'perspires' revealing hidden longings from the depths of Clarissa's soul. Identical with the vagrant in the gutter, and with Septimus Warren, hers is the primeval moaning 'of no age or sex' which is the true source of poetry. She is the unladylike, frumpish part of Clarissa, which only makes a public appearance in doggishly 'snuffing in' the scent of flowers. Divided by class, their passionate attachment is one of hatred instead of love.

It was a fundamental problem for early feminists that being a lady was as much a matter of class as of gender. Women who remained 'ladies' retained their class privileges, but they had to surrender their passionate nature. On the other hand, women who took over the 'masculine' privileges of education and politics lost their 'femininity': 'unsexed', they lowered themselves. This erupted in divisions in the women's suffrage movement such as the split in the Pankhurst family. Christabel preached patriotic chastity to conservative ladies, while Sylvia lived amongst the working-class women of the East End and gave birth to an illegitimate son. As we can see from Cicely Hamilton's novel *William*, and from *Mrs Dalloway*, it was a psychological problem for individual women too, which was experienced as a split in the psyche. It was necessary for either the 'feminine', ladylike side of the personality to atrophy, or for the liberated, 'masculine' part to be frozen out. It is clear from *Mrs Dalloway* that Virginia Woolf considered women just as vulnerable to male rapacity as Cicely Hamilton did. But a woman who 'played the man' would never 'come first' with someone of 'the opposite sex', whichever that was taken to be. Violated either way, women were left with a rankling sense of grievance, a gradual rusting and corrosion of the spirit which Septimus's death enacts. They were wounded by rusty spikes, a spear-thrust through their inmost self.

Virginia Woolf's novel covertly examines the Victorian notion of self-sacrifice, while displaying the implicit bullying which feminists had long claimed was an integral aspect of an imperialist, and hence militaristic, state. For her, at the heart of the darkness of imperialism lay the alienation of women which resulted from the perversion and suppression of personal feelings. Yet, despite the death of Clarissa's soul, the novel – like other elegies which it resembles, such as Milton's *Lycidas* – holds out hope for the future. While opposing 'Darwinian' ideas of evolutionary progress (since, for all their refinement and breeding, women remain emotionally primitive) it lends support to socialist-feminism through the consciousness of Clarissa's daughter, Elizabeth, who dreams of choosing a profession and joining the sisterhood of the 'republic of women' (152). Woolf makes plain in the historical 'placing' of her women characters, Aunt Helen, Clarissa, Elizabeth, that women born in the 20th century had choices not open to Victorian women. There is consolation in the perpetual change of the clouds, the endless van of life.

It seems to me that Jane Marcus's view that 'Writing, for Virginia Woolf, was a revolutionary act' (Marcus, 1981: 1) is well substantiated by placing *Mrs Dalloway* in its historical setting. Her novel is not merely revolutionary; it is part of the women's revolution. Other literary works which challenged the political, sexual, or religious *status quo*, such as Joyce's *Dubliners* or *Ulysses* had difficulty in finding a publisher; or, when they had found one, were banned for 'obscenity' or treason, like Allatini's *Despised and Rejected*, Lawrence's *The Rainbow* or Norah C. James's *Sleeveless Errand*. But Virginia Woolf even gets away with describing a woman's orgasm (36). Then she ironically remarks on the fact that despite 'the enormous resources of the English language, the power it bestows, after all, of communicating feelings' (196), people inwardly live in separate, isolated rooms. The silver *fountain*-pen which pertinaciously drafts civilised letters to *The Times* may be essentially phallic, masculine. But the 'sacred well' of lyricism, the primeval, eternal source of song and poetry, is vaginal, feminine. Gleefully, her novel subverts the coercive power of the State and its religion, celebrating resistance to domination and conformity; claiming a communion across class and gender; even asserting that if the atheist can conceive of God, 'then in some sort she exists', not like a father almighty, but as a figure of compassion, comprehension, absolution, who bestows a general peace, the 'figure of the mother whose sons have been killed in the battles of the world' (64–5).

Mrs Dalloway shares a common background of political analysis with other fiction of the period, such as Katherine Mansfield's short story *The Fly* (which first appeared in *The Dove's Nest and Other Stories*, 1923). Since this story was included in her *Collected Stories*, and reprinted in many anthologies since, it seems appropriate to consider it here among the best-sellers.

The Fly functions indirectly. It is probably for this reason that this is the story of Katherine Mansfield's that has attracted most critical attention. The unsettled controversy stems from the story's unpalatable implications, which are more easily understood within the context of other writing about the Great War, alongside other fiction like *Mrs Dalloway*. Then the hints gain their full significance, for the story's range extends far beyond its setting in a boss's cosy office in the City of London, several years after the War. It is a succinct exposition of patriarchal power, of 'bossiness'. Mansfield obliquely applies the plaint from *King Lear* to the missing 'middle-term' of the analogy; as flies to boys, and men to gods, so *boys to men*:

> As flies to wanton boys, are we to th' gods,
> They kill us for their sport.
> (*King Lear*, Act IV, scene 1, 36–7)

The story crystallises the Great War myth of the sacrifice of the sons to the selfish ambitions of the fathers. This was the generational myth, expressed by Wilfred Owen, Osbert Sitwell and others, in poems that parodied the bible: Abraham obstinately insisted on sacrificing Isaac.

The central character is 'the boss'. His old employee, five years his younger, is presented as peering out of his friend's arm-chair like a baby peering out of a pram, so by implication the boss is a boy. He is an egoistic, thoughtless bully. Exactly like an overgrown schoolboy, he persecutes a fly by dropping blots of ink on it. Pluckily the fly tackles the task of escaping and recovering from each 'horrible danger'. The reader is encouraged to identify with the 'little beggar': 'Now one could imagine that the little front legs rubbed against each other lightly, joyfully'. The boss continues testing it until finally the draggled victim is dead. It is then flung into the waste-paper basket like so much rubbish, alongside the *Financial Times*.

The story is haunted by the six-years' old photo of 'a grave-looking boy in uniform standing in one of those spectral photographer's parks'. It is the photo of a young man killed in the War, the boss's only son. Whereas the boss wants to remember his son, rosily, as boyish, bright and 'his natural self', the photo portrays him as 'cold, even stern-looking', with an 'unnatural' expression.

The Boss's peace of mind is guarded by Macey, a sycophantic office-messenger like a watch-dog in a kennel. Macey is employed to keep out whatever might disturb the boss's comfort, his 'snug' self-satisfaction. But he could not exclude the telegram announcing the son's death. That death is a fact that the boss tries to disguise from himself. It reveals the complete futility of his power, which did not keep his son alive, and the futility of his life, since everything in his life had been done to enable his son to step into his shoes, 'carrying on where he left off'. To apprehend that futility results in 'a grinding feeling of wretchedness' that he is anxious to avoid. 'Grinding wretchedness' is usually associated with the poor, not with the successful.

The sport with the fly distracts him from his sense of wretchedness. It does not distract the reader. On the contrary, it enables us to recognise the truth about his relationship with his son, that he was as cruelly destructive of the boy's joy in life as he was of the fly's; and that his use of power is a way of evading emotional reality, which would threaten his self-esteem. What men regard as sport, kills their sons.

The last line of the story is the final thrust of the scalpel: 'For the life of him he could not remember'. It is the hint that he could not go on living if he faced up to reality, but also that he has evaded the real task of living by the repeated indulgence of an over-dramatised grief. He has coddled himself and swamped his life. In the light of the annual Remembrance Day ceremonies, 'We will remember', the last line is vibrantly sardonic.

But it is not the only source of the faint unease left by the story. The opening paragraph delicately suggests a further irony. In old age these god-like men become like babies again, to be boxed up and have their pleasures rationed by their women-folk. These women are as insensitive and unimaginative about the men as *they* were about flies and sons. The women's petty meanness and impotent revenge is a parody of the men's despotism. In the last analysis, the gods are that other term so ironically absent from Lear's ratio: 'the ladies'.

Virginia Woolf's subtle challenge to the established gender norms of her society was published by the Hogarth Press, a press which she had founded with her husband and which they jointly owned. Her novel revealed the perverted power of repressed desire, but this determination to indicate what her society kept hidden went unremarked by the establishment. A less wily novel provoked outright confrontation. The story of the censorship of Radclyffe Hall's *The Well of Loneliness* (1928) has often been told. Within six months of its publication, the book was banned in Britain under the Obscene Publications Act of 1857, on the grounds that 'it would tend to corrupt those into whose hands it might fall'. The decision was upheld on appeal, the view being reiterated that not only was the book corrupting, but 'that this is a disgusting book when properly read – a disgusting book'. The Court of Special Service in

New York disagreed. There the matter was seen as involving the American Constitutional guarantee of freedom of the press. The Judges, noting that the book dealt with a delicate social problem, considered that it did not do so in a manner which was 'obscene, lewd, lascivious, filthy or indecent'. They therefore determined that *The Well of Loneliness* did not violate American Penal Law.

Marguerite Radclyffe-Hall had already won both the Prix Femina Vie Heureuse and the James Tait Black prize of 1927 for her fourth novel, *Adam's Breed* (against such competition as Liam O'Flaherty's *The Informer*). She now became a celebrity as her publisher engineered a *cause célèbre* which gained *The Well of Loneliness* worldwide sales. All three trials were highly publicised. Such famous authors as Virginia Woolf, E. M. Forster and Rose Macaulay were among 40 writers who had accepted an invitation to attend the first trial, prepared to speak on behalf of the book. (They were not called; the magistrate ruled that the book's literary merits were beside the question.) The book was widely and seriously reviewed. Its passage through the courts was recorded and its message was discussed in the dailies and in the Sunday newspapers. Indeed, it was an editorial in the *Sunday Express* which triggered off the legal proceedings:

> ... sexual inversion and perversion are horrors which exist among us today. They flaunt themselves in public places with increasing effrontery and more insolently provocative bravado. The decadent apostles of the most hideous and loathsome vices no longer conceal their degeneracy and their degradation ... they seek [publicity], and they take a delight in their flamboyant notoriety. The consequence is that this pestilence is devastating young souls. (Dickson, 1975: 149)

Jonathan Cape, Hall's publisher, had himself drawn these opinions to the Home Secretary's attention, thus precipitating the book's prosecution.

The Well of Loneliness is a surprisingly reticent work to have achieved such notoriety. The famous few words '. . . and that night they were not divided' could hardly have been more restrained. The novel is strongly moral and religious. And, perhaps even more surprisingly, it is a work which upholds 'respect for the normal': 'the love that existed between [ ] parents ... – children, a home that the world would respect, ties of affection that the world would hold sacred' (Hall, 1928: 501–2). But it ended with a plea for open acknowledgement of 'inverts', a public claim for the right to a homosexual existence. And it was that wish for the public recognition of lesbianism that was denied when the novel was banned.

Not that Radclyffe Hall's was the first novel to have dealt with a homosexual relationship between women. One of the best-sellers of the war-period, a work first brought out in 1917, frequently republished and still in print today, was Winifred Ashton's first novel, *Regiment of Women* (written under the pseudonym 'Clemence Dane'). It was concerned with the counter-claims of female bonding and heterosexual marriage. Broadly it follows the lines of earlier comic novels on the same theme, such as Mrs Lynn Linton's *The Rebel of the Family* (1880) and Henry James's *The Bostonians* (1886): an innocent girl is rescued from a predatory relationship with an older woman by an ardent young man. However, whereas the earlier novels were explicitly concerned with feminism and the fight for women's suffrage (feminists being caricatured as sour, man-hating lesbians), these particular political topics were steadfastly ignored by Winifred Ashton. Nor did they form any part of Radclyffe Hall's interest.

Born in the early 1880's, like Rose Macaulay and Virginia Woolf, Ashton and Hall belonged to the age of what Esther Newton has called the second generation of New Women (Newton, 1984: 562). By this time the first generation of New Women had gained access to higher education and the professions. They battled to maintain their autonomy through supportive romantic friendships in place of marriage, and they flourished in a segregated world of all-female institutions. *Regiment of Women* is concerned with the monstrosity of just such an all-female world as exemplified in a school for girls. It displays the evil selfishness inherent in the 'monstruous empire of a cruell woman', in order to show that 'naturally' one cannot weigh 'the most intimate, the most ideal friendship against the chance of getting married' (335). A friendship between women is vampirism; it deflects 'from its natural channel, the strongest impulse of any girl's life . . . [She] needs a good concrete husband to love' (334). A woman without a man is a failure, unfulfilled. Following the conventions of the romantic novel, *Regiment of Women* ends by reasserting orthodox gender distinctions. The fact that the monstrous woman with the significant name of Clare Hartill is not prepared to consider the happiness of her lover, Alwynne, before her own, is sufficient indication of the worthlessness of her love beside a man's.

Radclyffe Hall, concerned to query the dominant sexual paradigm, paradoxically also re-inforces it. Her monstrous woman, the 'invert' Stephen Gordon, cannot marry the woman she loves. To counter the charge of unnatural egoism levelled against such women as Clare Harthill, Hall shows Stephen's love to be as noble as any man's by having her heroically sacrifice her own happiness to prevent the 'spiritual murder' of the woman she lives with. Stephen arranges for Mary Llewellyn to have the social acceptability granted by respectable marriage to a man who loves her. As Jean Radford puts it: 'in Radclyffe-Hall's inverted romance, the heroine becomes a "hero" by renouncing the love of a woman' (Radford, 1986: 110). Radclyffe Hall's novel follows the other pattern of Victorian romance, displayed in such works as Harraden's *Where Your Treasure Is* and Delafield's *The Pelicans*. Rather than ending 'happily ever after' with marriage, an earthly, physical satisfaction is resigned in favour of the greater spiritual gain of triumphant self-sacrifice.

In the Victorian period there was no suggestion that relationships between women involved any sort of 'indecent' intimacy. Indeed, Esther Newton has convincingly argued that since sexuality was seen as essentially 'phallic', and women were regarded as the passive objects of male desire, whether genital intimacy was involved or not, a relationship between women could not be conceived of as sexual. Even such highly conventional writers as Mrs Humphry Ward represented 'the tender and adoring friendship of women for women' as intense and passionate, but with no intended implication of lust, or of the perverted or the unnatural physical expression of feelings. But for the second generation of New Women personal relationships presented more difficulty. Part of the male rebellion against Victorian values was a new sexual freedom. As women pressed for access to opportunities which had been male prerogatives, an active, lustful sexuality became a recognised aspect of women's personal autonomy. But if women were to develop a lustful sexuality, with whom were they to express it? In answering this problem, 'the old feminist movement began to split along the heterosexual / homosexual divide that is ancestral to our own' (Newton, 1984: 564).

In Ashton's novel, it was possible to write that Clare 'put her arms round Alwynne and kissed her passionately and repeatedly. "Good-night, my darling," said Clare' (73) because Clare was to be criticised for this as self-indulgence. Her conscience, although keen-witted, might irritate her but it could not influence her actions by one hair's-breadth. This conscience was little more than an 'epicurean appreciation of what was guileless and beautiful and worthy' and it co-existed with 'the intellectualized sensuality of her imperious and carnal personality' (182). Her final loneliness was due to her conceited contempt for other people, even those who loved her. At the end of the book, 'Faces rose about her, whispering reminders, forgotten faces of the many who had loved her' (345). These include one little girl who was driven to kill herself by jumping out of a window, as a result of thwarting Clare's capricious desires. Loneliness is the deserved retribution for perverted sensual appetite. And a woman's sensuality is perverted if it does not submit to its natural fulfilment in a carnal relationship that leads to children.

Hall's novel also ends with her homosexual heroine left alone. However, in place of the agonies of loneliness, Stephen suffers the rocketing pains of giving birth to a sterile burden of sound: 'the room seemed to be thronging with people . . . the quick, the dead, the yet unborn' (509–10). They are the socially stigmatised clamouring on Stephen to ask God why they were outcast. Named after the first Christian martyr, she becomes a fierce parody of the Virgin Mother, the Mater Dolorosa, suffering to articulate a birth-cry, the inverts' prayer for a right to exist. The book, *The Well of Loneliness*, is itself the fruit of the novelist's womb. It discharges not the thin, enigmatic song of the battered old vagrant in *Mrs Dalloway*, which merely stains the pavement, but, dropping scorching tears of fire on the spirit, 'a demand like the gathering together of great waters'. It is on this demand that the book climaxes: 'Acknowledge us, oh God, before the whole world. Give us also the right to our existence' (510).

Hall's use of the term 'invert' indicates her debt to the theories of Havelock Ellis. The original edition of *The Well of Loneliness* carried a foreword by Ellis, stating that the book possessed 'a notable psychological and sociological significance'. A friend of Edward Carpenter and, like Carpenter, a socialist, Havelock Ellis was one of the pioneers of the study of human sexuality. At that time psychology was a new discipline, and British psychologists were anxious to ensure its respectability as a 'positive science' in place of mental philosophy. Making every effort to document his evidence, Ellis commenced his monumental work, *Studies in the Psychology of Sex* at the end of the 19th century. The first volume, *Sexual Inversion*, was published in England and Germany in 1897. A

London bookseller was prosecuted for selling it and the book was suppressed as an 'obscene libel' under the Obscene Publications Act. Ellis did not attempt to defend the man or the book. He merely undertook never to publish 'sex books' in Britain again, and *Sexual Inversion* and the succeeding five volumes were published in America instead.

Another pioneering work on 'abnormal' sexuality, Richard von Krafft-Ebing's *Psychopathia Sexualis* (1886), had been published without trouble in London and Philadelphia in 1893. Neither the title nor the technical terminology were 'Englished'. The author explained that he had chosen that title in order to mystify 'unqualified persons'. He had felt 'compelled' to express himself in *terminis technicis*, and also 'to give certain particularly revolting portions in Latin'. As a socialist, Ellis had tried to write *Sexual Inversion* in a language accessible to the general reader. It was not reviewed in *The Lancet*. The editor, admitting the book's 'dispassionate and scientific style', gave as the reason partly that Ellis had not ensured that the book was restricted to a scientific audience, but also that Ellis (in agreement with Ulrichs, but differing from Krafft-Ebing) believed homosexuality to be natural and far more prevalent than was generally admitted. The editor concluded that Ellis's evidence would fail to convince medical men that 'homo-sexuality is anything else than an acquired and depraved manifestation of the sexual passion' and that it was 'especially important' that the matter should not be discussed by the man in the street, 'not to mention the boy and girl in the street' (Hynes, 1968: 162–3). Medical men were not, however, to be given the chance to judge for themselves. Nor were women, in the street, medical, or otherwise.

In her biography of Radclyffe Hall, Una Troubridge recorded that in June 1927 John (as Radclyffe Hall was known to her friends) discussed with her the possibility of writing a book about sexual inversion. John particularly wanted the book to be a novel in order to make the subject accessible to the general reader who did not have access to technical treatises. 'It was her absolute conviction that such a book could only be written by a sexual invert, who alone could be qualified by personal knowledge and experience to speak on behalf of a misunderstood and misjudged minority' (Troubridge, 1961: 81). Since Una had left her husband in order to live with John, and they had since been together for over ten years, any public condemnation resulting from a book based on John's own life would be bound to affect Una as well. However, Una pronounced herself 'sick to death of ambiguities' and only wishing to be known for what she was, so John went ahead. She worked compulsively on the book, long into the night, and completed it in under a year.

Havelock Ellis was not the only authority on homosexuality whose theories Radclyffe Hall consulted. Ellis's view was that 'true inversion' was natural, and therefore normal, because it was biologically determined. This relieved the true invert from guilt. Yet Krafft-Ebing, to whom Hall also refers, believed homosexuality to be degenerate. The woman who was a 'true invert' possessed masculine characteristics in a body which was masculine except for the genitals. Whereas Ellis, like Carpenter, believed in a 'third sex' (the 'effeminate man' or the 'masculine woman', who had the soul of one gender trapped in a body of the other – a theory dreamed up by Carl Heinrich Ulrichs, to whom Hall also refers), Krafft-Ebing thought homosexuality to be pathological, that is, abnormal. Lesbians were, for Krafft-Ebing, freaks. Furthermore, since women who were true inverts were masculine in all but genitals, they would wish to pair with 'womanly women' who were only lesbian by persuasion, being feminine in every way except for their attraction to a masculine woman. So a truly 'feminine lesbian' was a contradiction. Such women existed, but only through being perverted by born inverts, and were therefore decadent.

The central problem for all these theorists was the polarised way in which gender was conceptualised, and the fact that active sexuality was thought of as masculine, whereas feminine sensuality (if it existed at all, as modernists believed it did) was only reactive and had to be aroused. Such beliefs were self-fulfilling, and Radclyffe-Hall both as an author and in her personal life was caught up in the dilemma posed by the apparent contradiction in the idea of a feminine lesbian.

She was herself attracted to a non-materialist view of the psyche. Her 'War-service' consisted mainly in the attempted empirical investigation of spiritualism, and she saw no incompatibility between this and her devout catholicism. Radclyffe Hall must also have read what little had been published in English on the psycho-analysis of homosexuality. She refers to the work of the Hungarian psychoanalyst, Ferenczi, uses the Freudian terminology of 'libido' and 'complexes', and argues fluently about sexual repression. Her novel shows Stephen Gordon repeatedly involved in triangular relationships which echo the family nexus of her childhood, in which she rivals her father for her mother's affection which must be renounced in his favour. (Despite the attention which has been paid to the boy-child's Oedipal complex, there is still no clear understanding of the role of mother/daughter eroticism in lesbian sexuality.)

It is perhaps unfortunate that Radclyffe Hall saw her mission as popularising scientific theories of lesbianism, partly because these were all male-authored, partly because the theories were not mutually compatible, and partly because she perpetuated the gender polarisation on which were based. Had she been able to trust her belief in the invert's own authority of personal experience, she might have contributed to an improved comprehension of lesbianism. As it was, instead of penetrating her own life, Radclyffe Hall created a romantic fantasy. Although Lovat Dickson asserts that '*The Well of Loneliness* is the thinnest of disguises, with [Hall's] own upbringing romanticised' (Dickson, 1975: 9), in fact it significantly alters both the original family situation (Hall's father deserted her mother before she was born) and the character of the lesbian marriages that Hall knew from the inside. Seven years younger, Una Troubridge may have considered John's genius superior to her own, but she was herself a sculptress and a writer, and the mother of a daughter before she set up household with John in 1916. The year Una had married, 1907, was the year John went to live with the married woman, Mabel Batten, 'Ladye'. Ladye was 20 years her senior and taught her to take pride in herself. By contrast, Stephen Gordon does not take a mother substitute as her lover, nor a woman who is her social equal, but a sexually inexperienced girl. Radclyffe Hall wrote a polemic to defend the invert against the charge of depravity which implicitly conceded the evidence. And she left posterity with a stereotype of helpless femininity being mastered by 'butch' lesbianism which feminists have been trying to live down ever since.

However, whether or not *The Well of Loneliness* is the 'completely faithful and uncompromising' representation of social life as it existed in the 1920s which Havelock Ellis stated it to be, what is interesting is how Hall *imagined* the relationship between her lesbian hero, Stephen Gordon, and her 'wife', Mary Llewellyn. Stephen hates her own athletic, muscular body, 'like a monstrous fetter imposed on her spirit'; but her hate turns to self-pity, and she grieves over her desolate body. She only wishes to be manly in order to protect women, for women who are 'all woman' and 'purely feminine' are vulnerable. They cannot withstand the pressures of pain and poverty that result from their position in society, and from which marriage seems the only haven. Yet in marriage they are open to intimate cruelty from their husbands. Men are 'selfish, arrogant, possessive' (346). Like a man, Stephen is possessive; she wishes to 'bind Mary fast' in an exclusive relationship. But she does not wish to be masculine in two crucial respects: bullying or bloodlust. The horse, Raftery, (significantly named for an Irish poet) stands for Stephen's masculine joy in life, but she denies him the thrill of hunting that rouses in him the primitive, bestial memory of killing in battle, accompanied by an 'incredibly savage war-cry' of jubilation. Stephen is a good fencer, but she will not inflict pain. Unlike men she is merciful, and wants to succour and protect the helpless. In Krafft-Ebing's categorisation of lesbians, any aspiration to male privilege was a symptom of lesbianism, and the more masculine a woman was, the more degenerate a lesbian she was likely to be. For such a deviant, 'The consciousness of being a woman and thus to be . . . barred out from a military career, produces painful reflections' (Newton, 1984: 566). But militarism in itself has no appeal for Stephen. Yet she identifies with England at war, for England is a land 'of peace, of mothering hills, of home . . . fighting for her right to existence' (309). Although Marguerite Radclyffe Hall and Una Troubridge stayed in England during the First World War, mainly absorbed in private concerns, for Stephen Gordon the War was to be the opportunity to come into her own.

At first her pride is humbled because she can be of no use to her country. Every 'decent instinct of courage' that she has inherited, 'all that was male in her make-up', is frustrated since she is neither man nor woman:

She felt appalled at the realisation of her own grotesqueness; she was nothing but a freak abandoned on a kind of no-man's-land at this moment of splendid national endeavour. England was calling her men into battle, her women to the bedsides of the wounded and dying, and between the two chivalrous, surging forces, she, Stephen, might well be crushed out of existence. (311)

However, England at war needs even women of her sort. She joins the London Ambulance Column. Then she begins to recognise many more women like herself; each having 'crept out of her hole and come into the daylight' had been taken on to fill a man's place. They were accepted on their merits. The War gave such women the opportunity to find themselves, and 'a battalion was formed in those terrible years that would never again be completely disbanded' (316).

Stephen remains obsessed with one idea, 'to get out to the front'. Although an ambulance had managed to get to Belgium for a while and done fine service, Stephen Gordon lacks the influence to achieve anything similar. England does not send women to the front-line. Then in 1917 she is invited to join the *Breakspeare* Unit of Englishwomen attached to the French Army Ambulance Corps, as an ambulance-driver. In the forbidden zone, in Compiègne 50 yards behind the trenches, Stephen Gordon falls in love with another member of the Unit, the 20-year-old orphan Mary Llewellyn. Mary 'in all faith and innocence' turns to Stephen, and Stephen, engulfed by gentleness, tries to spare her the horror of the wounded. However, she puts her duty to the Unit before her anxiety about Mary's safety. They are all 'splendidly courageous and great-hearted women', and Stephen goes about her duties grimly, with unfailing courage and devotion. Her cheek is cut open by a splinter of shell, and she carries 'an honourable scar as a mark of her courage'. Then with other members of the Unit, she is awarded the Croix de Guerre, which is decorated with three stars each standing for a mention in dispatches. After the War, Mary goes to live with Stephen in Paris and is clearly in love with her, but Stephen's sense of honour restrains her from seducing the girl: 'A dastardly thing it would be to drag her through the maze of passion' without warning her that it would be impossible for Stephen to protect her from society's persecution of such love (347). She tries to 'play straight'. But Mary forces the issue '. . . and that night they were not divided' (361).

At first content with each other, they do not feel desolate outcasts, 'unwanted, despised of the world' (336). But gradually they need other friends. Their relationship gives them both 'loyalty, faith, consolation, devotion', a palliative for 'the wound of existence', but the social shamefulness of the arrangement is a chink in Stephen's armour. Stephen feels 'self-sufficient and strong, wonderfully capable of protecting', but this is an illusion. She cannot protect Mary from insults, from the social stigma attached to deviation from the sexual norms.

The War plays a similar function in several of Hall's works – making it possible for characters to display chivalrous qualities, especially courage, and to realise their own natures. Hall was typically Victorian in her belief that war releases human idealism, enabling people to serve the common good and to sacrifice themselves for others. As the disclaimer at the front of *The Well of Loneliness* indicates, Radclyffe Hall based her idea of the ambulance unit on historical facts. The reference to an ambulance that 'had managed to slip over to Belgium for a while and done some very fine service' (315), surely points to the Monro Corps which May Sinclair had helped to fund and which she accompanied to the Front in the first weeks of the War. The exploits of the corps were well-publicised (and Hall came to know May Sinclair personally). Its two heroic members, Mrs Knocker and Mairi Chisholm, seem to have been the inspiration for the friendship between Stephen Gordon and Mary Llewellyn. Although they were probably the most famous couple of war-heroines, Hall knew other women who had done similar war-service. Gertrude Stein and Alice B. Toklas drove their car around France, helping behind the lines. More importantly, Una Troubridge reports that Radclyffe Hall became very friendly after the War with 'Toupie' (Barbara) Lowther, another flamboyant lesbian (who was caricatured as Aurora Freemantle in Compton Mackenzie's lesbian satire, *Extraordinary Women*, 1928). Born in 1890, Lowther had been briefly married to an army-officer and divorced. In 1917, together with Miss 'Desmond' Hackett, she formed an all-women ambulance unit consisting of 20 cars and 25 women drivers, British, American and French. It operated alongside the French army on the Compiègne battlefront, and was mentioned in dispatches. Like Stephen Gordon, Lowther was awarded the Croix de Guerre.

In *The Well of Loneliness* Radclyffe Hall is concerned to deny that Stephen Gordon has the faults of masculinity – selfishness, possessiveness, lust, a bullying nature – whilst wishing to claim for Stephen the merits of manly chivalrousness. In fact she locks herself into the dilemma of her paradox: Stephen is to be manly but not like a man. Reciprocally, Mary Llewellyn must be a damsel, defined by her need for protection. She ends up as little more than an admiring mirror for Stephen's masculinity, a weak and trivial plaything kept solely for the amusement of her 'husband'. Stephen is revealed as selfish, possessive, lustful and cruel, despite her masochistic sacrifice at the end of the book. It is a sacrifice which, cruel to be kind, locks Mary into the passive, feminine role of a helpless victim with no say in her own fate.

An earlier work explores more openly the fantasy inherent in Hall's use of the war-time weakening of gender taboos. 'Miss Ogilvy Finds Herself' was a short story written just before *The Well of Loneliness*, in 1926. Boyish and athletic since childhood, vital, dauntless, commanding and domineering, at the outbreak of the First World War Miss Ogilvy was still a spinster at the age of 56. Feeling defrauded that she had not been born a man, she cut her hair and set up her own ambulance unit of English girls, 'fearlessly thrusting right up to the trenches' in their search for the wounded. The War had 'set Miss Ogilvy free'. It enabled her to live 'in a kind of blissful illusion', as competent, fearless, devoted and untiring, as any man could hope to be. Yet she still checks any deep emotion. After the War, she senses complete frustration again. Normal domestic life with her sisters seems trivial, and she suddenly sets off on an adventure. In a hotel on an island off the coast of Devon, she is shown a pre-historic skull. In response she experiences an overwhelming sense of outrage and unassuageable grief, so devastating she thinks it might be shell-shock. Then she apparently relives some former existence, as the consciousness (or the soul) in the male body to which the skull belonged. She is feeling immensely tall and 'the strongest man in our tribe'. Accompanying her is a woman, a 'hut of peace for a man after battle', who kneels at 'his' feet, whispering, 'My master'. His instinct is to menace beasts and slay his enemies, although thoughts of war always make his woman afraid. That night he possesses the woman for the first time, and while laying defenceless in their cave afterwards is apparently killed by his enemies. The next morning Miss Ogilvy is found dead in a cave by the sea.

The courage and sense of well-being experienced by Miss Ogilvy as a man is bound up with her physical strength, which is both admired and feared by her mate. The strength enables her to fight off rivals and possess the woman as 'mine', and the sexual act itself is expressed as a form of violent possession. It seems clear that for Radclyffe Hall masculine chivalry was militant and domineering, voracious and egotistical. In other words, while continually speaking of the virtue of courage, she is deflecting attention from the fact that masculinity was for her not merely freedom from domestic triviality, but competitive aspiration to power over women; femininity was the willing submission to superior force.

Although there is no accepted definition of a best-seller, a book that is still in paperback more than 50 years after its first appearance can at least be said to be a sales success. The reasons for that success must be as different in the case of the three novels I have just discussed as the novels are from one another. Presumably *The Return of the Soldier* has continued to please because of its genteel snobbery, its nostalgia for an innocent, romantic love that transgressed class-barriers, and its final endorsement of the institution of marriage. *Mrs Dalloway* shares most of those characteristics, but appeals to a more 'high-brow' readership due to its innovatory structure and use of metaphor. And in girls' schools round the world, *The Well of Loneliness* has been an underground classic as a 'safe', non-pornographic treatment of lesbian love, which also endorses bourgeois marriage. If we take John Sutherland's thesis that books which sell well are 'culturally embedded works' which are of interest for what they can tell us about society at the time they have done well, we may wonder what these particular books tell us about their 'host culture' of women's values (Sutherland, 1981: 5). (Remembering that *The Return of the Soldier* was dismissed by the *TLS*, *Mrs Dalloway* had the thumbs down from the Leavises, and *The Well of Loneliness* was actually banned, what sustained them when, for instance, the three war-time pacifist novels by women, which had a similarly in/auspicious beginning, disappeared leaving scarcely a trace?)

Contrary to Cockburn's views about best-sellers, those written for men-readers may very well largely take 'the situation on the private sector for granted', but best-sellers for women certainly regard the private status of women as requiring exposition. Women's personal relationships are their central theme, even in books dealing with one of the most public topics of all – war. However, the three later best-sellers are straightforwardly different from the three noteworthy pacifist novels by women that were published during the First World War and forgotten afterwards. In the earlier novels, women authors presented men as sensitive and vulnerable to the demands of the State, and permanent peace as not only desirable but a political possibility to be publicly worked for by women acting together. In the best-sellers which have remained in print ever since the War, women authors concentrate on women as the vulnerable ones. War and hostility are presented as a permanent, primitive feature of society, bound into the definition of femininity and the relation between the sexes. There is no suggestion that this could be intentionally altered. The books are not concerned to promote public political power; rather, they are about domestic power and social prestige. The books themselves may be public political acts, intended to influence opinion, but the question of, for instance, what women might do with their vote is not discussed within them.

What I myself find disturbing in these novels is that they all express very strong hatred between women. (This is surprising when one considers the mythology of supportive, loving relationships that were supposed to exist between women before the First World War, during the authors' formative years.) The hatred is between a cold, beautiful ladylike figure, and the sensuous woman who is branded a slut, an ugly monster, a freak: Kitty and Margaret, Mrs Dalloway and Miss Kilman, her mother and Stephen Gordon. The hatred becomes internalised as a hopeless sense of inferiority. Unlike the recent blockbusters Sutherland examined, these old best-sellers do not have the 'upliftingly happy or providential endings' that he invariably found. In each case the novel ends with the endorsement of a socially acceptable, restrained marriage between a lady and a gentleman, and the exclusion of the repulsive monster from an enchanted garden of paradise. However rebellious, they are recipes of despair.

It is conspicuous that, despite the example of Flora Sandes, none of these women writers wished to re-create the experience of men on active combat at the Front. Their imagination may have taken them into the Forbidden Zone behind the firing-line (from where they might view No-Man's-Land), but it goes no further. They do not attempt to relive trench-raids or bombing sorties, or bayonetting in self-defence, nor to explore the lives of men as comrades together without women. Since war inextricably involves the intentional killing and harming of other people, it is significant that these women do not imagine destruction from the point of view of the destroyer, but as passive sufferers or compassionate helpers of the victims. They can sympathise with pain and grief, which are the dominant emotions of all these novels. But never with the 'savage war-cry' of jubilant slaughter. Women imagine, not the world of male comradeship, but the extra-marital forbidden zone of free and equal women, where women are liberated from notions of ladylike behaviour or sexual sluttishness, and can become (gender-free) comrades, capable, competent people chivalrously succouring the weak and helpless.

However, just as for men the dream of fearless warriors gave way before the reality of the modern state: the military-machine, random death and shell-shock, followed by economic depression, so in these novels the women's dream of competent fellowship also melted away. Instead there is the re-assertion of female vulnerability masked by a hostile, ladylike control of sensuality. Men were left divided by generation; women by class.

It is worth recalling the comment by which Ray Strachey ended her history of the Women's Movement in Great Britain, *The Cause* (1928). Discussing the fiction of the period between 1837 and 1928 as exceedingly important to an understanding of women, she remarked that it could be used to measure the progress of the Women's Movement: 'The change in the type of heroine required for "best-sellers" is the real test, and it is not until the "strong, silent hero" ceases to "dominate" the gentle heroine that the end of the Women's Movement will have arrived' (Strachey, 1928: 420). I should like to adjust that prediction. It is not until women's imagination ceases to be dominated by ideas of the vulnerable maiden and the powerful married 'Lady', that the Women's Movement will have arrived.

6

Memoirs of a Generation

In *No Time Like the Present*, published in 1933, Storm Jameson wrote of herself as essentially a survivor of the Great War. Discussing what was being written from 1929 onwards she claimed that the only literature of any value that her generation would have to leave would be its war books. Their final value would be that they conveyed 'experience . . . that involved the whole self – of that time in the writer's life when he was most sharply alive' (Jameson, 1933: 149). (With fine judgement, she instanced *The Middle Parts of Fortune*, *Undertones of War*, *The Memoirs of an Infantry Officer*. These have indeed come to be considered an important part of our literary heritage.) It is curious that she assumed the authors of war books to be men, despite recognising that women were also affected by the War: women too, experienced 'the impalpable excitement fiddling on our nerves'. Yet, paying the inevitable tribute, which entailed the downgrading of women's lives, she explained in passing why the account of women's experience would be of less value: the war pressed more lightly on women '(we were not soldiers)'.

It is not merely the *sharpness* or depth of the experience conveyed which determined the subsequent value of the war-books Jameson mentions. Two other remarks she makes elsewhere in her book perhaps explain their continued importance. She repeats two clichés: first, that for the men who fought, the War would not be done with until the men died for whom such names as 'Givenchy, Thiepval, Gommecourt, Mametz have a meaning incommunicable to those who "were not there" ' (99) and second, that 'The distance measured in miles from . . . England to the Western Front is short. Measured in experience it is infinite. The gulf which divides the women of my generation and their men who fought in the War is impassable on any terms' (214). In other words the War did not die for those who took part in it, yet what it meant to them was incommunicable to others. Those others were particularly women. The war-books not only helped to perpetuate the comradeship of veterans, and their memories of those who died, but to re-assert the exclusivity of their fellowship. The retrieval, editing and preservation of war-writings was an act of cultural piety on the part of such ex-soldiers as Blunden. But in memorialising the 'men who fought', literary historians have excluded women from the collective memory of their culture.

Storm Jameson was a young wife during the War. Like Rebecca West, she was absorbed in her first child. Her husband was not posted abroad and she suffered little personal fear or grief except for her younger brother, who was shot down over France in 1918. It was through her second husband that she recognised the gulf in her generation. Guy Chapman was another respected academic who, like Blunden, having served on the Western Front, wrote his own war-memoirs and retrieved and edited the war-writings of other soldiers. Haunted ever after 1918 by the feeling of being one of a generation specifically marked out and separated from other generations, he called his autobiography *A Kind of Survivor*. Storm Jameson immediately contradicts her own appropriation of that idea. She talks of herself as a Great War survivor, and of 'my generation', whilst admitting she had no part in the experiences that marked that generation out as special, and that gave to men the memories conveyed in the books by which 'my generation' will speak. If she were right, women would not be able to speak for their generation, or to leave literature of any value. Was she right?

She was at any rate not typical of the women of her generation. The war had more direct impact on other women. For single women, in particular, the War meant something different, especially for those who served on one of the Fronts or who actively opposed the War. Like other members of her generation, Storm Jameson had her emotional memories of the Great War stirred by the songs sung by the troops on their way to the battlefront, such as *There's a long, long trail*. Her immediate reaction to hearing this sung again later, on 'War-Time Music Hall' on the wireless, was to switch it off: 'not because the tune is cheap and nauseous but because I will not have my heart torn out by thoughts I can neither mitigate nor use' (37). Other women of her generation did try to use, or to mitigate their thoughts about the War, through writing about it.

Storm Jameson speaks unself-consciously of her own generation and its literacy legacy. The idea of that generation as 'the lost generation', an epithet coined by Gertrude Stein, became one of the myths of literary history. The poet, Hilda Doolittle applied it to herself as much as to the men that she knew, like her own husband, the writer Richard Aldington (Doolittle, 1960: 8). Yet male critics have reserved the term for their discussion of men-writers (for instance, Aldridge, 1957). It is difficult to define precisely what is meant by a cultural generation: 'a vague, ambiguous, and stretchable concept ... people of roughly the same age whose shared experience significantly distinguishes them from contemporaries in other age groups' (Spitzer, 1973: 1353–4); or by 'the War generation' in particular: 'pronounced generational breaks which may affect an entire society apparently occur only after decisive historical events, such as wars' (Jaeger, 1985: 291). However, as both Vera Brittain and Storm Jameson claimed, experiences brought about by events such as war seem to affect the members of certain age groups more than those of others, even if the experiences are different for the two sexes. The reactions of those who were reared in the same culture and have reached a similar stage of development may not be identical, but shared historical events have for them a formative influence of the same depth of significance. The significance is determined by the beliefs and values which people also share, and act on enthusiastic-ally. 'A generation is only constituted when a system of references has been retrospectively set up and accepted as a system of collective identification' (Kriegel, 1978: 29).

In the case of the 'War Generation', the generation which Vera Brittain defined as having grown to consciousness during the Edwardian era (1901–10), the shared historical events between 1914 and 1918, and the aftermath until 1928, were not only disillusioning; they were profoundly traumatic. The strength of the trauma determined the force of the disillusion. But the precise experiences by which the events were brought home, and that determined the nature of the trauma, were different for the two sexes.

Men and women did not share precisely the same stressful experiences, since women were not permitted up to the trenches and it was the trench experience and events in No-Man's-Land which were peculiarly shocking for men. Moreover, most men between the ages of 18 and 40 either enlisted or were conscripted. Therefore, the majority of men were subjected to the prolonged emotional violence of active warfare and the incomprehension shown by the non-combatant population. Although many women of all ages did volunteer for war-work of various kinds, no woman was required to participate in precisely the activities which were so psychologically disturbing to the men. Women risked death, for instance, in munitions factories or as auxiliaries behind the lines, but they did not have to endure hours of incessant bombardment. Men who were their brothers, friends, lovers, died, but women did not have to see them blown to pieces before their eyes. War service was depersonalising for many women, subjecting them to the humiliation of discipline, of uniform, and of authority over their personal lives, but it did not carry with it the inhumanity that the armed forces meant for men, with the threat of field punishment or firing-squad. Above all, no woman was trained and expected to kill. Their emotional shock was different although, like the men's, it was compounded with fear and grief.

What men and women did share were the cultural myths and the behavioural inhibitions of their society. They suffered equally from the repression of their memories of traumatic experiences, and from a common vulnerability to the myths of imperialism. Writing was a means of purging the memory of shock, of bitterness and pain, and of anger. Discovering new ways of writing formed a way of exploring and rejecting the whole panoply of war-propaganda, especially the bombastic rhetoric that had supported it. Through writing both men and women tried to salvage something from all the destruction. It enabled them to recapture vivid excitement and lost happiness, which were grieved for. It was also a means to conceptualise the personal changes that had occurred, and to relate them to the wider society. And the enterprise of creating a book could be seen as the construction of a fitting memorial to the dead. It was a memorial women could erect as well as men.

Poetry written in response to the Great War was published as soon as war was declared, and plays about the War were performed while it was in progress. Although some war-stories and novels appeared in print during and shortly after the War, the most enduring prose works based on the First World War took years to gestate; 1928 to 1930 were the *anni mirabiles* for fictionalised war-memoirs such as Edmund Blunden's *Undertones of War*, and R. C. Sherriff's play, *Journey's End*, which date from 1928; Richard Aldington's *Death of a Hero*, Robert Graves's *Goodbye to All That*,

Ernest Hemingway's A Farewell to Arms, and the English translations of Ernst Jünger's *The Storm of Steel* and E. M. Remarque's *All
Quiet on the Western Front*, all came out in 1929; Frederick Manning's *Her Privates We*, Sassoon's *Memoirs of an Infantry Officer*, and
Henry Williamson's *Patriot's Progress* were published in 1930.
Autobiographies continued to appear throughout the decade. Later
critical studies, assuming like Storm Jameson that war-books are by
definition written by men, have concentrated on these works.
Although a great number of on-the-spot reports by women were
published in 1915–16, and most war-fiction by women appeared in
1918, the years from 1929 to 1933 were also the milestone for women's
autobiographies and fictionalised war-memoirs. They are not referred to in studies of 'war-books' or 'the Literature of the Great War'.

The concentration on the personal histories of young soldiers
has not only excluded women's memories. It has given support to
the idea that war is a men's affair. By perpetuating the myth of the
spirit of the trenches, it has persisted in glamorising the War,
despite all the anti-war propaganda. It has also obscured the
significance of what happened to women for our understanding of
social and cultural change. The battlefront is not the only theatre of
war. During the First World War what happened behind the
battle-lines and on the home-front was of crucial importance to the
development and outcome of the War. It was also of supreme
importance for the development and outcome of the war for
women's equality. Women had been fighting for more than half a
century for access to the zones of male power and prestige
forbidden to women. It seemed to many women writing at the time
that that access had been gained by the War. Women's war-writing
concerns the forbidden zones behind all the fronts of the War, not
only the Western Front.

The range of Great War-books which were based on women's
personal experience can be viewed as stretching across three
stages: from the diary, chronicle or journal, kept as an immediate
record but edited for public consumption, through the stage where
the experience, shaped by the imagination, has been developed
into stories, poems, or a novel, to the point where recorded and
imagined experience, having been filtered through the memory,
ordered and distanced, is presented by the intellectual imagination
as part of a total life-history, as autobiography. These three

theoretical stages are not completely distinct from each other, of course, and the picture is complicated by what may well be 'pseudo-memoirs', sensationalised or ghost-written in order to cash in on morbid curiosity.

The most far-seeing and trenchant record, which appeared during the war-books 'boom' (1928-33), was E. Sylvia Pankhurst's *The Home Front* (1932). Based on the articles she wrote during the War for her newspaper, *The Woman's Dreadnought*, *The Home Front* placed her anti-war-work in London's East End within a conscious political analysis of the government's war-aims and its control of dissent. Other comparable books, such as Mrs C. S. Peel's *How We Lived Then* (1929) and Carolyne E. Playne's *Society at War 1914–16* (1930) and *Britain Holds On, 1917, 18* (1933), are less radical attempts to describe events at home. Mrs Peel based her book on personal interviews, trying to allow women to speak for themselves about their war-time experience and the way in which the War had changed their lives; Playne's work, like her earlier book, *The Neuroses of Nations* (1925), tried to evoke the atmosphere of the time, to show, rather jauntily, what it felt like to live through historical events. The difference between their approaches is illustrated by their attitudes to queuing. Whereas Playne recollected that in 1917:

> For those who took life lightly or had little to do at home, 'queuing' could be an enjoyable pastime, for joking was rife, tales and rumours flooded about and merriment took on the exhilaration of a time of adventure and upheaval. (Playne, 1933: 67–8)

Mrs Peel, more of a social explorer, reported that:

> Anyone who penetrated the poorer neighbourhoods became familiar with the queue. In the bitter cold and rain of that depressing winter of 1917 women and children waited outside the shabby shops common to the poorer districts of all towns. (Peel, 1929: 96–7)

But both historians, by the middle-class standpoint which they take for granted and by their political tranquillity, reveal the inadequacy of Pankhurst's sub-title 'A Mirror to Life in England During the First World War'. Sylvia Pankhurst's book was both less than that and very much more.

Women's histories, these were not the first books to be written about life in England during the War. Some records were published earlier; others not until much later. Enid Bagnold's *A Diary Without Dates: Thoughts and Impressions of a V.A.D.*, which was based on her experiences as a VAD nurse at the Royal Herbert Hospital in Woolwich, appeared in 1918. (It led to her instant dismissal from the hospital.) It does not leap to the eye as a war-book, but its careful restraint is better appreciated when set against the blaring war-time propaganda about devoted nurses and the heroic wounded, from which it detached itself. (The titles alone of some of these books indicate their stance; for instance, Mabel Potter Daggett's *Women Wanted: The Story Written in Blood Red Letters on the Horizon of the Great War* (1918). Such women's-books as Daggett's, like Thekla Bowser's *The Story of British V.A.D. Work in The Great War* (1917) and the newspaper articles of Frith Tennyson Jesse and Rebecca West, did not sensationalise women's war-work and men's heroism merely as part of the inflated patriotism of the times. They wrote out of an intoxication with the idea that, after so much battling to show their worth, women could be seen to be publicly demonstrating that the country could not do without them: they stood equal with men as saviours of the Motherland.) Despite having been a suffragette, Enid Bagnold deliberately held her war-book aloof from all public controversy, explicitly disengaging herself from pacifists, jingoes or feminists: 'These are the sort of things they say in debating societies. But Life talks differently...' (Bagnold, 1918: 111). She was not going to argue.

The attitude of *A Diary Without Dates* is cool and reflective. Concerned with a large hospital, an institution organised to deal with pain and dying, Bagnold's is some of the little writing I have found which is firmly rooted in the First World War but transcends it. Bagnold makes a quiet choice of language. It recreates her gradual, tactful exploration of the interface between the physically efficient nursing-system and the patients' inner encounters with pain and their own death. Her diary records the development of her respect for the common soldier. Her calm contemplation is at the opposite pole from Sylvia Pankhurst's frenetic political activity and ceaseless noting of figures, names, dates, places. But in fact they seem to me to have the same ultimate concern: the importance of the dignity and suffering of common people, 'the stuff the world is made of ... men through and through – patchy, ordinary,

human' (Bagnold, 1918: 78–9). Whereas Bagnold holds a magnify-
ing glass over her 'illuminations', penetrating the glass-doors, the
masks, the hurried remarks that betray 'the locks on men's souls',
Pankhurst amasses an accumulation of data, case upon case upon
case, historical evidence of 'a society of brutish class division, so
callous in the administration of its own partial and biassed laws'
(Shirley Williams, 'Foreword'. Pankhurst, 1932: xi).

That the books were written at different times partly explains the
difference in their method and purpose. Sylvia Pankhurst was
primarily concerned with working-women and their power in
society. She saw this as part of a common cause with working-
men, but it was the women's case that she put and argued for.
Women's suffrage was fully gained in 1928, but this was only of
use to women if they were politically educated. *The Home Front* was
partly an attempt to enable women to understand their history and
the economic reality that constrained them.

Bagnold's book was written at a time of rampant propaganda,
both for and against the War. What she tried to do was to enable
the nature of the ordinary wounded soldier to speak for itself,
beneath the din, by creating a silence away from the preconceptions of the public world. In that sense her book is an act of cultural
piety every bit as important as the retrieval of the poetry of Isaac
Rosenberg. With its humble compassion, it achieves a less histrionic or patronising reproach than, say, Wilfred Owen's verse.
Remarking on 'How little women can stand!' she describes Waker,
who 'is not everything a man should be: he isn't clever. But he is so
very brave':

> After his tenth operation two days ago there was a question as
> to whether he should have his pluggings changed under gas
> or not. The discussion went on between the doctors over his
> bed.
> But the anaesthetist couldn't be found.
> He didn't take any part in the discussion such as saying 'Yes,
> I will stand it . . .' but waited with interest showing on his bony
> face, and when they glanced down at him and said, 'Let's do it
> now!' he rolled over to undo his safety-pin that I might take off
> his sling.
> Six inches deep the gauze stuck, crackling under the pull of
> the forceps, blood and puss leaping forward from the cavities as
> the steady hand of the doctor pulled inch after inch of the gauze

to the light. And when one hole was emptied there was another, five in all.

When we had finished and Sister told me to wipe the sweat on his forehead, I did so reluctantly, as though one were being too exacting in drawing attention to so small a sign. (140–1)

Her admiration is typical of the tribute paid by women to the men they helped: 'Man that is master of his flesh, / And has the laugh of death and pain' (Reilly, 1981: 32). This admiration was sincere. Bagnold combined it with an equally sincere contempt for women:

There is a certain dreadful innocence about [grown women at the Hospital] too, as though each would protest, 'In spite of our tasks, our often immodest tasks, our minds are as white as snow.'

And, as far as I can see, their conception of a white female mind is the silliest, most mulish, uncurious, unresponsive, condemning kind of an ideal that a human creature could set before it. (34–5)

A Diary Without Dates bears comparison with another journal kept during the same period, but not published until 50 years later: Lady Cynthia Asquith's *Diaries 1915–18*. While recording intimate matters about public figures, her diaries are also an unabashed display of the frivolous occupations of an intelligent but uneducated lady, who led the life of what Rebecca West called 'parasite women'. Beautiful, charming, affectionate Cynthia Asquith may have been. But the hours she passed in the trivial word-game of 'gibbets', and the ignorant superficiality of her chatter show the personal hollowness and narrow awareness that feminists were desperate to escape. Her flashes of perspective and insight, her odd felicitous phrases, betray the sensibility wasted. (For instance, she greatly admired *A Diary Without Dates*, finding it 'gripping, pitiless and true, and so vividly written' (Asquith, 1968: 425).) Tenderly sympathetic to her family and friends, nevertheless her petty vanity explains the misogyny of men like Siegfried Sassoon. Interestingly, she admired and privately justified his pacifist stand as moral courage: 'Certainly Siegfried Sassoon breaks the conspiracy of silence, but sometimes I strongly feel that those at home should be made to realise the full horror, even to the incidental ugliness, as much as possible' (381).

The continual whirl and excitement were partly an attempt to distract herself from the tragedy of her autistic son, and the deaths of so many close friends and relatives, as well as the worry over her husband, who was serving on the Western Front, and suffered from shell-shock. It is notable how surprised she was to find VAD nursing satisfying – perhaps not least because it relieved her of self-consciousness and the perpetual thirst for 'dewdrops' – compliments. But she did not persevere in the work, and social thrills could not sustain her. During a musical house-party, on 23 September 1918, she wrote:

> Found this orgy of music disagreeing with me – unless one is sufficiently musical for it to be an intellectual occupation I'm sure hours of just having one's emotions teased and tickled is demoralising and exasperating to the nerves. On a foundation of happiness I daresay it would be all right, its effect being just to dramatise my own thoughts not to give me any new ones. On my foundation of sorrow it seemed just to serve to take the skin off several wounds and for the first time I felt the germ of resentment, a wish to hit back at something. (477)

She had a breakdown shortly after.

Cynthia Asquith's diaries provide a foil for the literary remains of less self-centred lives. While Asquith was motoring between country-houses, playing word-games, visiting Dublin in 1916 in order to flirt with the Private Secretary to the Lord Lieutentant of Ireland, and in-between-times occasionally dressing up as a VAD to play at 'war-work' like making gas-masks, women in the East End of London were dying of starvation trying to earn their children's bread from such work. And real VAD's such as Vera Brittain and Enid Bagnold were learning, sometimes in foul conditions, to ameliorate the humiliating suffering of war-cripples who would never again be their family's bread-winner.

The first two types of war-book – the diary, and the collection of sketches or short stories which lead on to the novel – are bridged by such works as Nurse Shirley Millard's *I Saw Them Die* (1936), worked up by a ghost-writer (Adele Comandini) from the scanty diary-jottings of a young American nurse, to produce a conventional love story. A sophisticated French doctor falls in love with the nurse, who nevertheless sticks to her American GI, and the book is published as a momento for her son, born after the War. The narrator has adopted a *'verité'* method of rather clumsily interspersing quotes from the diary, and from the nurse's later memories, with snatches of narrative. The title suggests a lurid shocker, but the few lines of genuinely horrific description reveal the thinness of the rest:

> Gas cases are terrible. They cannot breathe lying down or sitting up. They just struggle for breath, but nothing can be done. Their lungs are gone – literally burnt out. Some have their eyes and faces entirely eaten away by gas and their bodies covered with first-degree burns. We must try to relieve them by pouring oil on them. They cannot be bandaged or touched. We cover them with a tent of propped sheets. Gas burns must be agonizing because usually the other cases do not complain even with the worst wounds but gas cases are invariably beyond endurance and they cannot help crying out. One boy today, screaming to die, the entire top layer of his skin burnt from his face and body. I gave him morphine. (Millard, 1936: 62)

But the popular genre of light romance wins out.

Neverthless, *I Saw Them Die* is more plausible than the war-book which Rebecca West authored anonymously, again originally for an American magazine: *War Nurse – The True Story of a Woman who Lived, Loved and Suffered on the Western Front* (1930). It is long and rambling in structure although the language has the precision one would expect from West. The American nurse's romance with a young English nobleman, his family's disdain, his death, her adulterous affair, an abortion, fall into the genre of gothic romance. Fall and fail. As do the anonymous, but best-selling *W.A.A.C.: The Woman's Story of the War*, and the putative memoirs of the real-life spy, Marthe McKenna, *I Was a Spy* (1933) and *A Spy Was Born* (1935), ghost-written by E. E. P. Tisdall. The fantastic improbabilities of all these works show how the War could be dreamed of by women as an opportunity for adventure, a chance to escape the tedious normality of domestic life. The defeat of this dream in each work reflects not only the limits of women's consciousness, but the inherent contradictions of their wishes; the adventure that war seemed to promise was still seen as a sexual adventure properly leading to marriage, a family, and happiness ever after. (Abortion figures sensationally, but contraception is never mentioned.)

Against such works, Mary Borden's later stories in *The Forbidden Zone: experiences as a nurse attached to the French Army* (1929) show the pressuring of real war experience. Like certain of Katherine Mansfield's short stories, they display the distancing and control necessary if story-telling is to rise above vindictiveness or self-pity. Two stories in particular pare their emotional subject down to the quick: *Moonlight* and *Blind*.

In *Moonlight* the cadences of the prose and the luminous beauty it captures contrast strangely with the mundane objects and remarks that punctuate it. Incongruously the telling-voice repeats that 'I don't mind – it is part of the routine' as a constant refrain to what is most abnormal, the smell of wet mud and blood, the sound of cannonading and human pain. What is accepted as normal, as part of the routine, are such events as having to push legs and arms wrapped in cloths out of the way '– they belong to no one and are of no interest to anyone – 'in order to drink cocoa at midnight. What threatens this normality of slop pail and iodoform is an intolerable nightmare which cannot be true because it is not part of the routine: the moonlight, the scent of new-mown hay. These are unbearable and sickening because they are lovely. The earth of whispering grass, lovesick for the floating moon, recalls a world of clean, normal real men and seemly love.

Borden gives flesh to what became a cliché: 'the obscenity of war'. In this world of war there are no men and no women:

There are heads and knees and mangled testicles. There are chests with holes as big as your fist, and pulpy thighs, shapeless; and stumps where legs once were fastened. There are eyes – eyes of sick dogs, sick cats, blind eyes, eyes of delirium; and mouths that cannot articulate; and parts of faces – the nose gone, or the jaw. There are these things, but no men; so how could I be a woman here and not die of it? (Borden, 1929: 60)

But the wounded have a mistress, a monstrous bedfellow: Pain. Pain is a harlot in the pay of War. Her insatiable delight is the refuse of suffering bodies. The foul odour of their festering flesh is no protection. She plies her trade shamelessly, never leaving them even when she has exhausted them: 'she lies beside them, to tease them with her excrutiating caresses, her pinches and twinges that make them moan and twist in sleep' (62).

In this world, officers on 'terrible business' are blind, deaf, dead, like the nurses. They cannot afford to feel, to consider men's spirit. They must be machines. The nurse is also a soulless machine who has killed her heart and deafened her ears in order not to mind. To hear Life crying and mewing is unbearable.

In *Blind* the depersonalisation is looked back on in disbelief. 'That woman, myself' works in a dream, happy, a little delirious, with 'a sense of great power, exhilaration and excitement' (146). The refrain has become 'It was my business . . . I had much to do'. In the reception hut of a field hospital, the ceaseless battle against death, 'the unseen thing that scurries and hides and jumps', keeps her occupied: 'I didn't worry. I didn't think. I was too busy, too absorbed in what I was doing'. We learn why 'It didn't do to think':

> When the dresser came back I said: 'His brain came off on the bandage.'
> 'Where have you put it?'
> 'I put it in the pail under the table.'
> 'It's only half his brain,' he said, looking into the man's skull. 'The rest is here.'
> I left him to finish the dressing and went about my own business. I had much to do. (143)

The nurses's one tool for dealing with physical pain is the hypodermic syringe of morphine. For chilled, dying flesh, she has a kitchen of implements and a bed in a rough wooden frame lined with electric light bulbs, where a man could be cooked back to life before going to the operating theatre. Cute eyes and hands seem to know of themselves what to do. The nurse didn't think about it. But for a blinded man there is no remedy and no hurry: 'There was plenty of time. He would always be blind' (141). She forgets about him, and later hears him calling out to her, thinking he had been abandoned: 'Sister! My sister! Where are you?' This voice of a lost man calls her out of her dream, and she awakes to realise the dreadful horror she is surrounded by but which he cannot see, 'the wounded packed round us, hemming us in' (158). She lies to reassure him. Then the machine of her body jerks and breaks down, and she runs to hide, cowered and sobbing behind her screen.

The elderly orderlies cannot decide what to do. Finally a tin cup of hot coffee is offered round the screen. 'He didn't know of anything else he could do for me' (159). What comfort could there be for any person in that dream-hell?

Borden's need to purge the horror impels a plain, flat vocabulary, occasionally relieved by surreal imagery. Together they convey the searing intensity which led to the protective withdrawal of automatism. The same psychological process appears in war-book after war-book, such as *All Quiet on the Western Front*. It was a process shared by men and women. A bald, dispassionate discipline, nostalgic for sensuous beauty, controls the self-pitying hysteria into which other memoirs such as *Death of a Hero* drive themselves hoarse. By contrast, an especially sensational book, *Not So Quiet . . . Stepdaughters of War* by 'Helen Zenna Smith', screams into hyperbole before reaching catatonic indifference. It was a runaway best-seller on publication, going immediately into several editions, and leading to two sequels, each – incredibly – even more crudely overwrought and melodramatic than its predecessor. I hazard that it was precisely their bitterness and resentment which made them sell well, if, as Sutherland suggests, best-sellers feed or express needs in the reading public.

Although presented as autobiographical, *Not So Quiet . . .* was written by the professional author, Evadne Price, who never reached the Continent during the War. Much of the detail about women's ambulance work on the Western Front is authentic. Price used the unpublished diaries of a real ambulance-driver, Winifred Young, to provide her colour, but the general information, as Cadogan and Craig point out, was available to any competent researcher. Probably even the girls' boarding-school atmosphere is accurate, and the Commander, 'Mrs Bitch', bears a strong resemblance to Mrs Graham Jones, who was in command of a Women's VAD Motor Ambulance Unit attached to a base hospital in Northern France from 1916, and was mentioned in despatches. The work of such a unit was far more arduous than that of women drivers in the WAAC, who were mainly employed chauffering cars for staff officers and spent many of their long hours emptily waiting. (It is a WAAC driver whom Enid Bagnold portrays in *The Happy Foreigner* (1920) as Fanny, who thoroughly enjoys her romantic adventures in France after the Armistice.) Mrs Jones insisted on 'strict and unquestioning obedience to Army discipline' (Maclaren, 1917: 114). During the rush when the Somme fighting began, her drivers were working shifts of eight hours on, four hours off, driving 130 miles a day, and also cleaning and maintaining the cars themselves. 'Helen Smith' graphically describes what that means: cleaning out the filth of 'stale vomit . . . temporary lavatories for all purposes, blood and mud and vermin and the stale stench of stinking trench feet and gangrenous wounds' (Price, 1930: 59).

The main aim of the book is to fill out this sordid reality behind the glowing war-time propaganda. Aged 21, Smithy is particularly virulent against her own mother and other older women with their patriotic committees and recruiting meetings, who believe the propaganda and encourage their daughters to be heroines and 'do their bit', with no understanding of what that actually means. The book, narrated in the present with more racy immediacy than a diary, addresses her mother and friends back home in Wimbledon: 'Oh, come with me, Mother and Mrs Evans-Mawnington. Let me show you the exhibits – lift your silken skirts aside . . . a man is spewing blood' (90–1). The drivers are 'gently-bred' and un-prepared for their exhausting work or for 'the stretchers of moaning men . . . men torn and bleeding and raving' (12).

Within this disgusting context a female drama is played out between the stereotypes of women's fiction. Mrs Bitch resembles the sadistic teachers of school stories such as 'Clemence Dane's' *Regiment of Women*: 'Why is it that women in authority almost invariably fall victims to megalomania?' (61) (This is a question posed in other war-books by women as various as E. M. Delafield, Vera Brittain, and Diana Cooper.) She sniffs out and punishes a couple seeking comfort in a lesbian relationship. They are por-trayed as skinny, pale and uninteresting. The heroine is 'Tosh', Georgina Toshington, the Amazonian niece of an earl. The book commences with Tosh 'unsexing' herself by cutting off all her generous red hair to get rid of her lice. This real 'lady', with coarse language she picked up from stable-boys and the laugh of a publican, reveals the false gentility of other characters such as 'B. F.', Bertina Farmer, who is 'fearfully "refeened and neece"' (24) and thinks short hair terribly unfeminine and blue-stocking. Much of the comedy stems from Tosh pulling B. F.'s genteel leg. The sardonic tragedy comes from Tosh's death in a bombing-raid:

> Tosh lies in my arms dead, killed by a splinter of bomb. Tosh the brave, the splendid, the great-hearted. Tosh is dead.
> And I, the coward, the funk, the white-livered . . . I am alive.
> It is funny. It is the funniest joke I have ever heard. (160–1)

Tosh satirised the War. She compiled a war alphabet: 'B for Bastard – obsolete term meaning war-baby . . . I for Illegitimate

– (See B) . . . V for Virgin – a term of reproach (ask any second loot)' (160). This attitude to sexual morality is the main change worked in women by the War. The book claims sympathy for these 'gentle-women' who have acquired 'barnyard morals' because they 'use love as a drug for forgetfulness'. There is certainly no pleasure in promiscuity, in Smithy's case performed out of pity for the beauty of men who are whole and sane, and in order to forget 'a shadow procession of cruelly maimed men'; in her younger sister's case it results in an abortion.

The book claims pity and understanding for the 'war-shocked woman who sacrificed her youth on the altar of the War . . . war made by age and fought by youth' (166). War makes young women 'war products', a race apart like young men, 'feared by the old ones, and resented by the young ones . . . a race of men bodily maimed and of women mentally maimed' (167). In Price's book young men and women understand each other; they have in common that they are 'war-sick'. Drained of emotion, they are a 'stricken generation' (203). By the end of the book Smithy is a machine, her body operating automatically, without hate, love or anger, with 'mental atrophy'. Like her fiancé, Roy, who, crippled, castrated and blinded, no longer cares about anything, she has become indifferent to life (217). The ending comes with a grand guignol finality: 'Her soul died under a radiant silver moon in the spring of 1918 on the side of a blood-spattered trench' (239).

Not So Quiet . . ., as its title suggests, deliberately counters the wartime 'rubbish praising the indomitable pluck and high spirits of "our wonderful war girls"' (134), 'England's Splendid Daughters' (13). In the process it satirises current conceptions of womanliness, femininity and ladylike behaviour, as hypocritical and sentimental, and as contributing to the cruelty of the War. Price makes an attempt to establish a kinship between the men and the women who served overseas and witnessed the misery, because they can speak to each other. Cut off from those older and younger than themselves, they belong to the same generation by virtue of their common experience. Her book is also a grovelling plea for a woman's share in the pity of war.

Whether or not *Not So Quiet* . . . *Stepdaughters of War* expressed the views of the large readership it acquired in the 1930s, it at any rate seems to meet the need of recent feminist literary historians to find an adequate example of a woman's war-book. Since its citation as 'a little-known autobiographical work' by Jean E. Kennard in

1985, no less than three new editions of it have been promised, each with a notable introduction. A less sensational, more comprehensive novel about women's experience of war service has received less attention. Irene Rathbone's *We That Were Young* (1932) is partly autobiographical. It deals with women's work in munitions factories, as VAD's and at YMCA's in France. Laying more stress on women's companionship, the overall message of Rathbone's novel is nevertheless the same as Price's: women sacrificed not their lives but their youth in war-work, work which was exhausting and unglamorous. Their reward was the emptiness of the post-War years.

The difficulty of using actual memories of the War as a basis or background for fiction is demonstrated by the sentimental old-hat of Mary Borden's wartime romance set on the Western Front, *Sarah Gay* (1931). Mary Hamilton's *Special Providence: A Tale of 1917* (1930), cast in the form of a court-room drama, displays the same problem but exacerbated. She has tried to make a murder-story, based on a love-triangle between a soldier, his wife and a pacifist, into a vehicle for the serious discussion of pacifism and the idea that war turns men into killers. The book has some chilling moments of psychological insight concerning the relations between the wife and her army-husband, as he tries to express his sense of alienation during his leaves from the Front, but to use this to heighten a melodramatic murder story not only reveals the thinness of the rest of the motivation. It reveals as a curiously repulsive form of sensationalism, that which battens on such anguish. The sensationalism does not enhance the political argument. In 1951 Eliza Butler incorporated her memories of a hospital unit on the Eastern Front, in Russia, into a ghost story. *Daylight in a Dream* is a rather weak effort to convey peacetime selfishness.

One of the few novels by women which successfully integrated the War into its plot was Joanna Maxwell Cannan's *High Table* (1931). This is a restrained, delicately witty portrait of an Oxford don. His life as an academic is arid, without faith or passion. It flowers once, briefly, when the War interrupts college routine and he enters wholeheartedly into a dream of fatherhood. Sadly it is an illusion. The intensity of the War, its pressures on personal relations, reveals the emotional impoverishment of his existence.

Winifred Holtby's *A Crowded Street* (1924) also concentrates on civilian life in England. The deep emotional power of a striking image from an incident early on in the plot, unfortunately works against the surface argument of her novel as a whole. The book's thesis is that marriage is not the only fulfilment of a woman's life; spinsterhood can be equally, if not more, rewarding. The incident, based on Holtby's own experience as a schoolgirl of the bombardment of Scarborough in 1914, is of a breathtaking escape from a town under enemy-fire. This 'Great Adventure' peters out at the town dump. It is a vivid allegory, which crystallises many young people's disillusionment with the War when finally seen at first hand, but it also sums up the great anti-climax of the heroine's life. She experiences neither the comradeship of shared danger, nor any other intense emotional relationship. The refuse-dump comes to stand not merely for the sordid backwash of war, but for a life of sexual rejection. Nothing else in the novel has the excitement or interest, or even the comedy, of that bourgeois flight into drab safety.

The incompatibility in these novels between the prosaic surface of conventional fiction, whether it be crime fiction, or light romance, or comedy of manners, and the underlying passions and miseries that the War forced into the open, reveals the shams which most women had to accept for reality, and why their writing tended to be superficial. Like the war-time pacifist novels, these books also show the difficulty of making conventional novel-forms the vehicles for political analysis. While the writing which did find methods of challenging the conventions continued to be censored, women had few models to learn from. No wonder if Aldington finds 'Victorian cant' to blame for everything, or if Helen Zenna Smith is reduced to crazy laughter. Fortunately for British culture, the very debt to war-victims that society piously recognised, resulted in the eventual unabridged publishing of ideas and language that had been rigorously prohibited before the War (Aldington, 1965: Manning, 1977).

One woman who would not stand for shams was Sylvia Pankhurst. Usually designated as 'social history', her book *The Home Front* is more helpfully regarded as part of her political autobiography, as she indicates after the dedication: 'Herein is told the story of my life and time during the War years 1914, 1915, 1916'. It follows on from what is, in effect, volume 1, *The Suffragette Movement: An Intimate Account of Persons and Ideas* (1931). The trilogy ought to have been completed with *In the Red Twilight*, the book she promised at the end of *The Home Front* (Pankhurst, 1932: 446), but this third volume of the autobiography, which would have dealt with her experiences following the Russian Revolution, was left uncompleted in 1935 and never published. Her political autobiography is complemented by a short piece she contributed to a book edited by Margot Oxford, the Countess of Oxford and Asquith (Cynthia Asquith's mother-in-law): *Myself When Young: by famous women of to-day* (1938).

To call *The Home Front* a political autobiography is not to deny its important contribution to our knowledge and understanding of social history. It is also a history book. But a history written in a highly raised state of political consciousness. Sylvia Pankhurst makes the reader aware at all times of her own viewpoint and particular perspective. Her ego intrudes. It is the ego of a heroine, a heroine passionately committed to raising the sights of working women in order that they might themselves improve their own conditions in life. The book forms an integral part of that life. Just as Katherine Mansfield and Virginia Woolf made themselves artists by converting their own lives into written works of art, so Sylvia Pankhurst made herself a socialist feminist by converting her life into political history.

Paradoxically the book opens with an explanation of how narrowed her horizon had become by 1914 and how she shrank from the imminence of the tragedy, as 'Hourly the War drew nearer'. Continuing with the strenuous struggle for Women's Suffrage, Sylvia was held in the grip of the 'Cat and Mouse Act' (The Prisoners Temporary Discharge for Ill-Health Act, which was being used to persecute suffragettes on hunger-strike). Hounded, she had seen little of Keir Hardie. He was at this time the chairman of the British section of the International Socialist Bureau, and had been aware of the threat of international war and speaking out against it. Her 'deep love and respect' for this man, like a father to her and equally her hero, is stated on the opening page of *The Home Front*. Throughout the book she pays tribute to him, to his courage and faith in internationalism: 'His example was a buttress against cynicism and despair' (Pankhurst, 1938: 278). His death is one of the most moving parts of her book, and is more evidence of how deeply she cared about other people.

Over and over again she feels overwhelmed by the tragedy of the War and the seemingly hopeless task of even mitigating its effects, let alone bringing about world peace. But always she is inspired by the same faith that had fired Hardie, and the book ends with a statement of her belief in the advance of humanity to a world where 'all shall co-operate gladly in giving to the common stock according to their abilities and in receiving from its abundance according to their needs' (Pankhurst, 1932: 447).

This may not be a creed that most people can agree with, but the book makes plain how the jingoist propaganda of the War, concentrating on what might be glamorised, obscured the worsened suffering that the War entailed for the poor. Her book also makes plain to us how the continuing focus on battle-tales diverts us from any vision of the soldier in his political context, or of the country in a state of martial law. Modern war is not, and cannot be, merely a matter of opposed armies. It involves whole nations. The story of the First World War must incorporate the story of the non-combatant part of the nation, including both women and the disabled soldiers who began to return home from 1914 and who, incurable, remained a burden for the next 60 years.

Sylvia Pankhurst's story of the War commences in Dublin, where she had gone to report for *The Women's Dreadnought* on the news that a company of British soldiers had fired on an unarmed crowd including old women and children. When war was declared she returned on the overnight boat, amid chaotic scenes of intoxicated men and distraught women.

Thus she returned from the blunt evidence of British military rule of the Empire, to an England now also in the open grip of militarism. If her analyses of the economic effects of war are hard to follow, her account of martial law is clear and straightforward: 'Civil liberty is ever the first victim of war'. The Defence of the Realm Acts nullified existing constitutional safeguards, and 'Anyone who contravened the regulations established under these Acts could be tried by court martial as though he were a soldier on active service' (36). Censorship under DORA was combined with pro-war propaganda to prevent the public from making informed judgements, especially about 'money mystery'. The rest of *The Home Front* is an account of Britain, and more especially of the East End of London, as fundamentally affected by the new economic conditions created by the War, and under the increasing control of martial law. But it is not an abstract, general account. It is a painstaking detailing of particular case after particular case of the callousness with which the new system of social order was operated. For, as Sylvia remarks about the tale of life's hardship that a mother told her daughters as she lay dying of phthisis in the small back-room of a working man's cottage, 'it was part of the history of the Great War'. History as Sylvia Pankhurst tells it is never boring. We come to agree with her, that 'Novels, romances, what is the need of them? Not one is so strange, so poignant as the true romance of Life' (238).

The misery she documents would be unbearable were it not for the passion with which she opposes it, the companionship which supports her, and the typical pieces of women's cheek which she quotes with glee. For instance, the letter published in *The Women's Dreadnought* from Rose Rosenberg of Bethnal Green, who suggested:

> Women should in future refuse to take over men's work, unless and until an undertaking is made by those who administer the law, that Members of Parliament who are of military age, be released, and enabled to join the colours with their pals, and women asked to fill *their* places. (272)

'Spurred by anxiety, which could find respite only in effort', Sylvia seethed with energy. A rage against the War and against poverty, that was motivated by an enduring desire to restore 'these faded women, these starved and stunted children', kept her ever active. Her angry activity keeps the reader edgy too: gratified to hear of her successes but never satisfied. The endless stream of stories is one aspect of her tireless attention to the lives of real people, her determination to speak on behalf of the 'voiceless millions of the submerged poor'. If countless war-memorials vow never to forget the young men who 'gave' their lives in the Great War, nor will she permit us to forget the poor char-woman who received ten years' penal servitude for strangling her own two-year-old starving child, having been without food for days. However Victorian her rhetoric, we cannot but believe Sylvia Pankhurst when she claims that, to the great mass of the poor 'my heart clove; I was theirs, theirs with all my strength' (86).

Such whole-hearted, uncompromising dedication must have made her very prickly in person. Perhaps this is shown most clearly by her acid vignette of a week-end house-party at the Waldorf-Astors' mansion near Maidenhead, which she attended to raise funds for her co-operative toy factory. Speaking of the 'hard, grey life in the East End' to women who 'looked like a bit of Dresden china', she says she was 'well-received' and comments: 'many people enjoy having their hearts touched – then pass to the

next sensation, quite unchanged' (142–3). Later, after an extrava-
gant dinner, the women rose and left the men to smoke alone.
Sylvia had forgotten 'such foolish customs still obtained' and was
amazed at 'the futility of this life, upborn by the underworld of toil
and striving' where she herself lived. But there is still amusement
to be gained from the icy disdain shown by one lovely being who,
having enquired 'What are you doing in war work?' and been
greeted with Sylvia's passionate reply: 'Nothing! I am not connected with the War!' had haughtily reminded her that 'Of course
we are all connected with the War!' This parasite's connection was
only too conspicuous to Sylvia Pankhurst.

After depicting the way in which such *toys* (as these shrill,
strutting women ironically appear to Sylvia) were ogled by old
fogeys like Balfour, 'in the manner of a dying epoch', she describes
the following day's visit to a small hospital for wounded soldiers in
the grounds. The matron refused entry to the house guests, who
had to content their curiosity with such patients as were taking the
air. Not surprisingly, the soldiers were surly, but one who
recognised Sylvia called her over to speak to himself and his wife.
He took advantage of a moment when his wife was distracted by
their child, to tell Sylvia what his wife did not yet know: that both
his legs had been amputated. On the way back to the main house,
an American journalist overtook Sylvia, expatiating on how
glorious it was 'to see all this wonderful selflessness and unity
amongst all classes'. Impelled by sorrow for the crippled, Sylvia
burst out hotly in reply with 'hatred for such canting untruth'
(146). We imagine the man's discomfiture.

The weekend raised £15. Afterwards, having heard of Sylvia's
connection with the Women's International Peace Congress, Mrs
Astor wrote regretting her help for the toy factory. She had
discovered that the wages were as high as £1 a week instead of the
6–10s. paid by the Queen Mary Workrooms. Sylvia Pankhurst
argued that this was sweated labour which would depress
women's wages generally, and at 3d an hour was below the
minimum rate fixed by the Clothing Trade Board. One of Sylvia's
campaigns was to ensure that the War was not used as an excuse to
avoid fair pay for women's work. It was another hard struggle.
Pirelli's was paying 1¾d an hour at the Southampton works. [By
comparison, Cynthia Asquith's annual (unearned) allowance of
£500 was not entirely spent on clothes; by the end of the War she
was able to earn another £500 working 2–3 days a week as

J. M. Barrie's untrained secretary. Her sister was not embarrassed to spend 7 guineas on a hat during the War (Asquith, 1968: 128, 424, 455).]

The difficulty of supporting a family on low wages had been itemised in Maud Pember Reeves' *Round about a Pound A Week* (1913), a report of the Fabian Women's Group research in Lambeth, 1909–13. The conclusions were that the cause of infant mortality was not that mothers were ignorant or degenerate, but that they had too little money to provide for their own and their families' essential needs (Reeves, 1979: xi). Before coming to England in 1896, Reeves had campaigned successfully for women's suffrage in New Zealand. She became Director of the Educational and Propaganda Department of the Ministry of Food during the First World War. Her name does not appear in *The Home Front*, but the names of other members of the Group do. The fact that Margaret Bondfield, Susan Lawrence and Mary Macarthur were appointed to the very administrative committee of the Queen's Workshop for Women Fund which fixed the sweated wage of 10s maximum a week is but one more instance of how the pre-War women's movement compromised with the war-time government. Contemptuous of appeals for the protection of young soldiers 'preyed upon and ruined by harpies', Sylvia Pankhurst was seriously worried that sweated labour and unemployment 'would bring recruits to the sad army of prostitutes' (104).

Although *The Home Front* is a record of Sylvia Pankhurst's life and time, it tells us very little about her personal life, if indeed she had much privacy during those years. There are brief references to the rift between herself and her sister and mother. She felt deeply hurt by their betrayal of her father's socialist ideals and by their public attack on Keir Hardie through the Suffragette paper (renamed *The Britannia* to fit its war-time jingoism). She continued the campaign with members of the East London Federation of Suffragettes instead: 'They were, to me, in Gladstone's phrase, *vox populi, vox dei*, the touchstone of eternal verities; my mothers, my sisters, my daughters. I had need of no other kin than they' (51). Above all, she could not forgive her mother for publicly wishing 'her boy had been marching with the armies' (67). Often, travelling by bus, Sylvia Pankhurst would look up at 'some young soldier lad' who had given up his seat to her, 'and stood there, steadying himself by the hanging strap, his slim wrist and hand unfit, as yet, for heavy labour, his throat still childish-looking and smooth, his head a little drooping, fatigued, it seemed by the weight of his knapsack and greatcoat'. She would see her dead brother, Harry, in all these soldier boys, and 'Anguish, almost unendurable, would seize me that this slender boy, here within touch, should be going out to the slaughter – and that all we adults should slavishly allow it' (289).

Her writing is seldom introspective, and although it is often pithy when dealing with matters written up for *The Women's Dreadnought*, her use of language is hardly innovative. It is the form of her book which is creative, bringing economic theory, political analysis and historical facts to life by her constant vivacity and eye for particulars.

She remarks frequently on the drabness of East End life, the dingy, dreary environment, but only by reading 'Myself When Young' can it be discovered just what she sacrificed to her political activity. Having won a studentship to the Manchester School of Art in 1898, when her father died, she had afterwards been awarded a travel scholarship to Italy and then a place at the Royal College of Art, coming top of the list for all England and Wales. She dreamed of being able to devote herself 'to the study and creation of beauty', to 'portray the world that is to be when poverty is no more'. Yet the struggle to better the world for humanity required a more directly political action which interfered with her artistic ambition. Crises of inner misery that resulted in neuralgia led to her putting the artist's life second, yet not entirely surrendering the study of colour and form, for 'to wear out one's life on the platform and the chair at the street corner was a prospect too tragically grey and barren to endure' (Pankhurst, 1938: 285). But she did wear out her life during the War.

The East End provided little to delight her eye, with the drab hopelessness of the slums: 'starvation, that strange, dull gaze, daily stared in my face from the eyes of mothers and children' (43). It drained the poetic imagination which had transmuted her experience of Holloway. Yet the alertness of her eye and ear recreate the irrepressible vitality of common life. On a visit to Sheffield, amongst the bombed wreckage of one of the dingiest parts of the city, she witnessed a scene which she recorded in detail. It was a scene that might have tickled Brecht. Following a zeppelin raid, heavy wooden barriers had been placed across certain streets, and soldiers with fixed bayonets were guarding the ruined warehouses. People stood gloomy and silent, gazing at the ruins. 'Only the dirty-faced, ragged little children retained their full activity, rushing pell-mell among the sightseers, bobbing under barriers, squeezing through boarded-up doorways.' Copying the soldiers, a noisy troop of children shouldered long strips of wood hacked out to represent guns, with smaller pieces nailed on for bayonets:

> At their head strutted a tiny, waggish girl, eight years old at most, with hair cropped short like a boy's, the leader and bully of the rest. Her stockings, stuffed with rag about the calves, were tied under her small bare knees. For her gun she had no long stake of wood like the other children, but a brick, precariously balanced against her shoulder. As the soldiers wheeled and stood at attention, grounded arms, and were drilled by the sergeant, she mimicked them, serenely impudent, with exaggerated contortions, bending her knees, as though horribly bandy, crying 'rr'ght t'rrn' like the sergeant, swinging out her leg grotesquely far, and bringing her heels together with a bang. By turns she pretended that the brick had cut her, rubbing her cheek with impish grimaces; caught the brick up in her pinafore like a baby, kissing and petting it; shouldered it; feigned to drop it on her toe; then swung it vigorously as though to hurl it at the soldiers, but let it fall harmlessly behind her. (373)

When one of the soldiers threatened this small tormentor, she dashed away, helter-skelter, with shrieks of laughter. Nearby, the front of a blitzed chapel had crashed down, revealing the text written large on a wall inside: 'A new commandment I give unto you; that ye love one another'.

Sylvia Pankhurst lived on the cusp between two ages: the Victorian and the modern. She was in the vanguard of the revolutionary political movements of her time, and yet she was fired by an almost revivalist evangelism. Inspired by William Morris, her prose is at times almost archaic in its fervid, biblical apostrophes, but her scorn and irony are the hallmarks of the modern age. Without giving way to cynicism, she humorously balances any tendency to mawkishness with her sense of the incongruous. In 1916, 'striving to rend from the wreck of things some brightness and joy for the beauty-starved people' of the East End, she set her cousin, Joan, to organise a children's festival. Sixty of the children were to dance, but alas! Joan had chosen white muslin, the thinnest and frailest, for their dresses. 'How it looked, that white muslin, transparent and flimsy, over the children's poor underclothes, made up of old garments cut down for them, all colours and patterns, hastily washed, hastily patched and darned by work-driven fingers!' As she watched the long, bedraggled train hurrying to the Park, her eyes watered for them: 'My dear little darlings, your poverty – oh, your appalling poverty!' and then a mother cried out, running in happy excitement to catch up with them: ' "Where is my Mary? I want to put a flower in 'er bloody 'air!" ' (339).

Relegated to bibliographies, *The Home Front* disappeared from popular view. That other celebration of the war-time working-class, *Oh What a Lovely War*, was first performed in the East End 30 years later. The playscript contains no reference to *The Home Front* or *The Women's Dreadnought* in its appendix of source material. In Act Two it apparently confuses Sylvia with her mother, having 'Mrs Pankhurst' speaking from a box: 'War cannot be won. No one can win a war'. She is shouted down and drowned out by 'Rule Britannia!' The play was more ironic than it knew.

The most famous women's book of the Great War is undoubtedly Vera Brittain's *Testament of Youth: An Autobiographical Study of the Years 1900–1925*, which was a best-seller on both sides of the Atlantic when it first appeared in 1933 and went on selling. Re-issued in a war-time format during the Second World War, the new edition sold out before publication day. It was republished in paperback in 1960. Dramatised by Elaine Morgan and adapted as a film for BBC Television in 1978, it became a paperback best-seller again, being reprinted annually. The book helped make a name for Vera Brittain as able to speak on behalf of women with regard to war, claiming adamantly that war was not the business of one age or sex alone. On the 50th anniversary of the 1914–18 War, she was the only woman invited to contribute to *Promise of Greatness* (1968), George A. Panichas's memorial volume of writings on the Great War.

Testament of Youth is promoted by her publishers together with Vera Brittain's two other works based on her own life: *Testament of Friendship: The Story of Winifred Holtby* (1940) (which tells of her friendship with Winifred Holtby from 1919 until 1935) and *Testament of Experience: An Autobiographical Story of the years 1925–1950* (1957).

As a trilogy, they add up to a picture of a woman's life over half a century, from the Diamond Jubilee of Queen Victoria, through the First World War, when Vera Brittain lost her first fiancé, to the Depression, when she married the political philosopher George E. Catlin; then from the Depression through the Second World War, to the World Peace Conference in India, and her own silver wedding anniversary in 1950.

The relation charted between private affairs and matters of world importance was not accidental. All three books try 'to put the life of an ordinary individual into its niche in contemporary history' in order to show the influence of worldwide events on personal destiny (Brittain, 1933: 12). This had a political objective. By the end of the First World War Vera Brittain was a dedicated pacifist, and she saw her work as an attempt to help create a mental revolution by enlarging the consciousness of humanity: 'The real cause of the two World Wars had been political unconsciousness' (Brittain, 1957: 472). One aim of *Testament of Youth* was to raise the political consciousness of her reader with regard to war.

Despite having graduated in history from Somerville, Vera Brittain retained a somewhat novelistic conception of history (apparently derived from George Eliot's *Daniel Deronda* [Panichas, 1968: 372]). She viewed it as a panoramic background to personal lives, a sequence of large-scale events which occasionally interfered with particular people, rather than as the temporal dynamic of a culture (Brittain, 1957: 78). (Of a culture as the total medium for human life and consciousness, changing from period to period, she seems to have had no conception at all, despite her constant awareness of generational difference.) At first sight her aims seem to be the same as Sylvia Pankhurst's in *The Suffragette Movement*: 'to introduce the actors in the drama as living beings; to show the striving, suffering, hugely hopeful human entity behind the pageantry, the rhetoric and the turbulence' (Pankhurst, 1931: Preface). But Sylvia Pankhurst never loses sight of the fact that she is writing social history: 'no history, whether of movements or of persons, can be truly expressed apart from the social and economic conditions and thought currents of its time' (ibid.). Although Vera Brittain paid lip service to the idea that 'no life is really private, or isolated, or self-sufficient', since each person is 'part of the surge and swell of great economic and political movements' (Brittain, 1933: 472), her account of her own life remains a descriptive chronicle of personal events.

This is not only a reflection of her own political ignorance during the First World War; it reveals that that idealistic ignorance remained essentially unaltered. Twenty years later, her own assessment of the limits of her consciousness represents her limitations as merely snobbery and sexual innocence. She never comes to examine her own elevated sentiments, still expressed in a Victorian rhetoric that continues to magnify the personal incidents of war. For instance, after graduating in 1921, she visited her brother's grave in Italy. (He had been killed in action during the Battle of Asiago, in June 1918.) Whilst in Florence, she watched a pageant about Dante and recorded her reflections on the Battle of Campaldino which took place in 1269. Having learned at university that 'the working out of time's inscrutable purposes' might take seven hundred years, she wondered whether an impulse to avenge that defeat had subconsciously inspired the Austrians at Caporetto: 'Had Edward's death lain so long ago in the logic of history?' (529). As she later remarked, 'I have only a personal and not a historical memory' (532).

Ultimately the rhetoric still veils the unpleasant fact of death. On a visit to her fiancé's grave, she found that 'the impetuous warrior slept calmly in this peaceful, complacent earth with its suave covering of velvet lawn' (533). There is a total lack of the kind of political analysis and explanation which informs the narrative of events in *The Home Front*, as Sylvia Pankhurst tries to identify the forces that govern historical direction, especially the chaos and convolutions of the thing we call Capitalism, 'wherein too often we are as corks, tossed on the ocean' (Pankhurst, 1932: 16). Vera Brittain remained an innocent, idealistic cork.

As a result, one of her aims in writing *Testament of Youth*, 'to show that war was not glamour or glory but abysmal grief and purposeless waste, although [acknowledging] its moment of grandeur' (Brittain, 1957: 80), remains at the level of emotional protest. She succeeds in demonstrating that war is sad and wasteful. Why it should ever have been believed to be glamorous, or glorious, or purposeful, she does not elucidate. Although her book may have contributed to the emotional revulsion against war which was so marked in Britain between the Wars, it can hardly have created any mental revolution in political consciousness such as she had hoped for.

It is significant for our idea of 'the War generation' that the First World War dominates the first volume of Vera Brittain's autobiography, fundamentally affecting how she conceived the shape of her whole life; whereas it is the subject of the second volume of Sylvia Pankhurst's autobiography. Born in 1882, Sylvia Pankhurst was a late Victorian. Like Virginia Woolf, Radclyffe Hall, Mary Hamilton and Rose Macaulay, she was ten years older than Vera Brittain and over 30 when the First World War was declared. She had already had the oppportunity to evaluate the dominant beliefs of her society and reject them. Vera Brittain was still finding her feet. Raised in the capital city of the North of England, Manchester, at the centre of social and political controversy, by a forceful mother and an egalitarian father, who both believed in feminism, Sylvia saw no obstacle to forming her personal destiny as an independent woman. Vera Brittain, on the contrary, was subject to conflicting views about womanhood. At the same time as benefitting from the changes achieved by the Women's Movement, she suffered from the backlash to them.

Brought up in a provincial Midlands town in accordance with the dominant conventions, Vera Brittain was expected to conform to her mother's example of submissive obedience to a domineering paterfamilias. However, she attended a school with a feminist headmistress. Exposed to orthodox feminism (but not to the radical doctrines of the suffragettes), she planned to go to university and earn her own living rather than make marriage her end in life. Yet her adolescent reading included both the two opposing spokeswomen on women's emancipation, Olive Schreiner and Mrs Humphry Ward. Against opposition, Vera Brittain gained a place at university. But once she fell in love, she immediately dreamed of marrying and having a child in preference to all other ambition (*supra* chapter 2).

Vera Brittain suffered the counteracting influence of the two competing goals for the girls of her class at that period: either New Woman or Ladylike wife, mother, and society hostess. This partly accounts for the lack of coherence between the three volumes of her life-story, where the story of a feminist friendship overlaps the two tales of heterosexual love (youthful romance and mature marriage). It also partly accounts for the tension between her view of herself as an independent heroine like Olive Schreiner's Lyndall, which fills the consciousness of her younger self, and the overall structure of *Testament of Youth*. In spite of her avowed feminism, the Testament follows the stereotype plot of a romantic novel. She states emphatically that 'Marriage, for any woman who considered all its implications both for herself and her contemporaries, could never, I now knew, mean a "living happily ever after" on the contrary it would involve another protracted struggle' (Brittain, 1933: 654). Yet her life is presented as being like the fairy-tale from Andrew Lang's *The Pink Fairy Book* that she places at the beginning of the book (and at the end of *Testament of Experience*): once upon a time, a long time ago ... and so she married and lived happily ever after.

This unresolved contradiction between independence and wifehood is not the only source of tension in *Testament of Youth*. Although the book follows the thread of a single life-story, a woman's life from birth to marriage, it was intended as a memorial to her brother, fiancé and two male friends who were all killed in the War.

As she remembers in *Testament of Experience*, the original inspiration lay in the numerous war-books by men that appeared in the late 1920s. Starting with a visit to *Journey's End* in 1929, she was provoked by *Undertones of War*, *Memories of a Fox-Hunting Man*, *Goodbye to All That*, *Death of a Hero*, *All Quiet on the Western Front*, and *A Farewell to Arms*, to ask: 'Why should these young men have the War to themselves? Didn't women have their war as well?' (Brittain, 1957: 77). Reacting against the portrayal of women in these books, as suffering wives and mothers, callous parasites, or mercenary prostitutes, she remonstrated that women did warwork too, beginning with high ideals but carrying on when disillusioned, just as the men did. Believing her own story to be just as interesting as that of Blunden, Sassoon or Graves, she also thought she had perceived things differently from them, and had seen other things besides. Her autobiography was to be 'the epic of the women who went to the war', speaking not just for those in high places but 'for my own generation of obscure young women' (77).

Yet in *Testament of Youth* she refers constantly to 'the men and women of my generation'. Quoting frequently from the correspondence between herself and the four young men who were killed, she aims to speak on their behalf too, for 'the generation of those boys and girls who grew up just before the War broke out' (Brittain, 1933: 11). Her own typical story was to illustrate the influence of worldwide events on the members of both sexes. Thus, although the War was different for women, her experience is to stand for the experience not only of other women, who had been omitted from the stories told by men, but also for the experience of men. It is to be the story of a complete generation, not merely one half of it.

Vera Brittain was in fact breaking new ground in more ways than one. *Testament of Youth* was not only a woman's story of the War, written as a historical autobiography rather than as a novel; it was also the first in a new genre, the generational autobiography. A year before Malcolm Cowley produce *Exiles Return: A Narrative of Ideas* (1934), which speaks continually in the plural of 'we' rather than 'I', Vera Brittain was already trying to identify herself and her middle-class contemporaries in terms of their common experience as a generation, to define them in terms of their joint participation in historical circumstances and events which changed their lives. In so doing, she produced what Robert Wohl has found to be 'the classic example of English lost generation literature' (Wohl, 1980: 110). As a project this was highly innovatory. Its theoretical failure is important for our understanding of women's history and of women's sense of their own identity.

The failure of *Testament of Youth* as a generational autobiography is due to two facts. Firstly, she does not understand the men she writes about, the male half of her generation. It is not simply that she can still, in 1933, make the crass claim that 'the noblest and profoundest emotions that men experience – the emotions of love, . . . can come to them only through women' (Brittain, 1933: 88) as if Plato and Shakespeare had never written. Whether or not the comradeship of fighting men was 'noble' (a chivalric term which in itself betrays her), or led to profound emotions, as so many men stated, she does not understand how men's experience of war changed their ideas. Her use of the term 'epic' is sufficient indication of this. Graves' war-book is a satire, Blunden's an elegy; for Hemingway, war made life absurd. Like Rupert Brooke, her young men may have set off in expectation of a Greek epic; as Roland Leighton tried to make clear to her, they did not find it. The only English writer who may have experienced the First World War as an epic was Lawrence of Arabia, but guerrilla warfare in the desert was not like trench warfare on the Western Front. Even by stretching the imagination the tale of Loos, the Somme or Passchendaele could not be regarded as an 'epic' of heroic deeds, and Vera Brittain's imagination does not stretch at all.

Like Storm Jameson, Vera Brittain was aware of a gulf between the men and women of her generation, but it was a gulf which she tended to dramatise rather than examine. Her very determination to continue conceptualising war in terms of nobility and courage identifies that gulf. Her sense of the waste of war is brought home vividly when she visits post-war Germany and witnesses the humiliation and starvation. She is appalled at such cruel destruction. But even then it is as the waste of 'noble emotion' and the 'laying down of life' that she complains of it. She wants to run away from the results, back to the past where 'abstract heroism is all that matters, and men acted finely and bravely, believing that the end would be quite other than this' (645). Although *Journey's End* may have enabled her to maintain this pious illusion about the sacrifice of men's heroism in war, Hemingway's *A Farewell to Arms* contains the classic statement of the men's reaction to that mode of thought:

> I was always embarrassed by the words sacred, glorious, and sacrifice and the expression in vain ... I had seen nothing sacred, and the things that were glorious had no glory and the sacrifices were like the stockyards at Chicago if nothing was done with the meat except to bury it ... Abstract words such as glory, honour, courage, or hallow were obscene beside the concrete names of villages, the numbers of roads, the names of rivers, the numbers of regiments and the dates. (Hemingway, 1929: 143–4)

As Aldington expressed it, he liked and respected the War soldiers, not as soldiers but as men, because they had developed an essential manhood and humanity which 'existed in spite of the War and not because of it. They had saved something from a gigantic wreck, and what they had saved was immensely important – manhood and comradeship, their essential integrity as men, their essential brotherhood as men' (Aldington, 1929: 258).

Secondly, she does not understand the experiences of women either. She does not understand what identified her as a member of a particular generation of women. Presenting the historical background to her life in terms of international politics and her family's origins, she gives no details of the history of the women's movement. She does not portray her own education and ideas as part of the social and cultural currents connected with women's political struggle for emancipation. She actually has very little interest in or respect for other women, even of her own class.

For instance, confessing that even by 1919 she had heard very little of the 'bitter tale of pacifism during the War', she gives the names of E. D. Morel and Bertrand Russell but not of any of the women who kept the movement going (473). So when she later mentions Mrs Helen Swanwick in connection with the League of Nations Union, the name appears, like the Union, out of the blue. She first came into intimate contact with the homes of the poor in Bethnal Green in the East End, in 1922. It was this encounter with the 'semi-barbarous' conditions of four-fifths of the population, and her recognition of the kinship between these men and women and the Tommies she had nursed for four years, who showed the same humour and compassion and courage, which converted her to socialism. She was apparently quite unaware of Sylvia Pankhurst's work in this part of London. Vera Brittain shows no sense of gender solidarity, identifying more with her brother than with friends of the same sex. Generally refusing to see herself as a typical woman, she nevertheless claims to speak on behalf of other women, presenting her story as having a wide general application.

Had she understood both men and women better, known more about them and been able to explain the differences between them, she might have realised that her idea of identifying a single historical generation of both men and women was one more example of the naïve idealism of her youth. As an adolescent she had dreamed of a new Renaissance inaugurated by the men and women of her generation, when women would no longer be considered second-rate and unimportant creatures, but 'the equal and respected companions of men' (Brittain, 1933: 41). Women did not get political equality with men until 1928; equal pay was not legally enforced until after the Second World War. Women may have been important, even crucial, to Britain's war-effort in 1914–18, but they were not companions of men. After the war women were conspicuously treated as second-rate, as Vera found at Oxford. This was despite struggle by several generations of women.

The unqualified use of the terms 'contemporaries' and 'generation' masks the crucial distinction of gender. Vera Brittain is quite able to conceptualise the problems facing the New Woman, for instance, in combining motherhood with an independent profession: 'for me and my contemporaries our old enemies – the Victorian tradition of womanhood, a carefully trained conscience, a sheltered youth, an imperfect education, lost time, blasted years – were still there and always would be' (Brittain, 1933: 655). Although this parallels Graves' recognition in the Epilogue to the 1957 edition of *Goodbye to All That*: 'a conditioning in the Protestant morality of the English governing classes ... is not easily out-grown' (Graves, 1957: 282), it is hard to suppose that the Victorian tradition of womanhood or the imperfect education a girl received at the turn of the century presented the same problems for Graves as for Brittain. That distinction, and the difference in experience which went with it, explain the fallacy in her view that 'the same prodigious happenings and the same profound changes of opin-ion' moulded her contemporaries of equal sex. The happenings and changes were not the same for contemporaries of different sex. If the changes were not the same, then the unqualified idea of a single historical or cultural generation is misleading.

Vera Brittain did not originate the idea of talking about a historical generation, although she was the first writer to insist that a historical generation consisted of both sexes. Robert Wohl discusses the genesis of the theory of historical generations in his book *The Generation of 1914*. He also discusses how the idea generated the myth of 'The Lost Generation'. In American myth-ology this is specifically a literary conception. In British mythology it is political as well as cultural: the best of a generation in body and spirit died on the Western Front. These were the younger generation, sacrificed by their elders. This myth was very widely held to explain Britain's post-War decline: 'and nobody, nothing will shift me from the belief which I shall take to the grave that the generation to which I belonged, destroyed between 1914 and 1918, was a great generation, marvellous in its promise' (Priestley, 1962).

The myth finds its most perfect expression in Vera Brittain: 'the finest flowers of English manhood had been plucked from a whole generation' (Brittain, 1933: 610). As she explained it, the con-sequences for civilisation were dire: 'the men who might, in co-operation with the women who were not too badly impaired by shock and anxiety, have contributed most to its recovery, the first-rate, courageous men with initiative and imagination, had themselves gone down with the Flood, and their absence now meant failure and calamity in every department of human life' (645). And the consequences for the world as a whole are apocalyptic: 'lacking first-rate ability and social order and economic equilibrium, it will go spinning down into chaos as fast as it can – unless some of us try to prevent it' (473).

In fact, as demographers have demonstrated, not only is there nothing to indicate that it was the 'finest' who died in the War, the guns being indiscriminate, but the population losses of the First

World War were made up within a matter of a few years (Winter, 1978: 254–5). Moreover, the myth of the lost generation has obscured the actual demographic gains of the war-period among the civilian population, due to improvements in public health and the war-time rise in the standard of living amongst the very poorest, so that 'after 1914 poverty meant deprivation rather than destitution for the working class' (Winter, 1985: 21). As Wohl says, 'the Lost Generation' is an élitest myth, based largely on losses among the sons of the governing classes. However, statistically justified or not, it has played an important role in the consciousness of succeeding generations: 'the best that we who were left could do was to refuse to forget, and to teach our successors what we remembered in the hope that they, when their own day came, would have more power to change the state of the world than this bankrupt, shattered generation' (Brittain, 1933: 645–6).

Women also died serving their King and country in the First World War, but it is never suggested that they formed part of the 'Lost Generation' of first-rate ability. Their loss did not contribute to Britain's parlous state. Even Vera Brittain never suggests that women's talent might replace the courageous talent lost on the Somme. One consequence of the Lost Generation myth is to reinforce women's sense of inferiority.

A further consequence is, paradoxically, to undermine the 'Somme Myth'. Recent commentators like A. J. P. Taylor and Paul Fussell, have argued that the Battle of the Somme sums up British attitudes to the Great War. The first day of the 'battle', 1 July 1916, became the archetypal original for the modern sense of irony; events on that day became a virtual allegory for the political and social disillusion of our time. The myth is built around a sense of the worthlessness of individual life to the modern State, and is combined with a profound distrust of the official ideology which suggests otherwise. This disillusion was stated as early as 1922 by C. E. Montague, in the book he entitled *Disenchantment*:

> The most bloody defeat in the history of Britain, a very world's wonder of valour frustrated by feckless misuse, of regimental glory and Staff shame, might occur on the Ancre on July 1, 1916, and our Press come out bland and copious and graphic, with nothing to show that we had not had a good day – a victory really. Men who had lived through the massacre read the stuff open-mouthed. (Montague, 1922: 102)

Alan Bishop, in an unpublished paper, 'The Battle of the Somme and Vera Brittain', has examined the way in which the Battle of the Somme appears in Vera Brittain's writings, as a way of testing Fussell's hypothesis about the ironic memory of the Somme typifying the dominant form of modern understanding. Vera's brother, Edward, a junior officer in Kitchener's Army, led one of the futile assaults on the morning of 1 July 1916, and was afterwards awarded the Military Cross for his behaviour on that day. He was wounded and, by chance, ended up four days later in the London hospital where Vera was nursing, so she heard at first hand what his experiences had been like, while they were still fresh in his mind. (He never voluntarily spoke about the matter again.) She recorded what he told her directly into her diary, and she used this record when writing her autobiography in 1933. She also implicitly referred to his ordeal in her poem, 'To My Brother', written in 1918 to express her admiration for him and to encourage him just before the battle on the Italian front in which he was killed leading a counter-attack. Between 1933 and 1935, she wrote several journalistic articles based on her diary record of a tour of the Somme battlefield, its cemeteries and memorials, which she made in 1933. So the Somme figures prominently in Vera Brittain's literary legacy about the Great War.

In her war-diary (later published as *Chronicle of Youth*), Vera Brittain records on 1 July 1916 that she has heard from the newspapers that 'a tremendous battle has opened on the Somme – very successfully they say' (Brittain, 1981: 410). On 5 July she transcribes what Edward has told her about 'all he had been through on that day – hereafter to be regarded as one of the greatest dates in history' (411). Edward's Company was in the second wave of the attack, and while they were waiting to go over his men were swamped in the trench, first of all by crowds of wounded returning from the first wave, and then by the panicking members of another battalion, running away from the carnage. The panic spread to Edward's men, who refused to move. 'Twice he had to go back to rally them. Finally he got them over the parapet . . .' (412). He was wounded twice within the first hundred yards of No-Man's-Land and eventually crawled back through the dead and dying. For this 'conspicuous gallantry and leadership' he was awarded the Military Cross. Of his Company (which would have consisted of approximately 200 soldiers and five officers) only 17 men and two officers came through 'unscathed'. This meant that the 20-year-old Edward Brittain was decorated for 'leading' nearly 200 men to certain maiming or death. The only way for a junior officer (presumably supported by his NCO) to 'rally' mutinous troops was to threaten them with his revolver. How else would he have persuaded them to walk straight into the German machine-gun fire? No wonder that Vera also remarks that a little while afterwards she and his friends 'realised that July 1st had changed him utterly & added ten years to his life' (411).

Although modern historians try to be scrupulously faithful to the remembered experience of 'the men who were there', they do not report any such resistance to orders. The mutiny at Étaples in 1917 went down in folk-memory, despite efforts at an official 'cover-up' (Brittain, 1933: 426). But 'cowardice in the face of the enemy' – or determination to preserve one's own life during a battle – is not what men care to recall. In his history, *The First Day on the Somme*, Martin Middlebrook includes details of Edward's Battalion, the 11th Sherwood Foresters, on that morning, including the wounded clogging up the trench. Immediately before, he expressly claims that, despite men seeing with their own eyes the devastation of the first assault-wave, 'There is no record of any battalion hesitating in its attack' (Middlebrook, 1971: 159). Later historians may not display quite the patriotic fervour of Mrs Humphry Ward in her novel '*Missing*': 'Then on the first of July, the British army . . . leapt from its trenches on the Somme front . . . In those days "there were no stragglers – none!" said an eye-witness in amazement. The incredible became everywhere the common and achieved. Life was laid down as at a festival' (Ward, 1917: 197). But neither do they stress the role of battle-police and the background of intimidation and coercion. In her history, *Somme* (1983), Lynn Macdonald includes just one reference to such a consideration, in a quotation from a sergeant in a Scots division (Scots are not renowned for hesitancy):

We knew it was pointless, even before we went over – crossing open ground like that. But, you had to go. You were between the devil and the deep blue sea. If you go forward, you'll likely be shot. If you go back, you'll be court-martialled and shot. So what the hell do you do? What can you do? You just go forward, because the only bloke you can get your knife into is the bloke you're facing. (Macdonald, 1983: 157)

Part of the Somme myth is that the men of Kitchener's Army were duped victims whose bravery was wasted. However, at this point Vera was not concerned with victims or sacrifice, or the examples of 'funk' her brother recalls. She is concerned only with Edward's heroism, confirmed by his decoration, which she described to her mother as 'too unspeakably splendid'.

In 1918 she wrote Edward a poem to tell him what she could never say to his face or put into a letter: 'how greatly I esteemed him for the brave endurance' which he had shown on 1 July 1916 and so often afterwards (Brittain, 1933: 434). This is the poem 'To My Brother (In Memory of July 1st, 1916)' which was published in her *Verses of a VAD* in 1919, and reprinted in *Testament of Youth*, and which (unfortunately in Bishop's opinion) gave the title to Catherine Reilly's collection of women's war-poetry, *Scars Upon My Heart* (1981). By 1918 Vera had served in hospitals in Malta and on the Western Front, as well as in London, and she had witnessed with compassion the terrible injuries war inflicted. She had written her mother a letter in 1917 about the acute medical ward she was working in, saying how she wished that the people who wrote so glibly about 'this being a holy War', and the orators who made speeches about carrying on with the war no matter what the cost, could only see the cases of mustard gas poisoning she was nursing: 'could see the poor things burnt and blistered all over' (395). Despite this rejection of war-propaganda and its talk of a holy war, her own poetry still uses the same chivalric conventions. Not remarking on the irony of a *military* cross, she praises it as a symbol of Edward's courage, received in the 'grand and tragic "show"' of the Somme, and hopes that he will endure 'And with your men pursue the flying foe, / As once in France / Two years ago'. Apart from the weak need for a rhyme, 'flying foe' is part of the archaic rhetoric associated with the pro-war propaganda; it only too manifestly bears no relation to what Edward did during that war of attrition, especially in the Battle of the Somme where his company did not cause the enemy to retreat one inch.

In *Testament of Youth*, she repeats what she had written in her diary about Edward's exploits, although she now speaks of the Battle of the Somme as 'that singularly wasteful and ineffective orgy of slaughter' (276). Yet she expresses no irony with regard to Edward's decoration, reporting that it was still comparatively rare and meant a good deal, being 'awarded only for acts of conspicuous courage' (289). The effect of propaganda is very powerful, and perhaps what especially prevents her from paying full attention to what Edward or Roland or Victor tell her is the ideology of femininity and masculinity imposed upon her: 'For us who cannot fight, it is a burden almost more than we can bear, to feel that we owe our safety to the lives and sight and strength of such as Roland and Victor and Edward' (Brittain, 1981: 426). She repeats this same idea from 1916 in 1933, when she wonders how far the women of her generation who accept new emotional relationships 'thereby destroyed yet again the men who had once uncomplainingly died for them in the flesh' (Brittain, 1933: 655). Although war is wasteful of youth and happiness, men die in war to save their womenfolk. The myth of the Lost Generation re-asserts those gender values, binding masculinity to heroism in battle, and femininity to dependent helplessness. After the War, there remained only 'fussy, futile, avid, ineffectual' men 'who wallowed in nauseating sentimentality and hadn't the brains of an earwig – [and] simply provided one proof after another that the best of their sex had disappeared from a whole generation' (608).

While visiting the cemeteries on the Somme brought home to Vera Brittain the numbers of men killed, and led her to repudiate even the dignified war-memorials as 'a cheating and a camouflage' since they continued to suggest that war itself was 'noble and glorious', the very numbers of lives 'lost' merely re-inforced her idea of a 'lost generation' (Brittain, 1985: 215). As Alan Bishop states, 'the "lost generation" aspect of the Somme myth deserves to be questioned; it accommodates a muted version of the myth of martial heroism in its concentration on the putative effects of lost leadership'. Vera Brittain's various responses to the Battle of the Somme qualify Fussell's argument: 'The Somme myth, as it established primacy and then patterned Brittain's final response, did not completely replace the old myth of martial heroism, but adapted and absorbed it as the "lost generation" theme that she so emphasised in her subsequent writing' (Bishop, 1986).

It makes sense to consider the Lost Generation myth in England as essentially a women's myth. It goes together with the Remembrance Day celebrations, to continue glamorising the dead as perfect and unchanging: 'To the end, to the end they remain'. While glamorising and mystifying grief for the dead: 'in the midst of desolation / . . . glory . . . shines upon our tears' it also glamorises death in war as martial heroism: 'They fell with their face to the foe' (Laurence Binyon, 'For the Fallen', 1914). Having encouraged men to go to war to demonstrate their manhood (as Vera encouraged Roland and Edward), it seems to have been impossible for women to admit it did no such thing. Glamourising the dead also veiled women's share in the moral responsibility for the waste of men's lives. This is made clear by the unironic ending of Iris Murdoch's later novel about the Irish uprising of 1916, *The Red and the Green*:

[The dead] had a beauty which could not be eclipsed or rivalled. They had been made young and perfect forever, safe from the corruption of time and from those ambiguous second thoughts which dim the brightest face of youth. In the undivided strength of their first loves they had died . . . and had it been for nothing? Because of their perfection she could not bring herself to say so. They had died for glorious things, for justice, for freedom, for Ireland. (Murdoch, 1965: 272)

This glamorisation is, I think, precisely what prevents a proper political consciousness of war, of why wars take place and what they result in. In the case of the so-called 'Great War' it set up a powerful barrier to understanding why the men who had fought felt so bitter, and so misunderstood.

7

'Old, Unhappy, Far-off Things'

In his historiographical study of three famous British battles, *The Face of Battle* (1976), the military historian, John Keegan, claimed that in a sense the Battle of the Somme has still not ended yet. Despite the acres of official war graves, 'the principal memorial which the Somme left to the British nation is not one of headstones and inscriptions. It is intellectual and literary' (Keegan, 1976: 285). The experience of the Western Front called forth 'a literature of immense imaginative power and sweep ... an expression of the feelings of a whole generation' (286). Mindful of the book market, Keegan is wary of interpreting the sudden outpouring of war literature at the end of the 1920s as the 'lifting of a collective amnesia' or the 'dissipation of a mass repression'. However, certain of these works have sustained a readership, notably Blunden's, Graves's, Hemingway's and Sassoon's. Keegan suggests that this is not because they offer documentary evidence about the Great War. It is because they are 'moving and enduring expressions of truth about how man confronts the inevitability of death' (288).

Keegan's interest in producing his study derived from the fact that neither he nor his peers had what his father and grandfather had had: any first hand knowledge of battle as combatants. His central question was, 'How would *I* behave in a battle?' It was a question which raises emotions that are 'a very powerful, if dormant, part of every human being's make-up', both the violent passions of hatred, rage and the urge to kill, and the deep fears of being wounded, of death, and of failing in one's ultimate responsibility to others (16). Quoting from Herbert Butterfield's *Man on his Past*, Keegan claims that battles are always a matter of men struggling to reconcile their instinct for self-preservation with their sense of honour; they are always a matter of fear, and of violence; above all, the study of battle is a study of solidarity and of disintegration. However, since the First World War, our notions of cowardice have changed radically, so that now armies are taught to accept that 'courage and cowardice are [not] alternative free choices that come to every man, overriding all emotional stress' (334). After 1915, 'shell-shock' or psychiatric breakdown gradually became recognised as an inescapable aspect of prolonged combat.

In other words, Keegan and other young men read battle tales both to find out about the nature of humanity in extreme circumstances, and to understand the character of masculinity in particular. Insofar as our idea of courage has changed since the Great War, so has our idea of heroism and of what is to be expected of and admired in men. The ideal of manliness plays a different role for women; it sets no goal for their own behaviour, only for what they might value in the men they know. Women read such books as outsiders, as beholders of the opposite sex.

Although rage and fear are also part of women's make-up, women in Western society are not expected to demonstrate physical courage in armed combat, nor judged to be less feminine on that basis. (That physical courage and endurance are necessary in childbirth is another matter.) There were heroines during the First World War, in the sense that certain women voluntarily risked death, injury, or assault, and also displayed moral courage in enduring experiences which were for them horrific and stressful. However, although we may read women's war-books because they thrill and excite us just as men's do, they share one of their main sources of inspiration with the men's testaments of war, and this is also a motive in our reading. Women not only recount how men faced death away from the battlefield; they also tell us how they themselves faced the deaths of others.

In his novel *Aaron's Rod* (1922), which Richard Aldington called 'improvised variations on Lawrence's own experience' (Aldington 1950: 7), D. H. Lawrence wrote about the First World War from the point of view of a non-combatant. At one point he describes the behaviour of an army-officer on leave, a character very probably based on Aldington himself, since he was one of the few combatants of Lawrence's acquaintance. As helplessly gripped as a man in search of a prostitute, this officer has to talk on and on about the subject that obsesses him, 'to talk war at' someone, with

the same hot, blind, anguished voice of a man who has seen too much, experienced too much, and doesn't know where to turn.

None of the glamour of returned heroes, none of the romance of war: only a hot, blind, mesmerised voice, going on and on, mesmerised by a vision that the soul cannot bear. / In this officer, of course, there was a lightness and an appearance of bright diffidence and humour. But underneath it all was the same as in the common men of all the combatant nations: the hot, seared burn of unbearable experience, which did not heal nor cool, and whose irritation was not to be relieved. The experience gradually cooled on top: but only with a surface crust. The soul did not heal, did not recover. (Lawrence, 1922; 139)

In 1968 Derek Patmore recalled Richard Aldington writing *Death of A Hero* in 1928: 'I can remember he went through great agony recalling his war experiences, and I can recall the picture of him lying on his bed crying when he remembered the terrible life in the trenches during the First World War' (Patmore, 1968: 23). Aldington himself said later that, 'By writing *Death of A Hero* I purged my bosom of perilous stuff which had been poisoning me for a decade' (Aldington, 1941: 339).

The use of literature to purge the soul of pain was widespread. Some years after the Armistice, Wyn Griffith also experienced what he called 'an upsurge of remembering that brought back the war ... There was a kind of emotional explosion within me' (Panichas, 1968: 290). Writing his war-memoir *Up to Mametz* (1931) enabled him to become 'accustomed to and even reconciled with remembering'. Once he had faced and recorded the high point of the war, there came a kind of peace within him: 'I had spent my emotional capital in this detailed recovery and had been purged of the pain of war' (290). In 1963 Henry Williamson wrote in the 11th volume of his fictionalised autobiography, *The Power of the Dead*, about Phillip Maddison recalling his experience of the Battle of the Somme and writing it down, 11 years later in 1927: 'He put down the pen and walked about the room, trembling, while tears dripped from his eyes' (Williamson, 1963: 119). This was the result of an overwhelming impulse to write down, while the immediacy of memory lasted, that which had overwhelmed him (116). Part of the pain of remembering stemmed from grief. The volume is haunted by Maddison's memories of the dead: 'the faces of friends in uniform – these phantoms were more real to him than the living. One must never go back among the living: one must, for ever, say goodbye to old comrades, so that one might always see them with young faces' (298). But by the end of the book he has come to surrender his 'homeless ghosts' into God's hands. Writers like Blunden and Sassoon and Williamson spent the rest of their lives recalling the War, and trying to purge themselves of it.

When Vera Brittain was writing her autobiography, *Testament of Youth*, her 'unworthy' memorial to her dead brother and fiancé, she found that when she had finished the second third of it, she had rid herself of the War and its memories. She wrote to her husband that she felt empty: 'For eighteen years I have thought about little else but the war and the men I lost in it; now it is all laid down on paper and I shall never, perhaps, write of it again' (Brittain, 1957: 80). She had not entirely escaped her grief. A few weeks later she was writing about visiting her brother's grave after the War, and 'I was ashamed to find myself ignominiously weeping' (81). In 'urgent need for reconciliation with the past' (79), she had written, she thought, to try to console others who like herself had known despair. She found that by enabling her to set down the sorrows of the First World War, and to remove their bitterness, '*Testament of Youth* became the final instrument of a return to life from the abyss of emotional death' (76). What she discovered was that 'the actual decanting into words of past grief for lost loves is a form of exorcism, leaving the way clear for new patterns of tenderness' (92). This metamorphosis she summed up in the moral: 'though we cannot forget the dead, we must not remember them at the expense of the living' (92). This pattern of emotional resurrection appears over and over in women's books inspired by the War.

Certain war-books were intentionally written as laments for the dead, laments which were also tributes. Fussell called Blunden's *Undertones of War*, 'an extended pastoral elegy in prose' (Fussell, 1975: 154). This does not quite explain the 'uneasiness' readers have experienced. H. M. Tomlinson attributes the uneasiness to the fact that Blunden's book is 'by a ghost for other ghosts' (Tomlinson, 1930). The younger critic, Alec Hardie, agrees, 'It is the ghost of the "unknown soldier" that makes the whole narrative universal and exact ... The ghosts have never left him, and, as with so many of his generation, have haunted him ever since' (Hardie, 1958: 6–9). But Tomlinson speaks with the authority and personal feeling of one who knew the Western Front: 'You may hear echoing, as one used to hear desolation murmuring ... the wonder and awe of the sacrificed who did not know why this had come to them; for Blunden's is a tribute to the unknown soldier more lasting than the pomps about a cenotaph'.

More angrily, in his preface to *Death of A Hero*, Aldington wrote: 'this book is really a threnody, a memorial in its ineffective way to a generation which hoped much, strove honestly, and suffered deeply' (Aldington, 1929: 8). And in the Prologue he called the book 'an atonement, a desperate attempt to wipe off the blood-guiltiness' by which the dead were poisoning the survivors, the war-generation. Such mourning-books performed a rite more significant to the veterans than the national annual ceremony of Two Minutes' Silence: 'Headstones and wreathes and memorials and speeches and the Cenotaph – no, no, it has got to be something *in* us' (35). Williamson found that 'something' to be joy in human brotherhood:

> I must return to my old comrades of the Great War – for I am dead with them, and they live again in me. There in the beautiful desolation of rush and willow in the forsaken tracts I will renew the truths which have quickened out of their deaths: that we must free the child from all things which maintain as pre-eminent the ideal of a commercial nationalism, the ideal which inspired and generated the barrages in which ten million men of my generation, their laughter corrupted, perished. (Williamson, 1963: 70)

Literature both laid the dead to rest and helped to reconcile the living to the unchangeable past. It achieved this by making a permanent statement of society's debt. Some war-authors resolved that that debt must be paid by changing the nation. Other authors, like Robert Graves, or Gerald Brennan, understandably washed their hands of Britain. In Vera Brittain's case, as in Henry Williamson's, a war-memoir was also a commitment to a new beginning, rescuing for future generations something out of the waste by *determining* that the dead should not have died for 'nothing'.

Whatever war-authors explicitly determined, Keegan suggests that the long-term political implications of the curious social confrontation between ex-public schoolboy officers and the 'Pals' Battalions' of Kitchener's Army made it one of the most significant events in British history. In the process of mutual discovery were conceived 'an affection and concern for the disadvantaged which would eventually fuel that transformation of middle-class attitudes to the poor which has been the most important social trend in twentieth-century Britain' (Keegan, 1976: 225). The relation was idealised in the poetry of young officers such as Herbert Read. In 'My Company' he cries: 'O beautiful men, O men I loved,' and describes the 'radiance' that seemed to give grace to their unity. Denis Winter found more prosaic examples which show that 'If not quite love, there was always mutual respect' (Winter, 1978: 62). For instance, J. Boyd Orr, a future Cabinet Minister, was an officer with the Sherwood Foresters, who were mostly miners: 'Ever since, when there are troubles and strikes with miners, my sympathies have always been with the men' (62).

The sense of common humanity which over-rode rank in the army was not an experience which could be shared by women. Class divisions between middle-class women and working-class men and women were not so obviously transformed by the War (Braybon, 1987: 74–8). The women of Vera Brittain's generation led a far more restricted life than the men, even if they went overseas. It was not open to them to become the comrades even of the men of their own class, let alone of the common soldier whom Blunden celebrates. They may have learned to admire the Tommy, as Enid Bagnold and countless other nurses did, and to discover that the German soldiers were no different, but they were not in a position to write about Tommies as friends. As memorials, their books remained both more particular: grieving for the few men they could know personally, brother, lover or husband; and more general: expressing horror over 'those thousands of poor chaps, with all their lives before them, shovelled together'. The pattern in women's war-books, of emotional death and resurrection, did not usually lead to a sense of 'common sisterhood' or to a political new life as in Brittain's case, but to the more traditional 'new life' of motherhood. A child was a new beginning, a commitment to the future.

Vera Brittain's experience of emotional death came during the worst part of the War. By this stage the 'psychological shutter which we firmly closed down upon our recollection of the daily agony' (Brittain, 1933: 384) had begun to work with a lethal clamp. During the general retreat of March 1918, the Base Hospital at Étaples where she was nursing turned into a Casualty Clearing Station, taking the wounded off ambulance-trains straight from the battle-line, day and night. For nearly a month the camp resembled one of Doré's illustrations to Dante's *Inferno*, with 'gassed men on stretchers, clawing the air – dying men, reeking with mud and foul green-stained bandages, shrieking and writhing in a grotesque travesty of manhood – dead men with fixed, empty eyes and shiny yellow faces' (423). Her world became a 'kingdom of death' (416). After her brother was killed she felt 'marooned in a kind of death-in-life' (430). Deeply isolated, she continued working mechanically. Her disillusion at the death of her friends made reflection about the war dangerous; resentful, she repressed ferocious dreams of assault and murder. By November 1918 she had changed into a 'complete automaton, moving like a sleep-walker . . . into a permanent state of numb disillusion . . . with the ending of apprehension had come a deep, nullifying blankness, a sense of walking in a thick mist which hid all sights and muffled all sounds' (458). Within ten years she had lost one world, the world of her youth, but 'after a time rose again, as it were, from a spiritual death to find another' through the friendship of Winifred Holtby (495). By 1925 she had found the courage to look forward again, convinced that that was part of fidelity to the dead. She agreed to marry and have children, and so influence the future.

The fictionalised war-autobiography by Ruth Holland, *The Lost Generation* (1932), uses the same pattern of death and resurrection, but more personally than Vera Brittain. Holland's heroine, Jinny, also works as a VAD but never leaves England to share what Brittain called 'the tragic, profound freemasonry of those who accepted death together overseas' (360). Jinny's childhood sweetheart, her cousin who is more than a brother to her, is killed. She meets other boys: 'They came and went . . . and yet somehow none of them seemed real, or could make her feel real again . . . One after another friends were killed' (Holland, 1932: 156). She lives in a 'state of numbness, of feeling that she herself had died, while through some ghastly chance her body was still alive, and had to go on through the tasteless routine of days' (154). In spirit and truth she was elsewhere:

She was out in the darkness, out in some black waste strewn with corpses, and she was going from one to another, looking, peering, yet dreading to see; she was looking for Eliot. There were bodies lying on their faces as if they had fallen as they ran and never moved, bodies on their backs with faces ghastly, upturned, bodies twisted terribly. They were everywhere. She had to go to them all, with the other ghosts that wandered like

herself in that black waste. Killed . . . blown to pieces, a voice
was saying in her head, but still she had to go on looking and
searching and wandering. (171)

Eventually she returns from this No-Man's-Land of death-in-life.
Frightened of the grown-up world, she nevertheless finally stops
being so self-centred. She reconciles herself to Eliot's death,
accepts a social responsibility, and, like Vera Brittain, commits
herself to the future by marriage and children.

In the comparatively light-hearted work by Enid Bagnold, *The
Happy Foreigner*, which appeared only shortly after the War in 1920,
the archetypal nature of the pattern of death and resurrection is
more obvious. Within the guise of a romance, the heroine
undergoes the autumn and winter of hardship in France following
the German withdrawal, she explores the 'underworld' of the
fortress of Verdun, and then emerges to foresee the vista of the
future and the re-building of France in the spring.

The most self-consciously mythical use of the pattern is the
war-book by the American poet H.D., *Bid Me To Live: A Madrigal*.

Hilda Doolittle's novel, *Bid Me To Live*, was not published until
1960, but it is based on motifs that she was working on during the
First World War. The first draft seems to have been composed in
1927, and it was revised heavily, first in the 1930s while she was
undergoing analysis with Freud and again in 1949. The book is a
roman á clef and the characters and events it deals with appear in
three other novels concerning the same period. The first was D. H.
Lawrence's *Aaron's Rod* (1922); the second was John Cournos's
Miranda Masters (1926); and the third was the war-book by her
husband, Richard Aldington's *Death of A Hero* (1929). These novels
are extraordinarily different, both in tone and in their interpreta-
tion of events. The simplest account occurs in the book by
Cournos, who was not present in London while the main events
were taking place, but who was in love with H.D. and corresponding regularly with her. The broad 'facts' as he gives them are
corroborated by Aldington's biography, *Life for Life's Sake*,
by Cournos' own *Autobiography*, and by biographies of D. H.
Lawrence and his novel *Kangaroo*.

After a romantic attachment with Ezra Pound as a student, H.D.
had followed him to Europe. In London he introduced her to
another imagist poet, Richard Aldington, whom she married in
1913. He was then 21 and she was 27. In 1915 she suffered a

miscarriage, which she felt Aldington had brought on by the insensitive way in which he told her the news about the sinking of the *Lusitania*. She was very distressed by the loss of their baby and the person who seemed best to understand this and offer her comfort was D. H. Lawrence, perhaps because of his grief over the death of his mother. With the War in progress and Aldington about to enlist, she was apparently advised not to get pregnant again before the War was over. She and Aldington had a flat in Mecklenburgh Square, where Cournos had a room upstairs which he had lent to his former girlfriend, Dorothy Yorke. During one of his leaves Aldington embarked on an affair with Dorothy. H.D. was meanwhile corresponding regularly with Lawrence. Later, when Lawrence and his wife, Frieda, were expelled from Cornwall as spies, they stayed with H.D. H.D. understood that Frieda intended to have an affair with a young composer, Cecil Gray, but she herself seems to have suffered a sexual rejection from Lawrence. Eventually in 1918 H.D. let herself be persuaded to accompany Gray to Cornwall, where she became pregnant. The War ended. She left Gray, Aldington cast her off in order to live with Dorothy, and H.D. left for the Continent to spend the rest of her life with her daughter, Perdita, and the millionairess, 'Bryher' (Winifred Ellerman).

There has been a great deal of critical speculation in general as to how writers transform events into works of art, and in particular as to why the transformations are so different in the case of the novels by Lawrence, Aldington and H.D. The three novels offer quite distinct pictures of the breakdown of the Aldingtons' marriage, and the part played by Lawrence (who does not appear at all in Aldington's version). It seems to me that the most useful discussion is provided by Peter E. Firchow. He demonstrates that there is no piece of unimpeachable, unambiguous evidence as to the precise nature of the relationship between H.D. and D. H. Lawrence, despite all the surmising by their biographers. However, he claims that 'there is unquestionably a textual dialogue going on in *Bid Me To Live*' addressed to Lawrence and to Aldington (Firchow, 1980: 66). Summarising his analysis, he claims:

> Ultimately, it suggests, I think, that *Bid Me To Live* is heavily indebted to both *Aaron's Rod* and *Death of A Hero*, just as the latter novel is heavily indebted to the former; and it suggests too that

the three novels can only be read and interpreted fully and satisfactorily when taken together as a kind of 'trilogy'. It suggests further that both Lawrence's and Aldington's novels are unsympathetic reactions to the growing independence (especially in sexual terms) of women in the first part of the century, and that H.D.'s novel is a reaction to that reaction. (Firchow, 1980: 72)

Lawrence wrote quite openly to Gray about the fact that he regarded H.D. as a disciple, a kind of Mary Magdalene to his Christ, but that he was frightened of the relation of knowledge between them, which was 'deeper than love' (65). He also stated baldly in *Kangaroo*, that the 'American wife of an English friend, a poet serving in the army', to whom he was very grateful, 'was beautiful, reckless, one of the poetesses whose poetry Richard [the DHL figure] feared and wondered over' (Lawrence, 1923: 291). Lawrence's poetry of this period was influenced by H.D. and there appear to be correspondences between their later writings too. Believing in women's necessary subservience to men, this influence probably was felt as threatening by Lawrence.

However, I am not here primarily concerned with H.D.'s relationship with Lawrence, sexual or otherwise, but with the gulf that opened up between H.D. and Aldington during the War. It is impossible to say whether a rift would have appeared in their marriage if the First World War had not taken place. H.D. was hyper-sensitive and she was undoubtedly the more creative writer of the two. (Her poetic talent was acknowledged by the other great poets of her generation, not only Pound and Lawrence, but also T. S. Eliot. Writing in *The Sacred Wood* (1920), Eliot praised H.D.'s translations from the Greek above those of Gilbert Murray, the most important translator of the day.) But it seems unlikely that Aldington would have devoted himself to his wife's emotional needs and artistic abilities as Middleton Murry and Leonard Woolf did. Indeed, Aldington gave H.D. little support at the time when she needed it most, after her miscarriage, and even seems to have taken the opportunity to have an affair while H.D. was in the nursing-home recovering. Conversely, he seems not to have appreciated her emotional numbness after such a shock and felt it primarily as sexual coolness. However, they both attributed the break-up of their marriage to the War, and it is pertinent to understand why.

At the beginning of the War, both women and men rushed to the Continent. The Defence of the Realm Act was introduced immediately to restrict both mental and physical initiative. By 1915 strict military control was being enforced, and it was difficult to gain authority even to cross the Channel, let alone to visit the military zone. The physical area covered by martial law not only included 'sensitive' areas of Britain near army barracks, the coast, or munitions factories, and the front-line in Flanders, but the whole extent of France from the ports and base-areas up to the trenches. In the early part of the War this military zone included civilians, as La Motte and Mansfield recorded (*supra*, chapter 3), so although no one could move freely there was some sort of regular domestic existence for soldiers to participate in when they returned from the trenches. There were families living there, including wives and daughters, and not much further back there were women nurses, and the auxiliaries attached to the base. Various writers have commented on the importance of this 'normal' life for soldiers to retain a sense of their ordinary identity and humanity.

> Confronted with good, gentle people, men recognised themselves, felt ashamed of their crudities of speech and manner which war and male society feed. They yearned for their old life, where they could be their real selves. This was the precious experience which French civilian life offered ... what estaminet and cottage offered men was beyond price. If there were small children or animals about, the temporary psychic infusion would be complete. (Winter, 1978: 145)

But this did not continue. Winter was wrong to claim that, 'This was the clue. In a hard war, in an institution which took from men many of the inhibitions of what they would once have regarded as decent behaviour, the soldiers never became wholly cut off' (145). For as Carrington demonstrated: 'As the intensity of war increased, absorbing more people more deeply into its soulless mechanism, the battle-zone from which all civilians were excluded spread wider, and the kindly processes of common life died away' (Carrington, 1965: 167). When the Germans retreated behind the Hindenburg Line in 1917, they deliberately laid waste a huge devastated area and cleared it of all civilians. For the last two years of the War half of the British Army was living in a virtual desert within which the only activity was military, and in which there were no women at all. Carrington's battalion was in the devastated area from February to June 1917, and those soldiers who did not get leave or go on a course during that time, 'Never saw a street, a shop window, a civilian, or a woman of any class' (167).

When George Winterbourne, the protagonist of *Death of A Hero* arrives in France in late 1916, he serves on a part of the line where there are no civilians, all buildings and trees have been smashed, and the only thing that flourishes on the bare landscape is graves: 'It was like living in the graveyard of the world – dead trees, dead houses, dead mines, dead villages, dead men' (Aldington, 1965: 268). Even the rest periods are spent in a ruined village where, although Winterbourne would not have been tempted by one, the men are disappointed to find no brothel. The description offered him of soldiers lining up outside a war-area bawdy-house in Béthune does not suggest the 'psychic transfusion' Winter speaks of:

> You can see 'em lining up outside the red lamps after dark under a Sergeant. Soon's the ole woman gives the signal, the sergeant says: 'Next two files, right turn, quick march,' and in yer go. The ole woman 'as a short-arm inspection and gives yer Condy's fluid, and the tart 'as Condy's Fluid too. She was a nice tart she was, but she was in a 'ell of a 'urry ... I 'adn't got meself buttoned up afore I 'eared the Sergeant shoutin': 'Next two files, right turn, quick march'. (293)

When Winterbourne finally gets leave and arrives back in London, he 'was amazed at the beauty, the almost angelic beauty, of women'. Like Aldington himself on his first leave in 1917: 'He had not seen woman for seven months' (339).

In such a context, letters became a vital lifeline, and their importance is stressed in both *Death of A Hero* and *Bid Me To Live*. (It is presumably for this reason that Aldington named his H.D. figure 'Elizabeth Paston', in humorous allusion to the Paston letters, an intimate correspondence maintained between members of the Paston family during the Wars of the Roses.) This was not merely a matter of 'keeping in touch'. It was a matter of preserving a man's sense of his own identity and personal worth, and thus of his own sanity. Once out of the firing-line Winterbourne became different from the 'dazed and haggard man' of battle, but was overcome with an 'apathetic weariness of mind' and became 'aimless, apathetic, listless': 'An immense effort of imagination was needed to link himself now with then [the old days before the War]' (339). The experience of battle 'made a cut in his life and personality . . . he was a little mad' (323). This madness, the result of extreme anxiety and fear, was accompanied by a deep sense of degradation.

The degradation was dual, a combination of physical humiliation and mental suffering. In order to achieve 'efficiency' the military machine was designed to depersonalise men: 'It would be much more practical to fight modern wars with robots than with men. But then, men are cheaper . . . the trouble is that most men have feelings; to attain the perfect soldier, we must eliminate feelings' (267). Winterbourne was humiliated by the constant filth and his resultant diarrhoea. His body was infested with lice and broke out in boils; his hands and face were coarsened and his feet deformed. There were no sanitary washing facilities and the latrines were disgusting. He was soiled, and he soiled himself. His mind also degenerated. He suffered from the shock of the abrupt change from surroundings where the things of the mind were valued, to surroundings where they were ignorantly despised. He found it difficult to read or think consecutively. 'He was less and less able to enjoy subtleties of beauty and anything intellectually abstruse. He came to want common amusements in place of the intense joy he had felt in beauty and thought' (288).

Winterbourne became conscious of this degradation through the imagined attitude of the women he knew. Women had acquired 'a sort of mythical and symbolical meaning for him'; they were 'havens of civilised existence' (227), and they did not understand the brutal strain he was living under. They were still human beings; he was a murder-robot:

> 'It's quite useless,' said Elizabeth; 'he's done for. He'll never be able to recover. So we may as well accept it. What was rare and beautiful in him is as much dead now as if he were lying under the ground in France.' (228)

The women Winterbourne loved receded far away from him: ' "Elizabeth" and "Fanny" were now names at the foot of sympathetic but rather remote letters' (279).

Poetic art required an exquisite sensibility, a mind finely attuned to nuances. As D. H. Lawrence showed in *Aaron's Rod*, any such sensitivity became intensely painful at the battlefront. In general any delicacy of response was coarsened by the animality of everyday life in the war-zone, and particularly by the horrifying way in which men were killed. There was no balm for such anguish of mind. The mindless, physical comfort Aldington craved on leave, H.D. could not provide after the trauma of the miscarriage; the fineness of spiritual sympathy she expected was torture to him. Aldington wrote in his autobiography that by the end of the War, 'my creative vein had practically dried up' (Aldington, 1941: 214). He was one of the spiritually war-wounded.

As Helen McNeil has pointed out, H.D. was also 'badly war-wounded' (H.D., 1984: xiii).

Aldington called *Death of A Hero* 'a jazz novel' (Aldington, 1965: 7) to indicate that it violated the conventions of the classical novel: 'good taste', emotional restraint, detachment. In the course of the novel, Aldington likens the 'stupendous symphony of sound' made by the barrage that procedes battle, to 'super-jazz'. During the first half-hour of the 'colossal harmony' of the bombardment 'hundreds upon thousands of men would have been violently slain, smashed, torn, gouged, crushed, mutilated' (321). Like jazz, *Death of A Hero* improvises its own form, a combination of narrative and violent political polemic. It has an individual lead voice which is passionate, vehement, strident. Modulating between lyricism and rancour, this is an instrument which refuses to play 'The Last Post' but hectors the reader instead in a way which critics dislike (Bergonzi, 1980: 186; Greicus, 1973: 16). With final contempt for British conventions, the 'Hero' of the title does not keep a stiff upper lip: his death is, ironically, a desperate suicide on the eve of the Armistice.

By contrast, *Bid Me To Live* was subtitled *A Madrigal*. Dating from the Renaissance, the madrigal was a standard lyrical form of great intricacy. The novel is prefaced by the poem from which its title is taken, *To Anthea, Who May Command Him Anything*, a love lyric by the 17th-century poet Robert Herrick. References and allusions to Herrick's poetry, particularly to *To Daffodils* ('We weep to see / You haste away . . . We have as short a spring'), form a leitmotif in *Bid Me To Live*. However, H.D.'s book does not share the bawdy wit of the final lines of *To Anthea*: '[Thou] hast command of every part / To live and die for thee'. Quite the contrary. H.D.'s protagonist is called 'Julia', the name of the imaginary woman to whom the celibate priest-poet, Herrick, addressed most of his lyrics. Julia's libido was depressed in the War, just as her husband's sensual desire became less biddable and more rampant. H.D. begins her novel by an explanation of Julia's total depression. With the death of her child in the womb, Julia has experienced annihilation of her inmost being. War means destruction and annihilation. So she had felt what the War was, in her own self, and was terrified that her husband, Rafe, would also be annihilated.

The War meant a complete break in time; the years of happiness before the war, the early years of her marriage, spent in France and Italy, were irrecoverable. The beautiful works of art they had seen together were now stored, as most of the furniture of their marriage was stored, in a basement. Similarly, although the past was dead, blasted to bits, traces of it lay in the minds of those who were rooted in the past. The ghost of her marriage lived on, although she was emotionally frozen, dead, and Rafe had become a stranger: 'She had married him when he was another person' (16). Yet the echo of his voice, the echo of the past, could still be heard within the coarseness of his present voice. An echo, a slightly varying repetition, is fundamental to the madrigal-form. Wittily, Herrick 'echoed' the sound of the madrigal by the way in which the phrases 'bid me to live' and 'a loving heart' modulate through his poem. Echoing is what gives H.D.'s novel its unifying style, and links the form of the novel to its content. Words and ideas resonate in the mind, so that although the past is dead it goes on living subliminally in the present.

Although her allusiveness is more consciously verbal, H.D.'s style has much in common with Virginia Woolf's in *Mrs Dalloway*. This is not, I think, so much a matter of Woolf's influence, as due to the fact that H.D.'s novel is also to do with the nature of the unconscious, of repressed memory and its imaginative power.

Nor is it purely coincidental, I think, that the word 'madrigal' (that H.D. insisted on, despite her publishers) is supposed to have derived from the Latin, meaning 'of the womb'. With the destructiveness of the war, the emptiness of her womb, Julia had receded to an empty black cavern, a state of frozen emotion in which her imagination had died. Like other poets such as Blunden, she despaired of the possibility of poetry in the face of war-reality: 'Beauty is truth, truth beauty. But could truth be beautiful? . . . Seasons revolved around horrors until one was numb' (37). It was out of that emotional death that 'Rico' summoned her, Orpheus-like, back to the light of poetic vision by which she could see the 'gloire', the inner radiance of the world. The imagery of Greek myth and Platonic philosophy runs through the novel.

The gap in Julia's consciousness, a pit of darkness, becomes identified with the room in Queen Square, where she is shuttered in against the carnage of the War, just as the remembrance of her loss is shuttered inside her, and the idea of death or any reference to it is excluded as unthinkable. At the heart of the room, a bed-sitting room, is the marriage-bed that she shares with her husband. It is also a death-bed. To revisit that room and what happened in it, and especially to recall what happened in that bed, is to recall the bliss of her marriage and the pain which wounded her (13); it is to remember the War and the unfeelingness war produces.

The pit of blackness in her consciousness is identical with her own empty womb, and with the pit of the cinema-theatre in which she sees a thousand soldiers as if in the pit of inferno: 'it seemed that all the soldiers in the world, symbolically were packed into this theatre' (122). Watching a film, they are the doomed, the dead watching their own destruction; singing *Tipperary*, they are voices 'surging toward their own destruction' (126). But the film they watch is a vision, a ghost of Beauty, of Persephone in Enna, of Demeter, of Primavera: 'Beauty was not dead' (125). The young composer who took Julia to the cinema is not a soldier. He takes her away, away from her dead marriage, away from London and the bombing, to Cornwall. There she begins to come back to life. But the actual instrument of her resurrection is the poet, Rico, whose poetic vision is like the sun. He bid her to do away with her 'frozen altar', and makes her feel that as a poet she has worth, and through him she writes poetry again. 'Don't you know, don't you realise that this is *poetry*?' (140). In Cornwall she becomes Demeter, who recovers the fruit of her own womb: Persephone and the love of flowers. (In real life, H.D. called herself 'HERmione' and her daughter 'Perdita', recalling Shakespeare's version of the Persephone myth in *The Winter's Tale*.)

But why had Julia's room/womb become a tomb in which she was a corpse (119)? Why had her marriage-bed become a frozen altar? The reason is an event she wants to forget, an event she attributes – in the final analysis – to the War.

Her husband had been her lover, 'the author of her psychic being' (19). Through their union, through their ability to communicate directly with each other, they had fed off each other, kept each other alive. This union was destroyed, partly because Julia fell 'cerebrally' in love with Rico who then replaced Rafe as the inspiration of her poetry, and partly because Rafe physically desired Bella and addressed his poetry to her in place of Julia. Yet they still loved each other. Sexually frozen, Julia 'condoned' Rafe's adultery. It did not seem like adultery since an army-officer, a stranger to her, had replaced her poet-husband. This stranger spoke a foreign language: 'You might let me have a little fun . . . Bella is a star-performer' (47–9).

Her husband had 'colourated' to an army-officer: he had taken on the markings of the military. He had become loud, hearty, violent, and had actually begun to enjoy the War: 'We have them on the run' (46). She could actually taste the War in him. When he kissed her, he breathed a taint of poison-gas and flayed carcasses into her lungs (39). Julia's explanation is that 'Rafe the last times back here [from the Front], had simply not been Rafe but someone else and what does it matter that a strange officer on leave spends half a day upstairs in [Bella's] attic bedroom?' (57). Julia herself cannot 'serve God and Mammon, not serve poet and hearty over-sexed young officer on leave' who mangles her emotions (46). While the officer spends his afternoons in bed upstairs, the poet leaves flowers for her to find in their room downstairs.

But the charade becomes untenable when, during an air-raid, she walks into the big room downstairs one afternoon, to find them together in her own bed: 'That had been the last human experience' (117). That is the traumatic experience that the War means for her. 'Well, that bed was that bed and she had not slept in it since, with or without Rafe' (129). The only explanation that Rafe gives for his behaviour is 'Bella makes me forget. You make me remember'. Julia, uncomprehending, responds 'Well, that at least was to her credit, she had kept the flame alight' (71). But the kind of thing Bella makes him forget is the kind of thing he has nightmares about: helping to drag out some officers buried in a dug-out during a gas-attack (175). Julia would need to 'live in two dimensions' simultaneously to cope with a soldier-poet: the military and the poetic. But the military is repugnant to her.

Aldington, too, gives an account of the estrangement between Winterbourne and his wife, of the alienation between the front-line troops, 'a new, curious race of men, the masculine men' and everyone else (Aldington, 1965: 255). From the first he finds something 'intensely masculine' about the troops, something stimulating: 'They had been where no woman and no half-man had ever been, could endure to be. They were Men' (253). It makes them 'better' than the women and the half-men. By comparison, even new soldiers seem babyish – rounded and rather feminine. Winterbourne humbly admires the men, wants to die with them rather than live without them. 'True, they were degenerating in certain ways, they were getting coarse and rough and a bit animal' (258), but they retained what was important: their essential manhood.

In other words, with the development of the War, Winterbourne despises his wife's femininity, which would make the front-line unendurable to her; conversely, Julia finds her husband's new-found masculinity repulsive. Women symbolise something which had been of extreme importance to Winterbourne: civilisation. But now he has found something of greater importance: basic human-ity, and by identifying it with masculinity, he depreciates the feminine. The War ethos has re-asserted gender values which are not only mutually exclusive, but mutually alienating. It is all the more poignant then, that Julia should have argued *against* Rico's theory that man-is-man and woman-is-woman. She had claimed that consciousness is sexless: 'Why should not she enter into the feelings of men?' (62).

The idea that *battle* 'made a man of you' was, of course, not unique to Aldington. It finds an idealised expression in William N. Hodgson's much anthologised poem, *Before Battle*, first published in June 1916: 'Make me a soldier, Lord. / Make me a man, O Lord'. Having enlisted in 1914, Hodgson made his 'fresh and sanguine sacrifice' in the Battle of the Somme, at the age of 23. Men who were not actually killed were nevertheless fundamentally altered by the ordeal of battle. H. Allen, listening to a man telling his battle-story, responded: 'He was a different man. Something had come to him which had not yet come to us. It was the trial of battle and no one who passes through it is ever quite the same again' (Winter, 1978: 189). Even E. Norman Gladden, who experienced the Somme, his first battle, as rather an anti-climax in which 'nothing much happened', nevertheless wrote 60 years later: 'but I had been in a battle and was henceforth a different being. For the first time I felt myself a man, indefinably changed' (ibid.). This is the gloss some men put on an experience that Gladden called 'more horrible than anything I had visualised'. All observers were agreed that men were dazed and haggard when they first came out of battle. Drawing on his own experience, Manning described the immediate reaction: 'They had been through it and lapsed little lower than savages. Life for them held nothing new in the way of humiliation' (188). Is this what Aldington really meant when he wrote that battle produced 'a cut in [Winterbourne's] life and personality', that he was left with a sense of anxiety and fear, and also a 'shrinking horror of the human race'? (323). Or as Ford Madox Ford put it: 'The war had made a man of him! It had coarsened and hardened him' (Ford, 1926: 266).

It is understandable that in *Death of A Hero* Aldington satirised elderly women jingoists such as Mrs Humphry Ward or May Sinclair in the person of Winterbourne's mother: 'Her view of the British Empire was that it should continue the war as a holy crusade for the extermination of all "filthy vile foreigners", making the world safe for . . . pure, sweet, kittenish Englishwomen of fifty' (Aldington, 1965: 23). But what he says about the war having an erotic effect on lots of women: 'All the dying and wounds and mud and bloodiness – gave them a great kick, and excited them to an almost unbearable pitch of amorousness' (18) seems to be a perversion of what Manning, talking about *men*, explained in another way: 'In the shuddering revulsion from death, one turns instinctively to love as an act which seems to affirm the completeness of being' (Winter, 1978: 150). The conclusions Aldington draws are little different from that masterpiece of stereotyping propaganda that Graves quoted, the 'Little Mother' letter. Aldington attributes people's war-time behaviour to physiology: 'There was the deep primitive physiological instinct – men to kill and be killed; women to produce more men to continue the process' (19).

In fact these 'deep instincts' were being denied by many pacifists and feminists. Not only was Julia/H.D. *not* erotically excited by war, being physically repelled by it, but Aldington's own narratorial voice also argues that war is violence and butchery, that is, murder, and 'when you approve of murder you violate the right instincts of every human being' (245). Like Herbert Read, Aldington boasted in his autobiography 'I am perfectly certain I didn't kill anyone' (Aldington, 1941: 127). He even claimed to have *saved* the lives of two wounded Germans. As Winterbourne's internal muddle indicates, Aldington was struggling to reconcile two completely antipathetic sets of values. One of them, which reduced women to 'WOMAN', H.D. tried to indicate as theatrical when she described Rafe Ashton in his uniform, as 'dressed up, play-acting . . . war-time heroics' (H.D., 1960: 150). Unfortunately it was woundingly real, despite being imaginary. (Bergonzi's choice of epithet to describe *Death of A Hero* is only too perspicacious: 'a massive ejaculation of pent-up venom' [Bergonzi, 1980: 183].) Julia's repudiation of her soldier-husband was a rejection of militarism and its definition of 'humanity', both masculine and feminine. Humanity should *not* entail *'a rendez-vous with death'*.

Fussell's main thesis in *The Great War and Modern Memory* is that the dominant form of modern understanding is ironic. Graves's *Good-bye To All That* is the prime example of his argument. Quoting Dürrenmatt to the effect that tragedy presupposes such conditions as despair, moderation, vision, a sense of responsibility, none of which we have, Fussell claims that in the modern age, 'comedy alone is suitable for us' (Fussell, 1975: 203). Graves, in eschewing tragedy and melodrama in favour of farce and comedy, ridicules 'the preposterous scientism of the twentieth century' (206). Above all he mocks the claimed objectivity of historical 'facts' based on documentary 'evidence', or 'texts'. His autobiography can be read as a satire of military history, a perverse historiography. By apparent contrast, Blunden's war memoir is a pastoral elegy. But Blunden uses the English pastoral tradition in the service of irony too. The very archaic nature of his style, the conscious literariness of his prose, is a way of indicating the 'otherwise unspeakable grossness of the war . . . Blunden's style is his critique' (268). The enduring qualities of a long tradition, manifested in a civilised sensibility, are the best weapons against the War.

H.D.'s target was not so much scientism, or historicism, as militarism. At the beginning of *Bid Me To Live* she demonstrated how war whirled cultural traditional distinctions out of joint: 'Punch and Judy danced with Jocasta and Philoctetes' (H.D., 1960: 7). Neither knockabout farce nor heroic tragedy was dominant. Julia's room became a stageset, characters made exits and entrances. She was in the middle of a trilogy, although she didn't know it. On the stage a charade is played, directed by Rico; a ballet is danced; a miracle-play is acted out. The War becomes 'this whole mad show' (50). While Rafe is playing at Sir Philip Sidney, with 17th- [sic] century gallantry, Julia sees herself as Electra. She is a heroine in a Greek tragedy; Rafe is 'metaphorically booted and spurred' and speaking a clichéd lingo, 'that's the stuff to give the troops'. Desperately trying to hold on to past values, Michelangelo, Botticelli, Julia eventually escapes from the theatricality to the real, sacred world of poetry, where she can be an artist, rather than WOMAN or tragedy queen, and other people can be what they are, 'human people, Englishmen, madmen' (164). Like other women of her period, such as Mary Borden and Katherine Mansfield, H.D. was ironic about both war and the idea of the soldier, and determined to re-assert sacred values in a profane world.

As H.D. pointed out, her generation may have been a war generation, and lost, but being in their mid-20s to early 30s they had roots in the past that the actual lost generation did not have. They were not totally lost. It was the generation after Vera Brittain's, the children who grew up in the War, who were really lost, as the writings of Pamela Hinkson and Antonia White reveal.

When Vera Brittain visited the Somme battlefields in 1933, she visited Roland's grave. 'Yet though I could still weep for Edward, my childhood companion, I had now no tears to shed for Roland ... only a deep impersonal sorrow for brilliant youth thrown remorselessly away' (Brittain, 1957: 91). At that period, when girls led such restricted lives, they were closely attached to their brothers, generally the only members of the male sex whom they knew closely before they married. Brothers played a special role in the imagination of their sisters, which does not seem to have been reciprocal. They were permitted and encouraged to do what was forbidden to a girl, and in a sense their sisters lived vicariously through them. It was by comparison with their brothers, their imagined 'comrade-twin' to use Adrienne Rich's epithet, that girls learned their own inferior and dependent role; often they knew themselves to be equal in talent, as the writings of Vera Brittain, Rose Macaulay, May Sinclair, Virginia Woolf, all indicate, but found resentfully that they were to be subordinate in the family enterprise. When girls imagined their future adventurously, they tended to fantasise through the experience of their brother (rather than, say, of their mother). The relationship between sisters and brothers could be seen as comradely, and formed a model for their imagined relationship with other men which proved to be delusive. (Their brothers did not tend to regard them as sex-objects or ornamental toys or a means to their immortality.)

Cynthia Asquith wrote that she first felt 'the full mad horror of the war' when her younger brother, Yvo, was killed at the age of

19, after only a few weeks at the Front (Asquith, 1968: 90). The deaths of other people had not really touched her; the death of Yvo hurt her physically:

> Somehow with the others who have been killed, I have acutely felt the loss of them but have so swallowed the rather high-faluting platitude that it was all right for them – that they were not to be pitied, but were safe unassailable, young, and glamorous for ever. With Yvo – I can't bear it for him. The sheer pity and horror of it is overwhelming. (91)

Cynthia cried herself into a state of merciful exhaustion. But the effect on her younger sister, Bibs, who was only 13, is far more piteous. Unable to cry, she curled up on the bed beside Cynthia and slept with her: 'Poor little darling, it is too awful! She moaned like someone in great physical pain. She tears one's heart' (93). At that age there is no comfort for bereavement. If, as Cynthia says, Yvo's death 'emptied the future for each of us', it did so most of all for the young girl, to judge by Pamela Hinkson's elegy, *The Ladies' Road* (1932).

One of the great myths of the Great War, which threads through Fussell's cultural study along with the Somme myth, is that of the loss of innocence. It is summed up in Philip Larkin's poem, *MCMXIV*, with its haunting last line: 'Never such innocence again' (Fussell, 1975: 19). This myth has combined with an idea of Britain's lost imperial splendour to support the current imagery by which the Great War was viewed over and over in diaries and memoirs: that the War was like the Flood, the Deluge, the Fall from Grace, and the world which was lost was Paradise. The idea was not new. Gaunt's speech in *Richard II* summed up this vision of England as the lost Garden of Eden. In Shakespeare's time the Garden was seen as having been lost to commercialism back in the Middle Ages. No matter how repeatedly historians assert that in 1914 Britain was a nation of great social unrest and of miserable poverty in industrial or agricultural slums (Marwick, 1963: 11), it is the prelapsarian view that prevails. This nostalgia for idealised childhood, a time of happy security in the rural surroundings of the family-garden, finds its perfect expression in Hinkson's novel, where it is combined with the irrevocable loss of Ireland to form an elegy for a generation, grieved over by a young girl. Grief for the past is also part of the romanticisation of Empire.

The Ladies' Road was first published in 1932 and re-issued by Penguin in 1946, when it sold over 100 000 copies in paperback. (It is one of almost a genre of lost-Ireland books, including those by M. J. Farrell, and Elizabeth Bowen's *The Last September*.) Pamela Hinkson dedicated her book to her mother, the Irish poet Katherine Tynan. Tynan, a member of the Celtic literary revival, wrote simple pastoral lyrics. Her daughter's novel has a similar pastoral, lyrical beauty, combined with fine psychological insight into her upper-middle-class characters. Their educated reticence is exacerbated by the strains of the War; sympathy must be careful, controlled, lest one go mad with the enormity of it all (Hinkson, 1932: 181). Hinkson delicately objectifies their emotions through the reactions of their dogs, which can demonstrate misery or joy quite openly. Yet the War cannot be completely shut off. Reminders of it appear constantly throughout the book, in parentheses: '(It was winter out there now, Stella thought – cold, there might be snow soon.)' (97); 'Branches coming out of the undergrowth in a line might have been rifles with fixed bayonets. The moon made them gleam like steel' (201). The War opens a gulf, a chasm, an abyss, between the women and the men they love: mother and son, wife and husband, sister and brother, who become strangers to each other. The young men share 'the companionship of a generation doomed to death, a companionship which no one outside could possible understand' (197). The women are left outside.

In particular, Stella is left, left behind like a ghost in her white dress. Stella was born in 1900. She is too young to do what she dreams of, to be an ambulance-driver near the Line. Her brother, David, is three years older. As the war progresses he becomes old enough to train and go out to fight. One of the themes of the book is Stella's belief that nothing could ever take the place of the friendship between brother and sister, nothing that came later could replace the experience of childhood. However, men who loved each other could go up the same road, one could follow the other. They could be killed together and then nothing could separate them. Stella cannot follow her brother. She tries in all ways to learn what it will be like for him, to understand and imagine his life – even down to army instruction books: 'Bayonet fighting produces lust for blood . . . a Platoon Commander [must be] bloodthirsty and forever thinking how to kill the enemy and helping his men to do so' (136). But she will never, for instance, be in a gas-attack. David would.

David is reported 'missing, believed killed', in the battle for *Chemin des Dames*. For Stella it is as if the track of her life led that far and ended (205). After that she experiences extreme loneliness. When the War is over there is no direction to her life: 'she faltered, staring at a road before her that seemed to lead nowhere – the Ladies' Road' (217). And because she was neither old enough nor young enough, she 'must live always in a No Man's Land left by the War with a country on either side that was not hers' (313). But other women also experience the same disorientation, confronted by men who have changed. Irene's husband, George, survives the War, but to Irene it is not George who returns: 'Someone else, not George. She saw George sometimes looking at her as though over someone else's shoulder, from an immense distance. She could not reach him. They wanted each other, but they could not find each other' (297).

Hinkson uses a haunting image from the war to picture the way in which both men and women have lost their bearings:

Soldiers going up to the line at night guided by a tape had passed other soldiers going down, ghostly figures, half hidden. Voices had spoken, felt for each other in the darkness. 'Who are you, chum?'

Some regiment they had never heard of, might answer. A regiment and a man they had never seen in their lives. Nor did they ever see them. They passed, coming from obscurity, going to obscurity. (212)

There is no guiding idea in people's lives, no tape. No chum to give them re-assurance. The women kept faith with the survivors, and with seven million dead men, but there lies between them 'an experience unshared, a chasm never to be bridged' (217). Men and women had travelled on different roads.

Wistful and melancholy, *The Ladies' Road* is a book about adolescent experience which is far-removed from the high-jinks jingoism of books written for girls during the war-period itself. Angela Brazil's patriotic schoolgirls uncovered German spies with a malicious gusto unsuspected by Stella. (Brazil was a member of the same generation as Mrs Ward.) Nevertheless, in its concentration on personal grief, *The Ladies' Road* camouflages the War's actual legacy to the survivors: social guilt for the deaths of so many young men (Winter, 1985: 300).

Antonia White fictionalised her life in a series of novels from 1933 onwards. The heroine, Clara Batchelor, is an adolescent schoolgirl during the Great War, and is bruised afterwards by the behaviour of young veterans. In reply to one who despises her for not knowing anything about the battlefront, she replies that it was not her fault: 'Being too young and not being a man. I did *try* to imagine it' (White, 1982: 44). He responds bitterly that he had been through things she *couldn't* imagine. In his opinion she was still a child in pinafores, mentally. Following an unconsummated marriage with another veteran, an alcoholic, Clara descends into madness.

Her distraction begins during the week celebrating Armistice Day. She attends a solemn Requiem Mass for all who had died in the War. In front of the altar stand four young men in uniform, heads bowed, guarding a catafalque. Clara becomes obsessed with remorse at how she had shut the War out of her mind as a schoolgirl.

> Suddenly, beyond the four bowed figures guarding the catafalque she saw a crowd of young men in torn and blood-stained uniforms. Their haggard faces were all turned reproachfully on her. She buried her own in her hands to shut them out, praying in utter abasement: 'Forgive me . . . forgive me'. (408)

Once she is shut up in the Royal Bethlehem Hospital for the Insane (Bedlam, now the Imperial War Museum . . .), she becomes totally deranged, unable to recognise people she knew, thinking the nurses are not what they seem.

> She knew quite well that they were not nurses: they were women whose sons had been killed in the war. Each time a woman came in, Clara went through a new agony. She became the dead boy. She spoke with his voice. She felt the pain of amputated limbs, of blinded eyes. She coughed up blood from lungs torn to rags by shrapnel. Over and over again, in trenches, in field hospitals, in German camps, she died a lingering death. Between the bouts of torture, the mothers, in their nurses' veils, would kiss her hands and sob out their gratitude. (428)

What would it be like, *really*, to 'imagine the Great War'? Ten years after the War 48 special mental hospitals still tended

65 000 shell-shock victims, men who were unable to forget their experiences. Men like Aldington, Williamson, Blunden, Sassoon never forgot either. The mental scars, different, but cutting to the quick of sensibility, were also borne by women.

Conclusion

'FORBIDDEN ZONE' – THE GREAT WAR AND WOMEN'S MYTHS

Each generation rewrites history. My generation, the generation of grandchildren to veterans of the First World War, has been concerned to rediscover 'the Great War'. This has resulted in both empirical research and imaginative re-creation, where 'History' has become indistinguishable from 'fiction'. Perhaps the best example of this is John Harris's novel, *Covenant With Death* (1961), the story of an imaginary battalion in Kitchener's Army from its formation to its destruction at the Battle of the Somme. As Harris made clear, he based his story on an immense amount of reading and on conversations with the old men of the city where he lived. The authenticity of his vivid illumination of 'the systematised murder we call war' gained admiring tribute from the First World War historian, Leon Wolff. It was a novel with scarcely any women characters; women wait at home. Since the resurrection of the Women's Movement in the late 1960s, there has grown up a special interest in the role of women in war. Amongst women there has also developed an interest in the way in which the Great War affected women and their self-consciousness.

There are certain demonstrable facts about the First World War. From numerical data we can establish that from 1916 the registered employment of women changed and expanded. Women entered what had previously been masculine occupations, such as engineering and transport; within ten years after the War these jobs were predominantly male again. Many women wore trousers or uniform during the War ('Look at all the pockets', murmured Elsie, admiringly, 'it's as good as being a boy'. [Mackay, 1986: 222]), but trousers did not become regular wear for women until after the next war. Some changes endured. The standard of health and nutrition of mothers and children improved during the First World War and remained better. After 50 years of campaigning, women were enfranchised in 1918. At least, women over the age of 30 were enfranchised. Those women who needed the vote for their economic protection, working women and young mothers – that is to say: women of precisely the age group who had aided the war-effort – did not get the vote until 1928.

But people's lives are conditioned not merely by the objective, quantifiable facts of their existence, by their economic or political power. Their lives are also conditioned by how they understand themselves and their own position in society. (Although we can ask them about what they think, which is the role of oral history, quantifiable responses to specific questions, 50 or 75 years later, may not be a good guide to how people thought years before.) We cannot examine people's consciousness directly. Nor can we measure the patterns of thought that even they themselves are not aware of. However, people manifested how they saw the world at the time of the First World War, through what they wrote. We *can* examine literature. As Althusser argued, literature represents the myths and imaginary versions of real social relationships. It embodies the ideology that governs people's understanding of the world they live in. We are none of us fully aware of how such 'given' ideas and values dominate our thought. We start to become aware when the effort to resist them results in anxiety and inner turmoil. Underlying patterns in social attitudes are reflected in the patterns of consciousness that reveal themselves in imaginative writing. The contradictions and inconsistencies in literature flow from the conflicts and changes being thrashed out in society, which is never static.

People's imagining concerns two inter-connected zones. It concerns how they imagine themselves, and how they imagine other people: the zone of their own, apparently familiar experience, and the zone of what is alien and unknown. These zones are defined against each other and are only fully comprehensible in terms of each other. Modes of imagining do not emerge out of thin air, but are part of what Sylvia Pankhurst called the 'thought currents of their time', the ideas that prevail. My study is particularly concerned with how British women imagined the Great War and their relation to it. This is connected with how they imagined No-Man's-Land and the strictly male battlefront, which constituted a zone forbidden to women (an area that increased in extent in the course of the War). Women's writing has transmitted myths about those two zones: the zone to which they gained access, and the zone from which they were excluded. How did the modes of imagining available to women enable them to understand their own experience of the War in relation to what men experienced? What is the nature of the myths that my generation of women inherited?

Almost immediately on the declaration of war in August 1914, the British government resolved on two means of promoting the War which were to be decisive for British culture: censorship and propaganda. Defence of the Realm Acts were slipped through Parliament, and a secret Bureau of Propaganda was established. By these means the government strengthened and institutionalised the management of ideas, which had previously been exercised more loosely under the Obscene Publications Act of 1857. This Act had been used to control sexual, political and religious dissent. Under DORA direct political censorship was more rigorously enforced, and the penalties were more stringent. The propagation of the government's political aims was co-ordinated by the Bureau through propaganda of all sorts. In the first year it had distributed over two and a half million copies of books, pamphlets, and speeches, in various languages. By late 1916 it was issuing not merely press releases, maps and cartoons, but over four thousand photos a week, as well as pioneering the production of such films as *The Battle of the Somme*. The result of this propaganda lies in dusty evidence along the shelves of museums and libraries. It is sedimented in layers of British culture. The results of censorship were themselves censored (Hopkin, 1970: 151). It requires a much greater effort of research to discover the difference they made. Despite the eventual repeal of DORA and the disbanding of the Bureau of Propaganda (which had later become the Ministry of Information), their effects on British culture lasted long after the end of the War.

The main thrust of the official propaganda was an essentially Victorian ideal of war, which has dominated the British imagination of the Great War ever since. It promoted a chivalrous myth of British soldiers as pure young men who sacrificed their lives, innocently and willingly, to save their Mother-country and their womenfolk from violation. All criticism of this myth which implied that the war was anything other than a holy crusade against the bestial hun, was ruthlessly suppressed. (To take but one example: copies of a pacifist children's book by the Quaker writer Theodora Wilson Wilson, *The Last Weapon; A Vision*, which suggested that the 'last weapon' to end the war would be Fearless Love, were confiscated and burnt [The Friend, 22 March 1918: 192].) The chivalrous thought-currents which 'prevailed' during the Great War were deliberately and determinedly enforced.

At that time, British women, like men, were still inspired by the mythology of the British Empire. The Victorian ideal of chivalry was an integral part of that mythology, glamorising the economic nature of imperialism. They were also deeply affected by the public struggle for women's equality with men, and the challenges to prevalent theories of gender. Those challenges contradicted the assumptions of chivalry, and the struggle brought the underlying sexual coercion out into the open. Both the Empire and male supremacy relied on theories of the just and natural submission of inferior frailty to domination by superior strength. During the 19th century Josephine Butler had led a campaign against the sexual exploitation of women's bodies by their so-called chivalrous 'protectors'. In the 20th century, under the leadership of Mrs Pankhurst, militant suffragettes had waged physical, guerrilla war on the male political establishment. They had been confronted by superior physical force. The political campaign had been represented as a war. In 1914 the British government declared traditional war on Germany, that is, a war between men only, as combatants in opposing armed forces. At the beginning women were encouraged to stay at home, and to leave war, a masculine concern, to men.

Many women did no such thing. If we look at journalism and diaries of the period, we can see that the war represented an opportunity for 'adventure' for many women. They used it to escape domestic restrictions, to get 'out of the cage'. Through war-work of a myriad different kinds, which women volunteered for and originated for themselves, they showed initiative and discipline, and they gained self-respect and respect from other women (Blodget, 1985: 23–4). If women became a mutual admiration society, it was about time *somebody* gave women the confidence and encouragement to behave like people, not toys. Continuing the pre-war precedent of the WPSU, women produced their own war-time propaganda, eulogising women and the part they played in war. However, a different picture emerges from the books which describe how women imagined men and their own relationship to men, especially in the years after the war.

Although single women of all classes certainly liked the freedom from chaperonage, and the opportunity to meet men on a footing where courtship was not the main aim, the War emphasised an essential difference between men and women. Women were not combatants. And they were not allowed near the firing-line. Even independent, adventurous women like Cicely Hamilton and Rose Macaulay expressed a humiliated sense of their own inferiority at being non-combatant burdens on the male part of the population. While the War permitted women to do all sorts of things which had been regarded as strictly masculine before the War, it required of men a more extreme form of masculine activity which was prohibited even to men in peacetime: not merely physical violence, but savage murder in battle. The war re-asserted gender distinctions that women had been contesting: women were frail and had to be defended by strong protectors, who were prepared to kill or die on their behalf. Whatever claims women had made to equality,and whatever rights to serve their country they claimed in war-time, women were not deafening in their clamour to be permitted to go into battle.

They did face danger. They faced it bravely, and many died for their beliefs. Edith Cavell is the most famous, and she may stand for the other anonymous women nurses, doctors, drivers, re-fugee-helpers, who were also killed. But women faced danger essentially on the 'home' side of the firing-line. There was never in the First World War any question of conscripting women to 'fill the gaps', even after the German breakthrough of March 1918 when any old crippled man was called on to help 'stand with our backs to the wall'. And women did not offer to bear arms. Those who were not campaigning to stop the war altogether saw their war-role as auxiliary, as help-mates to men: 'Women are only repairers, darn-ing socks, cleaning, washing-up after men, bringing up reinforce-ments in the way of fresh life, and patching up wounded men' (MacNaughtan, 1916: 31). They compassionately cared for the wounded, or they produced ammunition, or new babies. There did not exist in the British army anything corresponding to the women-soldiers of the Serbian army, or the women's battalion recruited by Yasha Bachkarova to man the Russian trenches (Farmborough, 1974: 299–300). The belligerence of Flora Sandes did not, apparently, capture popular imagination in the way that the compassionate Heroines of Pervyse did. It remained funda-mental to the Englishwoman's conception of herself that women do not kill.

Conversely, the dominant myths of the Great War, which speak continually of men laying down their lives in sacrifice, obscure the fact that it was fundamental to the idea of masculinity prevalent at that period that men do kill. Men were expected to kill; women were not.

Roland Barthes has demonstrated how national myths act as

cultural alibis. They disguise injustice and responsibility. There are two main myths that have come down to us from the Great War: one is 'The Somme Myth' as Paul Fussell calls it; the other is what Wohl identified as 'The Lost Generation Myth'. They are linked by the nostalgic attitude of 'Never Such Innocence Again': British soldiers were essentially brave young victims, sacrificed like innocent scapegoats for the sins of their elders. Both myths deal with the loss of English manhood, and they both strengthen the taboo on contemplating the fact that the army trained a whole generation of young men in the arts of killing. This taboo operates even in military history, as John Keegan points out: 'citation writers, flinching from "kill", deal largely in "account for", "dispatch", "dispose of"' (Keegan, 1976: 321). It takes the glib sensationalism of Philip Gibbs to try to indicate what such euphemisms hide. To convey how a group of 'decent Yorkshire lads' became 'beasts of prey' in one 'battle', where 300 Germans were bayoneted at the Chateau of Hooge, not one left alive, he described the 'bloody and terrible scene, not decent for words to tell' as it looked on the following day:

a shambles of human flesh, which had been a panic-stricken crowd of living men crying for mercy, with that dreadful screech of terror from German boys who saw the white gleam of steel at their stomachs before they were spitted. (Gibbs, 1920: 89)

He wonders in passing how the Yorkshire lads live with that memory (he is, of course, guessing how it was).

In her history of the Somme, Lyn Macdonald reports coolly: 'Prisoners were a nuisance' (Macdonald, 1983: 289) and quotes without comment from one private:

Life meant nothing to you. Life was in jeopardy and when you'd got a load of Jerries like that on your hands, all stinking to high heaven, you hadn't much sympathy for them with their *Kamerad* and all this cringing business. It brutalises you, war does. You don't find that you've got much sympathy. (290)

Killing, to save one's own skin or revenge the death of a friend, left no sense of remorse. One officer remembered killing the first German soldier he'd ever seen: 'I killed him with one shot. I felt nothing. All I felt was relief. I knew I had no option, but I didn't stop to think of the morality. It was either him or me' (137). Stuart Cloete recalled: 'I had no moral scruples about taking life ... men are born killers, savages, tamed by ordinary life' (Cloete, 1972: 192–3). The perpetual anthologising of Owen's *Anthem for Doomed Youth* and *The Parable of the Old Man and the Young*, and the quoting of his claim that his subject was 'the pity of War', have distracted attention from the vindictiveness of his *Apologia pro Poemate Meo*, where he explains quite what *is* worth the reader's tears:

> Merry it was to laugh there –
> Where death becomes absurd and life absurder.
> For power was on us as we slashed bones bare
> Not to feel sickness or remorse of murder.

Human killing was anathema to most women. It was the extreme form of male brutishness. Despite Mrs Pankhurst's Boadicea-like generalship, and Christabel's deliberate assumption of the image of St Joan of Arc, even they did not inflict personal violence on men, though outrages were committed on their own bodies. It was difficult for men to make plain to women the callousness with regard to individual life at the Front; it must have been nearly impossible to admit their own remorseless indifference to their part in the savagery. Meanwhile, propaganda dressed German boys up as The Dragon, or bestial rapists.

One of the most important myths we have inherited from the Great War was that the experience of battle was incommunicable; you had to have been there. 'Those That Had Been There' formed an exclusive, quasi-mystical fellowship. Exclusive, naturally, of women. As Paul Fussell has pointed out, with the resources of the English language 'incommunicable' cannot mean that there were no words to express the experience. It must mean rather, that women could not sympathetically share in the understanding of what the experience had been like.

Starting with Rose Macaulay's *Non-Combatants and Others* (1916), the incommunicability of the men's experience has been a constant theme of women's novels about the Great War. As if to contradict it, women authors such as Vera Brittain, with novels such as *Honourable Estate* (1936), have made a huge effort to convey the nastiness of trench life, the horrors of No-Man's-Land, what shell-shock and fugue are like, and what the pressures were that led to madness or suicide. In fact, if one of the most important legacies of the popular memory of the Great War has been an emphasis on the separateness of the sexes, one way in which women have used their literary imagination has been to try to make plain the horrifying nature of the experiences that men kept to themselves and which isolated their minds from women. However, with all the resources of men's war-memoirs now to draw on, the matter that evades every woman's imagination is the one matter most men are reticent about: what it was actually like to kill other men. Their heroes do not use the bayonet. No-Man's-Land is not portrayed as a killing-zone, a battlefield. The taboo on murder, the stigma on the murderer, acts like a shutter on women's imagination, preventing them from exploring this essential aspect of men's experience of war. It is part of the forbidden zone on which they do not trespass.

Following critical arguments with her General husband, the Victorian war-artist Elizabeth Butler confessed that, although she had painted in order to portray the pathos and heroism of war:

> If I had seen even a corner of a real battle-field, I could never have painted another picture. (Springhall, 1986: 66)

Although the Somme myth ascribes guilt for the deaths of thousands of young men to old men, the final burden of guilt is placed by literature on the shoulders of women. One of the best-known posters of the War, besides *Kitchener Wants You*, was *Women of England Say 'Go!'* These were not statements of the same degree of veracity. Kitchener himself initiated the idea of a volunteer army. There was no referendum to establish what women said. The poster seems designed as much to convince women of what to say, as to convince men that they were saying it. Actually many women tried to get their sons out of the army. Others were agitating to prevent conscription. Still others were working for a negotiated settlement to the War. It is only very recently that the suppressed history of this political dissent has been recovered, and related to the pre-War women's analysis of militarism and its debasing effects.

Although I can find little mention of it in the literature of the war-period, novels written since the Second World War all tend to mention the White Feather Campaign. This was supposedly inaugurated by the middle-aged novelist Baroness D'Orczy. That not all women appreciated the spirit of the campaign is demonstrated by Helen Hamilton's poem to *The Jingo-Woman*: 'Jingo-woman / (How I dislike you!) / Dealer in white feathers, / Insulter, self-appointed, / Of all the men you meet, / Not dressed in uniform . . . You shame us women. / Can't you see it isn't decent, / To flout and goad men into doing, / What isn't asked of you?' (Reilly, 1981: 47–9). The white feather symbolises the 'moral' pressure women exerted on men to enlist. Sylvia Pankhurst records that the unspeakable Nancy Astor was one such Jingoist, leaning out of a car-window to shout complacently at a young man: 'Why aren't you in khaki?' (Pankhurst, 1932: 142). Mary E. Pearce's novel *The Sorrowing Field* (1975) actually commences with a scene in a railway carriage, where a woman denounces a young man in civvies for not being in khaki, and in turn receives a mouthful from a wounded officer. Sarah Harrison's *The Flowers of the Field* (1980) has a crucial scene where one of her protagonists, a conscientious objector, is handed a white feather. The book ends with the emotional claim at his funeral that 'we all admired Maurice so much. He was the bravest of us all' (663).

Women have been left with a legacy of guilt for the misery and death of a generation of young men. If they were more aware of the punctiliousness with which the war-time British government eradicated women's attempts to counteract the dehumanising effects of its war-machine, they might realise the nature of this cultural alibi. Not all women were filled with hatred for huns; not all women pressured their men-folk to kill or die on their behalf. The story which Jane Marcus reveals about the statue of Edith Cavell is infinitely instructive about propaganda and censorship. The war-time government erected a prominent statue to Cavell (just near Trafalgar Square), after she had been shot by the Germans for aiding British as well as German wounded. Inscribed on the base of the statue in large letters is the motto: 'For King and Country', Lower down, in smaller letters, the post-War Labour government added what she herself had said: 'Patriotism is not enough: I must have no hatred or bitterness towards anyone' (Marcus, 1988: 53).

The American critic, Northrop Frye, wrote that 'the culture of the past is not only the memory of mankind, but our own buried life'. He thought that to study the past is to recover not merely the past but the total cultural form of our present life (Frye, 1957: 346). To recover women's literature of the past is to understand our 'memory' of the Great War better. It necessitates an understanding of how and why women's writing has been suppressed, and how 'memory' is created. The patient efforts women made to detail and analyse the dehumanising effects of militarism should not be forgotten.

Appendix 1

WOMEN WRITERS AGED OVER 40 In 1914

1847–1929	Alice Meynell	Poems	1923
1851–1920	Mrs Humphry Ward	England's Effort	1916
		'Missing'	1917
		The War and Elizabeth	1918
1856–1935	Violet Paget 'Vernon Lee'	Peace with Honour	1915
1862–1952	Elizabeth Robins	The Messenger	1919
1862–?	Mrs St Clair Stobart	The Flaming Sword in Serbia	1916
1862–1937	Edith Wharton	The Marne	1918
		A Son at the Front	1923
1863?–1946	May Sinclair	A Journal of Impressions in Belgium	1915
		Tasker Jevons	1916
		The Tree of Heaven	1917
		The Romantic	1920
1864–1936	Beatrice Harraden	Where Your Treasure Is	1918
1865–1941	Theodora Wilson Wilson	The Last Weapon	1916
		Those Strange Years	1937
1866–1941	Elizabeth Von Arnim	Christine	1916
1868–1941	Jessie Pope	War Poems	1915
1869–1947	Angela Brazil	A Patriotic Schoolgirl	1918
1872–1952	Cicely Hamilton	William, An Englishman	1919
		Life Errant	1935
1873–1961	Ellen La Motte	Backwash of War	1916
1873–1947	Willa Cather	One of Ours	1922

WOMEN WRITERS AGED UNDER 40 IN 1914

1879–1958	Dorothy Canfield (Fisher)	Home Fires in France	1918
		The Deepening Stream	1930
1881–1965	Eleanor Farjeon	E. Thomas: The Last Four Years	1958
1881–1943	Radclyffe Hall	The Well of Loneliness	1928
		'Miss Ogilvy Finds Herself'	1934
1881–1958	Rose Macaulay	Non-Combatants and Others	1916
		What Not: a Prophetic Comedy	1918
		Three Days poems	1919
1881–1963	Margaret Sackville	The Pageant of War poems	1916
1882–1966	Mary Agnes Hamilton	Dead Yesterday	1916
		Special Providence	1930

1882–1960	E. Sylvia Pankhurst	*The Home Front*	1932
1882–1941	Virginia Woolf	*Jacob's Room*	1922
		Mrs Dalloway	1925
		Three Guineas	1938

WOMEN WRITERS AGED UNDER 30 IN 1914

1885–?	Eliza Marian Butler	*Daylight in a Dream*	1951
1886–1961	Hilda Doolittle (H.D.)	*Bid Me To Live*	1960
1886–1968	Mary Borden	*The Forbidden Zone*	1929
		Sarah Gay	1931
1887–1960	Cynthia Asquith	*Diaries 1915–18*	1968
1887–1964	Dame Edith Sitwell	*I Live Under a Black Sun*	1937
1887–1956	Sheila Kaye-Smith	*Little England*	1918
1888–1923	Katherine Mansfield	'An Indiscreet Journey'/	
		'Spring Pictures'	1924
		'Late at Night'/'Two	
		Tuppenny Ones, Please'	1924
		'Six Years Later'/'The Fly'	1923
		Journal of Katherine	
		Mansfield	1954
1889–1958	F. Tennyson Jesse	*The Sword of Deborah*	1919
1889–1981	Edith Bagnold	*A Diary Without Dates*	1918
		The Happy Foreigner	1920
1890–?	Rose Allatini	*Despised and Rejected*	1918
1890–1943	E. M. Delafield	*The War Workers*	1918
1890–1973	G. B. Stern	*Children of No Man's Land*	1919
1891–1986	Storm Jameson	*That Was Yesterday*	1932
		No Time Like the Present	1933
		The Captain's Wife	1939
1892–1933	Stella Benson	*This is the End*	1917
1892–1980	Irene Rathbone	*We That Were Young*	1932
1892–1983	Rebecca West	*The Return of the Soldier*	1918
		War Nurse – the true story	
		etc	1930
1893–1970	Vera Brittain	*Testament of Youth*	1933
		Chronicle of Youth	1981
1893–1973	May Wedderburn Cannan	*In War Time* poems	1917
		Grey Ghosts and Voices	1976
1893–1983	Diana (Manners) Cooper	*The Rainbow Comes and*	1958
		Goes	
1893–1980	Margaret Postgate Cole	*Poems*	1918
1894–1977	Phyllis Bentley	*The Rise of Henry Morcar*	1946
1896–1985	Evadne Price	*Not So Quiet . . .*	1930
1898–1935	Winifrid Holtby	*The Crowded Street*	1924
		'The Bombardment of	
		Scarborough'	1915
1898–1961	Joanna Maxwell Cannan	*High Table*	1931
1899–1980	Antonia White	*Beyond the Glass*	1954
1900?	Pamela Hinkson	*The Ladies' Road*	1932

Appendix 2

EXTRACTS FROM THE DEFENCE OF THE REALM ACT, 1914

1. His Majesty in Council has power during the continuance of the present war to issue regulations ... for securing the public safety and the defence of the realm; and may, by such regulations, authorise the trial by courts martial and punishment of persons contravening any of the provisions of such regulations designed –

(a) to prevent persons communicating with the enemy or obtaining information for that purpose or any purpose calculated to jeopardise the success of the operations of any of His Majesty's forces or to assist the enemy or to prevent the spread of reports likely to cause disaffection or alarm;

in like manner as if such persons were subject to military law and had on active service committed an offence under section five of the Army Act ...

II. The Defence of the Realm Regulations

13. Any person authorised for the purpose by the competent naval or military authority, and any police constable or officer of customs, may arrest without warrant any person whose behaviour is of such a nature to give reasonable grounds for suspecting that he has acted or is acting or is about to act in a manner prejudicial to the public safety or the safety of the Realm, or upon whom may be found any article, book, letter, or other such document, the possession of which gives grounds for such a suspicion, or who is suspected of having committed an offence against these regulations.

21. No person shall by word of mouth or in writing spread reports likely to cause disaffection or alarm among any of His Majesty's forces or among the civilian population.

27. Any person contravening any of the provisions of the foregoing special Regulations shall be liable to be tried by court-martial and to be sentenced to penal servitude for life or any less punishment:

Provided that no sentence exceeding three months' imprisonment with hard labour shall be imposed in respect of any contravention of Regulation 21 if the offender proves that he acted without any intention to cause disaffection or alarm.

Bibliography

BIBLIOGRAPHIES

BAYLISS, Gwyn (1977), *Bibliographic Guide to the Two World Wars* (London: Bowker).

BLUNDEN, Edmund *et al.* (1929), *The War, 1914–18: a booklist* (London).

ENSER, A. G. S. (1979), *A Subject Bibliography of the First World War: Books in English 1914–78* (London: Grafton).

FALLS, Cyril, (1930), *War Books: a critical guide* (London: Davies).

HAGER, Philip E. and TAYLOR, D. (1981), *The Novels of World War I: an annotated bibliography* (New York: Garland).

MURDOCH, H., SPEAR, Hilda D., and VALENTINE, D. (1980), *A Catalogue of Books Relating to the Great War held in the Library of the University of Dundee* (Dundee: Blackness).

REILLY, Catherine (1978), *English Poetry of the First World War: a bibliography* (London: Prior).

SCHAFFER, Ronald (ed.) (1978), *The United States in World War I: a select bibliography* (Oxford: Clio).

WINTER, Denis (1978), *Death's Men: Soldiers of the Great War* (Harmondsworth: Lane) 269–74.

Catalogue of Birmingham Public Library: Reference Department, special collection of war books.

Catalogues of The Imperial War Museum, London: Departments of Documents and Printed Books.

PRIMARY SOURCES, BY YEAR

[PH] = Hager and Taylor Bibliography reference number.

(a) Works by women published before World War II, excluding those about the American Home Front.
PRE-WAR

GILMAN, Charlotte PERKINS (1911), *The Man-Made World, or Our Androcentric Culture* (New York: Charlton).

MACAULAY, Rose (1911), *The Valley Captives* (London: Murray).

MACAULAY, Rose (1914), *The Making of a Bigot* (London: H & S).

MANSFIELD, Katherine (1911), *In a German Pension* (London: Swift; rep. 1926 with an introduction by John Middleton Murry, Constable; rep. Penguin, 1964).

REEVES, Maud PEMBER (1913), *Round About a Pound a Week* (London: Bell [rep. Virago, 1979]).

SALT, L. Godwin (1911), *English Patriotic Poetry* (London: Cambridge University Press).

263

SCHREINER, Olive (1883), *The Story of An African Farm* (London).
SCHREINER, Olive (1911), *Women and Labour* (London: [rep. Virago, 1979]).
ST CLAIR STOBART, Mrs (1913), *War and Women* (London).
VON ARNIM, Elizabeth (1898), *Elizabeth and her German Garden* (London).
VON SUTTNER, Bertha (1894), *Lay Down Your Arms* (London).
VON SUTTNER, Bertha (1909), *Memoiren* (Stuttgart).
WILCOX, Ella WHEELER (1903), *Poems of Power* (Chicago and London).

1914

HALLOWES, Frances S., *Women and War: an appeal to women of all nations* (London: Headley).
LLOYD, Gladys, *An Englishwoman's Adventures in the German Lines* (London: Pearson).
SINCLAIR, May, 'Women's Sacrifices for the War', *Collier's Magazine* (New York, 21 November 1914).
SUTHERLAND, Millicent, *Six Weeks at the War. The Times* (London).

1915

ADDAMS, Jane, *et al.*, *Women at the Hague* (New York, [rep. NY, Garland 1971]).
ALDRICH, Mildred, *A Hilltop on the Marne* (London: Constable).
Anon, *Diary of a Nursing sister on the Western Front* (Edinburgh: Blackwood).
AYRES, Ruby Mildred, *Richard Chatterton, V.C.* (London: H & S. [PH 15]).
CAMPBELL, Phyllis, *Back of the Front: experiences of a Nurse* (London: Newnes).
CASTLE, Agnes, (Sweetman), *The Hope of the House* (New York: Cassell [PH 25]).
CASTLE, Agnes, *Little House in Wartime* (London: Constable [PH 26]).
CRAIG, Marion Wentworth, 'War Brides: a Play in One Act', *The Century Magazine* (February, 1915, London).
CREED, L., *A Woman's Experiences in the Great War* (London: Fisher Unwin).
DEARMER, Monica, *Letters from a Field Hospital* (London: Macmillan).
HALLOWES, Frances S., *Mothers of Men and Militarism* (London: Headley).
HOLTBY, Winifred, 'The Bombing of Scarborough' (*Bridlington Chronicle*, 1915).
HOUGHTON, Mary, *In the Enemy's Country* (London: Chatto & Windus).
JEPHSON, Lady H. Julia, *A Wartime Journal: Germany 1914* (London: Elkin Mathews).
'LEE, Vernon' (Violet Paget), *Peace with Honour* (London: UDC).
LOWNDES, Marie Adelaide (Belloc), *Good Old Anna* (London: Hutchinson [PH 37]).
MacNAUGHTON, Sarah, *A Woman's Diary of the War* (London: Nelson).
MARSHALL, Catherine E., 'Women and War', *Common Cause* (26 March 1915. London).

OGDEN, C. K. and FLORENCE, Mary Sargant, *Militarism versus Feminism* (London: Allen & Unwin [rep. Virago, 1987]).

POPE, Jessie, *War Poems* (London: Richards).

RINEHART, Mary, *Kings, Queens and Pawns: an American Woman at the Front* (New York: 1915).

RUCK, Berta (Mrs Oliver Onions), *The Lad with Wings* (London: Hutchinson [PH 44]).

RUCK, Berta, *Khaki and Kisses* (London).

SINCLAIR, May, *A Journal of Impressions in Belgium* (London: Hutchinson).

SINCLAIR, May, *America's Part in the War* (New York: The Committee for Relief in Belgium).

STANLEY, M. M., *My Diary in Serbia* (London: Simpkin).

SWANWICK, Helena, *Women and War. War and Its Effect on Women* (London: rep. New York, Garland, 1971).

THURSTAN, Violetta, *Field Hospital and Flying Column, Being the Journal of an English Nursing Sister in Belgium and Russia* (London: Puttnam).

1916

ALDRIDGE, Olive, *Retreat* (London).

Anon, *The Rector's Wife Writes a Letter* (Gloucester: Minchin & Gibbs).

ASKEW, Alice and Claude, *Nurse* (London: H & S).

BLACK, Dorothy, *Her Lonely Soldier* (London: H & S).

BLUNDELL, Mrs Francis, *Penton's Captain* (London: Chapman Hall).

BRAZIL, Angela, *The Luckiest Girl in the School* (London: Blackie).

CAMERON, Charlotte, *Zenia: A Spy in Togoland* (London: Werner Laurie).

CHIVERS DAVIS, Ellen, *A Farmer in Serbia* (London).

CLARKE, Isobel, *The Potter's Home* (London: Hutchinson).

CONYERS, Dorothea, *The Scratch Pack* (London: Hutchinson).

COSENS, Monica, *Lloyd George's Munition Girls* (London: Hutchinson).

EDWARDS, Betham, *Hearts of Alsace* (London: Smith Elder).

FINZI, Kate, *Eighteen Months in the War Zone: The Record of a Woman's Work on the Western Front* (London: Cassell).

GREVILLE, F. E., Countess of Warwick, *A Woman and the War* (London: Chapman).

HAMILTON, Mary Agnes (Adamson), *Dead Yesterday* (London: Duckworths [PH 72]).

HARDY, Mary, *Letters of a Grass Widow* (London: Heath Cranton).

LA MOTTE, Ellen, *Backwash of War* (London: Puttnam [2nd edn 1934]).

LOWNDES, Marie Adelaide (Belloc), 1968–1947, *Lilla: a Part of Her Life* (London: Hutchinson).

LOWNDES, Marie Adelaide, *The Red Cross Barge* (London: Smith, Elder [PH 83]).

MACAULAY, Rose, *Non-Combatants and Others* (London: H & S; rep. Methuen 1986 [PH 86]).

MARTIN-NICHOLSON, Sister Joan, *My Experiences on Three Fronts* (London: Allen & Unwin).

MATTHEWS, Dr Caroline, *Experiences of a Woman Doctor in Serbia* (London: Mills & Boon).

MITTON, G. E., *The Cellar-house of Pervyse* (London: Black).

NORMAN, Mrs George, *Just Ourselves* (London: Chapman & Hall).

ORCHARD, Evelyn, *The Greater Glory* (London: H & S).

PARADISE, Dorothea Chester, *If There Must Be Battles: Letters of Peggy Pollock* (London: Unwin).

PETTER, Evelyn Branscombe, *Miss Velanty's Disclosure* (London: Chapman & Hall).

RADZIWILL, Catherine, 'C. Kolb-Danvin', *Because It Was Written* (London: Cassell).

RICKARD, Mrs Victor (Jessie Louisa), *The Light Above the Crossroads* (London: Duckworths).

SACKVILLE, Margaret, *The Pageant of War* (London: Simpkin).

SANDES, Flora, *An English Woman Sergeant in the Serbian Army* (London: H & S).

SCHREINER, Olive, 'Conscientious Objectors', *The Labour Leader* (March 1916).

SCOTT, Edith H., *Mistress Reality: An Everyday Apocalypse* (London: Allen & Unwin).

SINCLAIR, May, *Tasker Jevons: the Real Story* (London: Hutchinson [New York: *The Belfry*]).

ST CLAIR STOBART, Mrs, *The Flaming Sword in Serbia and Elsewhere* (London: H & S).

SWAN, Annie S., *The Woman's Part* (London: H & S).

TWEEDALE, Violet, *Love and War* (London: Hurst & Blackett).

VAUGHAN, Gertrude, E. M., *The Flight of Mariette: A Story of the Siege of Antwerp* (with an introduction by John Galsworthy) (London: Chapman & Hall).

WARD, Mrs Humphry, *England's Effort* (London: Smith Elder).

WEST, Mrs J. C., *Women's War Work* (London: Pearson).

WEST, Rebecca, 'Women of England', *Atlantic Monthly* (Jan. 1916) 1–11.

WILSON, Theodora Wilson, *The Last Weapon; a Vision* (London: Daniel [PH 110]).

WYNNE, M., *An English Girl in Serbia* (London: Collins).

1917

ALDRICH, Mildred, *On the Edge of the War Zone* (London: Constable).

BENSON, Stella, *This is the End* (London: Macmillan [PH 115].

BOTTOME, Phyllis, *The Second Fiddle* (New York: [PH 116].

BOWSA, Thekla, *The Story of British VAD Work in the Great War* (London: Melrose).

CANNAN, May (Wedderburn), *In War Time* (Oxford: Blackwell).

CHARTRES, Annie (Vivanti), *Vae Victus* (Arnold; 'The Outrage' New York 1918, trans. from Italian [PH 123]).

'CHOLMONDELEY, Alice' (pseud. of Countess Elizabeth von Arnim), *Christine* (New York: Macmillan [PH 124]).

'DANE, Clemence' (Winifred Ashton), *Regiment of Women* (London: Heinemann).

DENT, Olive, *A VAD in France* (1917).

DIVER, (Katherine Helen) Maud (Marshall), *Unconquered: A Romance* (New York: Murray (PH 130]).

DIXON, Agnes Margaret (Powell), *The Canteeners* (London).

HOBHOUSE, Mrs H., *I Appeal to Ceasar: the case of the conscientious objector* (London: Allen & Unwin).

JAMESON, Anne Edith (Foster), 'J. E. Buckrose', *War Time in Our Street* (London: H & S).

KENNARD, Lady Dorothy, *A Roumanian Diary 1915–17* (London).

MACLAREN, Barbara, *Women of the War* (London: H & S).

MANSFIELD, Charlotte, *The Dupe: A British and South African Story of the Years 1914 and 1915* (Simpkin [PH 159]).

McDOUGALL, Grace, *A Nurse at the War: nursing adventures in Belgium and France* (New York: McBride).

PENNEL, Robins, Elizabeth (Robins) (pseud. 'N.N.'), *The Lovers* (London: Heinemann).

RUCK, Berta, *The Bridge of Kisses* (London: Hodder).

SIDGWICK, Mrs Alfred – Cecily (Ullmann), *Salt of the Earth* (New York, [PH 174]).

SINCLAIR, May, *The Tree of Heaven* (London: Cassell [PH 175]).

SPEARING, E. M. VAD, *From Cambridge to Camiers under the Red Cross* (Cambridge: Heffer).

WARD, Mrs Humphry (Mary Augusta Arnold), *Missing* (New York: Collins [PH 183]).

WARD, Mrs Humphry, *Towards the Goal: Letters on Great Britain's Behalf in the War* (London: Murray).

1918

ALLATINI, Rose ('A. T. Fitzroy'), *Despised and Rejected* (London: Daniel rep. New York: Arno 1975).

Anon, *War Nurse's Diary: Sketches from a Belgian Field Hospital* (New York: Macmillan).

BAGNOLD, Enid, *A Diary Without Dates* (London: Heinemann [rep. Virago, 1978]).

BOND, Aimée, *An Airman's Wife* (New York: H. Jenkins [PH 199]).

BRAZIL, Angela, *a Patriotic Schoolgirl* (London: Blackie).

BRAZIL, Angela, *For the School Colours* (London: Blackie).

BRITTAIN, Vera, *Verses of a VAD* (London: Macdonald).

CANFIELD, Dorothy (Fisher), *Home Fires in France* (London: Hutchinson, 1919).

CASTLE, Agnes (Sweetman), *Minniglen* (Murray [PH 205]).

DAGGETT, Mrs Mabel, *Women Wanted: the Story Written in Blood-Red Letters on the Horizon of the Great World War* (New York: Doran).

'DANE, Clemence' (pseud. of Winifred Ashton), *First the Blade: A Comedy of Growth* (New York: Heinemann [PH 211]).

'DELAFIELD, E. M.' (pseud. of Edmée de la Pasture), *The War-Workers* (London: Heinemann [PH 216]).

DIVER, Katherine Helen Maud (Marshall), *The Strong Hours* (*Boston [PH 218]).

FITZROY, Yvonne, *With the Scottish Nurses in Roumania* (London: Murray).

FORBES, Hon. Mrs Walter, *His Alien Enemy* (London: Murray).

GRAVES, Clothilde Ines Mary ('Richard Dehan'), *That Which Hath Wings* (London: Heinemann [PH 215]).

HARRADEN, Beatrice, *Where Your Treasure Is* (London: Hutchinson [PH 232]).

HOCKIN, O., *Two Girls on the Land: wartime on a Dartmoor farm* (London: Arnold).

HOPE, Sylvia, *The Lighter Side of War* (London: Stockwell).

JAMESON, Annie Edith (Foster) 'J. E. Buckrose', *The Silent Legion* (London: H & S [PH 202]).

JOLY, Mrs John Swift, *Those – Dash – Amateurs* (London: John Long).

LAING, Janet, *Before the Wind* (London: Dent [PH 245]).

LEAKE, R. E., *Letters of a VAD* (London: Melrose [PH 246]).

KAYE-SMITH, Sheila, *Little England* (London: Nisbet, (NY: *The Four Roads*) [PH 241]).

LOWNDES, Marie Adelaide (Belloc), *Out of the War?* (London: Chapman & Hall [PH 252]).

PARR, Olive Katherine ('Beatrice Chase'), *The Soul of Two Knights* (London: Longmans).

POSTGATE, Mary (Cole), *Poems* (London: Allen & Unwin).

REEVES, Amber, *Give and Take* (London).

RUCK, Berta, (Mrs O. Onions), *The Land-Girl's Love Story* (London: Hodder [PH 393]).

RUCK, Berta *The Years for Rachel* (London: Hodder [PH 274]).

SIDGWICK, Mrs Alfred (Cecily Ullmann), *Karen* (London: Collins [PH 276]).

SIDGWICK, Ethel, *Jamesie* (London: Sidgwick [PH 276]).

SPOTTISWOODE, Sybil, *The Test* (London: Skeffington).

STANLEY, Dorothy (Tennant), *Miss Pim's Camouflage by Lady Stanley* (Boston [PH 281]).

STOPES, Marie, *The Race – a play* (London: Fifield).

TROUBRIDGE, Lady, *All's Well, Billy* (London: Hurst & Blackett).

TWEEDIE, Ethel, *Women and Soldiers* (London: Lane).

VASSALL, Gabrielle, *A Romance of the Western Front* (London: Heinemann).

WARD, Mrs Humphry (Mary Augusta Arnold), *The War and Elizabeth* (New York: Collins [PH 294]).

WHARTON, Edith Newbold (Jones), *The Marne: A Story of the War* (New York: [PH 297]).

WEST, Rebecca, *The Return of the Soldier* (London: Nisbet [PH 296]).

WYLIE, Ida Alexa Ross, *Towards Morning* (London: Cassell [PH 300]).

YOUNG, Florence Ethel Mills, *Beatrice Ashleigh* (London: H & S [PH 301]).

1919

ADAM, Helen Pearl, *Paris Sees It Through: A Diary, 1914–19* (London: H & S).

ALLATINI, Rose, *Requiem* (London: Secker).

Anon, *Nursing Adventure: a FANY in France* (London: Heinemann).

BOND, Aimée, *A Pair of Vagabonds* (London: Jenkins [PH 316]).
BOTTOME, Phyllis, *A Servant of Reality* (London: H & S [PH 318]).
CANFIELD, Dorothy (Fisher), *The Day of Glory* (New York).
HAMILTON, Cicely Mary, William – an Englishman (London: Skeffington [PH 345]).
JESSE, Friniwyd Tennyson, *The Sword of Deborah: first-hand impressions of the British Women's Army in France* (London: Heinemann).
LAING, Jane, *The Man with the Lamp* (London: Dent [PH 366]).
LAWRENCE, Dorothy, *Sapper D. Lawrence, the Only English Woman Soldier, Late R E* (London: Lane).
MACAULAY, Rose, *What Not: A Prophetic Comedy* (London: Constable).
MACAULAY, Rose, *Three Days* (London: Constable).
RADZIWILL, Catherine (Rzewuska), *The Firebrand of Bolshevism, the True Story . . .* (Boston: [PH 410]).
RICKARD, Mrs Victor (Jessie Louisa Moore), *The House of Courage* (London: Duckworths [PH 388]).
ROBINS, Elizabeth, *The Messenger* (London: H & S [PH 390]).
STERN, Gladys Bronwyn, *Children of No Man's Land* (London: Duckworth [PH 401]).

1920–29

BAGNOLD, Enid (1920), *The Happy Foreigner* (London: Heinemann [rep. 1954; Virago, 1987]).
BORDEN, Mary (1921), *The Tortoise, A Novel* (New York: [PH 447]).
BORDEN, Mary (1929), *Forbidden Zone* (London: Heinemann).
BRAZIL, Angela (1920), *A Popular Schoolgirl* (London: Blackie).
BUTLER, Lady Elizabeth (1922), *An Autobiography* (London).
CATHER, Willa Sibert (1922), *One Of Ours* (New York: [PH 462]).
COHN, Clara (Viebig) (1920), *Daughters of Hecuba: A Tale of Our Times* (London: Unwin (trans. German, *Tochter von Hekuba*, 1917 [PH 464]).
COURTNEY, Kate (1927), *Extracts from a Diary During the War* (privately published).
GUEST, Carmel (Goldsmid) (1928), *The Yellow Pigeon* (London: Harrap [PH 533]).
HALL, Radclyffe (1928), *The Well of Loneliness* (London: Cape).
HAMILTON, Cicely M., *The Child in Flanders – a play* (London).
HOLTBY, Winifred (1924), *The Crowded Street* (London: Bodley Head).
JAMESON, Margaret Storm (1926), *Three Kingdoms* (New York: [PH 504]).
LEE, Mary (1929), 'It's a Great War!' (New York: [PH 563]).
MACAULAY, Rose (1920), *Potterism: a tragi-comical farce* (London: Constable).
MACAULAY, Rose (1923), *Told By An Idiot* (London: Constable).
MACKINTOSH, Elizabeth ('Gordon Daviot') (1929), *Kif: An Unvarnished History* (London: Benn [PH 555]).
MANSFIELD, Katherine (1923), 'The Fly', *The Dove's Nest and Other Stories* (London: Constable).
MANSFIELD, Katherine (1924), 'An Indiscreet Journey', *Something Childish and Other Stories* (London: Constable).

ONIONS, Maude (1929), *A Woman at War: Being experiences of an army signaller in France in 1917–19* (London: Daniel).

PEEL, Mrs C. S. (1929), *How We Lived Then 1914-18: A Sketch of social & domestic life in England during the war* (London: Lane).

PLAYNE, C. E. (1928), *The Pre-War Mind in Britain* (London: Unwin).

POORE, Ida (1920), *Rachel Fitzpatrick* (London: Lane [PH 439]).

RUSSELL, Mary Annette Countess (von Arnim) (1920), *In the Mountains* (London: Macmillan).

SEDGWICK, Anne Douglas (1921), *Adrienne Toner* (London: Arnold [PH 460]).

SHAW McLAREN, Eva (ed.) (1920), *A History of the Scottish Women's Hospitals* (London: Hodder).

SINCLAIR, May (1920), *The Romantic* (London: Collins [PH 442]).

THOMPSON, Sylvia (1926), *Hounds of Spring* (London: Heinemann [PH 511]).

WARD, Mrs Humphry (Mary Augusta Arnold) (1920), *Harvest* (London: Collins).

WHARTON, Edith Newbold (Jones) (1923), *A Son at the Front* (New York: [PH 482]).

WILLIS, Irene Cooper (1928), *England's Holy War* (New York: rep. Garland, 1971).

WOOLF, Virginia (Stephen) (1922), *Jacob's Room* (London: Hogarth [PH 475]).

WOOLF, Virginia (Stephen) (1925), *Mrs Dalloway* (London: Hogarth).

WOOLF, Virginia (Stephen) (1925 B), *The Common Reader* (London: Hogarth).

WOOLF, Virginia (Stephen) (1929), 'Women and Fiction', *The Forum* (March 1929).

1930–39

ALLEN, Alice Maud ('Allen Havens') (1931), *The Trap* (London: Woolf [PH 647]).

Anon (1930), *WAAC: The Woman's Story of the War* (London: Ward).

ASQUITH, Cynthia (1936), *The Spring House* (London).

BOILEAU, Ethel (1930), *The Arches of the Years* (London: Hutchinson [PH 591]).

BORDEN, Mary (1931), *Sarah Gay* (London: Heinemann).

BRITTAIN, Vera (1933), *Testament of Youth* (London: Gollancz).

BRITTAIN, Vera (1934), *Poems of the War and After* (Oxford: Blackwell).

BRITTAIN, Vera (1936), *Honourable Estate: A Novel of Transition* (London: Gollancz [PH 715]).

CANFIELD, Dorothy (Fisher) (1930), *The Deepening Stream* (New York: Harcourt [PH 593]).

CULLING, E. V. H., *Arms and the Woman: a canteen worker with the French* (London: Murray).

HALL, Radclyffe (1934), *Miss Ogilvy Finds Herself* (London).

HAMILTON, Cicely (1935), *Life Errant* (London: Dent).

HAMILTON, Mary Agnes (Adamson) (1930), *Special Providence: A Tale of 1917* (London: Allen & Unwin; Boston, *Three Against Fate* [PH 608]).

HINKSON, Pamela (1932), *The Ladies' Road* (London: Gollancz; rep. Penguin [PH 670]).

HOLLAND, Ruth (1932), *The Lost Generation* (London: Gollancz).

HOLTBY, Winifred (1938), *Letters to a Friend* (London: Macmillan).

JACOB, Naomi Ellington (1935), *Honour Come Back* (London: Hutchinson [PH710]).

JAMESON, Margaret Storm (1932), *That Was Yesterday* (London).

JAMESON, Margaret Storm (1933), *No Time Like the Present* (London: Cassell).

JAMESON, Margaret Storm (1939), *The Captain's Wife (Farewell Night, Welcome Day)* (London).

LUARD, Kate E. (1930), *Unknown Warriors* (London: Chatto).

McKENNA, Marthe (Cnokaert) (1932), *I Was a Spy!* [E. P. Tisdall] (London: Queenway).

McKENNA, Marthe (Cnokaert), (1935) *A Spy Was Born* (London: Jarrolds [PH 711]).

MILLARD, Nurse Shirley (1936), *I Saw Them Die* (London: Harrap).

PANKHURST, E. Sylvia (1938), in *Myself When Young* (ed: Margot Asquith, 259–312) (London: Muller).

PANKHURST, E. Sylvia (1932), *The Home Front* (London: Hutchinson [rep. 1987]).

PLAYNE, Carolyne E. (1930), *Society at War 1914–16* (London: Allen & Unwin).

PLAYNE, Carolyne E. (1933), *Britain Holds On, 1917, 18* (London: Allen & Unwin).

PRICE, Evadne ('Helen Zenna Smith') (1930) *'Not So Quiet . . .' Stepdaughters of War* (London: Marriott; New York, *Stepdaughters of War*) (rep. Lawrence & Wishart, 1987; Virago, 1988; Women's Press, 1989 [PH 633]).

RATHBONE, Irene (1932), *We That Were Young* (London: Chatto) (rep. Virago, 1988) [PH 675]).

SCHUTZE, Gladys Henrietta (Raphael) (1930), *Mrs Fischer's War* (London: Jarrolds [PH 617]).

SITWELL, Edith (1937), *I Live Under a Black Sun: A Novel* (London: Gollancz [PH 739]).

STEIN, Gertrude (1933), *The Autobiography of Alice B. Toklas*.

WEST, Rebecca ('Anon.') (1930), *War Nurse: The True story of a Woman who Lived, Loved, and Suffered on the Western Front* (New York: [PH 637]).

WILKINSON, Iris Guiver ('Robin Hyde') (1936), *Passport to Hell* (London: Hurst & Blackett [PH 721]).

WILSON,Theodora Wilson (1937), *Those Strange Years* (London: Daniel [PH 741]).

WOOLF, Virginia (1931), 'Professions For Women', rep. in *The Death of the Moth*, 1942 (London: Hogarth).

WOOLF, Virginia (1938), *Three Guineas* (London: Hogarth).

(b) Works published after 1939, written by women born before 1900

ASQUITH, (1968), *Lady Cynthia Asquith: Diaries 1915–18* (ed. E. M. Horsley) (London: Hutchinson [New York: 1969; rep. 1988]).

BAGNOLD, Enid (1969), *Autobiography* (London: Heinemann [rep. Century, 1985]).

'BRIDGE, Ann' (pseud. of Mary Dolling (Sanders), Lady O.Malley) (1952), *The Dark Moment, a Novel* (London: Chatto; [PH 784]).

BRITTAIN, Vera (1945), *Account Rendered* (London: Macmillan [rep. Virago, 1982]).

BRITTAIN, Vera (1957), *Testament of Experience* (London: Gollancz [rep. Virago, 1979]).

BRITTAIN, Vera (1940), *Testament of Friendship* (London: Macmillan).

BRITTAIN, Vera (1968), 'War Service in Perspective' in George A. PANICHAS (ed.), 365–75.

BRITTAIN, Vera (1981), *Chronicle of Youth: War Diary 1913–7* (eds Bishop & Smart) (London: Gollancz [rep. Fontana, 1981]).

BRITTAIN & HOLTBY (1985), *Testament of a Generation* (eds Berry & Bishop) (London: Virago).

BUTLER, Eliza (1951), *Daylight in a Dream* (London: Hogarth [PH 783]).

CANNAN, May Wedderburn (1976), *Grey Ghosts and Voices* (Kineton: Roundwood).

COLE, Margaret (Postgate) (1949), *Growing Up into Revolution* (London: Longmans).

COOPER, Diana (Manners) (1958), *The Rainbow Comes and Goes* (London: Hart Davis [rep. Century, 1984]).

DAYUS, Kathleen (1986), *Where's There's Life* (London: Virago).

DOOLITTLE, Hilda (1960), *Bid Me to Live: (A Madrigal)* (New York: rep. London, Virago, 1984 [PH 800]).

FARMBOROUGH, Florence (1974), *Nurse at the Russian Front: A Diary 1914–18* (London: Constable [rep. Futura, 1977]).

HAMILTON, Mary (1944), *Remembering My Good Friends* (London: Cape).

HAMILTON, Peggy (1978), *Three Years or the Duration* (London: Owen).

JAMESON, Storm (1969), *Journey from the North: Vol I* (London: Collins [rep. Virago, 1984]).

MANSFIELD, (1954), *Journal of Katherine Mansfield* (ed. J. M. Murray, London: Constable).

MANSFIELD, (1977), *The Letters and Journals of Katherine Mansfield* (ed. C. K. Stead) (Harmondsworth, Penguin).

MORRELL (1964), *Ottoline at Garsington: Memoirs of Lady Ottoline Morrell, 1915–18* (ed. Robert Gathorne-Hardy) (New York: 1964).

PATMORE, Brigit (1968), *My Friends When Young* (ed. D. Patmore) (London: Heinemann).

PRICHARD, Katherine Susannah (1948), *Golden Miles* (London: Cape [rep. Virago, 1984]).

TROUBRIDGE, Una Lady (1961), *The Life and Death of Radclyffe Hall* (London: Hammond).

T'SERCLAES, Baroness de (Mrs Knocker) (1964), *Flanders and Other Fields* (London: Harrap).

WEST, Rebecca (1982), *The Young Rebecca: Writings of Rebecca West 1911–1917* (ed. Jane Marcus) (London: Macmillan [rep. Virago, 1983]).

WHITE, Antonia (1954), *Beyond the Glass* (London: Eyre & Spottiswoode); rep. in: (1982), *Frost in May (1) & (2)* (London: Fontana).

WOOLF, Virginia (1953), *A Writer's Diary* (ed. L. Woolf) (London: Hogarth).

WOOLF, Virginia (1977), *The Diary of Virginia Woolf, I: 1915–19* (ed. Anne O. Bell) (London: Hogarth).

WOOLF, Virginia (1979), *The Sickle Side of the Moon: The Letters of Virginia Woolf Vol. 5: 1932–35* (ed. Nigel Nicolson) (London: Chatto).

SECONDARY SOURCES

Anthologies 1914–45

Anon, ed. (1916, 1917) *Soldier Poets* (London: Macdonald).

BRERETON, Frederick, ed. (1930), *An Anthology of War Poems*. With an introduction by Edmund Blunden (London: Collins).

BROPHY, John, ed. (1929), *The Soldier's War* (London: Dent).

BROPHY, John and Eric PARTRIDGE, (eds) (1931), *Songs and Slang of the British Soldier, 1914–18* (3rd edn; republished 1965) (London: Partridge).

CHAPMAN, Guy, ed. (1937), *Vain Glory: A Miscellany of the Great War 1914–1918* (2nd ed. 1968) (London: Cassell).

CLARKE, G. H., ed. (1919), *A Treasury of War Poetry* (London: Hodder & Stoughton).

CLARKE, G. H., ed. (1919), *A Treasury of War Poetry, 2nd Series* (New York: Houghton Mifflin).

CUNLIFFE, J. W., ed. (1916), *Poems of the Great War* (New York: Macmillan).

FORESHAW, Charles Frederick, ed. (1916), *One Hundred of the Best Poems on the European War* (New York: Crowell).

FORESHAW, Charles Frederick, ed. (1916), *One Hundred of the Best Poems on the European War, Volume 2: By Women Poets of the Empire* (New York: Crowell).

FOXCROFT, Frank, ed. (1919), *War Verse* (New York: Crowell).

HOUSMAN, Laurence, ed. (1930), *War Letters of Fallen Englishmen* (London: Gollancz).

LLOYD, Bertram, ed. (1918), *Poems Written During the Great War 1914–1918* (London: Allen & Unwin).

LÖHRKE, Eugene, ed. (1930), *Armageddon: The World War in Literature* (New York: Cape).

MACKLIN, A. E., ed. (1918), *The Lyceum Book of War Verse* (London: Macdonald).

NICHOLS, Robert, ed. (1943), *Anthology of War Poetry, 1914–1918* (London: Nicholson & Watson).

OSBORN, E. B., ed. (1917), *The Muse in Arms* (London: Murray).

SYMONS, Julian, ed. (1942), *An Anthology of War Poetry* (Harmondsworth: Penguin).

TROTTER, Jacqueline, ed. (1920), *Valour and Vision: Poems of the War 1914–18* (enlarged edn, 1923) (London: Hopkinson).

WILLIAMS, Oscar, ed. (1945), *The War Poets: an Anthology of the War Poetry of the 20th Century* (New York: Day).

Anthologies published after World War II

BLACK, E. L., ed. (1970), *1914–18 in Poetry* (London: Hodder & Stoughton).
BRUCE, G., ed. (1983), *Short Stories of the First World War* (London: Methuen).
FERGUSON, John, ed. (1972), *War and the Creative Arts* (London: Macmillan).
GARDNER, Brian, ed. (1964), *Up the Line to Death: The War Poets 1914–1918* (Foreword by Edmund Blunden) (London: Methuen).
HARVEY, Anne, ed. (1987), *In Time of War* (London: Blackie).
HIBBERD, Dominic and John ONIONS, eds (1986), *Poetry of the Great War: An Anthology* (London: Macmillan).
HUSSEY, Maurice, ed. (1967), *Poetry of the First World War* (London: Longman).
MOYNIHAN, Michael, ed. (1975), *A Place Called Armageddon: Letters From the Great War* (London: David & Charles).
MOYNIHAN, Michael, ed. (1980), *Greater Love: Letters Home 1914–1918* (London: Allen).
PARSONS, I. M., ed. (1965), *Men Who March Away: Poems of the First World War* (London: Heinemann).
REILLY, Catherine, ed. (1981), *Scars Upon My Heart: Women's Poetry and Verse of the First World War* (London: Virago).
SILKIN, Jon, ed. (1979), *The Penguin Book of First World War Poetry* (Harmondsworth: Penguin). (2nd ed, 1981).
STEPHEN, Martin, ed. (1988), *Never Such Innocence: A New Anthology of Great War Verse* (London: Buchan & Enright).
VANSITTART, Peter, ed. (1983), *Voices From the Great War* (Harmondsworth: Penguin).

Journal articles

ANNAN, Noel (1978), '"Our Age": Reflections on three Generations in England', *Daedelus*, Vol. 107, 81–109.
ALTHUSSER, Louis (1971), 'Ideology and Ideological State Apparatuses', *Lenin and Philosophy and Other Essays*, trans. Brewster (London: New Left Books).
BARASH, Carol L. (1986), 'Virile Womanhood: Olive Schreiner's narratives of a master race', *Women's Studies International Forum*, Vol. 9, No. 4.
BAYLEY, John (1963), 'But For Beaumont Hamel . . .', *Spectator*, 4 October 1963, 419.
BISHOP, Alan (1986), 'The Battle of the Somme and Vera Brittain', unpublished.
BLACK, Naomi (1984), 'The Mothers' International: the Women's Co-operative Guild and Feminist Pacifism', *Women's Studies International Forum*, Vol. 7, No. 6.
BLODGETT, Harriet (1985), 'What Price Change? The Great War and

Englishwomen's Diaries', *Turn-of-the-Century Women*, Vol. II, No. 1, 18–29.

BYLES, Joan Montgomery (1985), 'Women's Experience of World War One: Suffragists, Pacifists and Poets', *Women's Studies International Forum*, Vol. 8, No. 5, 473–87.

COSTIN, Lela B. (1982), 'Feminism, Pacifism, Internationalism and the 1915 International Congress of Women', *Women's Studies' International Forum*, Vol. 5, No. 3/4, 301–15.

CROSTHWAIT, Elizabeth (1986), ' "The Girl Behind the Man Behind the Gun" – The Women's Army Auxilliary Corps, 1914–18', *Our Work, Our Lives, Our Words: Women's History and Women's Work*, eds DAVIDOFF, Leonore and WESTNER, Belinda (London: Macmillan) 161–81.

CULLETON, Claire A. (1988), 'Gender-Charged Munitions: The Language of World War I Munitions Reports', *Women's Studies International Forum*, Vol. 11, No. 2, 109–16.

DAVIE, Donald (1964), 'In the Pity', *New Statesman*, 28 August 1964, 282–3.

DAVIN, Ann (1978), 'Imperialism and Motherhood in History', *History Workshop Journal*, Vol. V.

EDWARDS, Lee R. (1977), 'War and Roses: The Politics of *Mrs Dalloway*', in *The Authority of Experience* eds C. DIAMOND and L. EDWARDS (Amherst) 160–77.

FENTON, Charles A. (1960), 'A Literary Fracture of World War I', *American Quarterly*, Vol. 12, 119–32.

FIRCHOW, Peter E. (1980), 'Rico and Julia: The HD–DHL Affair Reconsidered', *Journal of Modern Literature*, 8, 1, 51–76.

FRIEDMAN, Susan S. (1985), 'H.D.', *Contemporary Literature*, XXXVI, 1, 107–13.

GILBERT, Sandra (1983), 'Soldier's Heart: Literary Men, Literary Women, and the Great War', *Signs*, Vol. 8, Spring, 422–50.

GOLDRING, Douglas (1920), 'The War and the Poets', *Reputations: Essays in Criticism* (London).

HINDLE, Wilfred H. (1931), 'War Books and Peace Propaganda', *Bookman*, Vol. 81, 158–60.

HOPE, Francis (1965), 'Tommy's Tunes', *The Review*, 15, 139.

HOPKIN, Deian (1970), 'Domestic Censorship in the First World War', *Journal of Contemporary History*, Vol. 5, No. 4, 151–69.

INGRAM, Angela (1986), ' "Unutterable Putrefaction" and "Foul Stuff": Two "obscene" novels of the 1920's', *Women's Studies International Forum*, Vol. 9, No. 4.

JAEGER, Hans (1985), 'Generations in History: Reflections on a Controversial Concept', *History and Theory*, Vol. 24, No. 3, 273–92.

JOHNSTONE, J. K. (1968), 'World War I and the Novels of Virginia Woolf', in *Promise of Greatness*, ed. PANICHAS, 528–40.

KENNARD, Jean E. (1985), 'Feminism, Pacifism, and World War I', *Turn-of-the-Century Women*, Vol. II, No. 2, 10–21.

KRIEGEL, Annie (1978), 'Generational Difference: The History of an Idea', *Daedelus*, Vol. 107, 23–38.

LLOYD, Genevieve (1986), 'Selfhood, war and masculinity', *Feminist*

Challenges: Social and Political Theory, eds PATEMAN, Carole and GROSS, Elizabeth (Australia: Allen & Unwin) 63–76.

MACKAY, Jane and THANE, Pat (1985), 'The Englishwoman', *Englishness: Politics and Culture 1880–1920*, eds COLLS, Robert and DODD, Philip (London: Croom Helm) 191–229.

MARCUS, Jane (1988), 'The asylums of Antaeus: Women, war and madness. Is there a feminist fetishism?', *The Difference Within: Feminism and Critical Theory*; eds MEESE, E. and PARKER, Alice, (Amsterdam: John Benjamins) 49–81.

NEWTON, Esther (1984), 'The Mythic Mannish Lesbian: Radclyffe Hall and the New Woman', *Signs*, Vol. 9, No. 4, 557–75.

PIERSON, Ruth Roach (1987), ' "Did Your Mother Wear Army Boots?" – The Impact of the First World War', *Images of Women in Peace and War – Cross-Cultural and Historical Perspectives*, ed. MacDONALD, Sharon (London: Macmillan) 213–17.

PUGH, Martin D. (1974), 'Politicians and the Woman's Vote 1914–1918', *History*, Vol. 59, No. 197.

RADFORD, Jean (1986), 'An Inverted Romance: *The Well of Loneliness* and sexual ideology' in *The Progress of Romance*, ed. Jean RADFORD (London: Routledge) 97–111.

RICKWORD, Edgell (1940), 'War and Poetry (1914–18). Part 2: From Rhetoric to Realism', *Life and Letters Today*, 26 August 1940, 29.

RIVERS, W. H. R. (1918), 'The Repression of War Experience', *The Lancet*, 1, 171–8.

RUEHL, Sonja (1985), 'Inverts and Experts: Radclyffe Hall and the lesbian identity' in *Sex, Class and Race in Literature and Culture*, eds Judith NEWTON and Deborah ROSENFELT (New York: Methuen) 165–80.

SHOVER, Michele J. (1975), 'Roles and Images of Women in World War I Propaganda', *Politics and Society*, Vol. 5, 469–86.

SHOWALTER, Elaine (1981), 'Feminist Criticism in the Wilderness', *Critical Inquiry*, 8.

SPACKS, Patricia M. (1981), 'Stages of Self: Notes on Autobiography and the Life Cycle', *American Autobiography*, ed. A. Stone (NJ: Prentice Hall) 40–50.

SPITZER, Allen B. (1973), 'The Historical Idea of Generation', *American Historical Review*, Vol. 78, 1353–85.

SPRINGHALL, John (1986), ' "Up Guards and At them!": British Imperialism and Popular Art' in MACKENZIE, J. (1986), 49–72.

STIMPSON, Catherine R. (1982), 'Zero Degree Deviancy: The Lesbian Novel in English', in *Writing and Sexual Difference*, ed. Elizabeth ABEL (Brighton: Harvester) 243–56.

SUMMERS, Anne (1976), 'Militarism in Britain before the Great War', *History Workshop*, Vol. 2, 104–23.

SUTHERLAND, John (1987), 'Taxonomy of the Clandestine', *Times Literary Supplement*, 1001.

THOMAS, Edward (1914), 'War Poetry', *Poetry and Drama II*, No. 8, December.

TOMLINSON, H. M. (1930), 'War Books', *The Criterion*.

TYLEE, Claire M. (1988), ' "Maleness Run Riot": The Great War and

Women's Resistance to Militarism', *Women's Studies International Forum*, Vol. 11, No. 3.

VELLACOTT, Jo Newberry (1977), 'Anti-war Suffragists', *History*, Vol. 52, 411–25.

VELLACOTT, Jo Newberry (1987), 'Feminist Consciousness and the First World War', *History Workshop Journal*, Vol. 23, 81–101.

WRIGHT, D. G. (1978), 'The Great War, Government Propaganda and English "Men of Letters" 1914–16', *Literature & History*, Vol. 7, 70–100.

Books and Theses

ALDINGTON, Richard (1929), *Death of a Hero* (London: Chatto; Unabridged edition: London: Consul 1965).

ALDINGTON, Richard (1941), *Life for Life's Sake* (New York: Viking).

ALDINGTON, Richard (1950), *Lawrence: Portrait of a Genius But* ... (London: Heinemann).

ALDRIDGE, John W. (1957), *After the Lost Generation: A Critical Study of the Writers of Two Wars* (London: Vision; rep. 1959).

ALPERS, Antony (1980), *The Life of Katherine Mansfield* (London: Cape).

ASQUITH, Herbert (1937), *Moments of Memory* (London: Hutchinson).

AYLING, Ronald, ed. (1985), *Seven Plays by Sean O'Casey* (London: Macmillan).

BABINGTON SMITH, Constance (1972), *Rose Macaulay* (London: Collins).

BADEN-POWELL, R. S. S. (1908), *Scouting For Boys* (London: rep. 1963).

BAKER, Michael (1987), *Our Three Selves: a life of Radclyffe Hall* (London: Hamilton).

BANERJEE, A. (1975), *Spirit Above Wars* (Delhi: Macmillan).

BARTHES, Roland (1972), *Mythologies*, trans. Lavers (London: Cape).

BEAUMAN, Nichola (1983), *A Very Great Profession: The Women's Novel 1914–39* (London: Virago).

BEAVER, Patrick (1979), *The Spice of Life: Pleasures of the Victorian Age* (London: Elm Tree).

BENSEN, Alice R. (1969), *Rose Macaulay* (New York: Twayne).

BERGONZI, Bernard (1965), *Heroes' Twilight: A Study of the Literature of the Great War* (London: Constable; rep. 1980).

BLACK, E. L., ed. (1970), *1914–18 In Poetry* (London: Hodder & Stoughton).

BLUNDEN, Edmund (1928), *Undertones of War* (London: Penguin).

BLUNDEN, Edmund (1958), *War Poets, 1914–1918* (London: Longman; rep. 1969).

BOLL, Theosophilus, E. M. (1973), *Miss May Sinclair: Novelist* (New Jersey; Fairleigh Dickinson University Press).

BOND, Brian (1984), *War and Society in Europe, 1870–1970* (Leicester: Leicester University Press).

BOWRA, Maurice (1961), *Poetry and the First World War* (London: Oxford University Press).

BRAYBON, Gail (1981), *Women Workers in the First World War* (London: Croom Helm).

BRAYBON, Gail and SUMMERFIELD, Penny (1987), *Out of the Cage: Women's Experiences in Two World Wars* (London: Pandora).

BROWER, Reuben A. (1951), *The Fields of Light* (New York: Oxford University Press).

BROWN, Constance Adams (1978), *The Literary Aftermath: English Literary Responses to the First World War* (PhD, Columbia University, 1983).

BURGESS, Alan (1963), *The Lovely Sergeant* (London: Heinemann; rep. 1965).

BUSSEY, Gertrude and TIMS, Margaret (1965), *The Women's International League for Peace and Freedom* (London: Allen & Unwin; rep. 1980).

CADOGAN, Mary and CRAIG, Patricia (1978), *Women and Children First: The Fiction of Two World Wars* (London: Gollancz).

CAEDEL, Martin (1980), *Pacifism in Britain 1914–1945* (London: Oxford University Press).

CARRINGTON, Charles E. 'Charles Edmonds' (1929), *A Subaltern's War* (London: Davies).

CARRINGTON, Charles E. (1965), *Soldier From the Wars Returning* (London: Hutchinson).

CARSTEN, Florence (1982), *War Against War* (London: Batsford).

CHAPMAN, Guy (1933), *A Passionate Prodigality* (London: Nicholson).

CHAPMAN, Guy (1975), *A Kind of Survivor* (London: Cassell).

CHAPMAN, Jean (1981), *The Unreasoning Earth* (London: Macdonald).

CLAPHAM, M. (1930), *Mud and Khaki* (London: Hutchinson).

CLARKE, Ian F. (1966), *Voices Prophesying War, 1763–1984* (London: Oxford University Press; rep. 1983).

CLOETE, Stuart (1972), *A Victorian Son* (London: Collins).

COCKBURN, Claud (1972), *Bestseller – The Books that Everyone Read 1900–39* (London: Sidgwick).

COLE, George, D. H. and POSTGATE, R. S. (1949), *The Common People 1746–1946* (London: Methuen; 4th edn).

CONDELL, Diana and Jean LIDDIARD (1987), *Working for Victory? Images of Women in the First World War* (London: Routledge).

COOPERMAN, Stanley (1967), *World War I and the American Novel* (London: Johns Hopkins; rep. 1970).

COPPARD, George (1969), *With a Machine-gun to Cambrai* (London: HMSO).

COWLEY, Malcolm (1934), *Exile's Return* (New York: Vision; rep. 1962).

CRAIG, Alec (1962), *The Banned Books of England and Other Countries* (London: Allen & Unwin).

CROZIER, F. (1930), *A Brass Hat in No-Man's Land* (London: Cape).

DANIELS, Jonathan (1954), *The End of Innocence* (Philadelphia).

DARRACOTT, Joseph and LOFTUS, Belinda (1972), *First World War Posters* (London: Imperial War Museum; rep. 1981).

DEAKIN, Morley F. (1980), *Rebecca West* (Boston: Twayne).

DELANY, Paul (1978), *D. H. Lawrence's Nightmare* (New York: Basic Books).

DICKINSON, Jean E. (1980), *Women Novelists and War: A Study of Seven Women Novelists, 1914–40* (M. Litt., University of Edinburgh unpub.).

DICKSON, Lovat (1975), *Radclyffe Hall at the Well of Loneliness; a Sapphic Chronicle* (New York: Scribner's).

DYHOUSE, Caroline (1981), *Girls Growing Up in Late Victorian and Edwardian England* (London: Routledge).

ELLIS, John (1976), *Eye-deep in Hell; The Western Front, 1914–18* (London: Croom Helm; rep. 1979).

FERGUSON, John, ed. (1972), *War and the Creative Arts* (London: Macmillan).

FORD, Ford Madox (Hueffer) (1926), *A Man Could Stand Up*; rep. as part of trilogy *Parade's End*, 1960 (London: Bodley Head).

FRYE, Northrop (1957), *Anatomy of Criticism* (New Jersey: Princeton).

FUSSELL, Paul (1975), *The Great War and Modern Memory* (London: Oxford University Press).

GARNER, Les (1984), *Stepping Stones to Women's Freedom* (London: Hutchinson).

GIBBS, Philip (1920), *Realities of War* (London: Heinemann).

GILBERT, Sandra M. and Susan GUBAR (1979), *The Madwoman in the Attic; the Woman Writer and the Nineteenth-Century Literary Imagination* (London: Yale University Press).

GILBERT, Sandra and Susan GUBAR (1987), *No Man's Land: the Place of the Woman Writer in the Twentieth Century* (London: Yale University Press).

GIROUARD, Mark (1981), *The Return to Camelot: Chivalry and the English Gentleman* (London: Yale University Press).

GOLDRING, Douglas (1920), *Reputations: Essays in Criticism* (London).

GORDON, Ian A. (1954), *Katherine Mansfield* (London: Longman. rev. edn, 1971).

GOSSE, Sir Edmund (1916), *Inter Arma* (New York).

GRAVES, Robert (1929), *Goodbye to All That* (London: Cape; rev. edn, Cassell, 1957).

GRAVES, Robert (1950), *Occupation Writer* (New York: Grosset).

GRAY, Martin (1987), *Poets of the Great War* (London: Longmans).

GREEN, Martin (1980), *Dreams of Adventure, Deeds of Empire* (London: Routledge).

GREGSON, J. M. (1976), *Poetry of the First World War* (London: Arnold).

GREICUS, M. S. (1973), *Prose Writers of World War I* (London: Longmans).

GRIFFITH, Wyn (1931), *Up to Mametz* (London: Faber).

GUEST, Barbara (1984), *Herself Defined: The Poet H. D. and Her World* (New York: Doubleday).

HACKETT, Alice Payne (1956), *Sixty Years of Bestsellers* (New York).

HANKIN, C. A. (1983), *Katherine Mansfield and her Confessional Stories* (London: Macmillan).

HANSON, Clare and Andrew GURR (1981), *Katherine Mansfield* (London: Macmillan).

HARDIE, Alec M. (1958), *Edmund Blunden* (Harlow: Longman: rev. edn., 1971).

HARDWICK, Mollie (1975), *'The War to End Wars'* (London: Sphere).

HARRIES, Meirion and Susie (1983), *War Artists* (London: Michael Joseph).

HARRIS, John (1961), *Covenant with Death* (London: Hutchinson; rep. Pan, 1963).

HARRISON, Fraser (1977), *Dark Angel; Aspects of Victorian Sexuality* (London: Sheldon).

HARRISON, Sarah (1980), *The Flowers of the Field* (London: Macdonald).

'HAY, Ian' (John Hay Beith) (1915), *The First 100,000* (London: rep. Corgi, 1975).

HEERKENS, Lidwien (1984), *Becoming Lives: English Women's Autobiographies of the 1930's* (MA, University of Leicester unpub.).

HEMINGWAY, Ernest (1929) *A Farewell to Arms* (London: Cape).

HENTY, G. A. (1905), *In the Hands of the Malays & Other Stories* (London: Blackie).

HIBBERD, Dominic ed. (1973), *Wilfred Owen: War Poems and Others* (London: Chatto).

HIBBERD, Dominic, ed. (1981), *Poetry of the First World War* (London: Macmillan).

HILL, Susan (1971), *Strange Meeting* (London: Hamilton [rep. Penguin, 1972; Longman, 1984, with an introduction by the author]).

HOFFMAN, Frederick J. (1949), *The Twenties* (New York: Collier; rep. 1962).

HOLLAND, Vyvian (1954), *Son of Oscar Wilde* (London: Chatto; rep. Penguin, 1957).

HOLTBY, Winifred (1932), *Virginia Woolf* (London: Wishart).

HOUGHTON, Walter E. (1957), *The Victorian Frame of Mind* (New Jersey: Yale).

HOWARTH, Patrick (1973), *Play Up and Play the Game: The Heroes of Popular Fiction* (London: Methuen).

HYNES, Samuel (1968), *The Edwardian Turn of Mind* (London: Oxford University Press).

JOHNSTON, J. H. (1964), *English Poetry of the First World War* (Princeton, N.J.: Princeton University Press).

JOHNSTON, Jennifer (1974), *How Many Miles to Babylon?* (London: Hamilton).

JONES, David (1937), *In Parenthesis* (London: Faber).

KEATING, Peter, ed. (1976), *Into Unknown England, 1866–1913; Selections From the Social Explorers* (London: Fontana).

KEEGAN, John (1976), *The Face of Battle* (London: Cape).

KEMPF, Beatrice (1972), *Woman For Peace: the Life of Bertha Von Suttner* (London: Wolff).

KENT, Susan Kingsley (1987), *Sex and Suffrage in Britain, 1860–1914* (Princeton, N.J.: Princeton University Press).

KIPLING, Rudyard (1940), *Rudyard Kipling's Verse: Definitive Edition* (London: Hodder & Stoughton).

KLEIN, Holger, ed. (1976), *The First World War in Fiction* (London: Macmillan).

LAMBERT, Angela (1984), *Unquiet Souls: The Indian Summer of the British Aristocracy* (London: Macmillan).

LAWRENCE, D. H. (1922), *Aaron's Rod* (London: Heinemann).

LAWRENCE, D. H. (1923), *Kangaroo* (London: Heinemann).

LEED, Eric J. (1979), *No Man's Land: combat and identity in World War I* (Cambridge: Cambridge University Press).

LEHMANN, John (1981), *English Poets of the First World War* (London: Thames & Hudson).

MACDONALD, Lynn (1980), *The Roses of No Man's Land* (London: Joseph).

MACDONALD, Lynn (1983), *Somme* (London: Macmillan).

MACKENZIE, John (1984), *Propaganda and Empire: the Manipulation of British Public Opinion 1880–1960* (Manchester: Manchester University Press).

MACKENZIE, John, ed. (1986), *Imperialism and Popular Culture* (Manchester: Manchester University Press).

MANNING, Frederick (1929), *The Middle Parts of Fortune* (London: Davies).

MARCUS, Jane (1981), *New Feminist Essays on Virginia Woolf* (London: Macmillan).

MARWICK, Arthur (1963), *The Explosion of British Society 1914–62* (London: Pan).

MARWICK, Arthur (1965), *The Deluge: British Society and the First World War* (London: Bodley Head; rep. Penguin).

MARWICK, Arthur (1977), *Women at War, 1914–1918* (London: Fontana).

MEYERS, Judith Marie (1985), *'Comrade-Twin': Brothers and Doubles in the World War I Prose of May Sinclair, Katherine Anne Porter, Vera Brittain, Rebecca West, and Virginia Woolf* (PhD, University of Washington).

MIDDLEBROOK, Martin (1971), *The First Day on the Somme: 1st July 1916* (London: Allen Lane; rep. Penguin, 1984).

MITCHELL, David (1966), *Women on the Warpath* (London: Cape).

Modern Fiction Studies, 24, 3 (1978–79), devoted to K. Mansfield.

MONTAGUE, C. E. (1922), *Disenchantment* (London: Chatto).

MOODY, A. D. (1963), *Virginia Woolf* (Edinburgh: Oliver & Boyd).

MOYNIHAN, Michael (1975), *A Place Called Armageddon: Letters From the Great War* (London: David & Charles).

MURDOCH, Iris (1965), *The Red and the Green* (London: Chatto; rep. Penguin, 1967).

NEWBOLT, Margaret, ed. (1942), *The Later Life and Letters of Sir Henry Newbolt* (London: Faber).

OLDFIELD, Sybil (1984), *Spinsters of this Parish* (London: Virago).

OREL, Harold (1986), *The Literary Achievement of Rebecca West* (London: Macmillan).

PANICHAS, George A., ed. (1968), *Promise of Greatness* (London: Cassell).

PARFITT, George (1988), *Fiction of the First World War: A Study* (London: Faber).

PARKER, Peter (1987) , *The Old Lie: The Great War and the Public School Ethos* (London: Constable).

PARROT, Sir Edward (1917), Vol. 6 of *The Children's Story of the War* in 10 vols (London: Nelson).

PATMORE, Brigit (1968), *My Friends When Young* (London: Heinemann).

PEARCE, Mary E. (1975), *The Sorrowing Field* (London: Macdonald).

PEARSALL, Ronald (1969), *The Worm in the Bud: The World of Victorian Sexuality* (London: Weidenfeld).

POOLE, Roger (1978), *The Unknown Virginia Woolf* (Cambridge: Cambridge University Press).

POUND, Reginald (1964), *The Lost Generation* (London: Constable).

PRIESTLEY, J. B. (1962), *Reminiscences and Reflections* (London: Heinemann).

QUINN, Vincent (1967), *Hilda Doolittle* (Boston: Twayne).

RAEMAKER, Louis (1917), *Collected Cartoons* (New York).

RAY, Gordon N. (1974), *H. G. Wells and Rebecca West* (Yale).

RAYMOND, Ernest (1922), *Tell England: A Study in a Generation* (London: Cassell).

READE, Peterson *et al.* (1927), *Propaganda Technique in the World War* (New York).

REYNOLDS, E. E. (1942), *Baden-Powell* (London).

ROSE, Phyllis (1978), *Woman of Letters: a Life of Virginia Woolf* (New York: Oxford University Press).

SHOWALTER, Elaine (1977), *A Literature of Their Own* (Princeton: rev. edn, 1982).

SHOWALTER, Elaine, ed. (1985), *The New Feminist Criticism* (London: Virago).

SHOWALTER, Elaine (1985), *The Female Malady: Women, Madness and English Culture 1830–1980* (New York: Pantheon; rep. London, Virago, 1987).

SILKIN, Jon (1972), *Out of Battle* (London: Oxford University Press).

SIMPSON, Colin (1972), *Lusitania* (London: Longmans).

SPEAR, Hilda D. (1979), *Remembering, We Forget* (London: Poynter-Davies).

STALLWORTHY, Jon (1974), *Poets of the First World War* (London: Oxford University Press).

SUTHERLAND, John (1981), *Best Sellers: Popular fiction of the 70's* (London: Routledge).

SWARTZ, Marvin (1971), *The Union of Democratic Control in British Politics* (London: OUP).

SWINNERTON, Frank (1938), *The Georgian Literary Scene* (London: Dent).

TAYLOR, A. J. P. (1963), *The First World War: An Illustrated History* (London: Hamilton).

TAYLOR, A. J. P. (1965), *English History 1914–1945* (Oxford: Oxford University Press; rep. Penguin, 1970).

THEATRE WORKSHOP (1965), *Oh What a Lovely War* (London: Methuen).

TOMALIN, Claire (1987), *Katherine Mansfield: A Secret Life* (New York: Viking).

TREVELYAN, G. M. (1942), *A Shortened History of England* (New York: Longman's; rep. Penguin, 1959).

TUCHMAN, Barbara (1962), *The Guns of August: August 1914* (London: Constable).

TURNER, E. S. (1975), *Boys Will Be Boys* (London: Joseph; rev. edn, 1975).

VELLACOTT, Jo (1980), *Bertrand Russell and the Pacifists in the First World War* (Brighton: Harvester).

WALSH, Jeremy (1982), *American War Literature: 1914 to Vietnam* (London: Macmillan).

WHORPLE, Ken (1984), *Reading By Numbers: Contemporary Publishing and Popular Fiction* (London: Comedia).

WILLIAMSON, Henry (1963), *The Power of the Dead* (London: Macdonald; rev. edn, Panther, 1966).

WILSON, John (1966), *Hamp* (London: Evans).

WILSON, Trevor (1987), *The Myriad Faces of War* (London: Macmillan).

WILTSHER, Anne (1985), *Most Dangerous Women: Feminist Peace Campaigners of the Great War* (London: Pandora).

WINTER, Denis (1978), *Death's Men: Soldiers of the Great War* (Harmondsworth: Allen Lane).

WINTER, J. M. (1985), *The Great War and the British People* (London: Longmans).

WOHL, Robert (1980), *The Generation of 1914* (London: Weidenfeld).

WOLFF, Leon (1958), *In Flanders Fields: the 1917 Campaign* (New York: Viking).

WOOLF, Leonard (1967), *Downhill All The Way* (London: Hogarth).

ZEGGER, Hrisey Dimitrakis (1976), *May Sinclair* (Boston: Twayne).

Index

(Texts are indexed under their author)